The Arab Spring
Five Years Later

The Arab Spring Five Years Later

Volume 2
Case Studies

Hafez Ghanem
Editor

Brookings Institution Press
Washington, D.C.

The Brookings Institution is a private nonprofit organization devoted to research,
education, and publication on important issues of domestic and foreign policy. Its
principal purpose is to bring the highest quality independent research and analysis
to bear on current and emerging policy problems. Interpretations or conclusions in
Brookings publications should be understood to be solely those of the authors.

Volume 1 has been cataloged by the Library of Congress as follows:
Names: Ghanem, Hafez, author.
Title: The Arab Spring five years later : toward greater inclusiveness /
    Hafez Ghanem.
Description: Washington, D.C. : Brookings Institution Press, [2016–] |
    Includes bibliographical references and index. | Description based on
    print version record and CIP data provided by publisher; resource not
    viewed.
Identifiers: LCCN 2015045078 (print) | LCCN 2015040104 (ebook) | ISBN
    9780815727194 (epub) | ISBN 9780815727200 (pdf) | ISBN 9780815727187 (pbk.
    : alk. paper)
Subjects: LCSH: Arab Spring, 2010– | Arab countries—History—21st century.
Classification: LCC JQ1850.A91 (print) | LCC JQ1850.A91 G432 2016 (ebook) |
    DDC 909/.097492708312—dc23
LC record available at http://lccn.loc.gov/2015045078

9 8 7 6 5 4 3 2 1

Typeset in Sabon and Myriad Pro

Composition by Cynthia Stock
Silver Spring, Maryland

Contents

Preface

The Arab revolutions of 2010–11 were earth-shaking events that completely changed the sociopolitical landscape in this part of the world. Of course what happens in the Arab world has an impact on the rest of humanity through variables such as oil prices, migration, and violence. Therefore, in March 2012 a group of Brookings scholars published a monograph entitled *After the Spring: Economic Transitions in the Arab World*. There we argued that the Arab transition to democracy will be long and tortuous with many twists and turns along the way. We said that successful economic transition is necessary for a successful political transition. Specifically, we concluded that four main economic transitions—each with its own short- and long-term strategies—are needed in the region. These include: (1) expanding opportunities for young people; (2) building a modern state; (3) transforming the private sector; and (4) expanding global and regional integration. The research carried out at the Brookings Institution emphasized that these transitions must be addressed in a holistic way by framing a broad, long-term economic strategy to create expectations that growth, fairness, equity, and economic justice will play major roles in the transition to a new economy.

It was clear that the Arab countries in transition were at a critical juncture. The two or three years following the eruption of the Arab Spring would determine whether they would move to an "inclusive" political and economic system that fosters growth and social development, or revert back to an "extractive" system, where elites appropriate rents and power and exclude the majority of the population from participation in decisionmaking and from sharing economic benefits.

Or even worse, would they disintegrate into little quasi-states based on ethnic or sectarian affiliation and descend into a spiral of civil war and violent extremism.

The period of euphoria and optimism about the future that immediately followed the revolutions quickly came to an end. Arab Spring countries had to deal with the serious issues of agreeing on a vision for a new society and building the institutions necessary for implementing this vision. This required different political factions to make compromises in order to reach a national consensus, a difficult challenge for societies that have a limited culture of democracy and very little experience with democratic processes.

In this context, the Japan International Cooperation Agency (JICA) and the Brookings Institution initiated a three-year (2012–15) academic research program on Arab economies. In spite of respectable economic growth between 2000 and 2010 in Egypt and Tunisia, opinion polls showed increasing popular dissatisfaction and unhappiness. Thus, our initial research (carried out in 2011–12) concluded that this was probably because growth was not inclusive. Vast segments of society saw a small elite reap most of the benefits of growth while they got very little or nothing at all. It seemed clear to us at the time that moving toward greater social justice and economic inclusion was a prerequisite for successful democratization. That is why our research focused on the question of how to achieve inclusive economic growth in the Arab world.

We had three objectives:

—raise awareness in the Middle East and North Africa (MENA) of the importance of inclusive economic policies to provide opportunities for youth, reduce gender bias, and develop lagging rural areas, and start a debate on the subject of inclusiveness with academics, civil society, and thought leaders;

—provide policymakers in MENA with a menu of options that can be used to achieve growth that ensures equity and broad participation, particularly for young men and women; and

—better inform donor agencies of opportunities to develop grassroots programs and promote inclusive growth.

Which populations suffer most from economic exclusion in the Arab world? We identified three groups: (1) youth who feel economically and socially marginalized; (2) women (especially young women) who receive education, but face huge constraints to participating in the economic life; and (3) inhabitants of lagging regions (for example, Western Tunisia or Upper Egypt) who are usually dependent on low-productivity agriculture and have limited access to social and physical infrastructure.

But achieving inclusive (or shared) growth requires inclusive institutions. How can you achieve inclusion and social justice without hearing the voices of those you want to include? Hence, institutional and governance reforms that aim at providing voice to youth, women, and inhabitants of lagging regions need to be at the center of any economic reform agenda in the Arab world. In addition to providing voice, governance reforms need to aim at rendering decisionmaking processes more transparent and government officials more accountable.

Economic and political stability in the Arab world is a global public good, and the international community can support inclusive growth in MENA through economic and financial aid, foreign direct investment, technical assistance, and the free movement of goods and people. But donors also face financial and political constraints. Hence it is important to identify priority areas and approaches for international economic intervention that would have the greatest impact.

The joint research program produced papers (presented in this volume) covering all of the subjects identified as key for inclusive growth in the Arab world: (1) youth inclusion through entrepreneurship and education reforms; (2) governance reforms for more inclusive decisionmaking and effective implementation of policies, programs, and projects; (3) development of lagging regions and support for smallholder and family farmers; (4) gender policies and the empowerment of women; and (5) international cooperation and the role of donors in a fragile and unstable environment.

Two points are worth noting. First, this is a truly collaborative, scholarly effort between JICA and Brookings. It is not a typical donor-researcher program. While Brookings experts provided overall direction, quality assurance, and peer review, most of the papers presented here were produced by JICA researchers and experts. Second, the approach adopted in this research is based on country case studies, focusing on Egypt, Iraq, Jordan, Morocco, Tunisia, and Yemen. The individual chapters will continue to be relevant for those countries for several years. Moreover, many of the general lessons from the country studies could be useful for other Arab countries.

The world has changed quite a bit since these papers, now chapters, were originally written. The Arab transitions have turned out to be much messier than most had expected. Syria and Yemen are in the midst of murderous civil wars that are further complicated by foreign interventions. Libya seems to have disintegrated as different tribes vie for power. The so-called Organization of the Islamic State (DAESH) has taken over large swaths of territory in Syria and Iraq and is committing some terrible atrocities. There are about 15 million refugees and internally displaced people in the Middle East and North Africa today. The fall of the Muslim Brotherhood in Egypt through an intervention by the military, and the subsequent increase in violence and terrorism, marked a halt in this country's transition. Even Tunisia, where the transition to democracy is most advanced, was rocked by two terrorist attacks in 2015 (at a museum and a beach resort) that have put a halt to its tourist industry and hence to its hopes for rapid growth and a reduction in unemployment.

The focus today is on how to prevent violent extremism and bring about peace and stability in the Arab world. Very few people are talking about an Arab transition to democracy. This does not mean that all hopes for Arab democratic transitions are lost. However, it seems to be generally accepted now that the transition to democracy will take many years, maybe even decades.

Are the chapters presented in this book still relevant in a world that is mostly focused on preventing violent extremism rather than on democratic transition? The answer is obviously yes. I have just attended a meeting of the Club de Madrid, which is an organization of democratic former presidents and prime ministers. They continue to work on issues that are important for the world even after leaving office. The topic of discussion was how to prevent violent extremism. They developed a ten-point framework, and one of the points was inclusion. According to these wise former world leaders, "Systematic exclusion creates injustice and unfair treatment; it can produce a toxic mix that allows violent extremism to flourish." They added that "political leaders everywhere have a duty to represent all their citizens, empower women and young people, and ensure that individual, group, and community has equal access to economic development and other opportunities." This is exactly what this book is all about: achieving economic and social inclusion by ensuring that all citizens are empowered and have equal access to economic opportunities.

Acknowledgments

This book represents the culmination of a three-year academic project undertaken by the Japan International Cooperation Agency (JICA) and the Brookings Institution, exploring how to achieve inclusive growth after the Arab spring, with the goal of contributing to development and stability in the region. The project aims to inform Arab policymakers, thought leaders, as well as bilateral and multilateral development partners and donors that are reviewing their programs and projects to reflect new realities in the region.

This work would not have been possible without the support of many people inside and outside of JICA and Brookings. Kemal Derviş and Homi Kharas provided overall support and guidance. I am particularly grateful to Homi Kharas for his comments on the various papers and on volume 1. Participants in various author workshops provided valuable advice, comments, and suggestions. These included Mayyada Abu Jaber, Perrihan Al-Rifai, Uri Dadush, Shanta Devarajan, Mourad Ezzine, Marc Schifbauer, Djavad Salehi-Isfahani, Ehab Abdou, Tamara Wittes, Bernard Funk, Shinichi Yamanaka, Akihiko Koenuma, Daniela Gressani, Inger Andersen, Heidi Crebo-Rediker, and Andrew Baukol.

Kristina Server provided invaluable management support. Aki Nemoto, Misaki Kimura, and Yamillett Fuentes provided excellent administrative and financial management support. The authors are also grateful to Neil O'Reilly, Christina Golubski, Michael Rettig, and the Brookings Press team led by Janet Walker for their help with editing.

This work was carried out while Hafez Ghanem was a senior fellow at the Brookings Institution, before rejoining the World Bank in March 2015. Hence, it does not necessarily reflect the views of the World Bank.

Brookings is grateful to JICA for its financial and intellectual support of this project. Brookings recognizes that the value it provides is in its absolute commitment to quality, independence, and impact. Activities supported by its donors reflect this commitment, and the analysis and recommendations contained in this volume are not determined or influenced by any donation. The chapters reflect the views of the authors and not the official position of any specific organization.

The Arab Spring
Five Years Later

1

Egypt's Difficult Transition: Options for the International Community

HAFEZ GHANEM

Change is under way in Egypt. But, its end is not clear and the road ahead is likely to be long and difficult.

—BRUCE K. RUTHERFORD, Princeton University

On June 30, 2013, millions of Egyptians took to the streets demanding that their first democratically elected president, Mohamed Morsi, of the Muslim Brotherhood, step down and calling for new elections. Three days later, on July 3, the minister of defense—surrounded by the country's leading secular politicians, Salafist leaders, and the heads of Al-Azhar (the highest Islamic authority in Egypt) and of the Coptic Orthodox Christian Church—announced the president's ouster. The announcement sparked notably different responses around the country. Tahrir Square was filled with cheering crowds happy to be rid of what they considered to be an Islamist dictatorship. In other parts of Cairo, Nasr City and Ennahda Square, Brotherhood supporters started sit-ins to call for the return of the man they deemed their legitimate president.

On August 14, 2013, security forces moved to break up the Brotherhood sit-ins. Hundreds were killed. Armed clashes occurred all across the country, with more victims. Coptic churches, Christian schools, police stations, and government offices were attacked, apparently by angry Brotherhood sympathizers.[1] At the same time, other citizens, exasperated by the Brotherhood, joined the security forces in attacking them. The new interim government closed Islamist television stations and jailed Brotherhood leaders. It also passed a stringent law governing demonstrations and even jailed some secular activists who opposed this new limitation on political freedom. Yet the violence continued. Pro-Brotherhood demonstrations did not stop, nor did police repression of the demonstrators. Moreover, antigovernment groups escalated armed attacks against police and military targets, leaving many victims. The Brotherhood denied any role in those attacks and insisted that it had given up violence and was only protesting through peaceful means. Nevertheless, the interim authorities reacted to the attacks by declaring the Brotherhood a "terrorist organization," effectively criminalizing all its members.[2]

The youth who led the January 25 revolution demanded liberty, prosperity, and social justice. In the three years following the revolution very little has been done to meet those demands. What went wrong? Is the hope for democracy in Egypt dead? What can the international community do? Those are the three questions that I address in this chapter.

All major political actors in Egypt made mistakes that contributed to the present situation. However, the hope for democracy, while fading, is not dead yet, and the international community should remain engaged in Egypt. The youth who sparked the January 25 revolution will continue pushing for democracy, and they have learned how to use "people power." They used it twice in three years: first against Mubarak and then against Morsi. On the other hand, all parties need to understand that it will take many years (maybe even decades) for Egypt to build a stable democratic system, and there will probably be more setbacks along the way. Egyptian democrats, and their international partners, should work to ensure that clear steps are taken toward establishing a true democracy, focusing initially on building institutions, and changing the political culture. This needs to be undergirded by a growing economy with a much fairer distribution of income.

---

1. The Brotherhood denied any involvement and blamed security forces for those attacks.

2. Human Rights Watch (2013a) argues that there is no hard evidence linking the Brotherhood to terrorism and that therefore the terrorism tag is politically motivated.

Historical Perspective: Is National Reconciliation a Realistic Goal in the Short Run?

Immediately following the fall of Morsi, many observers, including me, believed that national reconciliation was possible.[3] However, both sides in the current political struggle in Egypt have toughened their positions and seem prepared for a long existential struggle. Can history shed some light on why dialogue and compromise appear virtually impossible at the moment?

Egypt's political scene is similar to that of most countries with a conservative right wing, a liberal-nationalist center, and a socialist-leaning left wing. Nevertheless, it is important to review modern Egyptian political history (starting in the late nineteenth century) to understand the roots of the different political currents in Egypt and the ongoing struggle over the country's identity and to appreciate the critical role that the military has played in Egyptian political life over the past 130 years.

The oldest political movement in Egypt is the liberal-nationalist (which could be considered centrist), whose ideas derive from Ahmed Orabi's 1879 revolution against the Ottoman khedive and Saad Zaghloul's 1919 revolution against British occupation. Islamists (mainly the Muslim Brotherhood) lead the conservative right wing. Their ideology is based on the work of Hassan al-Banna, who started the movement in 1928, partly in response to Ataturk's abolition of the caliphate in Turkey. The left wing in Egypt derives its inspiration mainly from the work and ideas of Gamal Abdel Nasser, who led the 1952 revolution that deposed the king and succeeded in obtaining the withdrawal of British troops. The military is the strongest and most popular institution in the country and has played an important political role since the late nineteenth century, supporting and even promoting certain political currents and ideologies at different points in time, while always remaining anchored in a strong nationalist tradition.

The brief history presented below shows how Islamism is based on principles that are in sharp contradiction with liberal-nationalism as well as with Nasserism. In a sense, political Islam could be considered as the antithesis of Egyptian nationalism (whether liberal or left-leaning

---

3. See Ghanem (2013a).

Nasserist), which may explain the deep polarization in Egyptian society today as it is divided between those two very different views of national identity. The bitter and often bloody struggle between nationalists and Islamists has been going on for more than eighty years, leaving many scars on both sides. That is probably why calls for national reconciliation in Egypt today are not gaining much traction.

Liberal-Nationalism: Can Egyptians Claim the Heritage of the Pharaohs?

Modern liberal-nationalist sentiment in Egypt dates back to the late nineteenth century, when Ahmed Orabi, the head of the Egyptian armed forces, revolted against the khedive, who represented the Ottoman Empire. In response to the khedive's claim that he was the legitimate ruler of Egypt and everybody had to bow to him, Orabi famously replied, "Our mothers bore us free; we were not created as slaves to anybody." All Egyptian children are taught this history and learn these words by heart. Orabi's revolution failed, as the British intervened to support the khedive. Orabi's army was defeated in 1882, Orabi was exiled, and Egypt became a British protectorate.

Nevertheless, Orabi continues to be a revered figure in Egypt. He is the first nationalist leader in modern Egyptian history. He also established two traditions: Egyptian nationalism is in conflict with pan-Islamism, which at the time was represented by the Ottoman Empire, and the Egyptian military is a bastion of nationalist sentiment. That Orabi was Egypt's military leader and also its first modern nationalist is important. He was the son of Egyptian peasants who stood up to the Ottoman khedive. His movement had broad-based popular support, as a statement of indigenous Egyptians' rejection of the hegemony of Ottomans and of European powers. Orabi established a nationalist tradition in the Egyptian military. The military is still perceived by the Egyptian public as the "sons of Egypt," who are committed to safeguarding the nation's interests and its dignity.

Orabi's nationalist mantle was taken over by Saad Zaghloul, a civilian, who started a revolution against British colonial rule in 1919. Zaghloul established the Wafd Party, which continued to be Egypt's largest party, winning 179 parliamentary seats out of 211 in the 1924 elections and 157 seats (with 89 percent of the vote) in 1936, until it was dissolved by Nasser in 1952. Throughout its history the Wafd was in constant conflict with the king and with the British, who effectively ruled Egypt despite its nominal independence in 1922. The party continues to play an important role in Egyptian politics today under the name of the New Wafd.

The Wafd's platform can be summarized as having three prongs: nationalism, secularism, and liberalism.[4] Zaghloul's movement opposed British occupation of Egypt. It developed a view of the Egyptian nation as an old and established civilization with roots going back to the pharaohs, from whom they traced their lineage. Nationalists of the early twentieth century, many of whom had studied in Europe, cultivated Egyptians' pride in their ancient heritage. The idea, therefore, was of an independent Egyptian nation that does not need to be part of a bigger entity formed by pan-Islamism or pan-Arabism.

While the Wafd's nationalism put it on a collision course with the colonial power, its call for a true constitutional democracy put it on a collision course with the king, who saw it as a threat to his prerogatives. Those two conflicts, with the king and the British, actually helped enhance the party's popularity.

Since the Wafd defined Egypt by its history and culture, and not its religion, it was only natural that its platform would be secular and that many Coptic Christians joined the Wafd and reached high leadership positions in it. A rallying cry of the liberal-nationalists of the time was "Religion is for God; the nation is for all." The Wafd Party also had a feminist wing, which was initially led by Zaghloul's wife, Zafiya, who led demonstrations and encouraged Egyptian women to take off the traditional veil.

This does not mean, however, that the liberal-nationalists were opposed to Islam or to Arab unity. Many of their leaders were pious and upheld Islamic traditions. But they considered Islam to be only one of the many variables that define the Egyptian national identity. For them, Egypt as a nation predates Islam. As noted by Rutherford (2008), modern Egyptian liberals are different from those in the West because they accept a role for religion in public life. They support article 2 of the 1971 constitution, which declares that the principles of sharia

---

4. The Arabic term for "secular," *elmany*, has been recently given a negative connotation by Islamist thinkers who sometimes appear to use it as a synonym for "atheist" (*kafir*). In this chapter I use the traditional definition of *secular* to refer to a person who believes in separating religion from politics.

will be the main source of legislation. Moreover, the Wafd, under the leadership of al-Nahas (Zaghloul's successor), played a key role in the creation of the Arab League.

The Wafd espoused liberal economic policies. It was supported by businessmen and owners of large landholdings, united by the nationalist narrative and a desire to free Egypt from British rule. On the other hand, it did not provide sufficient support to Egypt's nascent labor movement, nor did it focus on raising standards of living of the masses, particularly landless peasants. This left the Wafd open to attacks from both the left wing and the Islamist right wing.

The first half of the twentieth century was also a period of cultural revival in Egypt. This included a literary revival led by writers such as the Nobel laureate Naguib Mahfouz and a musical revival led by artists such as Um Kalthoum. The Cairo opera was active. The Egyptian movie industry and theater became popular all across the Arab world. A new elite, consisting of writers, poets, musicians, actors, and movie producers, appeared in Egypt. Nearly all members of this elite, who played a crucial role in creating national identity, belonged to the liberal-nationalist tradition.

Nasserism: Could Social Justice and Arab Unity Be Achieved?

Nasserism is Egypt's second secular ideology. It is inspired by the thoughts and actions of Gamal Abdel Nasser, who led the 1952 military revolt against King Farouk and who was president of Egypt from 1956 until his death in 1970. Nasser was probably the most popular Arab leader of the twentieth century, with his popularity spreading beyond Egypt to nearly all of the Arab world. He remains an iconic figure even today.

Nasserism is also a nationalist ideology. One of the key objectives of Nasser's Free Officers was to liberate Egypt from British occupation. However, Nasserism differs from the Wafd ideology in that it stresses the importance of pan-Arabism and Arab nationalism. Nasser's aim was the creation of a united Arab nation led by Egypt.

A distinguishing feature of Nasserism is its emphasis on social justice and its adoption of Arab socialism. Nasser implemented land reform in Egypt, confiscating land from feudalists and distributing it to landless peasants. He nationalized all large industries and the entire banking sector. Nasser's government invested heavily in large public sector manufacturing enterprises. One of his objectives was to have Egypt produce everything "from the needle to the rocket." Nasser also introduced free universal education and free health care, as well as large rural water and electrification projects. He introduced an article in the Egyptian constitution that requires that one-half of the members of all elected bodies be either peasants or workers. He also introduced laws guaranteeing a public sector job for all university graduates and put in place a large system of price controls and subsidies to protect low- and middle-income consumers.

The Nasserist political system was not democratic.[5] It was a one-party (Arab Socialist Union) system, and no opposition was allowed. All the political parties that existed before the 1952 revolution were banned. The state controlled all media outlets, and strict censorship was put in place. Nasser's opponents (mostly Islamists and communists) were dealt with harshly through a strong security apparatus. Thus Nasser put in place a system of political repression that was maintained and further developed by his successors—Anwar Sadat, Hosni Mubarak, and, to some extent, Mohamed Morsi.

As a nationalist army officer, Nasser could be considered a successor of Orabi. However, his views differed from mainstream Egyptian liberal-nationalist thought in three important ways: he stressed Egypt's Arab identity over its ancient pharaonic one; he prioritized social justice and implemented socialist economic policies; and he did not support multiparty democracy.

Today's Nasserists continue to prioritize pan-Arabism and social justice. However, they now espouse multiparty democracy.

The Muslim Brotherhood: Can Egypt Become Part of an Islamic Caliphate?

While Egypt has always been a deeply religious country, modern political Islam only appeared on the national scene in 1928 with the creation of the Muslim Brotherhood by Hassan al-Banna. The Brotherhood was created as a pan-Islamic social and political movement, partly in response to the fall of the Ottoman Empire and the abolition of

---

5. According to the Egyptian writer Tawfiq al-Hakim, "Nasserism rested on the basis of the destruction of minds and wills, other than the will of the leader" (quoted in Hopwood 1991, chap. 11).

the caliphate in Turkey by Mustapha Kemal Ataturk. This abolition was seen as an important setback by many pious Muslims, including al-Banna, who considered the caliphate to be a necessity in Islam. This put the Brotherhood in direct confrontation with Egyptian nationalists.[6]

The Brotherhood was based on two important principles. The first was the adoption of sharia law as the basis for conducting the affairs of state and society. For the Brotherhood, "Islam is a state as well as a religion." This is sometimes understood to imply that secular ideas are inherently un-Islamic and therefore Muslims who call for a secular state could be considered nonbelievers. The Brotherhood holds conservative views on gender equality and the role of women in society. They argue for a "modest" dress for women and the separation of the sexes at schools and workplaces. They also believe that cultural products should reflect the Islamic nature of society and have called for censorship of books and movies that they consider un-Islamic. Thus the Brotherhood has always been at odds with Egypt's cultural and artistic elite.

The second principle is to unify Islamic states and free them from foreign imperialism. The Brotherhood considers Egypt to be just one small part of a large Islamic empire (or caliphate) stretching from Spain to Indonesia. A previous general guide (chairman) of the Brotherhood, Mohamed Akef, generated an outcry when he commented in one of his interviews "to hell with Egypt." Of course he meant to emphasize the pan-Islamic ambitions of his organization, but his statement was interpreted by nationalists as indicating that the Brotherhood does not care for Egypt.

The Brotherhood has not presented a detailed economic program. But one can deduce from its pronouncements on economic policies that it would not be much different from that of the liberal-nationalists. The Brotherhood believes in a market economy with social protection and safety nets for the poor. It also emphasizes the fight against corruption.

The history of the Muslim Brotherhood is marred by violence. During the Second World War, the Brotherhood was accused of collaborating with the Axis powers in the hope that they would help rid Egypt of British imperialism. They were involved in several bombings and assassinations. As a result, in 1948 the Egyptian government banned the Brotherhood and arrested many of its leaders. The Brotherhood

6. For a more detailed history of the Brotherhood, see Wickham (2013).

retaliated by assassinating the prime minister, making the point that they were as powerful as the Egyptian state and could even hit the head of the executive branch of government. Al-Banna himself was later assassinated, probably in retaliation. The Brotherhood was also accused of taking part in the great fire of Cairo in 1952, in which some 750 buildings (mainly nightclubs, theaters, restaurants, bars, and hotels in the downtown area) were burned.

The Brotherhood initially supported Gamal Abdel Nasser and the Free Officers movement that took over power and sent the king into exile in 1952. However, they soon separated from the Free Officers when the latter passed a secular constitution. They were accused of trying to assassinate Nasser in 1954 during a public rally in Alexandria. Nasser retaliated by banning the Brotherhood once again and imprisoning thousands of its members. After another assassination attempt against Nasser in the mid-1960s, the state started another round of repression against the Brotherhood, and several of their leaders were executed. Nasser is considered to have been the Brotherhood's nemesis. Even today anti-Brotherhood protesters often carry pictures of Nasser, and videotapes of his speeches attacking the Brotherhood (which are on YouTube) are widely publicized and shared on secular social-media channels.

When Sadat came to power after Nasser's death in 1970, his main preoccupation was to reclaim the Sinai, which was occupied by Israel in the 1967 war. This required that he start shifting Egypt away from the Soviet camp and closer to the West, particularly the United States, who he believed held "99 percent of the cards in the Arab-Israeli conflict." Naturally, he faced stiff resistance from the left wing, whom he tried to neutralize by opening up to the Muslim Brotherhood. He started releasing members from jail and allowing them to carry out some activities, although they remained officially banned.

Sadat was a devout Muslim, but he was also a military man and a nationalist, in the tradition of Ahmed Orabi. Hence it was probably inevitable that he would clash with the Brotherhood. This happened after he signed the Camp David accords and the peace treaty with Israel. He was assassinated by an Islamist group that is an offshoot of the Brotherhood. Many Egyptian liberal-nationalists as well as members of the armed forces who admire Sadat continue to hold the Brotherhood responsible for his death.

The Brotherhood has officially announced that it now supports democracy and rejects violence. However, its detractors argue that it is difficult to have a true democracy in the context of a religious state that is governed by sharia. They say that it is hard to have a reasonable political debate when one party insists on using quotations from the Quran to validate its point of view. They also point out that many Brotherhood members continue to use violent means against their opponents and that Brotherhood demonstrators are sometimes armed.

Elusive Reconciliation: Is Political Islam Consistent with Egyptian Nationalism and Democracy?

This brief, and admittedly selective, review of Egypt's modern political history suggests three broad conclusions that can help explain the present situation. First, while the differences between liberal-nationalists and Nasserists are mainly around economic policies, the two parties' difference with the Muslim Brotherhood centers on national identity. The former difference can be dealt with in the course of normal political dialogue, but the latter has so far proved impossible to resolve through dialogue. This could explain why both the liberals and the Nasserists supported Morsi's ouster. Second, throughout its history the Brotherhood has been associated with violence. It sometimes instigated violence, but it was also often the victim of violent repression. The current cycle of violence is in some sense a continuation of a war that started in the 1930s and has already claimed thousands of victims on both sides, including a prime minister (Mahmud Fahmi al-Nuqrashi, assassinated in 1948), the Brotherhood's first general guide (al-Banna, assassinated in 1949), and a president (Anwar Sadat, assassinated in 1981). Third, Egyptians have never known true democracy and have lived under more or less repressive systems for millennia. This may explain why they are not particularly shocked by the current wave of repression against the Brotherhood. In fact, it appears that a majority supports it. There is a sense of déjà vu in what is happening in Egypt now.

Is political Islam consistent with democracy? There is no agreement on this point, neither among Egyptian politicians nor among Western scholars. The Brotherhood claims that it is democratic, while its opponents believe that its only aim is to get into power, and once it gets there, it will never leave. Opponents of the Brotherhood subscribe to the view of the United States' former undersecretary of state, Edward Djerjian, who, following the 1991 Islamist electoral victory in Algeria, described the Islamist political agenda as "one man, one vote, one time."[7] That is, an Islamist party might use democracy to get into power, but once in control it would never hand power back to a secular opposition.

The same debate is currently taking place among Western scholars. Wickham (2013) argues that the Brotherhood has evolved, especially owing to some of its members' participation in political life under Mubarak as leaders in professional associations or as members of parliament. She believes that this experience has made the Brotherhood more open to political debate and dialogue and more accepting of democratic values. In a sense the Brotherhood joined the formal political system to change it but ended up being changed by it. Nevertheless, she warns, one cannot conclude that the Brotherhood has embraced the liberal and inclusive ethos of democracy because its insistence on an Islamic frame of reference implies the existence of an authority above the electorate.

Bradley (2012, p. 71) is less nuanced. He argues that the belief that the Brotherhood has evolved "has more to do with its recruitment of spokesmen who spout to gullible western experts the virtues of its pro-democracy platform" than with any real change in its position. He examines the Brotherhood's 2007 platform and concludes that it does not meet democratic standards. The platform states that laws have to be consistent with sharia and establishes a body of religious scholars to review draft laws. It does not allow women to run for president. And it does not allow non-Muslims to run for president or prime minister. However, the Brotherhood dropped mention of those three controversial points in its postrevolution documents. It is not clear whether this reflected a real change in the group's values and perspectives or was just a tactical move for electoral purposes.

A key question is whether the Brotherhood, or anyone else for that matter, has the right to define Islam for the rest of society. The Brotherhood has been providing mixed messages. On one hand, they have adopted an apparently progressive discourse on freedom and democracy. On the other hand, they continue to hold a traditional, and illiberal, conception of Islam and its role in society. To be credible and assuage liberal fears, the Brotherhood will need to find a way

7. Quoted in Aliboni (2012).

to reconcile traditional Islam and sharia law with notions of human rights, respect for minorities, women's rights, and individual freedom.

The Mubarak Years: Why Did Egyptians Revolt?

Mubarak presented himself as the only protection Egyptians had against political Islam. And many secular Egyptians were happy to support him. He seemed secure in his position. Only three years before the revolution, Rutherford (2008, chap. 6) reflected the view of most observers when he stated that "in the Egyptian case, the prospects for democratization are poor. The [Mubarak] regime retains a stranglehold on political life which it shows little signs of loosening." How can one then explain the rapidity with which Mubarak fell?

Mubarak's thirty-year rule was characterized on the political side by overreliance on a security apparatus and repressive policies and on the economic side by an unequal distribution of the benefits of growth. He weakened all the secular parties except his own (the National Democratic Party). He continued to cling to power even when he passed the age of eighty, and he appeared to be grooming his son to succeed him. This greatly increased political tensions. Although the Egyptian economy was growing at healthy rates, the middle class did not expand fast enough, and youth were left out of the economic growth, which increased socioeconomic tensions. If Mubarak had stepped down in 2005 in favor of a younger leader (other than his son) who could start to gradually implement democratic reforms and policies to make income distribution more equitable, the 2011 revolution and all the turmoil that Egypt is going through now might have been avoided. However, Egyptians did not see any hope of peaceful democratic evolution, and revolution became unavoidable.

Lack of Progress on Democracy:
How Long Did Mubarak Plan to Stay in Power?

When Hosni Mubarak came to power in 1981, Freedom House classified Egypt as partially free, with a political rights index of 5 and a civil liberties index also of 5.[8] In 2010, Mubarak's last year in power, Egypt was classified as not free, as the political rights index had risen

8. www.freedomhouse.org.

(which implies a deterioration) to 6. This reflects worsening political conditions in the later Mubarak years, as he relied increasingly on the security forces and rigged elections to remain in power.

In 2005 the Mubarak regime made some signs of wanting to gradually open up the political system and start implementing democratic reforms. It introduced a change in the constitution that allowed for multicandidate presidential elections (in previous elections Mubarak ran unopposed). In 2005 Mubarak ran against two other candidates, Ayman Nour of al-Ghad Party and Numan Gumaa of the New Wafd. The regime also allowed Muslim Brotherhood members to run in parliamentary elections as independents; members won 88 seats (60 percent of the seats they competed for) out of a total of 518 and became the largest parliamentary opposition bloc.

But the regime's efforts were unconvincing. Presidential candidates confronted so many constraints that none of the candidates who might have threatened Mubarak were allowed to run. Moreover, the elections themselves were marred by many irregularities. Voter turnout was low, as most Egyptians did not expect the elections to be fair. Official figures put turnout at 23.9 percent, but other observers claimed that actual turnout was much lower. As expected, Mubarak won reelection, with 88.6 percent of the vote, while Ayman Nour received 7.3 percent.

Mubarak's conduct after the presidential election indicated that he was not serious about expanding political rights. Nour contested the election results and requested an investigation of irregularities and a revote. Not surprisingly, his request was rejected. To make things worse, Nour himself was tried on what appeared to be trumped-up charges of forgery and was sentenced to five years of hard labor. The message was clear: the regime would retaliate against those who went too far in claiming their political rights.

The 2005 parliamentary elections were also marred by irregularities, particularly in the runoff phase, when it became clear that the Brotherhood was making important inroads. There were widespread allegations that government employees stuffed ballot boxes, bought votes, and bused nonresidents in efforts to defeat opposition candidates. Police blockaded access to polling stations where the opposition was strong and even opened fire to disrupt voting, which led to several casualties.

The 2010 parliamentary elections, which took place in November and December (a few weeks before the start of the 2011 revolution) were even worse and are considered to have been the most fraudulent in Egypt's history—which is saying a lot, given the scale of fraud in previous elections. Mubarak's National Democratic Party increased its majority from 330 to 420 seats. The Muslim Brotherhood's share of parliamentary seats fell from 88 to only 1. Fraud was so blatant that it appeared that the regime no longer cared about presenting even a façade of democracy and rule of law.

The regime's policies have probably helped expand the Brotherhood and make it more popular. Most activist youth joined Islamist movements, which provided them with an alternative moral and cultural community.[9] Islamist organizations also provided youth with services, such as libraries and sports facilities, that the Mubarak regime did not deliver. Thus the Brotherhood gradually built its grassroots support and strengthened its organization across the country, especially in poor rural areas.

As a result of lack of political freedom it is not surprising that in 2010 Egypt scored far below all other comparators except China on voice and accountability in the Worldwide Governance Indicators index (table 1-1). Egyptians, especially youth, faced serious constraints to expressing themselves. The result was that most young people refrained from any civic activities or volunteer work. They felt that their voices could not be heard.

Lack of government accountability led to high corruption and added to Egyptians' sense of unfairness. As shown in table 1-1, Egypt ranked in the bottom half of all countries on corruption control in 2010. Among the five comparators, only China had a similar ranking. Egypt's record on corruption control is far below that of Chile, Brazil, Malaysia, and South Africa. Corruption was (and still is) pervasive, ranging from small payments to traffic police to huge sums in return for access to government contracts.

Egypt also scored poorly on government effectiveness. The middle class were (and still are) highly dependent on government services: health, education, transportation, and security. They suffered from the continual deterioration of those services. Children attending public schools are required to pay their own teachers for private tuition in

---

9. See Bayat (1998) for a more detailed exposition of this argument.

TABLE 1-1. Selected Governance Indicators, by Country, 2010

Percentile rank

Indicator	Egypt	Brazil	Chile	China	Malaysia	South Africa
Control of corruption	34	60	91	33	61	61
Government effectiveness	40	57	84	60	82	65
Rule of law	52	55	88	45	65	58
Voice and accountability	13	64	82	5	31	65

Source: Worldwide Governance Indicators, World Bank.

order to pass exams, and patients in government hospitals often need to pay bribes to get service.

Revolution became inevitable because Egyptians saw no end in sight. The National Democratic Party announced in 2010 that Mubarak would be once more its candidate in the 2011 presidential elections. Mubarak appeared set on remaining president for life. To make matters worse, he seemed to be grooming his son, Gamal, to succeed him. Gamal held the position of deputy secretary general of the party and headed the all-powerful policies committee. He and a group of businessmen close to him already played a large role in determining the country's policy directions as well as in the appointment of ministers and other high officials. Egypt appeared to be turning into some kind of presidential monarchy, and the Mubarak regime seemed set to continue long after its founder's death.

Noninclusive Growth: Can Rising Inequality Explain the 2011 Revolution?

During the period leading to the January 25, 2011, revolution, the Egyptian economy appeared to be doing well (table 1-2).[10] GDP was growing at 5 to 7 percent a year (supported by high foreign and domestic investment), while the current account was under control and foreign reserves were high. This strong performance continued even during the global financial crisis. In 2009 and 2010 the country's economy was growing at a healthy 5 percent and had reserves equivalent to seven months' imports, despite a decline in foreign direct investment

10. For more on the evolution of the Egyptian middle class see Ghanem (2013b), and for an analysis of the political role of the Arab middle classes see Diwan (2013).

TABLE 1-2. Selected Macroeconomic Indicators, Egypt, 2000–10

Year	Current account balance (% of GDP)	Foreign direct investment, net inflows (% of GDP)	GDP growth (annual %)	GDP per capita growth (annual %)	Gross fixed capital formation (% of GDP)	Total reserves in months' imports
2000	−1	1	5	3	19	7
2001	0	1	4	2	18	7
2002	1	1	2	0	18	8
2003	5	0	3	1	16	9
2004	5	2	4	2	16	7
2005	2	6	4	3	18	7
2006	2	9	7	5	19	7
2007	0	9	7	5	21	7
2008	−1	6	7	5	22	6
2009	−2	4	5	3	19	7
2010	−2	3	5	3	19	7

Source: World Development Indicators, World Bank.

and some deterioration in the current account balance. At 11 to 12 percent, inflation was high by international standards but still within the Central Bank's comfort zone. The problem was not the level of growth but its distribution. In particular, economic growth was not leading to the rapid development of a middle class, youth felt excluded, and rural areas, especially in Upper Egypt, were left behind.

I use here a definition of the middle class developed by Homi Kharas at the Brookings Institution. According to this definition, the middle class consists of "those households that have a certain amount of discretionary income that goes beyond the necessities of life to include consumer durables, quality education and health care, housing, vacations and other leisure pursuits. This group is differentiated from the poor in that they have choices over what they consume. They are differentiated from the rich in that their choices are constrained by their budget; they are price and quality sensitive."[11] By this definition, middle-class Egyptian households are those that spend between $10 and $100 a person per day.

11. See Kharas (2010).

According to estimates available at the Brookings Institution, the Egyptian middle class has grown from 12 percent of the population in 2000 to 22 percent in 2010, which appears to be a positive development. However, this expansion was not sufficient to reduce the absolute number of people living below the middle-class level (hence poor, according to this definition), whose number increased from 60 million in 2000 to 63 million in 2010. Egypt's experience in this regard is very different from that of emerging markets such as Brazil or India, where the middle class expanded at a much faster rate.

Youth suffered from economic exclusion during the Mubarak years, which can be best illustrated by examining labor market outcomes. The Egyptian public sector has traditionally provided jobs to the large numbers of graduates entering the labor market each year; currently, about 850,000 young people enter the labor market annually, and 70 percent of them have completed at least secondary education.[12] This changed with the economic reforms that aimed at controlling government spending and rationalizing the public sector; and given the high fiscal deficit and overemployment in the public sector, it is unlikely that this sector will be able to absorb many new graduates. As a result, it has become increasingly hard for young people to find jobs, and youth with secondary education or above represent about 95 percent of the unemployed in Egypt. The problem is particularly acute for young women, who are 3.8 times as likely to be unemployed as young men. Of the young men and women who do find jobs, only 28 percent find formal sector jobs—18 percent in the public sector and 10 percent in the formal private sector. The vast majority, 72 percent, end up working in the informal sector, often as unpaid family workers. For those who are paid, many have no labor contract, no job security, and no social benefits.

Rural-urban and regional inequalities are also serious problems. Economic growth does not seem to have benefited rural areas and Upper Egypt. The probability of being extremely poor in Egypt is nearly four times as high for people living in rural areas as for those in urban areas. About 6.7 percent of the population of Egypt is extremely poor, defined as unable to afford basic necessities. For urban areas that figure is only 2.6 percent, and for rural areas, 9.6 percent. That is, nearly one of every

12. See Assaad and Barsoum (2007).

ten rural inhabitants in Egypt is extremely poor and food insecure. In addition to the rural-urban differences, poverty in Egypt also varies by region. Upper Egypt has about 50 percent of the country's population but 83 percent of the extremely poor and 67 percent of the poor. The problem in Upper Egypt is especially serious in the rural areas. Urban Upper Egypt has 11.6 percent of the extremely poor and 11.3 percent of the poor; rural Upper Egypt has 71.5 percent of the extremely poor and 55.8 percent of the poor. Lower Egypt has less poverty. About 30 percent of Egypt's population lives in Lower Egypt, and the region is home to 13.7 percent of the country's extreme poor and 27.6 percent of the poor. However, it is important to note that the vast majority of the poor and extremely poor in Lower Egypt also live in rural areas.

Messy Transition: Why Did Things Fall Apart?

Bradley (2012, p. 199) concludes that "the Arab Spring has been a dismal failure." Many Egyptians would agree with him. What went wrong?

The initial success of the 2011 revolution led to a surge of optimism among Egyptians. In 2010, before the fall of Mubarak, 69 percent of Egyptians were dissatisfied with the way things were moving in the country. A year later, 65 percent of Egyptians were satisfied with the way things were moving. Egyptians were looking forward to a new era of democracy, human dignity, and economic well-being.

When Mubarak stepped down on February 11, 2011, he transferred his powers to the Supreme Council of the Armed Forces (SCAF). According to the Egyptian constitution at the time of Mubarak's resignation, when the office of the president is vacant the speaker of parliament acts as interim president. Hence this transfer of power to SCAF had no legal basis. However, it made political sense. The military is the most respected institution in the country, with a 67 percent approval rating, while parliament (especially after the rigged 2010 elections) was considered corrupt and illegitimate. Thus Egyptians were happy to see SCAF take responsibility for leading the transition.

However, the eighteen-member SCAF, which was led by the seventy-six-year-old Mohamed Hussein Tantawi, had no experience in running a country or in leading a political transition. Under SCAF's stewardship the economy declined at a worrisome rate, and political unrest continued. At the time when Morsi was elected in 2012, the country still had no constitution, and the courts had dissolved the lower house of parliament. And Egypt was moving steadily toward an economic crisis. The Supreme Council seemed relieved to be able to hand over power to the elected president and let him handle the remainder of the transition.

But Morsi's management of the transition was even worse than SCAF's. During the one year of Morsi's rule the economy nearly collapsed, corruption increased, a nonconsensual constitution was passed, and the country became polarized between Islamists and secularists. The youth who started the revolution felt betrayed as their political and economic exclusion during the Mubarak era continued. This led to the rise of the Tamarod (rebellion) movement. Supporters collected millions of signatures on a petition calling for Morsi to step down and for the organization of early presidential elections. They also organized massive anti-Morsi demonstrations in late June 2013. Morsi, supported by the Muslim Brotherhood, refused to compromise and argued that his electoral legitimacy gave him the right to ignore opposition demands.

Finally, in June 2013 the people rose against Morsi, and he was deposed. The head of the constitutional court was named as interim president, and he, in turn, appointed an interim government. The new transitional authorities announced a road map for the future that involved writing a new constitution as well as parliamentary and presidential elections. Nevertheless, Morsi's overthrow led to increased political violence and even more polarization. It remains to be seen whether the interim government will be able to lead the country toward democracy or whether Egypt will slide back to a Mubarak-like era of police repression and constraints on political and civil liberties.

A Leaderless Revolution: How Did Mubarak Fall in Eighteen Days?

The Egyptian revolution had no clear political agenda and no leadership.[13] It was started by secular youth (liberal-nationalists as well as leftists and Nasserists) whose stated objective was to bring down the Mubarak regime and to put in place a system that would ensure "bread, liberty, social justice and human dignity." Those lofty revolutionary ideals were not backed up by a detailed program, and the revolution had no

---

13. Ghonim (2013) describes the role that Mohamed el-Baradei, the former head of the International Atomic Energy Agency, played as an agent of change who could not, or maybe would not, take over as the leader and spokesperson of the revolution.

spokespersons to represent its views and push for its demands. Initially, Islamists did not join the revolution. The Brotherhood believed that the revolution was doomed to failure and wanted to avoid becoming a victim of yet another round of repression by the Mubarak regime. The Salafists were not interested in politics, and several Salafist leaders issued fatwas stating that revolting against a Muslim ruler was un-Islamic.

As the revolution progressed and appeared to be nearing victory, the Muslim Brotherhood decided to join. The Brotherhood is well organized and has a large number of disciplined followers. When they joined the secular youth in Tahrir Square, the Mubarak regime appeared to be in grave danger.

Mubarak ordered the army into the streets. Tanks and armored personnel carriers moved into Tahrir Square but did not attack the demonstrators. The military establishment had decided not to support Mubarak. According to the renowned Egyptian journalist Mohamed Hassanein Heikal, SCAF had discussed as early as 2010 what they would do if in July 2011 they discovered that the ruling party had nominated Mubarak's son for the presidency and the people, angered, took to the streets.[14] Heikal states that the generals agreed that in this case they would not obey orders and would not attack the demonstrators. Popular anger came six months earlier than the generals had predicted, and they stuck to their strategy of remaining neutral.

The Mubarak regime could not survive without the support of the military. February 11, 2011, when Mubarak stepped down, was a day of national unity in Egypt. Liberal-nationalists, Nasserists, leftists, and Islamists celebrated together the end of the autocratic regime, and they were supported by the military. They promised a new beginning, when all the political factions would work together to build a democratic and prosperous Egypt. However, this unity proved to be short-lived, and the dream of democracy much more difficult to achieve than the people in Tahrir Square envisioned.

First Phase of the Transition: Could SCAF Have Done Things Differently?

The Supreme Council of the Armed Forces was in charge of the transition, and Field Marshal Tantawi became the de facto head of state. The first political disagreement he had to deal with centered on the

---

14. Interview with *Al-Shorouk* newspaper published on January 4, 2014.

timing of elections and the writing of a new constitution. After the dissolution of Mubarak's National Democratic Party, the Brotherhood was the only organized group left in the country and therefore would win in any early election. They pushed for elections to take place before a constitution was written. The liberal-nationalist, Nasserist, and the leftist parties wanted time to prepare and organize their bases. Therefore they argued for agreement on a new constitution before elections. At this point the Brotherhood promised not to field candidates for more than 50 percent of the seats in parliament, so that they would rule only in a coalition government, and they also promised not to field a presidential candidate. The Supreme Council sided with the Brotherhood and started preparing for elections before the constitution.

As the politicians were arguing about constitutions and elections, the revolutionary youth were still on the streets demonstrating against military rule and calling for achievement of the revolution's objectives. The first major clash occurred on Maspiro Street, in front of the national television building, on October 9 and 10, 2011. A group of young Copts were demonstrating against the destruction of a church by extremists. The peaceful demonstration came under attack by security forces who used live ammunition and even crushed some protesters under armored personnel carriers. The result was twenty-four dead and more than 300 injured, nearly all of them Coptic Christians.

This was followed by huge demonstrations in Tahrir Square and on nearby Mohamed Mahmoud Street (leading to the Ministry of Interior) protesting police brutality against families of those killed or injured during the revolution. The repression of the demonstrations reached another level of violence, particularly on November 19. The revolutionary youth chanted against military rule and against Field Marshal Tantawi. They called for the cancelation of the parliamentary elections, which they felt were pointless under the circumstances. It is important to note that the Brotherhood did not participate in those demonstrations. It maintained good relations with SCAF and continued to prepare for the elections. It had already broken its first political promise and was fielding candidates for all the seats in the lower house.

The treatment of women demonstrators was shameful. Many women were sexually assaulted or even raped during demonstrations. Egypt was shocked to learn that army officers carried out humiliating "virginity tests" on female demonstrators whom they detained. Several human rights groups organized protests and marches to demand gender equality and an end of sexual violence against women.

The incident of "the woman in the blue bra" shocked the nation and probably helped set the stage for continuing revolt by youth against both the military and the Brotherhood. Young people were demonstrating against SCAF and what they considered SCAF's deals with the Brotherhood. On December 18, 2011, during one of those demonstrations, security forces grabbed a female demonstrator, tore her clothes, exposing her bright blue bra, and dragged her through the street. A young male demonstrator who rushed to help his fallen female colleague was savagely beaten by the security forces. His beating, as well as the attack on the woman, was caught on video and widely watched by Egyptians. Hassan Shaheen, the young man who was beaten, is one of the leaders of the Tamarod movement that eventually succeeded in overthrowing the Brotherhood's president.

Notwithstanding the boycott by the revolutionary youth and continued demonstrations and unrest, elections for the lower house of parliament took place as planned in three stages between November 28, 2011, and January 8, 2012. As expected, the results were catastrophic for the secularists. The Brotherhood won 37.5 percent of the popular vote, which translated into 45 percent of the seats in Parliament. The Salafists came in second, winning 27.8 percent of the popular vote and 25 percent of the seats in parliament. Thus Egypt's first postrevolution parliament had a crushing Islamist majority of 70 percent. Elections for the upper house were also carried out on January 29 and February 22. They solicited little enthusiasm, and voter turnout was low. Islamists won nearly 80 percent of the seats, with the Brotherhood holding an absolute majority of about 58 percent.

Secular forces, and particularly the revolutionary youth, felt betrayed by SCAF and by the Islamists. Questions about the funding of Islamist campaigns were raised, and it was alleged that the two large Islamist parties received generous donations from individuals in Qatar for the Brotherhood and in Saudi Arabia for the Salafists. This was a step toward polarization as secular parties played to Egyptians' nationalist sentiments by implying that the Islamists received foreign financing and were therefore agents of foreign interests.

The Brotherhood-dominated parliament elected a constituent assembly to start drafting Egypt's postrevolutionary constitution. It included 66 Islamists out of 100 members. It had only six women and five Copts. Secular parties boycotted the assembly, and ultimately the courts declared the results unconstitutional because members of parliament had elected themselves to the assembly. Agreement was reached between secularists and Islamists on the structure of the second constituent assembly, but the secularists claimed that the Islamists broke that agreement. Many secular parties followed the call of Mohamed el-Baradei (liberal-nationalist) and Hamdeen Sabbahi (Nasserist) to boycott the second constituent assembly. Other groups, including Coptic Church representatives, also joined the boycott. According to a poll carried out by Al-Ahram news agency, more than 80 percent of Egyptians wanted the constituent assembly to be reformed to better reflect all forces in society. The schism between the Islamists and the rest of society appeared to be getting wider.

In the meantime, a presidential election was held in two rounds, the first on May 23 and 24, 2012, and the second on June 16 and 17. The Brotherhood broke its second political promise and fielded a presidential candidate. In fact, it fielded two candidates. Its preferred candidate was Khayrat al-Shatter, a millionaire businessman and deputy general guide of the Brotherhood. However, al-Shatter had legal problems that could have disqualified him, so the Brotherhood also fielded a second candidate, Mohamed Morsi, president of its political party, Freedom and Justice. This earned Morsi the nickname of "the spare-tire candidate." In the end the Brotherhood was proved right: al-Shatter was disqualified, and Morsi became the official Brotherhood candidate.

The Supreme Council clearly stated that it was not supporting any political group or candidate. However, most Egyptians felt that they were in fact supporting Ahmed Shafik, a former air force general and the last prime minister under Mubarak. The choice of Shafik as the standard-bearer of the liberal-nationalist-military alliance was unfortunate. He was closely associated with the Mubarak regime, and it would have been difficult for the people of Tahrir Square to vote for him. Another liberal-nationalist candidate, Amr Moussa, a former minister of foreign affairs and secretary general of the Arab League, presented himself in the elections, but he did not receive much support from SCAF and its followers.

Morsi won the first-round presidential election and Shafik came in second (table 1-3). Thus the second round was between those two. In

TABLE 1-3. Results of First Round of Presidential Elections, Egypt, 2012

Percent

Candidate	Political current	Share of vote
Mohamed Morsi	Muslim Brotherhood	24.8
Ahmed Shafik	Liberal-Nationalist	23.7
Hamdeen Sabbahi	Nasserist-Socialist	20.7
Abdel Moneim Abul Fotouh	Moderate Islamist	17.5
Amr Moussa	Liberal Nationalist	11.1
Other		2.2

Source: Egyptian Supreme Committee for Elections.

that first round of voting Islamists (Morsi and Abul Foutouh) received 42.3 percent of the vote. The liberal-nationalists (Shafik and Moussa) received 34.8 percent, and the Nasserist Sabbahi 20.7 percent. Sabbahi's strong showing demonstrates that the Nasserist and leftist message still attracts substantial support in Egypt, particularly among the working class. It is noteworthy that Sabbahi won pluralities in Egypt's two largest cities, Cairo and Alexandria.

Morsi won the second round of presidential elections with 51.7 percent of the vote to Shafik's 48.3 percent. Many secularists voted for Morsi because they did not want to support someone whom they considered to be a Mubarak clone. Others simply stayed home on election day. It is hard to predict what the elections' outcome would have been had the liberal-nationalist-military coalition selected someone other than Shafik as their standard-bearer. But an opinion poll by Al-Ahram shows that had the second round of presidential elections been between Mohamed Morsi and Amr Moussa, Moussa would have won with 77.6 percent of the vote to only 22.4 percent for Morsi.

Second Phase of the Transition: Why Did Morsi's Presidency Fail?

Egyptians of all political leanings who were worried that the elections might get rigged in favor of Shafik celebrated Morsi's electoral victory. His inauguration on June 30, 2012, was reminiscent of the day that Mubarak resigned. Tahrir Square was filled with huge crowds representing all political forces. The nation seemed united once more, and all the violence on Maspiro and Mohamed Mahmoud streets appeared to have been forgotten. A few weeks later, Morsi fired Field Marshal

Tantawi from his post as minister of defense and appointed a new chief of staff of the armed forces. This move was widely supported. Democracy seemed to be working, as the elected civilian president was taking control of the military.

Morsi promised to be the president of all Egyptians and to appoint two vice presidents, a woman and a Copt. But those promises were not kept, and the euphoria following Morsi's election quickly dissipated as Egyptians slowly came to believe that he as president served only the Brotherhood.

Morsi's term in office started with a clash with the judiciary. In early June, before the presidential elections, the courts ordered the lower house of parliament dissolved on grounds that the election law was unconstitutional, and the SCAF quickly complied. On taking office Morsi tried to reinstate the lower house, but this was interpreted as an attack on the independence of the judiciary and was resisted by the judges, the media, and the political parties. In the end the president had to retreat and accept the dissolution of the lower house. Another battle with the judiciary involved the change of prosecutor general, which Morsi tried to implement in an extralegal manner and was strongly resisted.

The battle between the elected president and the judiciary was often presented as an attempt by Morsi (and the Muslim Brotherhood) to encroach on the prerogatives of the judicial branch of government, which under a democracy is supposed to be independent from the executive. There may have been some truth to that. However, it is also true that the Egyptian judiciary (like the military, police, and civil service) comes from a long nationalist tradition. Moreover, all the judges that Morsi had to deal with were Mubarak appointees. They were happy to make life as difficult as possible for the new president and his Islamist supporters. Society became even more polarized as secularists united to defend the beleaguered judges from what they considered unwarranted Islamist attacks. The Brotherhood would have been well advised to avoid entering into such a divisive battle so soon after its accession to power.

But the Brotherhood's worst mistake was yet to come. On November 22 Morsi issued a seven-article constitutional declaration. Article 2 stated that all decrees, constitutional declarations, and laws issued by Morsi since his inauguration on June 30 could not be appealed or canceled by any authority of the country (effectively ending parliamentary and judicial oversight) and that all pending lawsuits against his

decisions were void. Article 6 authorized the president to take any measure he saw fit to protect the revolution and safeguard national unity
(effectively giving him unlimited dictatorial powers). Reaction against
this declaration was quick and vehement.

People took to the streets to protest what they considered a dictatorial
move by the Brotherhood. The police responded to the demonstrations
forcefully, and many young people were killed. Sexual violence against
female demonstrators continued and even increased. It appeared as if
the Brotherhood, now in power, was using the same repressive techniques that previous governments had used against them.

Finally, Morsi had to retract and annul his ill-fated constitutional
declaration, but the harm was already done. The Brotherhood then
committed another serious mistake. It decided to quickly push through
a new constitution before the judiciary could dissolve the second
Islamist-dominated constituent assembly, which was being boycotted
by nearly all secular groups. The new constitution was passed in a referendum that was carried out in two stages on December 15 and 22,
2012. It was approved by a 63.8 percent majority, but voter turnout
was only 32.9 percent and a majority of voters in Cairo (the capital and
largest city) voted against the constitution.

The new constitution reflected an Islamist vision of Egypt rather
than a broad societal consensus. Copts were against this constitution
because it did not sufficiently protect minority rights. Women's groups
opposed it because it did not ensure equality of the sexes, and the media
opposed it because it did not protect freedom of the press.

An open confrontation emerged between the Brotherhood and
nearly all of Egypt's mainstream media. Many leading media figures
were being sued either for "contempt of religion" or for "insulting
the president," both charges punishable by prison sentences. Islamist
demonstrators surrounded Media City, where many media offices are
located, for many days and even threatened to kill some leading report-
ers and press figures. The media's response was to escalate its attacks
on the Brotherhood and on its political leader, President Morsi.

Morsi also started a needless battle against Egypt's artists and leading intellectuals. He appointed a conservative Islamist as minister of
culture. The new minister tried to impose an Islamic code on Egypt's
influential cultural elite. He fired many of the ministry's top officials,
including the highly respected director of the Cairo Opera House, in

order to replace them with people who could implement his conservative vision. This led to another uproar, and leading artists, writers, musicians, actors, and film producers started an open sit-in in front of the ministry's building.

Thus in a matter of few months the Brotherhood was able to antagonize a huge segment of Egyptian society who felt that Morsi and his supporters were imposing their vision of postrevolution Egypt without sufficient consultation. For many among them it became an existential struggle. Two political parties that historically have been sworn adversaries, Sabbahi's Nasserists and el-Badawi's New Wafd, agreed to coordinate and join el-Baradei's Salvation Front against the Brotherhood. Even Abul Foutouh's moderate Islamists joined forces with the secular parties in the Salvation Front.

By early 2013 Morsi's position was starting to look shaky. He was facing a united opposition of secularists and moderate Islamists who were supported by the revolutionary youth, the judiciary, the media, and the cultural elite. Owners of large businesses also joined the ranks of Morsi's opponents because the economy was quickly heading toward a major crisis. Officially, the military, the police, and the civil service were neutral. However, it was an open secret that those intensely nationalist institutions, filled by Mubarak appointees, did not trust the Brotherhood.

Thus when a group of revolutionary youth started the Tamarod movement and began collecting signatures on a petition for early presidential elections, they received tremendous moral support from political, cultural, and media elites as well as financial support from the business community. They claim to have collected 22 million signatures on the petition, which is much more than the 13 million votes that Morsi obtained in the second round of elections. They then organized massive anti-Morsi demonstrations in all Egyptian cities. At this point SCAF stepped in with an ultimatum to both sides in the confrontation (but clearly directed mainly at Morsi) to reach a compromise. Otherwise, they said, they would impose their own road map for a new transition.

Morsi responded with a long speech in which he rejected opposition demands for early elections, as well as the military's ultimatum to reach a compromise that would be acceptable to Egyptians on the streets. He insisted that he was the legitimate president of Egypt and would complete his four-year term in office. Did this mean that the millions demonstrating in Tahrir and other squares all around Egypt did not respect legitimacy? That is not the way they saw it. They argued that legitimacy is given to a president by his people. Morsi failed to meet Egyptians' expectations. In the absence of a parliament that could impeach the president, the people were impeaching him directly by going to the streets. The demonstrators believed that they, and not the president, represented true legitimacy in Egypt.

With the benefit of hindsight, it would have made much more sense for Morsi to negotiate a compromise with the opposition and with SCAF. It was clear that Egypt's transition was in trouble and a change of direction was needed. It may have still been possible for him to lead this change and start a process of healing and national reconciliation. But he chose not to, and on July 3 he was deposed. At least as many people swarmed into Tahrir Square to celebrate his fall as had celebrated his election a year earlier.

Back to Square One: Has the Egyptian Spring Failed?

Regardless of how one evaluates the Morsi presidency, the prevailing view among political scientists seems to be that the ouster of Egypt's first democratically elected president is a setback to the democratization process. In a series of articles, Amr Hamzawe, a prominent Egyptian political scientist turned politician and opponent of the Brotherhood, argues it was necessary that Morsi leave the presidency, but it should have been done through democratic means, such as early elections.[15] Thus, according to Hamzawe, the way in which Morsi was forced to leave office was a mistake. At best Morsi's ouster takes Egypt back to where it was in February 2011, when it had to start building democratic institutions more or less from scratch. At worst it takes the country back to the Mubarak era of police repression and lack of political freedom and civil liberties.

Mohamed Hassanein Heikal has a different analysis. According to Heikal (2014), SCAF recognized that a mistake had been made in the way the initial phase of the transition was managed, which allowed the Brotherhood to achieve political control, crush the opposition, and move away from the liberal-democratic ideals of the revolution. The council felt a certain responsibility to fix this error. Heikal argues that this is why the generals took the initiative to meet with all political

---

15. Hamzawe presents his views in a daily column in Cairo's *Al-Shorouk* newspaper.

forces, including the Brotherhood, to try to find a way out of the political crisis that the country was facing. He adds that SCAF and the political parties asked Morsi to organize early presidential elections, but Morsi refused and left them with no other option than to force him out.

The new transition team is led by a civilian interim president (the head of the Constitutional Court) and a civilian interim prime minister (a well-known economist). However, the military continues to be the most respected as well as the most powerful institution in the country. The minister of defense, General el-Sissi, is the most popular politician in Egypt today and will probably easily win the next presidential elections if he chooses to run. So far he has said that he has no presidential ambitions, but he has stopped short of completely ruling out running for president. El-Sissi appears to be very different from the Soviet-trained Field Marshal Tantawi, who led the country after the fall of Mubarak. El-Sissi is American trained, youthful, and charismatic. His discourse is nationalist, and he is perceived to be the heir to a long military-nationalist tradition started by Orabi and continued by Nasser and Sadat.*

In view of the central role that General el-Sissi is playing in the current phase of Egypt's transition, it is useful to examine his views on democracy in the Middle East, which he presented in a 2006 paper written as part of his studies at the United States Army War College. In this paper the general describes the constraints to democracy in the region, namely poverty, lack of a democratic culture, religious extremism, the Arab-Israeli conflict, and the negative perception Arabs have of the West, particularly the United States. He clearly sees democratization as a long-term process. He states,

> It is one thing to say that democracy is a preferred form of government, but quite another to adjust to its requirements and accept some [of] the risks that go along with it. . . . The economic, religious, education, media, security and legal systems will be affected. As a result, it will take time for people and the nation's systems to adjust to the new form of government. . . . In my opinion democracy needs [a] good environment like a reasonable economic situation, educated people and a moderate understanding of religious issues.[16]

*The chapter was written in early 2013. On July 2013 Abdel Fattah el-Sissi led a coalition to oust President Morsi from power. On June 8, 2014, he was sworn in as the president of Egypt.

16. El-Sissi (2006, pp. 2–3).

The chapter concludes by arguing that in order to develop democracy in the Middle East, four things need to happen. First, the education system should be strengthened and the media should play a bigger role in spreading a culture of democracy. Second, a consensus needs to be reached on the appropriate role of religion in government. Third, there needs to be greater regional integration and exchange of lessons and experiences. Fourth, as the Middle East develops, the rest of the world needs to assist in promoting democratic values, perhaps by supporting education.

The new authorities set out a transition road map to put the country back on the road to democracy. It starts with revisions of the constitution, to be followed by parliamentary and presidential elections.[17] At the time of this writing, a referendum on the new constitution has been called for mid-January. It is expected that the new constitution will be approved by a large majority, in spite of the Brotherhood's opposition. Nevertheless, it is important to note that some secular movements are also calling for a no vote on the constitution, mainly because it allows for the trial of civilians in military courts in cases where the civilian is accused of attacking military personnel or facilities.[18] The constitution also provides the military with other protections. It specifies that SCAF has to approve the selection of the minister of defense during an eight-year transition period, and it limits parliamentary discussion of the defense budget.

Progress on a new constitution has not led to an easing of tensions and a reduction of violence. In August, the security forces forcibly disbanded two Brotherhood sit-ins, resulting in hundreds of dead and thousands of injured. It also led to the resignation of Mohamed el-Baradei from the post of interim vice president. El-Baradei was a strong supporter of Morsi's ouster, but he disapproved of the security forces' tactics. The new authorities jailed Morsi and nearly all of the Brotherhood's leadership, including their general guide. They also closed down their television stations and newspapers.

Brotherhood sympathizers have also used violence. The interim government blames the Islamists for terrorist attacks against police stations

17. At the time of this writing, a debate is still going on in Egypt about which election should come first.

18. Notably, the April 6 movement, which was one of the main youth groups that started the revolution in 2011.

and military targets that left many dead and injured. The Brotherhood is also being blamed for attacks on churches as well as on Christian schools and businesses. As a result the interim government declared the Brotherhood a terrorist organization, which implies that anybody joining the Brotherhood could face criminal prosecution. The level of violence and counterviolence is such that it is not realistic to talk of national reconciliation in the near future.

As described by Youssef (2013), the news media are leading intensive anti-Brotherhood campaigns with calls to destroy the organization. Several political parties and associations have joined the clamor. The Brotherhood is being demonized and accused of plotting with foreign powers against the Egyptian state. Liberal thinkers and politicians (for example, Mohamed el-Baradei), who oppose the use of force against Brotherhood sit-ins and demonstrations, are also being attacked by the media and other secular political parties. They are alternatively being called traitors or accused of being too weak on national security.

Howeidy (2013–14) warns that political confrontation is straining the very fabric of Egyptian society. He describes the case of three secular political activists who are imprisoned for breaking the new antidemonstration law.[19] The three jailed activists have gone on a hunger strike to protest their mistreatment in prison, which apparently includes solitary confinement and refusal to let them meet with their lawyers. Howeidy expresses surprise that Egyptian intellectuals and human rights activists have not mobilized to support the three young men. He concludes that "one of the tragedies of the present moment in Egypt is that political convictions and ideological struggles have destroyed what is humane, what is based on human rights, and even what is ethical."[20]

Some of the revolutionary youth seem to be developing a new movement that opposes both the military and the Brotherhood. The movement, sometimes known as the third way, uses three slogans: Down, down with the rule of soldiers; Down, down with the rule of the guide (referring to the Brotherhood's general guide); and As long as Egyptian

---

19. These are Ahmed Doma, Ahmed Maher, and Mohamed Adel. They are among the group of young people who sparked the revolution against Mubarak in January 2011.

20. Author's translation from the Arabic original that was published in *Al-Shorouk* newspaper on January 5, 2014.

blood is cheap, down, down with every president.[21] The third way defines itself in terms of opposition to military rule, to religious rule, and to violence. It will probably need to develop a positive vision of Egyptian society if it wants to attract more followers.

Economic Crisis: Why Have Successive Interim Governments Ignored the Economy?

Economic recovery will have to be the top priority of any future government.[22] Economic decline contributed to the current situation in Egypt. Morsi's ouster underlines the importance of both consensus building and economic growth for the success of the transition process. The Tamarod movement was started by revolutionary youth who felt that Morsi and his Muslim Brotherhood had excluded them from the political process. They argued that the Brotherhood was not willing to listen to the opposition and was not interested in forging consensus around major national issues.

Although those political grievances may have been real, it is unlikely that Tamarod would have been able to mobilize millions of Egyptians had the economy been doing well. Polls show that 65 percent of Egyptians felt that their standard of living had declined since President Morsi came to office.[23] About the same percentage (64 percent) believed that corruption had increased since the 2011 revolution. And many of those who joined the Tamarod demonstrations on June 30, 2013, did so because they were suffering from unemployment, rising prices, and shortages of key necessities.

The Brotherhood started by tackling divisive political and identity issues. Economic issues that affected the daily lives of ordinary Egyptians were put on the back burner. Morsi appointed a prime minister who, according to many observers, had neither the experience nor the stature for the job.[24] He changed three different ministers of finance in less than a year. The government appeared incapable of dealing with Egypt's admittedly difficult economic challenges.

To be fair to Morsi, the economic decline started before he took office. The Supreme Council's record of economic management was

21. See Soueif (2013–14) for a more detailed description of this third way.
22. This section draws on the work of Ghanem and Shaikh (2013).
23. Pew Research Center (2012).
24. For example, Howeidy (2013–14).

not brilliant. It kept a strong exchange rate after the revolution and allowed capital flight to reach a point where Egypt lost more than half of its international reserves. It tried to appease different interest groups by increasing public spending, and the fiscal deficit reached new highs. It did nothing to support the private sector that was suffering from the political unrest and the high interest rates caused by government borrowing. And it refused to accept international financial support in the form of an International Monetary Fund program that was offered in 2011 with virtually no conditionality.

The economic situation worsened under Morsi. The Egyptian economy did not collapse suddenly. However, in the absence of a serious macroeconomic stabilization program it deteriorated gradually, with low growth and increasing unemployment and inflation. Even corruption rose. The Egyptian people were also feeling the pinch in terms of higher prices and shortages of some imported necessities.

Loud grumbling was heard all over Egypt, and even nostalgia for autocratic rule. According to the Pew Center's Global Attitudes Project (2012), more than 70 percent of Egyptians were unhappy with the state of the economy, 33 percent felt that a strong leader was needed to solve the country's problems, and 49 percent believed that a strong economy was more important than a good democracy. The number of people disillusioned with the revolution continued to increase as the economy weakened further.

In addition to freedom and dignity, the young men and women who started the Egyptian revolution on January 25, 2011, were demanding better living conditions and greater social justice. Their demands were far from being met as growth declined and unemployment rose (figure 1-1). Industrial growth, which stood at a healthy 5 to 7 percent a year before the revolution, fell to about 1 percent, and the official unemployment rate rose from 9 to 12.5 percent. About 95 percent of the unemployed were youth with at least a secondary education. Nearly three-fourths of those who were lucky enough to find jobs ended up working in the informal sector, where wages range between $2.60 and $3.70 a day.

Government fiscal policy was not conducive to growth and employment generation. Figure 1-1 shows that the government deficit rose from about 8 percent of GDP in 2010 to nearly 11 percent in 2011. It exceeded 13 percent of GDP in 2013 (not shown). The increasing

FIGURE 1-1. Selected Economic Indicators, 2008–12

Percent

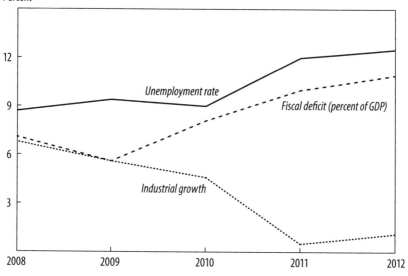

Source: Economist Intelligence Unit.

deficits were financed almost entirely domestically, and the public domestic debt rose from some 60 percent of GDP in 2010 to 70 percent in 2012.[25] At some point in 2012 the Egyptian government was paying 16 percent interest on its short-term domestic debt.[26] That is, the government has been sucking liquidity from the domestic financial system and crowding out the private sector, discouraging investment, growth, and employment creation.

Surprisingly, corruption seems to have increased after the revolution. Ending corruption has been a key demand of the revolutionaries, and the country has witnessed more than 6,000 corruption investigations and several high-profile incriminations since February 2011.[27] Investigations and police action send a political signal, but they do not constitute an effective anticorruption program. Data for 2012 from the Worldwide Governance Indicators show deterioration in corruption control. According to Transparency International's 2013 Global

25. Economist Intelligence Unit.
26. Ministry of Finance, Egypt.
27. African Development Bank and others (2012).

FIGURE 1-2. International Reserves, Egypt, 2008–12

Billions of U.S. dollars

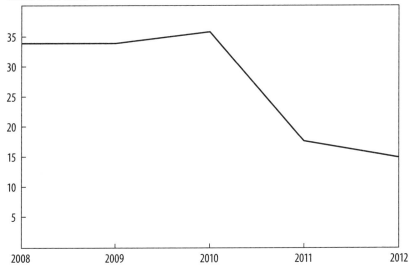

Source: Worldwide Governance Indicators, World Bank.

Corruption Barometer, only 16 percent of Egyptians believe that there has been an improvement in corruption control since the revolution. Nearly 65 percent of Egyptians feel that corruption has increased by a lot or a little since the revolution. The perception that democracy was associated with more rather than less corruption could provide some explanation for youth disillusionment.

Falling tourism and foreign direct investment, together with increasing capital flight, led to a decline in foreign reserves from more than $35 billion in 2010 (covering seven months' imports) to less than $15 billion in 2012, which covered less than three months' imports (figure 1-2). As a result, foreign exchange became scarce, and the Egyptian pound started depreciating rapidly. It depreciated against the U.S. dollar by about 15 percent in the first three months of 2013. Moreover, a black market in foreign exchange emerged. Egypt's credit rating suffered a setback as Moody's downgraded Egypt's debt to "caa," meaning that it is of poor standing and entails very high risk.

Imports became more expensive and increasingly difficult to procure. Egypt is highly dependent on the import of many necessities, including food and fuel. The pound's depreciation meant that domestic prices for imports rose, which affected millions of poor and middle-class families. Scarcities of some imported goods (for example, diesel fuel) became commonplace as foreign exchange was increasingly difficult to obtain, and foreign banks were wary of providing credit to Egyptian importers. Some businessmen complained that it took more than six weeks to open a letter of credit, while it had taken only three days before the revolution.

The government argued that there was enough fuel in the country to ensure supply to all the petrol situations as well as for electricity production. It stated that fuel shortages and power outages had been created on purpose by civil servants loyal to the Mubarak regime who wanted to sabotage the democratic transition. This may very well have been true. However, the Egyptian people continued to be angered by the shortages. They did not care whether those shortages were caused by financial problems or by the government's inability to control the bureaucracy.

In those difficult economic circumstances Morsi's decision to appoint a member of an Islamist group who was involved in past attacks on tourists as governor of Luxor (the site of ancient Thebes and Egypt's most important tourist destination) was hard to understand. The decision was met with outrage, especially from tourism professionals and business people in the city, who were already suffering from a sharp drop in tourist visits. The minister of tourism presented his resignation in protest. Sit-ins were organized in front of the governor's offices to prevent the new governor from entering them. Finally, the new governor resigned without ever setting foot in his office, and Morsi's image was further tarnished.

There was general agreement that Egypt needed to implement credible reforms to stabilize the economy, control corruption, and lay the foundations for inclusive growth. Such reforms would normally include a reduction in the fiscal deficit to bring the domestic debt under control and a further depreciation of the Egyptian pound to encourage exports and tourism.[28] The Morsi administration had been negotiating for a whole year with the International Monetary Fund to obtain support for such a stabilization program, without much success. It was doubtful that under the situation of extreme political polarization the government could implement the type of difficult measures that were needed.

---

28. For example, see Freund and Braga (2012) or Ghanem (2013b).

The Morsi administration was facing a sort of catch-22. It could not implement needed economic reform because it was facing stiff opposition and unrest. But failure to reform the economy made the opposition stronger and the unrest more widespread.

The Way Forward: What Can the International Community Do?

Many analysts argue that it is in the interest of the international community, and particularly the United States, to promote democracy in Egypt and the rest of the Arab world.[29] They call for an active policy of supporting democratization. But can the international community really influence short-term political developments in Egypt?

As worries that Egypt is returning to the repressive ways of the Mubarak regime and back-tracking on democratic reforms increase, many voices in the United States and Europe are calling for suspension of economic aid. However, a decision to suspend Western economic aid to Egypt would probably be counterproductive for at least two reasons. First, a suspension of aid by the West would not be understood by the Egyptian public as a position of principle in support of democracy. Instead, it would be interpreted as a sign of Western support for the Brotherhood. It could play into the nationalist argument that the Brotherhood is a foreign-supported organization with international ambitions and is not loyal to the Egyptian nation. This could be used to drum up additional public support for even more repression.

Second, a suspension of Western economic aid would encourage Egypt to turn to the East. Western economic aid is small relative to Egypt's economy and is dwarfed by financial assistance from oil producers in the Gulf. Compare the United States' annual economic assistance of US$250 million with the Gulf states' recent decision to provide Egypt with exceptional support of US$12 billion over six months. Thus a suspension of Western aid is unlikely to have much impact on the Egyptian economy, and it would lead to a reduction of Western influence in Egypt.

Therefore, it is important for the international community to remain engaged in Egypt. However, it may also be necessary to reexamine the nature of this engagement and reorient aid flows toward areas and

29. For example, Wittes (2008).

sectors that directly enhance economic and political inclusiveness. Examples of such areas would be institution building, support to small-scale enterprises, and agriculture and rural development.

This does not mean that the international community should provide unconditional support to the current Egyptian government. Continued support could be linked to the implementation of the authorities' road map for a transition to democracy, and the level of support could be adjusted to reflect progress on the democratic transition.

Adopting a Long-Term View: Can the West Be Patient?

The international community would like to see an end to violence in Egypt and the start of a process of national reconciliation, but this is unlikely to happen in the short run for three reasons. First, most Brotherhood leaders who have sufficient authority to enter into reconciliation talks are in jail. It would be hard for the interim government to take a political decision to release them immediately because it would anger the masses of Egyptians who rose against the Brotherhood and would thus weaken the government's support. It is the courts that will have to issue such a decision. Judicial proceedings have started against them, and it would probably be necessary to let the process take its course. Monitoring by human rights groups and the international community would help ensure that they get a fair trial. Second, the Brotherhood has boxed itself into a maximalist position, demanding that Morsi be reinstated. This is not realistic, given the strength of anti-Morsi feeling in the country. It will take time for the Brotherhood to be able to change that position. Third, neither the Brotherhood's rank and file nor the anti-Brotherhood groups are in a mood for reconciliation. The pain from the violence is still too sharp.

Achieving the goal of a stable democracy requires peace. It also requires important institutions, such as a free press, an independent judiciary, and political parties that ensure transparency, voice, and accountability. Most important, it requires a change in political culture toward greater inclusion and acceptance of the other. Those changes take years to materialize. Therefore, patience and a long-term vision are needed. Western aid could be used strategically and be combined with knowledge sharing and technology transfer to influence the path of the transition and help achieve the Egyptian people's dream of "bread, liberty, social justice, and human dignity." By remaining engaged with Egypt the international community could maintain a high-level policy dialogue aimed at gradually achieving reconciliation and greater inclusiveness.

Economic aid to Egypt could focus on fixing the problems with the growth model adopted during the Mubarak years. It could tackle questions of social justice and inclusiveness. Achieving inclusive growth that is associated with the development of institutions that provide for transparency, voice, and accountability in decisionmaking, an expansion of the middle class, and the growth of small business would be important for the democratization process. International economic support for Egypt could prioritize inclusiveness and social justice by supporting institutional development, helping small business, and investing in agriculture and rural development.

Developing Inclusive Economic Institutions: How Can Donors Overcome Political Sensitivities?

Inclusive institutions are important for democracy, and they are important for social justice. Most Egyptian governments over the past four decades have at least given lip service to the goal of social justice and have taken some symbolic steps toward implementing parts of this agenda. However, no serious attempt has been taken so far to fully implement an agenda for achieving social justice and economic inclusion. Even after the revolution neither the transition governments nor the Muslim Brotherhood government took any significant moves toward achieving this key goal.

Egypt's failure to act decisively on social justice issues could be explained by the fact that the lower middle class and the poor, who would benefit from such an agenda, have little or no voice in the economic decisionmaking process. This could explain why their interests were not served by economic policies while a system of crony capitalism flourished.[30] Inclusive economic institutions that would give voice to ordinary citizens in economic policymaking and empower them to hold government officials accountable would increase the probability that an agenda for achieving social justice is actually adopted and implemented. It would provide important support for the democratization efforts.

---

30. For example, see Richter and Steiner (2008) for a description of cronyism in the tourism sector.

The allocation of public investment in Egypt is biased toward relatively better off regions and groups, which reflects the noninclusive nature of the planning and economic decisionmaking process. In his analysis of Egypt's planning system, Sakamoto (2013) finds that lack of a structured dialogue among key stakeholders is a key feature of the planning process in Egypt. Six five-year development plans were prepared during the Mubarak era. Budget allocations were decided before economic goals and strategies were determined. The first planning step was the production of the investment-budget allocation sheet by the Ministry of Planning based on the line ministries' investment-budget requests. The five-year development plan was then drafted by the Ministry of Planning based on the budget allocation sheet. This system was simple, with drafting being fully completed inside the Ministry of Planning without official outside contacts. Thus the system excluded major stakeholders, such as the private sector, civil society organizations, labor organizations, and farmer organizations. Even line ministries had little voice in the preparation of the plan document.

Kharas and Abdou (2012) look at the role that civil society organizations (CSOs) could play in achieving inclusive growth and social justice in Egypt. They argue that CSOs can make four important contributions to inclusive growth. First, they can play an advocacy role for small business, the informal sector, and other marginalized groups, ensuring that government takes their concerns into account when formulating policies and programs. They can also act as whistleblowers, denouncing corruption and other unfair practices that harm small or weak economic agents. Second, they can provide important economic services that the public sector is unable to provide (or provides inefficiently): for example, by helping small enterprises get access to finance and to technical assistance. Third, they can act as think tanks, developing ideas and promoting best practices that support inclusive growth. Fourth, they can be an important source of employment opportunities for youth. Currently, only 3 percent of Egypt's labor force work in CSOs compared with, for example, 9 percent in the Netherlands. Kharas and Abdou (2012) conclude that the legal framework governing CSOs in Egypt needs to be reformed to provide the organizations with greater flexibility and incentives to expand their activities.

Farmer organizations and cooperatives are a special type of CSO that can play an important role in strengthening the governance system of the agriculture sector, particularly in developing and supporting family farmers. Problems caused by the large number of very small family farms in Egypt can be tackled through the development of strong producer organizations that group farmers together to ensure that their voice is heard in policy discussions and also help enhance access to technology, inputs, and markets. Existing farmer organizations and cooperatives are weak and are dependent on government for financial and technical support, which erodes their independence and limits their areas of action. Cooperatives and farmer organizations sometimes act more as government agencies, informing farmers of policy decisions that are taken at the central level and helping implement them, rather than as bodies that represent farmers and advocate for policies that protect their interests.

These are just three examples of areas where support for institution building is badly needed. International support in institution building could be a sensitive subject as it may raise political issues. Recent experience with U.S. funding for Egyptian CSOs is an example of how things can go wrong.[31] But this should not be an argument for doing nothing. Instead, it should be an argument for engaging the Egyptian government in a serious dialogue on the issue. Neither democracy nor social justice can be achieved without institutions that ensure transparency in decisionmaking, provide voice to all stakeholders, and hold government officials accountable.[32]

Some members of the international community are particularly well equipped to provide support to the development of inclusive economic institutions. The United Nations Development Program, which has a strong presence in Egypt, has a clear mandate in the area of human rights that includes the principles of transparency, voice, and accountability. Moreover, it is a neutral UN agency that can provide needed support to nongovernmental organizations, legislatures, and the free press without necessarily being accused of political meddling. Another UN agency, the Food and Agriculture Organization, has long experience of working with farmer organizations. The International Monetary Fund and the World Bank have vast experience in the area of

31. See Human Rights Watch (2013b).
32. For more on the role of institutions in development see Acemoglu and Robinson (2012).

public financial management, procurement policies, and civil service reforms. The Japan International Cooperation Agency is already working with the Egyptian government to support inclusive planning. This project will greatly enhance transparency in economic policymaking and provide greater voice to different stakeholders as they participate in the planning process. Similarly, the European Commission, Canada, and the United Kingdom have established human rights policies and experience in supporting organizations that promote transparency, voice, and accountability, including in Egypt.

Supporting Small Business: Could Donors Move Beyond Simple Credit Programs?

The expansion of the small and medium enterprise (SME) sector would help promote both democracy and economic inclusiveness. When the private sector consists of a small number of large firms, those firms tend to build special links to government. Those connected firms are happy to support autocratic regimes that provide them with protection and other privileges, such as access to financing, government contracts, and public infrastructure. Thus a system of autocracy and crony capitalism grows and tends to perpetuate itself. Owners of large businesses have no interest in promoting democracy, as it could disrupt their special relations with government. In his study of Egypt under Mubarak, Rutherford (2008) argues that autocracy can be countered by supporting a large number of small business owners who would normally exert pressure to institute legal and institutional reforms that would level the playing field and break the link between corporate capitalists and autocratic governments. They would also call for democratic reforms so as to use electoral politics to push for policy reforms to support small businesses.

Development of SMEs is also important for economic inclusiveness and social justice. According to Ghanem (2013c) about 56 percent of Egyptians live on $2 to $4 a day, and they depend mainly on SMEs, typically in the informal sector, for their livelihood. More than 70 percent of young first-time job seekers end up working in SMEs, with wages of about $3.70 a day. That is why expanding and modernizing the SME sector so that it can provide more and better-paying, higher-productivity jobs should be a component of any program that aims at achieving inclusive economic growth.

Most donors have programs to support SMEs and youth entrepreneurship, and they need to be refined and scaled up. In addition to providing access to financing, those programs need to prioritize technology transfer and market access. Vocational and entrepreneurship training programs are also important to correct some of the weaknesses of the Egyptian education system. Successful SME development programs are usually based on partnership between governments (which provide funding), civil society organizations (which provide training), and the organized private sector (which provides technology and markets). In the case of Egypt, those partnerships still need to be developed. In particular, donors can help connect domestic SMEs with foreign investors and export markets.

Access to regional and international markets is important for business development and job creation. The international community could make a huge contribution to the development of exports and job creation in Egypt. It could facilitate exports of manufactured goods from Egypt, especially for materials for construction, mechanical, and electrical industries, by negotiating mutual recognition agreements to reduce technical barriers to trade. Agriculture and agro-processing is an important sector for Egypt, and it is also a sector where SMEs could easily develop. The international community could improve Egypt's access to its agricultural markets by removing nontariff barriers to agricultural trade. This would require, among other things, the abolition of quotas, reference prices, and seasonal restrictions, especially for exports of fruits and vegetables.[33]

Support to Lagging Regions and the Rural Poor: Is It Possible to End Decades of Neglect?

A strategy to achieve inclusive growth in Egypt will have to deal with the problems of regional inequalities and rural poverty. For many years no real action has been taken to develop lagging regions or support the rural poor. This had serious political consequences as some lagging regions became centers for extremism and sometimes even violence. It also had serious social and economic consequences. Illiteracy, child malnutrition, and even stunting of growth continue to be unacceptably

---

33. For more on the importance of opening up developed country markets to Arab country exports, see Chauffour (2012).

high in rural areas, particularly in Upper Egypt. Intervention is needed in two areas: social protection for the rural poor and the development of agriculture and agro-industries.

In Egypt social protection is provided to the populations of large cities through a system of untargeted price subsidies. In the rural areas social protection is usually project based and therefore fragmented. There is a need to move to a systems-based approach to social protection. Egypt can benefit from Latin America's experience in this area, especially Brazil's Bolsa Familia and Mexico's Progresa-Oportunidades. This experience shows that direct cash transfers can be used to achieve poverty reduction as well as development objectives. By providing cash to poor families those programs help raise their consumption and get them out of poverty. It is a much more direct method than generalized price subsidies for products that can be consumed by the poor as well as the nonpoor. By making part of the transfer conditional on school attendance or immunization, the programs also encourage investment in human capital and thus help achieve long-term development objectives. There is also some evidence that recipients of cash transfers in rural areas tend to save part of it and use it for investments in productive physical capital.

Agriculture is crucial for Egypt's economy and particularly for poor households. It accounts for around 14 percent of GDP, employs 30 percent of the labor force, and is responsible for about 20 percent of total exports. Nearly 40 percent of the poor in Egypt rely directly on agriculture. All of the poor in rural areas are either directly or indirectly affected by agriculture. Therefore, agriculture growth and the resulting growth in the nonfarm rural economy would have significant poverty reducing effects. It would also have strong equalization effects as it reduces the large income gaps between urban and rural areas and between Upper Egypt and the rest of the country. The Ministry of Agriculture has developed a long-term strategy for developing the sector. It includes investments in irrigation (to deal with water scarcity), research and extension, and rural infrastructure. It also includes incentives for processing of agricultural products and support to farmer organizations and CSOs operating in rural areas. This strategy needs to be implemented.

The international community has a great deal of experience in social protection and agricultural development and could provide important support in achieving inclusive growth through financing and knowledge sharing. The World Bank has done extensive work on social safety nets and can support reforms in this area. Several donors are funding agriculture development, and UN agencies (mostly the Food and Agriculture Organization) are providing technical assistance and knowledge sharing. They could scale up their interventions and focus them on supporting smallholding farmers, particularly in the poorest areas of Upper Egypt.

Assessing Risks: Where Is Egypt Heading?

There is no doubt that the present situation presents serious risks. Some observers believe that the Muslim Brotherhood is prepared for a long struggle and therefore predict a period of continued violence and civil strife similar to what happened in Algeria after the 1991 elections. Others point to the rise in the level of repression by the security forces (and the criticism leveled at moderate and liberal politicians) and predict that Egypt will become a military dictatorship reminiscent of Chile under Pinochet.

While those two scenarios present real risks and should be taken seriously, there is also the possibility of a third scenario materializing. Under this more optimistic scenario, the current authorities implement their road map and hand over government to a freely elected president and parliament, who then proceed to gradually strengthen democratic institutions and create more inclusive political and economic systems, and perhaps a societal dialogue on the appropriate role of religion in government. The international community could increase the probability of Egypt returning to the road toward democracy and inclusiveness by remaining engaged and by prioritizing support to areas that enhance social justice and promote inclusive economic growth.

References

Acemoglu, D., and J. Robinson. 2012. *Why Nations Fail: The Origins of Power, Prosperity, and Poverty*. New York: Crown Publishers.

African Development Bank and others. 2012. "Egypt." In *African Economic Outlook 2012: Promoting Youth Employment*. OECD Publishing.

Aliboni, R. 2012. "Societal Change and Political Responses in Euro-Mediterranean Relations." In *Arab Society in Revolt: The West's Mediterranean Challenge*, edited by O. Roy and C. Merlini. Brookings.

Assaad, R., and G. Barsoum. 2007. "Youth Exclusion in Egypt: In Search of Second Chances." Wolfensohn Center for Development, Brookings.

Bayat, A. 1998. "Revolution without Movement, Movement without Revolution: Comparing Islamic Activism in Iran and Egypt." *Comparative Studies in Society and History* 40, no. 1: 136–69.

Bradley, J. 2012. *After the Arab Spring: How Islamists Hijacked the Middle East Revolts.* New York: Palgrave Macmillan.

Chauffour, J. 2012. *From Political to Economic Awakening in the Arab World: The Path of Economic Integration.* Washington: World Bank.

Diwan, I. 2013. "Understanding Revolution in the Middle East: The Central Role of the Middle Class." *Middle East Development Journal* 5, no. 1.

el-Sissi, A. 2006. *Democracy in the Middle East.* Strategy Research Project, United States Army War College. Mimeo.

Freund, C., and C. Braga. 2012. "The Economics of Arab Transitions." In *Arab Society in Revolt: The West's Mediterranean Challenge,* edited by O. Roy and C. Merlini. Brookings.

Ghanem, H. 2013a. "Egypt Needs Truth and Reconciliation" (www.brookings. edu/research/opinions/2013/08/16-egypt-democracy-truth-reconciliation-ghanem).

———. 2013b. "First Confront Discontent: Egypt's Teetering Economy." *Milken Institute Review,* January 14, pp. 24–34.

———. 2013c. "The Role of Micro and Small Enterprises in Egypt's Economic Transition." Working Paper 53. Global Economy and Development, Brookings.

Ghanem, H., and Shaikh S. 2013. *On the Brink: Preventing Economic Collapse and Promoting Inclusive Growth in Egypt and Tunisia.* U.S. Relations with the Islamic World, Brookings.

Ghonim, W. 2013. *Revolution 2.0: The Power of the People Is Greater than the People in Power: A Memoir.* New York: Mariner Books.

Heikal, M. 2014. "El-Sissi Is the Solution of Necessity, and Circumstances Will Force Him to Do What He May Not Wish." *Al-Shorouk,* January 4, 2014 (www.shorouknews.com/news/view.aspx?cdate=04012014&id=2dae7402-87db-4ec3-b292-8cc20d27e6a9) [in Arabic].

Hamzawe, A. 2013–14. "Collection of Articles" (www.shorouknews.com/columns/amr-hamzawe) [in Arabic].

Hopwood, D. 1991. *Egypt: Politics and Society, 1945–1990.* London: Routledge.

Howeidy, F. 2013–14. "Collection of Articles" (www.shorouknews.com/columns/fahmy-howeidy) [in Arabic].

Human Rights Watch. 2013a. "Egypt: Terrorist Tag Politically Driven." December 28 (www.hrw.org/news/2013/12/28/egypt-terrorist-tag-politically-driven).

———. 2013b. "Egypt's NGO Funding Crackdown." April 9, 2013 (www.hrw. org/news/2013/04/09/egypts-ngo-funding-crackdown).

International Monetary Fund. 2010. "Arab Republic of Egypt Article IV Consultation Staff Report." Washington.

Kharas, H. 2010. "The Emerging Middle Class in Developing Countries." Working Paper 285. OECD Development Center.

Kharas, H., and E. Abdou. 2012. "Regulatory Reforms Necessary for an Inclusive Growth Model in Egypt." Global Economy and Development, Brookings.

Pew Research Center. 2012. Global Attitudes Project.

Richter, T., and C. Steiner. 2008. "Politics, Economics, and Tourism Development in Egypt: Insights into the Sectoral Transformations of a Neo-Patrimonial, Rentier State." *Third World Quarterly* 29, no. 5: 939–59.

Rutherford, D. 2008. *Egypt after Mubarak: Liberalism, Islam, and Democracy in the Arab World.* Princeton University Press.

Sakamoto, K. 2013. "Efforts to Introduce Inclusive Planning in Egypt." Working Paper 54. Global Economy and Development, Brookings.

Soueif, A. 2013–14. "Collection of Articles" (www.shorouknews.com/columns/ahdaf-soueif [in Arabic]).

Wickham, C. 2013. *The Muslim Brotherhood: Evolution of an Islamist Movement.* Princeton University Press.

Wittes, T. 2008. *Freedom's Unsteady March: America's Role in Building Arab Democracy.* Brookings.

World Bank and Organization for Economic Cooperation and Development. 2013. *Integrating Human Rights into Development: Donor Approaches, Experiences, and Challenges.* Washington: World Bank.

Youssef, B. 2013. "Collection of Articles" (www.shorouknews.com/columns/Basem-youssef [in Arabic]).

2

Introducing Inclusive Planning in Egypt

KEI SAKAMOTO

High economic growth in Egypt between 2000 and 2010 was associated with increasing popular discontent. Favorable macroeconomic growth tends to hide the qualitative changes taking place in a society (Shimizu 2011), as can be seen in Middle Eastern countries, where steady macroeconomic growth occurred while economic and social structures with unequal access to social services were also emerging. This was demonstrated in Egypt, where obtaining social justice became a slogan in the 2011 revolution. Figure 2-1 shows the level of discontent toward the government among the citizens. The chart indicates that the number of people who felt they were thriving was decreasing despite positive macroeconomic growth. As shown in figure 2-2, citizens' decreasing satisfaction in terms of the freedoms they enjoy implies the same result. The Arab economies of the 1970s and 1980s had one of the highest global rates of economic equality, but several factors, such as changes in migration patterns, demographic pressures, fiscal retrenchments, and the rise of corruption, have strained the traditional sources of inclusive growth (African Development Bank 2012). The growth seen in Egypt could be expressed as jobless growth or unfair growth, which was no longer acceptable to the citizenry.

The Japan International Cooperation Agency states that "inclusive development represents an approach to development that encourages all people to recognize the development issues they themselves face, participate in addressing them, and enjoy the fruits of such endeavors."[1]

---

1. Japan International Cooperation Agency, mission statement (www.jica.go.jp/english/about/mission/index.html).

FIGURE 2-1. GDP Growth and Share of Egyptian Population Self-Identifying as Thriving

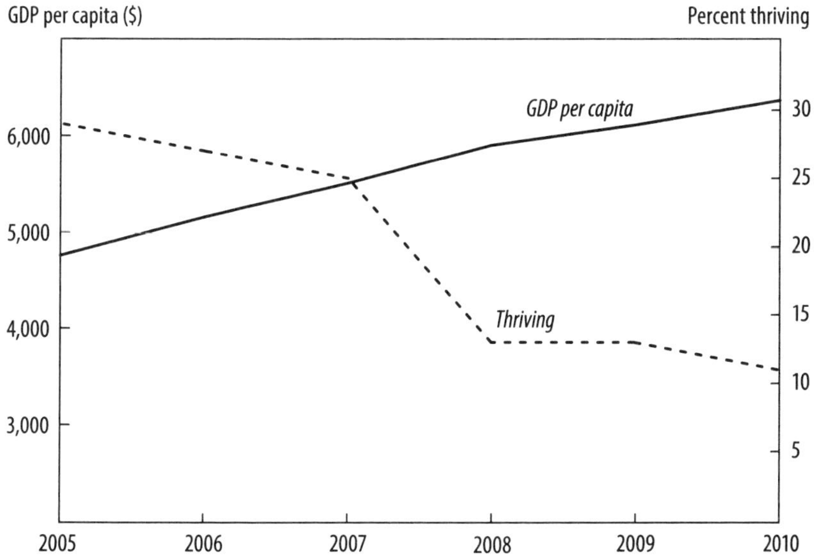

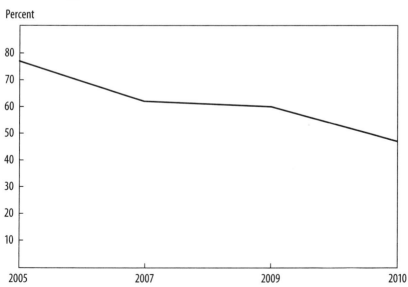

Source: Gallup (2011a). Data on GDP per capita from the International Monetary Fund, *World Economic Outlook* database.

FIGURE 2-2. Egyptians' Satisfaction with Freedom in Life

Percent

Source: Gallup (2011a).

There has been considerable discussion of the importance of inclusive development, which shares benefits equally among people, the importance of which has reached a consensus in international society. The Arab Awakening showed that it is not only the quantity but also the quality of macroeconomic growth that should be emphasized.

The concept of inclusive development is broad and includes fields of good governance, education reform, strengthening of vocational training, labor market reform, and development of small and medium-size enterprises. Implementing inclusive development requires effective decisionmaking processes that ensure an equal voice for all citizens. Voice and accountability are critical weaknesses in Egypt, where the government has failed to provide for the meaningful participation of stakeholders in decisionmaking. This, together with a lack of transparency in government decisionmaking, has led to a widespread lack of accountability. There is a strong need in Egypt to build a political basis for sustainable economic and institutional reforms to enhance inclusiveness.

Challenges for Development Plans in Egypt

As in other countries worldwide, development planning was introduced in Egypt after its independence. The five-year industrial plan (1957–62) aimed to enhance domestic industrialization and was the first such plan in Egypt. This was followed by the first five-year plan (1960–64), drafted by the National Planning Committee in President Nasser's era. Based on the introduction of Arab socialism in 1962, state intervention and central planning were regarded as increasingly important during this time (Ikram 2004).

President Sadat, who adopted the open-door economic policy, Infitah, implemented several policies to introduce liberalization and economic deregulation, strengthening the economic capacity for foreign direct investment. The revised investment law became the five-year development plan (1977–82). With the end of Arab socialism, the influence of central development planning began to decline with a commensurate increase in private sector development.

It was during the era of Hosni Mubarak, who became president in 1981, that the system of five-year development plans was settled. As economic policies based on the free market economy were continued and enhanced, development plans turned out to be too rigid, having a

TABLE 2-1. History of Planning in Egypt, 1956–2012

President	Plan
Nasser (1956–70)	First five-year plan (1960–64)
Sadat (1971–81)	Five-year plan (1977–82)
Mubarak (1981–2011)	First five-year plan (1982–86)
	Second five-year plan (1987–91)
	Third five-year plan (1992–96)
	Fourth five-year plan (1997–2001)
	Fifth five-year plan (2002–06)
	Sixth five-year plan (2007–11)
Transitional, Morsi (2012–)	Proposal for New Development Plan (2012–22)

negligible impact on the economy. Although Prime Minister Nazif's privatization reforms brought strong economic growth, they also caused increased corruption. In this context, Egypt's economic growth, with concomitant corruption, actually brought about what can be termed unfair growth. Consequently, there was broad discontent among the millions who were left without any benefit or, in many cases, even worse off than they had been before the reforms. Fakhouri (2010) characterizes the shift from Nasser to Sadat and then to Mubarak as "a shift from the government-directed economic model to the free economic model, then a shift to the uncontrollable economic model." Table 2-1 shows the brief history of economic planning in Egypt.

A Plan without an Institutional Dialogue Mechanism

Lack of dialogue among key stakeholders is a key feature of the planning process in Egypt. Findings from the field research show that the budget allocation was determined before the economic goals and strategies in the previous master plan had been drafted. The first planning step was the production of an investment-budget allocation sheet, which was created by the Ministry of Planning based on the investment-budget requests prepared by each of the ministries.[2] The five-year development plan was then drafted by the ministry based on the budget allocation

2. The Ministry of Planning became the Ministry of Planning and International Cooperation in 2011.

sheet. The plan was initially drafted by university scholars, whose names never appeared in the plan, and the drafted plan was then integrated into a division inside the Ministry of Planning. This system was simple: drafting was completed inside the Ministry of Planning without official outside contacts (Tinbergen 1964).[3]

Although it was efficient, the system also led to the exclusion of major stakeholders, such as the private sector, civil society organizations, labor organization, and the media, all of which were neglected in the development-planning process. Indeed, one executive of an international company in Egypt stated that the "private sector was excluded during the decision-making process, where the government decided the policy on its own."[4] Another executive, a member of a business association, revealed that "the development plans never attracted the private sector, which was a plan that no one has ever read."[5] Consequently, development plans, which were created with little external interaction during the planning process, lacked mechanisms for building consensus among the major stakeholders for economic development.

A Dialogue without a Mechanism

Conversely, studies show the existence of strong interactions between the government and the private sector (Wakabayashi 2007). From July 2004 to January 2011, the cabinet introduced wide-ranging reforms to strengthen relations between the public and private sectors, spearheaded by Prime Minister Nazif, who appointed ministers from the private sector, as represented by Mohamed Rachid, the minister of trade and industry. During the Nazif administration, it is said that the executives of major private companies in Egypt were able to directly communicate with Minister Rachid by mobile phone.[6]

Although there was a strong relationship between the public and private sectors, communication and cooperation were implemented without a rule-based institutional dialogue mechanism (Benhassine 2009), leading to numerous collusive relationships that resulted in corruption. Some privileged private companies benefited, while others were left

3. Tinbergen (1964) notes the importance of outside contacts during the planning process.

4. Field interview, July 2012.

5. Field interview, July 2012.

6. Field interview, July 2012.

in the lurch. This imbalanced social structure was one element in the background to the Egyptian uprising in 2011, where demonstrators singled out an individual person, Ahmad Ezz, as the model of a corrupted business person.

A Dialogue without a Mechanism and the 2011 Uprising

The absence of an institutional dialogue mechanism resulted in an increase in corruption, which the Egyptian people decided to combat. It is often said that the corruption during the 2010 election, the death of Khaled Saeed (a young man who was brutally killed by the police), and the labor demonstration in El-Mahalla el-Kubra in the Nile delta were the major incidents that triggered the uprising in Egypt. These incidents, along with the demonstrations in 2011, reveal that the Egyptian people were determined to achieve social justice by fighting against suppression and cleaning out corruption (Nagasawa 2012). During the labor demonstration in El-Mahalla el-Kubra, the demonstrators claimed that corrupt companies in turn corrupted the country, causing dissatisfaction to surge nationwide. This spreading discontent exploded in Egypt in 2011, triggered by similar movements in Tunisia.

While numerous demonstrators were youths, wide-ranging stakeholders, such as government officials, media officials, professors, lawyers, engineers, court judges, farmers, and businesspersons, also joined the movement. Businesspersons who participated in the demonstration claimed that Prime Minister Nazif's privatization policies were corrupt. People were opposed to economic development that benefited only the privileged, and they called for free and fair growth.

The Egyptian people were dissatisfied with the opaque political decisionmaking process. Even the Egyptian labor organization, which normally represents the interest of workers, was mired in corruption. The International Labor Organization positively evaluated the decision of the new minister of finance, who allowed the people to create trade unions after the revolution. Egypt was counted as one of the twenty-five worst countries in the world in terms of violating the international labor agreement (Nagasawa 2012). Few people shared the benefits of growth, and many citizens felt they were unable to express their views to the government, as indicated in figure 2-3. Only 4 percent of Egyptians said they were able to express their opinion to a public official, which was the lowest level in Gallup's 150-country database.

FIGURE 2-3. Voiced Opinion to Public Official

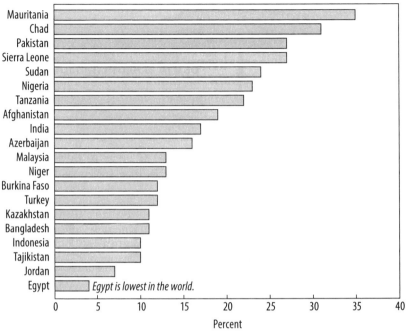

Source: Gallup (2011a).

Increasing Corruption

Previous studies (Amin 2011; Nagasawa 2012) explain the growing level of corruption by dividing postindependence Egypt into three periods: the monarchy era, the Nasser era, and the Sadat-Mubarak era. These studies show that there was little corruption in the monarchy era, when the country suffered from colonial rule. Nasser's era experienced a growth in suppression but little in corruption, based on the modesty of the president's personal character. It was in the third era that corruption spread nationwide, owing to the loss of the war in 1967, Sadat's character, and globalization resulting from the open-door economic policy. This era suffered from the burden of what Gunnar Myrdal describes as the "soft state" (Myrdal 1968, p. 869) (see table 2-2).[7]

7. Myrdal introduced the term *soft state* in 1968 to describe a state with weak governance. Nagasawa (2012) cites Amin (2011), who indicates that Egypt became a soft state in the Sadat-Mubarak era. The Muslim Brotherhood often uses the term "deep state" to refer to the old regime's holdovers.

TABLE 2-2. Burden for Citizens after Independence in Egypt

Three eras	Type of burden	Key issues
Monarchy era (1922–53)	Burden of subordination	Colonial rule
Nasser era (1956–70)	Burden of tyranny	Independence but suppression
Sadat-Mubarak era (1971–2011)	Burden of soft state	Corruption

Source: Author, based on Amin (2011) and Nagasawa (2012).

Nagasawa (2012) describes the existence of a "pyramid of corruption" during the Mubarak era, with the president at the top and family members, politicians, ministers, and businesspeople supporting the regime. The corruption in the administration, particularly involving Prime Minister Nazif, Mubarak's son Gamal Mubarak, and Ahmad Ezz, is often said to be the best example of the pyramid of corruption.[8] This pyramid structure was hard to remove, leading Egypt to become a soft state, with growing corruption (Nagasawa 2012).

The extent of corruption can also be confirmed by governance indicators. Countries in the Middle East and North Africa showed a decline in governance indicators for voice and accountability, corruption control, and government effectiveness (trust in government, consistency of policy direction, consensus building, and public satisfaction with services) (figure 2-4). Egypt showed a significant decrease from 2000 to 2010 in voice and accountability (24.5 to 13.3), corruption control (43.4 to 34.4), and government effectiveness (46.8 to 40.2). These figures indicate the lack and decline of transparency in the government decision-making process and the reality of Egypt being essentially a soft state.[9]

A lack of fairness and transparency in governance resulted in unfair competition, insufficient support for the poor, and the creation and preservation of an income gap in society (World Bank 2009). In particular, corruption disturbed the efficiency of government services in addressing disparity. To achieve inclusive growth, where the benefit of growth reaches the poor, corruption must be controlled with a mechanism that includes the voices of people from various classes, creating

8. Mubarak was a former deputy secretary general of the National Democratic Party; Ezz was the former owner of Ezz Steel and a former chairman of Egypt's national assembly's budget committee.

9. World Bank, World Governance Indicators (http://info.worldbank.org/governance/wgi/index.asp).

FIGURE 2-4. Governance Indicators in Egypt

Percentile rank (0–100)

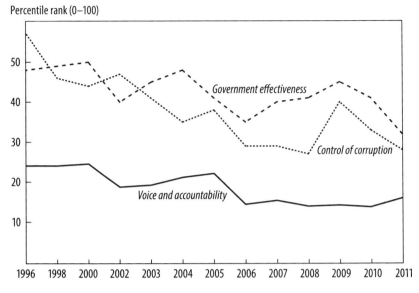

Source: World Governance Indicators, World Bank.

a policy consensus that benefits all. The pursuit of social justice was the engine that led the people, discontented with the lack of inclusion, to demonstrate. The planning procedure and the history of the fall to a soft state reveal the background to the growing discontent in the country.

Scattered Knowledge

One of the challenges related to the absence of an institutional dialogue mechanism during the planning process was the dispersal of plans and knowledge, which requires integration. Although the five-year plans were regarded as the major national plan, our surveys have found that forty-one plans existed in various forms: fourteen "plans," three "visions," seven "strategies," and three "programs," among others. These forty-one plans were individually drafted by ministries and relevant organizations with support from international donors. The problem here was the absence of interrelation among them and of linkage to the five-year plans, which should have acted as the guiding vision for each of the individual plans. There is a large challenge in integrating these scattered plans in a functional way to act as a guiding vision for national development. An organization or system to integrate knowledge, and wisdom to draft an effective plan, was also missing.

A Plan Lacking Implementation Guidelines

Another challenge was the lack of a strategy for implementation. A plan shows its value when it has been implemented. Development experts suggest that "development is a process that must be undertaken at the level of the nation-state as the implementing unit" (Ohno and Shimamura 2007). The problem with the planning in Egypt was the lack of execution.

Since the five-year plans in Egypt were drafted inside one section of the ministry without building consensus among major stakeholders, including each of the ministries that were the real implementers, the national plan was simply a concept paper that did not call for execution. Accordingly, many plans, visions, and strategies were well prepared but never implemented.

The idea of inclusion of major stakeholders in the planning process was not a new concept in Egypt. For example, Handoussa (2010) proposed a mechanism for including academics and civil society organizations. However, the proposals were difficult to execute owing to the absence of a strong implementation unit. Inadequate administrative capacity at the ministry level was another factor hampering implementation.

Postrevolution Obstacles

The uprising in 2011 succeeded in razing the suppressive regime. However, a significant number of challenges remain for the new government. Demonstrations in Tahrir Square reflected a discontent that lingers, and they remain the only outlet for some marginalized individuals to voice their concerns. Furthermore, news sources indicate a rise in the crime rate after the revolution, while Gallup polls indicate increased anxiety among citizens (see figure 2-5).

Growing uncertainty about the economic situation has also amplified national anxiety. Since the uprising, the unemployment rate has risen from 9.0 to 12.4 percent, and foreign reserves have declined from

FIGURE 2-5. Egyptians' Fears after the Revolution

Percent expressing fear

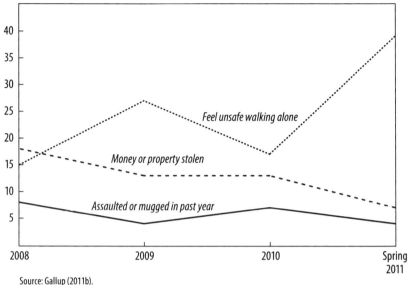

Source: Gallup (2011b).

$43 billion to $15 billion.[10] Moreover, the number of stakeholders in Egypt has rapidly increased, a balkanization that carries with it the potential of future divisiveness and resulting chaos.[11]

In light of these factors, the National Dialogue conference, which invited various stakeholders in the country, was carried out by the transitional government to help forge a sense of national consensus (Galal 2011). While this represented an initial step toward establishing dialogue, participants indicate that "the National Dialogue did not create a solution or consensus but brought chaos where people were expressing and pressing their own ideas."[12] Accordingly, the evidence indicates that an institutional system, one with the necessary capacity for creating national consensus and a guiding vision to overcome pressing after the revolution, was urgently needed.

10. Data from the Central Bank of Egypt, July 2012.
11. For example, a comparison with the elections results after the revolution indicates the diversification of political parties in politics.
12. Based on field interview, July 2012.

Inclusive Planning as a Way to Meet the Challenges

We have examined how dialogues without a proper institutional mechanism, scattered knowledge, and barriers to implementation represent the three primary challenges confronting Egyptian development objectives. Indeed, inadequate dialogue mechanisms contributed to the perception of Egypt as a soft state. In this context, the revolution was driven by the exasperation of the Egyptian people, who were fed up with increasing levels of corruption. However, the revolution did not resolve these challenges, and concerns are rising that the fractured society may be moving toward a period of increasing tension. A clear vision to stabilize and overcome the postrevolution difficulties is needed.

In light of these factors, the need to establish a defined mechanism for dialogue, and one free from corruption, cannot be overstated. It is the foundation and the necessary first step in building a national consensus. The Egyptian people have voiced their discontent and their hopes. Now, as the evidence resoundingly reflects, they demand a credible national decisionmaking framework. As a prerequisite to achieving this credibility, the mechanism must be one based on uniform, fair rules; and the institutional capacity of Egyptian implementation agencies must be bolstered to properly carry out their functions. To achieve these goals, a new role for development plans and a new institutional planning procedure is going to be examined.

The Importance of Procedures

There are two main sources of economic planning in modern history: communist planning and Western macroeconomic planning (Tinbergen 1964). The latter was introduced to most capitalist societies after World War II.[13] Economic planning has declined in several developed and developing countries, while the importance of the private sector, local governments, and civil society organizations has grown. There are also studies from the 1990s suggesting the decreasing effect of central planning (Balassa 1990).

13. Only the Soviet Union had economic planning before World War II (Keizaiki-kakucho, 1997).

This chapter suggests a new and important role for central economic planning in the twenty-first century based on recent studies that claim central planning plays a vital role during the early stages (that is, the recovery stage) of development, where development planning serves as an instrument for achieving sustainable economic growth and social justice (Ohno and Shimamura 2007). There are two basic roles of the new plan: the introduction of democratic procedure into policymaking and the creation of a growth vision for a mid- to long-term economic recovery.

Indonesian president Susilo Bambang Yudhoyono, in his presentation of the new economic plan in 2011, stated that "it is impossible to achieve our long-term economic goals without the master plan. We also can't rely wholly on market mechanisms. The government's role, as a 'visible hand,' is important" (Sato 2011, p. 107). This chapter emphasizes the possibility that a development plan can play an important role as a "visible hand" in Egypt in terms of sustaining its economic growth while promoting consensus building among major stakeholders.

As noted previously, institutional dialogue between stakeholders remains a crucial factor in keeping the national consensus equitable and in encouraging fair economic growth. Here, the process of establishing an institutional dialogue mechanism to include major stakeholders in the planning process (that is, the decisionmaking process) is defined as inclusive planning and is analyzed in accordance with the East Asian experience. A clear definition of inclusive planning does not exist. The phrase is used variously on different occasions, sometimes in the field of urban planning, which seeks to build a barrier-free planning method, and occasionally in the field of health, which attempts to address the significance of a disability inclusive planning process.

In this chapter, the term *inclusive planning* is used to describe the central planning procedure (inclusive process) for achieving inclusive development (inclusive aim) (figure 2-6). This requires the inclusion of major stakeholders (inclusive actors) in the planning process to build a national consensus while integrating the country's knowledge (see figure 2-7).

Inclusive planning requires that plans be a guiding vision for development. An inclusive plan must adopt a mid- to long-range perspective, moving beyond short-term goals (inclusive time frame) where new governments often address attractive, populist short-term policies. Inclusive planning reminds us of the importance of including long-term perspectives during the planning procedure. It should be noted here

FIGURE 2-6. Inclusive Planning in the Policymaking Process

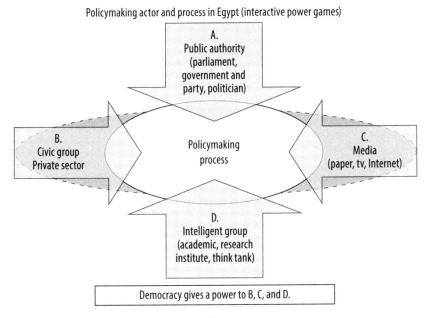

Policymaking actor and process in Egypt (interactive power games)

A. Public authority (parliament, government and party, politician)

B. Civic group Private sector

Policymaking process

C. Media (paper, tv, Internet)

D. Intelligent group (academic, research institute, think tank)

Democracy gives a power to B, C, and D.

Source: Based on JICA expert presentation materials, 2012.

that introducing a democratic planning process takes time. With a view to developing democracy and stabilizing the political and economic situation after the revolution, this chapter stresses the importance of institutionalization and the capacity development of planning organizations in policy planning procedures, as the initial measures to be taken. The excessive inclusion of stakeholders in the initial stage will create political anarchy rather than harmonization.

To achieve inclusive planning, the first step is to establish a fair institutional mechanism for increasing outside contacts. Tinbergen (1964) presents three main reasons for the importance of outside contacts during the planning period.

First, participation from outsiders in the planning process allows opinions to be exchanged with those operating the economy and thus introduces some features of democracy.[14] Second, detailed information

14. This chapter adopts the stance that the definitions of governance and democracy need to be carefully studied, since the development experiences of individual countries differ.

FIGURE 2-7. Inclusive Planning for Inclusive Development

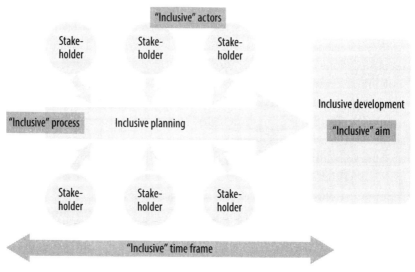

Source: Based on draft master plan and JICA expert presentation materials, 2012.

can be obtained from a number of outside experts, which indicates the quality of the economic plan will improve, being made more strategic. Third, the features of democracy will help facilitate the plan's acceptance, as well as its implementation.

I add another aspect to Tinbergen's analysis: aiming for the long term is an important factor in inclusive planning, creating a mutual and shared vision toward inclusive growth among major stakeholders and citizens. Table 2-3 illustrates the relation between the challenges and necessary reforms to create a inclusive planning process following Tinbergen's suggestion in earlier studies.

Lessons from the East Asian Experience

The fast-growing tiger economies of East Asia that emerged in the 1960s and 1970s were the first group of postindependence developing countries to develop strategies for inclusive growth (African Development Bank 2012). The East Asian growth experience, especially after World War II in Japan and after the Asian economic crisis in Indonesia, illustrates the success of these governments in developing mechanisms for effective dialogue and setting priorities for public actions to

TABLE 2-3. Matrix Relation: Challenges, Necessary Reforms, and Earlier Studies

Objective	Challenges facing development planning	Necessary reforms	Tinbergen's analysis of the importance of outside contacts	Method
Inclusive development	Dialogue without mechanism	Consensus building based on rules	1. Creating features of democracy ⟶	Inclusive planning
	Scattered knowledge	Integrating national knowledge	2. Integrating expertise	
	Lack of plan implementation	Strengthening of implementation mechanism	3. Facilitating implementation	
	Postrevolution obstacles	Guiding vision for stability and economic recovery		

Source: Author, based on Tinbergen (1964).

foster inclusive growth (African Development Bank 2012). It is often suggested that the creation of central economic agencies responsible for development planning and coordination was the key factor behind the so-called East Asian miracle (National Graduate Institute of Policy Studies 2008), and mobilization of all stakeholders toward a long-term economic goal is said to be a strong feature of growth in East Asia (Benhassine 2009). Of course, the effects of development plans differ in each country; however, their experience with inclusive planning provides a useful reference against which to introduce the concept. The experience of three countries in East Asia—Japan, Indonesia, and Malaysia—is assessed considering three factors: establishing an institutional consensus-building mechanism, integrating knowledge, and securing and strengthening the implementation of plans based on Tinbergen's studies (see table 2-4).

In addition, participatory policymaking, including as many stakeholders as possible in the policymaking process, is theoretically important for enhancing democracy. However, compared with Western society, with its long experience of developing democracy, states with less democratic experience confront certain difficulties in adopting a participatory system. The experience of East Asian countries shows that as well as the participatory policymaking process, a plan for a guiding vision is important in inclusive development.

TABLE 2-4. Japanese Economic Council

Role activities	—Economic planning	Drafting the indicative economic plan
	—Long-term visions	Providing a twenty-year vision and helping create a future vision among citizens
	—Policy recommendation	Specific topics or areas
Members	The chosen members were fewer than thirty people, including economists, academics, representative of labor unions, representative of consumers, media, and government officials. Under the council, there were several task forces (about 200 members).	
Achievements	Building a consensus between government and citizens, through objective and technical knowledge. —Providing mid- to long-term guidelines for activities for the private sector, contributing to economic development.[a] —Contributing to sharing of information between government and citizens.	
Developmental dissolution	In 2001 the function was succeeded by the Council on Economic and Fiscal Policy, strengthening the leadership of the prime minister as chief of this council. In 2009 the National Policy Unit was established.	

Source: Author, based on Keizaikikakucho (1997).

a. Providing a vision to the private sector was possible since the private sector was also included as a member of the planning committee.

Kondo lists four positive conditions (the prior experience of democracy, prior experience of civilian leadership, less experience of military domination, and prior achievement of economic development) required for democracy to be settled (Kondo 2011, based on Huntington 1991; Linz and Alfred 1996; Diamond 1999; Lipset 1959). Egypt seems to be one of the countries that has less experience with these conditions. However, East Asian countries also had the same problem. Kondo (2011) states that it is more important to target political institutionalization (including enhancement of bureaucratic structures and institutionalizing public-private partnerships) and economic achievements rather than to aim at deepening democracy (Kondo 2011). Establishing and rooting democracy will certainly take time, and it is important to adopt a long-term perspective and vision.

Lessons from Japan

Economic plans played a significant role in Japan's economic recovery from the ravaging effects of World War II. Indeed, Japan developed fourteen economic plans after the end of the war. If the draft plans, which were not officially approved, are included, the total number is twenty-four. The first economic plan was established immediately after the war, with economic recovery as its core objective. Following the first officially approved plan in 1955, the Japanese economic plans can be divided into four groups: the first targeted reconstruction and independence (first plan), the second aimed for high economic growth (second and third plans), the third tried to balance economic growth with social development (fourth to sixth plans), and the fourth strived for stable growth (seventh to fourteenth plans) (Keizaikikakucho 1997).

The Economic Council

Japanese economic plans were designed not only as guidelines for growth but also as instruments to guide future policy decisions. Japan's Economic Council was the planning mechanism employed to achieve these objectives.

The Economic Council was designed as an organization to create a national consensus and integrate expertise within the country. Japanese economic plans were drafted by the Economic Council, while the contents were implemented under each ministry. The council was established in 1952, under the Ministry of Economy and Trading Industry, as an advisory body for the prime minister. This was one of the official councils established under article 8 of the National Government Organization Act and articles 37 and 54 of the Cabinet Office Establishment Act. There are currently 115 official councils in Japan.[15] The Economic Council integrated the wisdom and knowledge from other sectors, such as the academic, economic, private, media, and social organization sectors, and played a key role in coordinating interests and conflicts among stakeholders. Academics praised the council for its externality, expertise, and communicative function (Keizaikikakucho 1997). Based on the official reports, table 2-5 describes the characteristics of the organization (Keizaikikakucho 1997).

The inclusion of the implementer—the ministries—during the planning procedure was the key factor in the implementation of Japanese plans. It is important to note that inclusive planning with the

15. Data from 2010. The Economic Council was one of the councils, but it was dissolved in 2011.

TABLE 2-5. Summary of Planning Experience of East Asia, Japan, Indonesia, and Malaysia

Japan	Stakeholder inclusion through Economic Council ("Shingikai"). Income-Doubling Plan as a guiding vision.
Indonesia	Stakeholder inclusion through Development Planning Committee ("Musrenbang").
Malaysia	Prime minister's office as a strong implementation body. Strong monitoring system.

participation of implementers binds each ministry and creates responsibility in implementing the discussed contents of the plan (figure 2-8).

The Income-Doubling Plan

The greatest achievement of the economic planning council in Japan is often said to be the creation of the income-doubling plan in 1960. This was the third plan to be drafted after World War II, aiming to double real national income within ten years and achieve full employment. The plan, which contributed significantly to Japanese reconstruction and development, also provided a guiding vision for public and private sectors in Japan. According to the Economic Planning Agency, the plan demonstrated three characteristics (Keizaikikakucho 1997).

First, the plan divided the public and private sectors, with the government fully responsible for achieving the public sector goals while private sector goals were simply predictive. It was the first time that Japanese planning had integrated the private sector into the plan and sent a strong message that the engine of development should be led by the private sector. This was important in that the plan not only was for public policy but also provided a vision for development for the private sector. The plan also clarified the public sector's role in enhancing social capital, improving human capacity, promoting science and technology, enhancing social security, improving social welfare, and introducing private industry.

Second, human resource development was a significant area of focus in the plan. The plan emphasized the importance of education, vocational training, and science technology from a long-term perspective.

Third, approaches to correcting gaps in various fields were comprehensively taken into account for the first time in Japanese planning. Income gaps, productivity differentials, and urban and rural gaps were discussed and reviewed during the planning process. Antipoverty was

FIGURE 2-8. Planning Process in the Japanese Economic Council

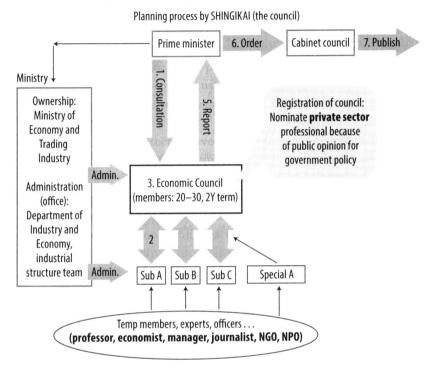

Source: Based on JICA expert presentation materials, 2012.

regarded as the central issue of social security, and the plan emphasized the promotion of social welfare measures. In Japanese history, the plan is often criticized as overemphasizing economic development, creating a regional gap and pollution nationwide. Indeed, the plan could not be highly rated as a success story in Japan in this respect, but its concept and idea provide lessons for achieving economic growth as well as strengthening social security.

The plan achieved its goal within just seven years, allowing Japan to step in as a member of the developed world.[16] This plan can serve as a benchmark for the new development plan in Egypt, which is examined later.

16. Conversely, negative aspects such as environmental pollution were expanded across Japan.

Japanese development plans have recently become less effective. Although the fifteenth Japanese development plan shows frequent consultation among citizens of Japan, no nationwide social consensus was achieved. This reality shows the importance of the plan as a guiding vision rather than just a means of participation. The income-doubling plan should be reevaluated, not only for Egypt but also for current Japanese development.

Lessons from Indonesia

Several common factors can be observed between Egypt under Mubarak and Indonesia under Suharto, such as the experience of a long dictatorship, high GDP growth, improvements in human development indicators, and the existence of major corruption in public and private sectors. With the success story in democratization after the collapse of the Suharto regime in 1997, many experts suggest that Indonesia offers some lessons for Egypt (Amin and others 2012; Kaufman 2011; African Development Bank 2012).

In Indonesia, it was during the Suharto era that the five-year development plan Repelita (Rencana Pembangunan Lima Tahun) and the twenty-five-year long-term vision were drafted and implemented. The Ministry of National Development Planning (Bappenas, Badan Perencanaan Pembangunan Nasional) was in charge of preparation, and the budget plan was drafted based on these plans. It also coordinated and monitored foreign aid. Under the Suharto regime, Bappenas was the engine of development, and it drafted six economic plans.

Democratization Reform after 1997

The Indonesian case demonstrates the importance of stakeholder inclusion during the planning process. The Asian economic crisis in 1997 and the collapse of the Suharto regime brought dramatic changes to Indonesia. From this incident, Indonesia started down the path to becoming a democratic nation. Development through a democratic and transparent process was needed following strong criticism of corruption in the Suharto regime. Many reforms were implemented, such as the introduction of the decentralization law, the establishment of a new partnership between government and civil society to fight corruption,

FIGURE 2-9. Governance Indicators in Indonesia

Percentile rank (0–100)

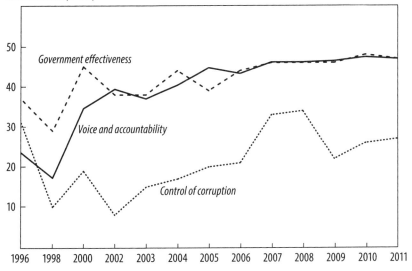

Source: World Governance Indicators, World Bank.

the establishment of the Corruption Eradication Commission, and the formation of an independent Socioeconomic Monitoring and Research Unit (Amin and others 2012). The dramatic improvement in governance indicators indicates successful results (figure 2-9). In addition, although the direct impact of these measures was small, the impact in terms of confidence and the sense of inclusion among people was significant (African Development Bank 2012).

A Transparent Inclusive Planning System

The fall of the Suharto regime brought some changes in the decision-making process, from a top-down planning process to a bottom-up approach, including citizens at several levels. The National Development Planning System Law, formulated in 2004, changed the composition of the development planning committee, Musrembang (Musyawarah Perencanaan Pembangunan). Citizen representatives joined this committee during the planning procedure, working to adjust the stakeholders' perspectives. Of course, this took considerable effort and time, but the government of Indonesia recognized the step as a necessary cost for democratization and good governance (Iijima 2005). Consequently, by establishing the Development Planning Committee, coordination between stakeholders became institutionalized, creating a consensus, which allowed the voices of citizens to be reflected in policies (African Development Bank 2012). Beginning in the second Yudhoyono administration in 2009, national dialogues with the thirty-two governors and chief executive officers of the chambers of commerce were organized once every several months to build consensus and ownership of the major implementers (local government and the private sector) for the new economic plan that was announced in 2011 (Sato 2011). This trend can be recognized as the achievement and development of inclusive planning.

Lessons from Malaysia

A 1993 World Bank report implies that the Malaysian economic growth resulted largely from the prime minister's strong leadership and the organizational strength of the economic planning bureau, which drafted, monitored, and evaluated the economic plans under the prime minister's office (World Bank 1993, cited in Torii 2005). A later United Nations evaluation report also stressed that a system for planning, monitoring, and evaluation contributed to Malaysia's socioeconomic success (United Nations 2001).

After attaining independence in 1957, the Malaysian government invited the World Bank evaluation unit to draft a report for central development planning. Based on its findings, a small economic planning bureau was established. In 1961 the bureau was upgraded to the Economic Planning Unit, which was attached to the prime minister's office. It is often said that the unit functioned as a superministry, which took the leading role in formulating the coordination plans with the National Budget Office (Ohno and Shimamura 2007). The unit was also in charge of drafting five-year plans, as well as midterm reviews.[17]

The implementation function was strengthened during the period of the second prime minister, Abdul Razak Hussein, as he adopted the New Economic Policy. In 1971 he established the Implementation Coordination Unit under the prime minister's office. This was a unit

17. Nine development plans have been drafted to date.

to implement the plan and make arrangements with each ministry. By placing the Economic Planning Unit and the Implementation Coordination Unit under the authority of the prime minister's office, the government created a strong administrative body. Furthermore, the two units inside the prime minister's office collaborated, united by common objectives. In sum, the system helped bolster the efficiency and success of planning implementation.

The fourth prime minister, Mahathir bin Mohamad, strengthened the implementation function further by including various stakeholders and introducing a public-private dialogue system, at regional as well as federal levels. For example, in 1988 a system for an annual public-private dialogue meeting was introduced, institutionally securing the participation of the private sector in the national planning process. This system was comparable to the Japanese Economic Council system.

Malaysia had two levels of decisionmaking institutions for national planning: one at the administrative level (the National Development Planning Committee) and one at the ministerial level (the National Development Council). In addition, the National Development Working Committee, in charge of monitoring the implementation at the administrative level, was established to enhance implementation, while at the state level, the State Development Council and State Development Working Committee were established to plan and implement the development plans within the state.

While impact evaluation at the project level was undertaken by each of the ministries, it was the Implementation Coordination Unit that conducted the impact evaluation at the macro level. The unit also developed various monitoring systems, which involved the periodic collection and analysis of physical and financial data. Some examples of a strong monitoring system were the Red Book System, which provided a monthly reporting format for rural development, and the Integrated Scheduling Application System, a physical monitoring system for development projects. This Malaysian experience of a strong implementation and monitoring unit could provide positive lessons to Egypt.

A New Role of the Development Plan in Egypt

The efforts to reform the planning procedures taken in Egypt were led by the Ministry of Planning, with the support of a Japan International

Cooperation Agency expert.[18] The newly established central planning organization, the Planning Committee, was responsible for drafting the new development plan.

The new plan had two characteristics. First, it served as a guiding vision. The plan aimed to provide a long-term development vision, while in the short term, it aimed to state a clear national vision for the country to overcome its economic difficulties after the revolution. Second, the plan introduced the idea of the democratic inclusive planning procedure.

The plan clearly stated that social justice will be realized through two main objectives: doubling the national income of Egypt within a decade and achieving full employment.[19] Egypt was showing steady macroeconomic growth during the Mubarak era, based on its open economic structure. The new plan emphasized the importance of growth with this economic framework, supplementing factors that were lacking in the previous plans, in particular, inclusiveness.

In fact, the Japanese income-doubling plan was the model for this new plan. Considering not only positive lessons but also the downsides of the Japanese plan (environmental disruption and overconcentration) (Honma 1999), social and environmental sustainability was added to the Egyptian version.

A Plan as a Guiding Vision

The first major feature of the plan was its strategic framework, acting as a guiding vision for national development. The plan considered eight social goals, ten challenges and opportunities for Egypt, and five key issues to be studied, as illustrated in figure 2-10. The plan also included the fundamental idea of comprehensively using the country's strength and opportunities. Taking into account the crisis of revolution and future economic development, the plan adopted a phased approach, dividing the decade into three phases, as shown in table 2-6, so that the objectives and inputs could be adjusted according to the development level. The plan was to serve as the master plan or a strategic framework for a decade and is to be followed by an execution plan in each phase.

18. The Japan International Cooperation Agency dispatched an expert to the Ministry of Planning as an adviser.

19. Doubling the national income is defined as doubling the real national income, which requires an average annual growth rate of 7.5 percent GDP growth a year. Achieving full employment is defined as reducing the unemployment rate to less than 4 percent.

FIGURE 2-10. Planning Approach

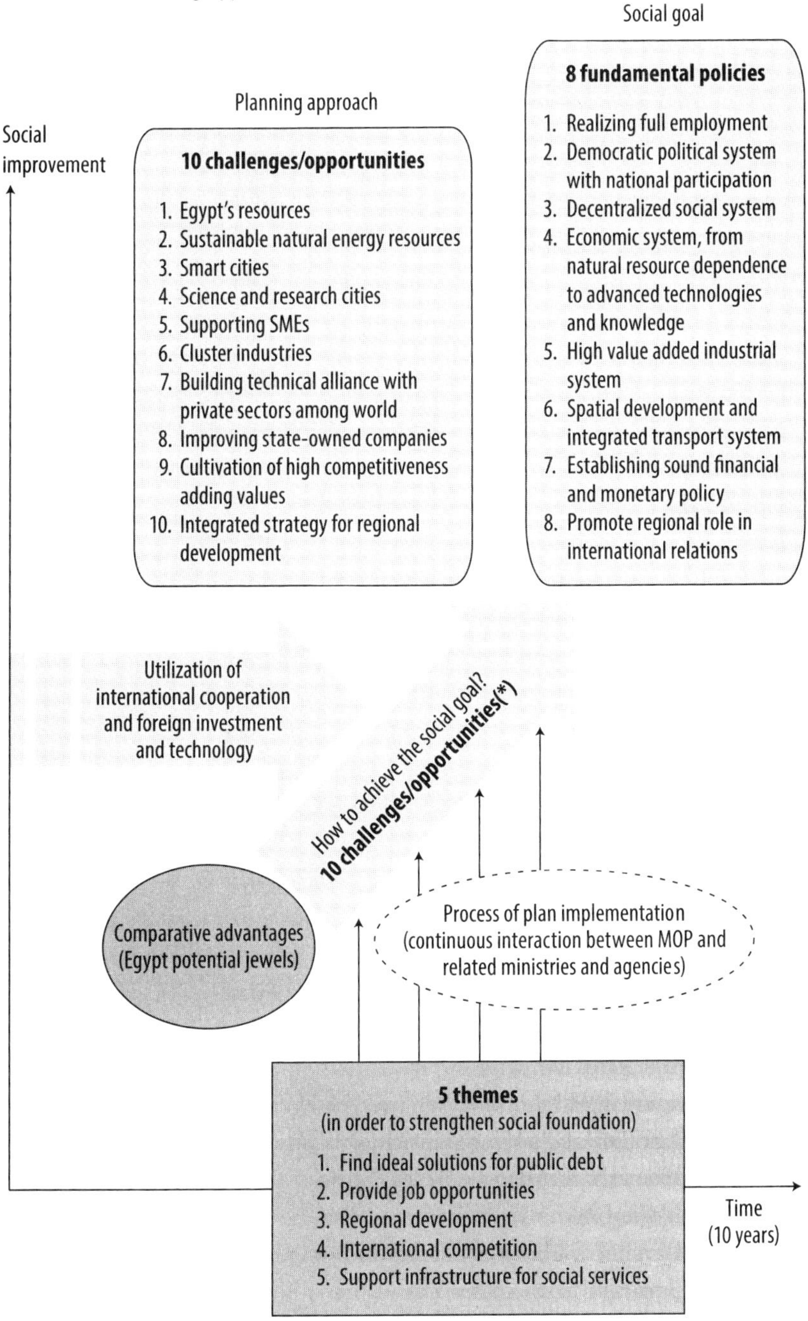

Social goal

Planning approach

8 fundamental policies

Social improvement

10 challenges/opportunities

1. Egypt's resources
2. Sustainable natural energy resources
3. Smart cities
4. Science and research cities
5. Supporting SMEs
6. Cluster industries
7. Building technical alliance with private sectors among world
8. Improving state-owned companies
9. Cultivation of high competitiveness adding values
10. Integrated strategy for regional development

1. Realizing full employment
2. Democratic political system with national participation
3. Decentralized social system
4. Economic system, from natural resource dependence to advanced technologies and knowledge
5. High value added industrial system
6. Spatial development and integrated transport system
7. Establishing sound financial and monetary policy
8. Promote regional role in international relations

Utilization of international cooperation and foreign investment and technology

How to achieve the social goal?
10 challenges/opportunities(*)

Comparative advantages (Egypt potential jewels)

Process of plan implementation (continuous interaction between MOP and related ministries and agencies)

5 themes
(in order to strengthen social foundation)

1. Find ideal solutions for public debt
2. Provide job opportunities
3. Regional development
4. International competition
5. Support infrastructure for social services

Time (10 years)

Source: Based on draft master plan and JICA expert presentation materials, 2012.

TABLE 2-6. Economic Targets of the Plan Based on Three Phases

Phase 1 Social recovery: 2012–14 (2 years ±1)	Stabilization of the political environment (election, president, and constitution) Social institution design and implementation Socioeconomic recovery start (3–5 percent GDP growth)
Phase 2 Socioeconomic independence: 2014–19 (5 years ±1)	Private sector leads economy Investment by domestic capital Industrialization balancing (1st, 2nd, and 3rd industries)
Phase 3 Socioeconomic growing shift: 2019–22 (3 years ±1)	Social stabilization and living standard enhancement Socioeconomic system shifts to industrial structure

Source: Author, based on JICA expert presentation materials, 2012.

This idea was based on the Japanese development approach phased in after the Second World War.

Building an Institutional Consensus-Building Mechanism

The introduction of inclusive planning was one of the achievements of the Ministry of Planning during the transitional government period. Currently, the plan's greatest challenge is to include the interests of civil, public, and private sector stakeholders. Given the varied and often conflicting interests of these sectors, a structured dialogue mechanism was necessary to help build consensus on policy-related issues. Indeed, in the absence of such a mechanism, many experts agree that attempts to increase dialogue might only lead to an increase in chaos. Based on these points, the Japanese Economic Council served as an exemplar in building institutional consensus.

The purpose of establishing the Planning Committee under the direction of the Ministry of Planning was to unify the ideas and voices of major stakeholders and build a national vision based on the consensus in the committee. The committee's mission involved integrating the varied interests and opinions of the public sector (represented by public social organizations), technicians and professionals (academics, engineers, and experts), and stakeholders (social group representatives) (figure 2-11). Within the Planning Committee, nine study groups and one editing team were established. This was just a first step but important for the introduction of inclusive planning. Fixing and strengthening this institution as the system evolves is important and necessary for Egypt.

FIGURE 2-11. Mechanism of the Egyptian Planning Committee

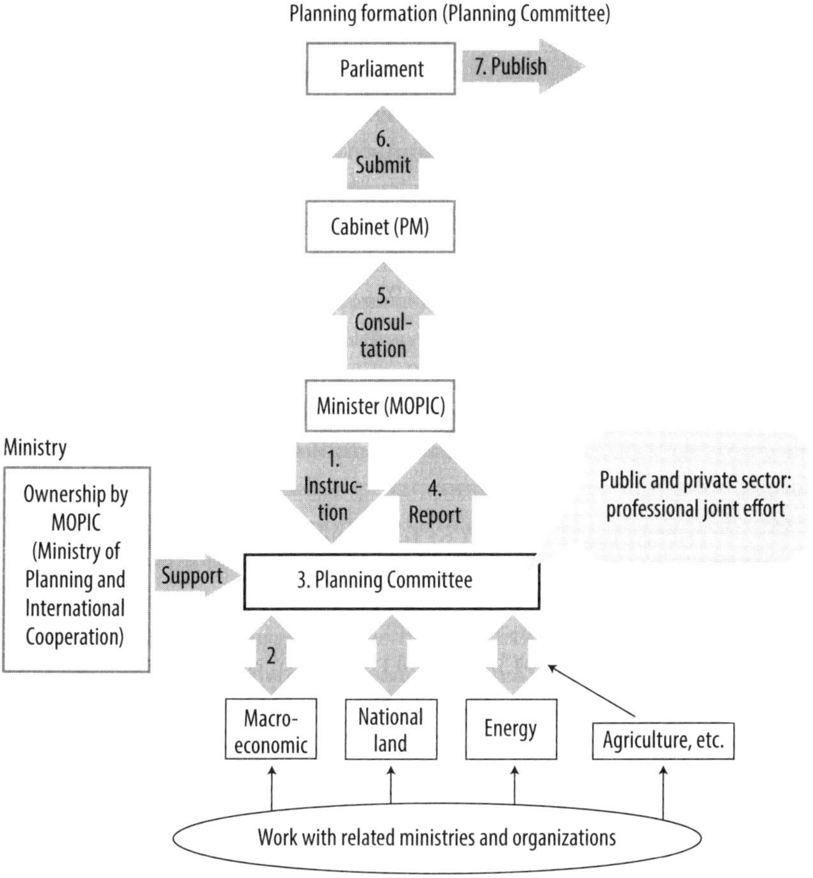

Planning formation (Planning Committee)

Parliament   7. Publish

6. Submit

Cabinet (PM)

5. Consultation

Minister (MOPIC)

Ministry

Ownership by MOPIC (Ministry of Planning and International Cooperation)

Support

1. Instruction   4. Report

Public and private sector: professional joint effort

3. Planning Committee

2

Macroeconomic   National land   Energy   Agriculture, etc.

Work with related ministries and organizations

Source: Based on draft master plan and JICA expert presentation materials, 2012.

The major contribution of the Planning Committee was the establishment of a national consensus-building mechanism, which also facilitates the integration of knowledge and strengthens plan implementation. For decades, people in Egypt were expected to follow the president's decisions, but the establishment of the Planning Committee will empower people to decide their future visions for themselves.

Integrating Scattered Knowledge

The Planning Committee played an important role in integrating existing wisdom and knowledge in Egypt. Experts from various fields gathered in the Planning Committee, and nine working groups were established, with twenty-one experts, to draft the plan. The authors' names, which did not appear in the previous versions of the plan, were given for reasons of accountability.

The effort to integrate this expertise is just beginning. Private and civil sectors have not yet been included in the planning process, in which around 200 members gather to draft the Japanese Income-Doubling Plan. The future challenge for Egypt is to include various experts from the private sector, civil organizations, the media, and so on. There is still much knowledge and great Egyptian wisdom that could be integrated into the plan.

The Planning Committee also contributed toward reorganizing existing plans in Egypt. The existing forty-one plans were listed and studied to consider the strength and potential in Egypt, assuming that the existing plans were not used effectively enough. From this effort, the potential strength in Egypt has been reconsidered, allowing them to devise a strategic framework, as described in the previous section. The Planning Committee contributed to integrating the wisdom and knowledge that had accumulated in Egypt.

Strengthening the Capacity of Research Institutions

The Institute of National Planning was another effort to integrate the scattered knowledge involved in strengthening the Ministry of Planning to support the planning process, both technically and academically. The institute was a research think tank under the Ministry of Planning that played an important role in the planning process. During the process of integrating knowledge, the Planning Committee and the institute found that existing laws were scattered and that they had difficulties in referring to important laws and documents while drafting a new plan.

To correct this problem, an electronic library was established inside the Institute of National Planning and all existing laws and important government documents were scanned electronically to create a large database maintained in the e-library. Work on knowledge integration in the institute is still under way.

Strengthening the Implementation Mechanism

When drafting and implementing a plan, the importance of linking national planning and policymaking was considered during the planning process, and the Japanese plan applied a phased approach. The income-doubling plan was defined as a master plan, as it holds the perspective of long-term growth and acts as a guideline for midterm and annual plans. The idea of strengthening and structuring the relation between the master plan and the execution plan is important for implementation.

The Malaysian experience shows the importance of a strong implementation system and body in achieving the goals stated in the plan. Egypt needs an implementation structure, and for this the new plan proposed to establish the Strategic National Project Execution Unit under the Ministry of Planning and promotes that unit as the national project manager in an effort to link the planning and implementation functions.

Challenges for Inclusive Planning

Establishing a planning committee was a first and important step toward reforming the planning process in Egypt. However, there are still numerous challenges to overcome. First, the participation of stakeholders was incomplete. Members from line ministries, private sectors, local governments, and media were missing from the Planning Committee. To build consensus and strengthen implementation, efforts and coordination to ensure implementers participate in the planning procedure is crucial. Second, the plan was prepared by the interim government just after the 2011 revolution, and it needs to be reevaluated and utilized by the current government. Third, the inclusion of the military as a large stakeholder in Egypt will be a big challenge. A large portion of the economy is run by the military. Including the huge economic activities of the military in the plan is one important task for inclusive planning. With the increase in stakeholders, which was examined in the previous section, more and more topics require further examination. However, with the effective inclusion of stakeholders within the institutional mechanism framework, the knowledge gained from other states' experiences, and Egyptian potential strengths, these challenges should be controllable.

Conclusion and Future Prospects

The Egyptian revolution in 2011 was a historical event that will have a lasting impact on world politics and economic and social commentary.

Years have passed, and the country still faces various challenges moving forward. Before the revolution, Egypt showed steady economic growth, but growth that was inequitable and in which the benefits were grossly unequal. The Arab uprising highlighted the fundamental desires of the Egyptian people, who simply sought social justice and were desperate to prevent their country from becoming further enmired in the insidious effects of endemic corruption. Moreover, the absence of a consensus-building dialogue system significantly helped fuel an environment of escalating corruption, a knowledge diaspora, and an impotent implementation process.

As applied in Japan, Indonesia, and Malaysia, the inclusive planning model demonstrates how economic growth and inclusiveness go hand in hand. The Japanese economic planning council system, the Indonesian experience of a participatory planning process during the democratization period, and the Malaysian experience of strengthening the implementation mechanism provide a frame of reference, indeed a malleable blueprint, which could be applicable to Egypt.

Egypt's movement just after the 2011 revolution toward drafting a master plan and establishing a planning committee represents important steps toward achieving inclusive development. The interim government also took steps toward building an inclusive planning procedure, which, once firmly established, could be fully utilized. Inclusive planning transcends political regimes. Indeed, it is apolitical as it is based on the facilitation of varied stakeholders. This feature in particular could help provide the necessary framework for establishing a national consensus, one built on integrated knowledge, visions, and strategies.

East Asian economic growth and growth experiences worldwide demonstrate that international assistance can be effectively used to support development. The incidents of 2011, including Japan's devastating earthquake, tsunami, and nuclear disaster, further demonstrate the immense value of international cooperation in supporting Japan's recovery. Indeed, it is reminiscent of the global cooperation that helped fuel Japan's remarkable recovery after the Second World War. Similarly, in nations such as Egypt and Tunisia, with histories of social, political, and economic instability, experts such as Kaufman (2011) believe that close collaboration with other nations may help ensure stability. Similarly, the importance of establishing links with countries such as Indonesia would offer similar benefits.

Finally, while economic assistance plays an indispensable role, it should not be used as a vehicle to impose a particular political ideology. Rather, it should be an apolitical instrument that facilitates a nation's rediscovery of its inherent strengths and collective wisdom—national treasures long buried under a pyramid of corruption in Egypt. Inclusive planning, in this context, implies the inclusion of, and respect toward, a country's people, culture, thoughts, and history.

References

African Development Bank (AfDB). 2012. *Jobs, Justice, and the Arab Spring: Inclusive Growth in North Africa.* Tunis (www.afdb.org/fileadmin/uploads/afdb/Documents/Publications/Jobs%20and%20Justice%20-%20en.pdf).

Amin, Galal. 2011. *Egypt in the Era of Hosni Mubarak: 1981–2011.* Cairo: American University in Cairo Press.

Amin, Magdi, and others. 2012. *After the Spring: Economic Transitions in the Arab World.* Oxford University Press.

Balassa, Bela. 1990. "Indicative Planning in Developing Countries." Working paper. Washington: World Bank.

Benhassine, Najy. 2009. *From Privilege to Competition: Unlocking Private-Led Growth in the Middle East and North Africa.* Washington: World Bank.

Daily News Egypt. 2012. "Mohamed Gouda Discusses 'Nahda' Project." June 28.

Diamond, Larry. 1999. *Developing Democracy: Toward Consolidation.* Johns Hopkins University Press.

Fakhouri, Hani. 2010. "The Negative Consequences of Egypt's Economic Planning." *Middle East Today,* May 27. http://mid-east-today.blogspot.com/2010/05/negative-consequences-of-egypts.html.

Galal, Ahmed. 2011. "Egypt Post–January 2011: An Economic Perspective." *Policy Perspective,* no. 3 (July). Economic Research Forum.

Gallup. 2011a. "Arithmetic of Revolution."

———. 2011b. "Egypt from Tahrir to Transition."

Handoussa, Heba. 2010. "Situation Analysis: Key Development Challenges Facing Egypt." United Nations Development Program.

Honma Yoshito. 1999. *Kokudo Kaihatsu Keikaku wo Kangaeru: Kaihatsu Rosen No Yukue* [Consideration about national spatial plan: The trace of development]. Tokyo: Chukoshinsho.

Huntington, Samuel. 1991. *The Third Wave: Democratization in the Late Twentieth Century.* University of Oklahoma Press.

Iijima Satoshi. 2005. "Indonesia Kokka Kaihatsu Keikaku Shisutemuhou No Seitei to Sono Igi Ni Tsuite" [Enactment of Indonesian National Development Planning System Act and its significance]. Development Finance Institution Working Paper. Tokyo: Japan Bank of International Cooperation.

Ikram, Khalid. 2004. *The Egyptian Economy, 1952–2000: Performance Policies and Issues.* New York: Routledge Studies in Middle Eastern Economies.

Kaufman, Daniel. 2011. "Governance and the Arab World Transition: Reflections, Empirics, and Implications for the International Community." Brookings Blum Roundtable Policy Brief. Washington.

Keizaikikakucho [Economic planning agency], ed. 1997. *Senngo Nihonkeizai no Kiseki Keizaikikakucho Gojyuunenshi* [Tracks of the postwar Japanese economy: The fifty-year history book of the Economic Planning Agency]. Tokyo: Ministry of Finance Press.

Kondo Hisahiro. 2011. "Minshuka no Jouken: Ikou to Teichaku" [Condition of democratization: Transition and establishment]. In *Kaihatu Seijigaku Nyumon* [Introduction to development politics], edited by Kimura Hirotsune, Kondo Hisahiro, and Kanamaru Yuji. Tokyo: Keiso Shobo.

Linz, Juan, and Stepan Alfred. 1996. *Problems of Democratic Transition and Consolidation: Southern Europe, South America, and Post-Communist Europe.* Johns Hopkins University Press.

Lipset, Seymour. 1959. *Political Man: The Social Bases of Politics.* New York: Doubleday.

Myrdal, Gunnar. 1968. *Asian Drama: An Inquiry into the Poverty of Nations.* 3 vols. New York: Pantheon.

Nagasawa Eiji. 2012. "Egypt Kakumei: Arab Sekaihendo no Yukue" [The Egyptian revolution: The path of fluctuations in the Arab world]. Tokyo: Heibonshashinsho.

National Graduate Institute of Policy Studies. 2008. "Atarashii Africa Seichoshien Initiative no Teigen [Policy recommendations for a new African development assistance initiative]. Development Forum Policy Note 4. Tokyo.

Ohno Izumi. 2009. "Higashi Asiateki hassou ni yoru Africa Seicho senryaku heno kouken" [Contribution to African development strategy by East Asian views]. *Kokusaikaihatukenkyu* [Research on international development] 18, no. 2.

Ohno Izumi and Shimamura Masumi. 2007. "Managing the Development Process and Aid: East Asian Experience in Building Central Economic Agencies." Tokyo: GRIPS Development Forum.

Okita Saburo. 1992. *Keizai Gaiko ni Ikiru* [Living in economic diplomacy]. Tokyo: Toyo Keizai Shinposha.

Sato Yuri. 2011. *Keizaitaikoku Indonesia: 21seikino seichou jouken* [Economic large-state Indonesia: Conditions of development in the twenty-first century]. Tokyo: Chuko Shinsho.

Shimizu Manabu. 2011. "Arab no Haru to Houkatsuteki Hatten [Arab spring and inclusive development]. Seisaku Teigen Kenkyuu [Policy recommendation research]." October. Asia Keizai Kenkyujyo [Institute of Development Economies, Japan External Trade Organization].

Tinbergen, Jan. 1964. *Central Planning.* Yale University Press.

Torii Takashi. 2005. "Malaysia ni Okeru Kaihatsugyousei no Tenkai: Seido Kouchiku wo Chuushin Ni-" [Performance of development policy in Malaysia: Focus on system establishment]. Discussion Paper Series 05 J-008. Tokyo. Research Institute of Economy, Trade, and Industry.

United Nations. 2001. "Malaysian Experiences of Monitoring in Development Planning." Development Planning in a Market Economy, Least Developed Countries Series No. 6. New York.

Vergianita Asra. 2010. "Indonesia ni Taisuru Kokusaiteki Minshuka Shien: Nihon Beikoku EU no Hikaku" [International support for democratization in Indonesia: Comparison with Japan, the United States, and the EU], *Asia Kenkyu* [Asian research] 56, no. 4.

Wakabayashi Hiroyuki. 2007. "Minkanjin Toyo de Susumu Egypt Keizaikaikaku" [Egyptian economic reform through private appointment]. *Kikankokusaiboueki to Toushi* [Institute of International Trade and Investment], no. 68 (Summer).

World Bank. 1993. *Lessons of East Asia*. Washington.

―――. 2009. *Economic Growth Report*. Washington.

3

Establishing Good Governance in Fragile States through Reconstruction Projects: Lessons from Iraq

SEIKI TANAKA and MASANORI YOSHIKAWA

Some of the Arab countries currently going through democratic transition (for example, Yemen) have experienced conflict and a collapse of some key institutions. They exhibit a number of the characteristics of fragile states. There is concern that this may lead to a decline in the volume of aid going to them at a time when they need it most. Aid can harm developing countries by distorting their incentive systems, especially when there is not an appropriate environment in which it can work. Particularly in weak, fragile governments, aid can be diverted by corrupt bureaucrats and politicians and have no positive effect on political stability and economic growth (Burnside and Dollar 2000; Collier and Dollar 2002).

Accordingly, the idea that good governance is a necessary prerequisite for aid to be effective has become a stylized fact (Epstein and Gang 2009).[1] In the past decade, the strengthening of good governance in developing countries has been both an objective of and a condition for development assistance. Furthermore, while donors did not hesitate

We would like to thank officials of the Iraq government and the United Nations Development Program Iraq, as well as JICA and the JICA Iraq office, for their invaluable assistance and collaboration, and scholars at the Brookings Institution for useful comments.

1. The concept of governance captures "the manner in which power is exercised in the management of a country's economic and social resources for development" (Santiso 2001, p. 1).

FIGURE 3-1. Long-Term Trend in Aid Disbursement, by Quality of Government, 1960–2004[a]

Average amount of aid (% GDP)

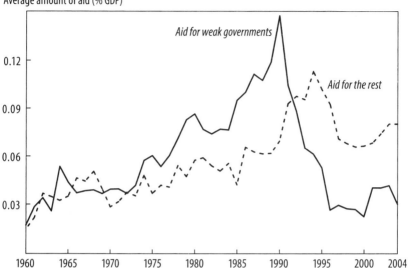

Source: Aid data from the World Bank; government data from the Polity IV project (Marshall, Jaggers, and Gurr 2011).

a. The polity score codes the qualities of democratic and autocratic authorities for each country for every year from 1800 and 2010. It ranges from 10 (consolidated democracy) to −10 (hereditary monarchy). We define *weak governments* as countries whose polity score is in the 25th percentile.

to implement large-scale projects in those countries with weak governance during the cold war, a recent trend of development assistance to such countries is to start from small-scale projects rather than risk losing the investment to corruption or incompetence. Figure 3-1 shows the decreasing trend in aid disbursement to countries with weak governments (or autocratic governments) after the end of the cold war.

This chapter, in contrast to the recent trend, proposes that aid can have a positive impact in a fragile state if certain conditions are met. Of course, the idea that aid sometimes results in increased political and economic development is not new (for example, Clist and Morrissey 2011; Dalgaard, Hansen, and Tarp 2004). For instance, Burnside and Dollar (2000) argue that foreign aid raises economic growth in a good policy environment, while Kosack (2003) finds that aid can improve the quality of life in democracies.[2] However, since most previous research

2. Burnside and Dollar's (2000) argument has been scrutinized and challenged by a number of scholars (for example, Easterly, Levine, and Roodman 2004).

employs a cross-country analysis with macro indicators, we still do not know what kinds of micro-level factors explain the positive relationship between economic aid and the recipient nation's development. Furthermore, given that donors tend to avoid disbursing aid to fragile states, analyses focusing on fragile states are scarce, and little is known about what leads to positive results in such circumstances.

By contrast, we examine the successful implementation of aid projects in Iraq by Japan's aid agency, the Japan International Cooperation Agency (JICA), and thereby identify the conditions under which aid can work in a fragile state. Although we may limit the external validity of our analysis by focusing on only one case, the existence of unique observational data, which include interviews, allows us to come close to identifying which micro-level indicators lead to a positive impact of aid in a fragile state. Whereas our observational data raise endogeneity concerns, we attempt to establish a relationship between JICA's interventions and the outcome by testing competing hypotheses.

We argue that the JICA project in Iraq resulted in positive development because of the presence of one or a combination of the following factors: the quantity and quality of the donor's involvement are high; there existed a social recognition system in the recipient government that evaluates their achievements in front of their peers; and a neutral mediator facilitates the communication between the donor and recipient agencies. By using a time-series analysis with novel micro-level indicators, we test the first two hypotheses; owing to data limitations, we conduct a bivariate analysis to examine the impact of third-party presence.

To examine the hypotheses, we first need to demonstrate that the JICA projects in Iraq led to positive results, although the purpose of our analysis is not to examine whether the JICA projects worked. Then, after confirming that the project is a successful case, in terms of whether Iraqi officials became more efficient, we investigate what mechanisms led to a positive aid impact in Iraq. Ultimately, by extracting mechanisms from the case study, we aim to generalize our findings to other cases. In other words, we believe that our attempt to identify the mechanisms not only helps accelerate postconflict reconstruction efforts in Iraq but is also of critical importance to policymakers and social scientists alike, in implementing large-scale projects and reestablishing good governance in other countries.

Difficulties of Postconflict Reconstruction

A donor of aid would generally encounter two main challenges in a postconflict society where the governance structure has been destroyed. First of all, there are considerable security risks. Not only do donors face recurrent terrorist attacks and a high crime rate, but they also face a risk that conflict itself will resume. By one conservative estimate, 36 percent of civil wars that ended between 1945 and 1996 were followed by an additional war (Walter 2004). This implies that a donor will have significant difficulty in maintaining a local office in postconflict societies; and even if the donor establishes an office, donor officials are more likely to remain in the office rather than in the field, because of security risks.

Second, and not necessarily owing to a conflict, war-torn countries historically have not had good governance records ex ante; the governments did not have the capacity to govern because of political and administrative weaknesses, corruption, ethnic tensions and conflict, economic depression, financial crises, or totalitarianism. These reasons are frequently cited as factors that explain why external or indigenous efforts at regime change occurred in the first place (Rondinelli and Montgomery 2005). To make matters worse, during the previous authoritarian regime or civil war, the normal incentive to maintain a reputation for honesty is often disrupted, switching the society into a persistent high-corruption equilibrium (Tirole 1996). In the end, donors often have to improve or rebuild government capacity for public services from scratch, while facing significant security risks.[3]

Given the anticipated difficulties (security risk and underdeveloped government capacity), the World Bank and other donors tend to avoid investing in some postconflict societies, although the media selectively capture cases and moments where donors have pledged to disburse aid, such as in Afghanistan, East Timor, and Bosnia. Yet in reality,

3. Some scholars argue that aid helps the dramatic recovery of conflict-torn societies. For example, Collier and Hoeffler (2004) find that aid leads to economic growth in postconflict societies. Yet their findings also need to be framed within a context: aid in conjunction with good policies has a positive effect on growth. The study also suffers from an endogeneity problem of the so-called phoenix factor (for example, see Kang and Meernik 2005).

as Flores and Nooruddin (2009) point out, donors such as the World Bank tend to select aid recipients according to their probability of conflict recurrence.

Reconstruction Projects in Iraq

Iraq is a typical example of a fragile country that is reconstructing without an effective government or political stability. After the Iraq war, the first election was held in 2005, and since 2007, the violence in Iraq has decreased and foreign commercial activities have become more vibrant. Yet despite signs of improvement, the country still faces instability in political, security, and economic matters. According to the Worldwide Governance Indicators of the World Bank (2011), Iraq is ranked twentieth from the bottom, after Liberia and the Republic of the Congo, in government effectiveness, and fifth, after Sudan and Afghanistan, in political stability. In addition, in Iraq's case, government officials have less knowledge and experience in international commercial activities, owing to decades of economic sanction, further discouraging donors from implementing large-scale projects. Moreover, security risk and capacity building, mentioned previously among the difficulties in implementing reconstruction projects, are apparent in Iraq.

As a result, as figure 3-2 shows, most donors avoid committing large amounts of aid to Iraq. Japan constitutes an exceptional case: JICA aid accounts for 85.0 percent of all loans Iraq receives and accounts for 26.7 percent in total grants that Iraq has received since 2004.[4]

The initial platform was established in 2008 between the Iraqi government and JICA, and in 2009 the United Nations Development Program (UNDP) joined the platform as a third-party fiduciary-monitoring agent and evaluator. In total, the platform includes twelve loan agreements amounting to $2.8 billion (subsequently, the number of loan agreements increased to nineteen) and covers various sectors such as electricity, transportation, water and sanitation, and oil.

While Japan expected to face difficulties in implementing large-scale projects in Iraq, it did not write a blank check; rather, JICA came up with several mechanisms for aid to work in a war-torn society. More

---

4. The United States provides exceptionally large amounts of technical cooperation aid and grant; we omit the data from the analysis as outliers.

FIGURE 3-2. Aid Commitment to Iraq, by Country and Type

Billions of U.S. dollars

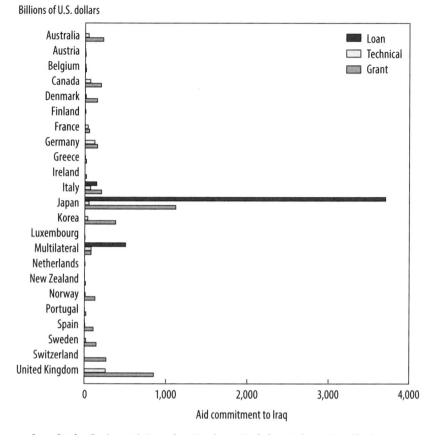

Source: Data from Development Assistance Committee, Organization for Economic Cooperation and Development.

specifically, to address the above-mentioned difficulties, JICA and the Iraqi government agreed to introduce a unique monitoring platform composed of increased interaction, a multilayer structure, and the presence of the UNDP.

Increased Interactions

Given that one difficulty in implementation was expected to be insufficient knowledge and experience regarding international standards, JICA increased the level of interaction with the recipient. More specifically, JICA agreed with project entities to set up a project management team (PMT), consisting of local officials, for each project. Whereas typically there would be high turnover among local officials in a fragile state, JICA asked the Iraqi government to retain the officials in a PMT for the long term. Then, JICA asked that each PMT submit a project progress report every month, after which JICA would review the report carefully and provide detailed feedback. The progress report and feedback cover important aspects of project management and contribute to establishing the project management framework. Since Iraqi officials do not have much experience or knowledge in project management with international finance organizations owing to decades of conflicts and economic sanctions, the increased interactions between JICA and Iraqi officials and the provision of constructive feedback are expected to direct communication between JICA and project entities to the important issues in project implementation and increase the effectiveness of project implementation.

Multilayer Structure

To facilitate the PMT's activity in project implementation, JICA further introduced a multilayer monitoring system. To increase the degree of monitoring, JICA agreed to establish a committee to oversee the reconstruction projects periodically, working with the Iraqi government's high-level authority and oversight agencies such as the Prime Minister's Advisory Commission, the Ministry of Finance, and the Ministry of Planning. A quarterly monitoring meeting follows the multilayer structure. In this meeting, project entities are expected to discuss best practices and common problems, while JICA, the high-level authority, and oversight agencies evaluate project entities based on measurable factors of their performance. More specifically, the latter three institutions praise PMTs that had good performance records, while they prod PMTs that have bad performance records.

Presence of the UNDP

While there is a need to increase monitoring in situations such as postconflict Iraq, limited access to project entities owing to security concerns often leads to ineffective and time-consuming project management (for example, communication only with official letters). In contrast, by collaborating with the UNDP, which has direct access to project entities even in a war-torn country, JICA attempted to solve such accessibility problems. The UNDP plays a unique role in this monitoring mechanism, as actual problems in implementation are captured by direct access rather than through e-mails or phone calls. Based on the findings, they provide analyses and evaluations in monthly reports and quarterly monitoring meetings. Furthermore, in addition to its physical advantage, it appears that the presence of the UNDP alleviated an unequal relationship between a donor and a recipient. Such unbalanced relationships or feelings between donors and recipients are often observed in implementation of aid projects. But being a recognized international organization, the UNDP's assessments are considered as an independent third-party's opinion, which contributes not only to maintaining a well-balanced relationship among stakeholders but also to improving effectiveness of monitoring.

Effectiveness of the JICA Reconstruction Projects

Any development project takes time, but it sometimes takes a decade for completion, owing to many factors, including a recipient country's dysfunctional bureaucracy, and further delay will be expected in a weak state. Such delay has a nonnegligible consequence on the development of a recipient country. For instance, one of JICA's reconstruction projects in Iraq is to construct pipelines and facilities for crude-oil export. Although Iraq is well known for rich proven oil reserves, its exports are still limited because of the lack of export facilities. The project aims to establish facilities to export nearly 2 million barrels a day, which accounts for almost 80 percent of Iraq's current oil exports. This means that if the construction of the oil export facilities were delayed one day, the expected cost would be $160 million at $80 a barrel, amounting to $4.8 billion for one month's delay. As oil constitutes a major portion of the Iraqi economy, this eventually affects the Iraqi people's livelihoods. Although we agree that efficiency may not be straightforwardly connected to the overall success of an aid project, we believe that it can be one of the important indicators of project success.

Since JICA started its projects in Iraq, the efficiency of project management by Iraqi officials who are in charge of loan execution has improved. For example, during the course of implementation, the average lapse of JICA's review of documents on each procurement process has become shorter, as shown in table 3-1, suggesting that the quality of the documents prepared by the Iraqi government has improved

TABLE 3-1. Average Lapse Taken by JICA in Reviewing Procurement Documents

	2008–09	2010	2011
Prequalification documents average lapse	41	14	n/a
Prequalification result average lapse	115	34	14
Bidding documents average lapse	53	48	26
Bidding result average lapse	32	29	42

Source: Data from JICA.

and the completion of aid projects will occur faster.[5] We assume that JICA's work for the review process is constant, so a decrease in the lapse should indicate an improvement of Iraqi officials' submissions.

Furthermore, to present counterfactual analyses, we compare work efficiencies of JICA projects across different countries. Comparing different projects by the same agency allows us to reduce omitted variable bias caused by differences in donors. Figure 3-3 shows scatter plots tracking the efficiency of project management by the quality of government. As a proxy for efficiency, the current analysis employs variables measuring how long a project takes to complete its assignment (same as in table 3-1). Although there is some variation, given that a possible selection bias leads to an underestimation for the fitted lines, we can see that the Iraq government manages JICA projects more effectively than average (except the top-right panel), suggesting that the efficiency improvement in Iraq shown in table 3-1 is partially supported.

Next, to corroborate the analysis, we compare work efficiencies of the JICA project in Iraq with the ones of the International Development Association's projects in Iraq. Though there are differences in donors and in the nature of their projects, this can complement the analysis with the cross-country comparison among JICA projects. Since the World Bank's procedure to review procurement documents may differ from JICA's procedure, the current analysis employs the ratio between

5. In each step of procurement, JICA requires project entities to submit procurement documents and reviews the documents against JICA's procurement guidelines, which indicates basic guidance in the international bid procedure. "Prequalification documents average lapse" and "bidding documents average lapse" mean days taken by JICA for review of prequalification documents and bid documents, respectively. In the case of prequalification and bidding results, JICA reviews the evaluation process and result described in the evaluation documents.

FIGURE 3-3. Recipient's Governance Index and JICA Project Effectiveness

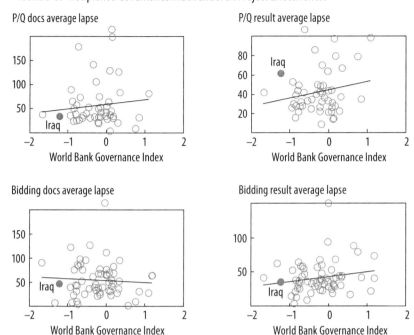

Source: Governance indexes derive from the World Bank; Japan International Cooperation Agency (JICA) project effectiveness data are from JICA.

commitment and disbursement as a proxy of project efficiency, expecting that if Iraqi officials improve their quality of work, they are more likely to make more disbursements. Figure 3-4 compares the indicators for JICA and World Bank projects. According to the figure, efficiency rates improve over time for both. However, the efficiency rate for the JICA projects exceeds the one for the World Bank over time, while the efficiency rate for the World Bank's projects are better than JICA's at the beginning.[6]

Although the analysis is only bivariate, the evidence indicates that the JICA projects in Iraq can be considered an example of success. However, the finding is less important than specifying the reasons for efficiency, as it does not allow us to extract an underlying mechanism and replicate it in other settings. Thus the following sections attempt to

6. We attempt to match time horizons (*x*-axis in figure 3-4), as project periods of the JICA and the World Bank are not exactly same.

FIGURE 3-4. Project Efficiencies, JICA and the World Bank

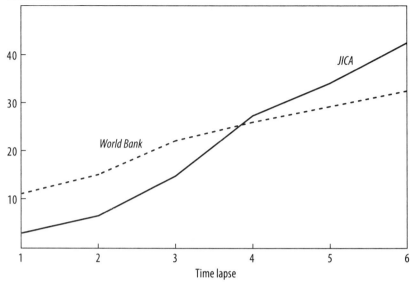

Source: Data from the World Bank and JICA.

identify how JICA's projects contribute to the increased efficiency of the Iraqi government's work by introducing some generalizable hypotheses.

Effective Aid Implementation in a Weak State

It has been demonstrated that the JICA projects in Iraq are effective compared with other projects in similar settings. Yet it is still unclear why this is the case. To learn from best practices and replicate them in other projects, we need to identify a causal relationship that explains why the JICA projects in Iraq increase the effectiveness of PMT officials. To identify the causal relationship, this section proposes hypotheses that connect the interventions to the results.

Because JICA introduced its three monitoring mechanisms at the same time, it is difficult to disentangle them and determine which one led to the positive result. To identify the mechanisms' effects, we thus derive several hypotheses by drawing on existing studies. By extracting distinct hypotheses, we attempt to differentiate the mechanisms that led to the positive results in the JICA Iraq projects from those that did not. From the three mechanisms introduced by JICA—which we identify as the information mechanism, the social recognition mechanism, and the mediation mechanism—we derive six testable hypotheses that allow us to explain the positive impact of the JICA interventions on the efficiency of Iraqi officials' work. We now explain each mechanism.

Information Mechanism

To overcome a lack of knowledge and conduct capacity building, JICA increased interactions with Iraqi officials. Although interactions can be defined in many ways, we focus on two aspects of interactions: the quality and the quantity. While we expect the increase in interactions and information provision to generally lead to an increase in work efficiency of Iraqi officials, the following question remains: Of quality or quantity, which is more important in this monitoring process?

The debate of quality versus quantity in education studies has a long history (for example, Ng 2008). Theoretically speaking, a significant body of education literature argues that the quality, not just quantity, of education matters to improve economic performance (for example, Hanushek and Woessmann 2007). Therefore we expect both increased quality and quantity of monitoring to increase Iraqi officials' work effectiveness.

Although it has been reported that an increase in the quantity of work is sometimes detrimental to work efficiency (for example, Barling, Rogers, and Kelloway 2001), the current analysis defines *quantity* as the amount of communications rather than the amount of work JICA and Iraqi officials complete. We thus expect that an increase in communication levels between JICA and Iraqi officials can reduce misunderstanding between them, while Iraqi officials can accumulate knowledge through frequent consultation with JICA. Similarly, JICA improved the content of monitoring and gave more detailed feedback to Iraqi officials to help them learn how to manage their projects. From this, if our expectations are true, we should observe a positive impact in both the quality and the quantity of interactions:[7]

---

7. Since the high quantity of JICA interventions can be correlated with the high quality of JICA interventions, we may not be able to disentangle the two hypotheses. Yet we can exploit variation in our data on JICA interventions: project entities that receive higher quality of JICA interventions are not the same entities that receive higher quantity of JICA interventions.

Hypothesis 1: *An increase in monitoring quantity leads to higher efficiency in project management.*

Hypothesis 2: *An increase in monitoring quality leads to higher efficiency in project management.*

Social Recognition Mechanism

A large body of the public administration literature indicates that good managers make positive change happen in their organizations (Fernandez and Rainey 2006). Thus the introduction of the multilayer monitoring system involving influential Iraqi high-level authorities such as the Prime Minister's Advisory Commission should result in positive changes. The existence of influential high-level authorities, however, tells us little about how they facilitate Iraqi officials' becoming more efficient in terms of project management.

The UNDP and JICA jointly publish a project-entity ranking based on their performance every year. Based on the ranking, the high-level authorities in Iraq praises project entities that performed well, while they give critical comments to project entities that did not. In development economics, some scholars find that provision of performance-linked financial incentives can encourage greater effort and improve performance in public service provision (Duflo, Dupas, and Kremer 2011). On the other hand, there is also evidence suggesting that relying on nonpecuniary incentives that come from social recognition, appreciation, or sanction can be more effective in motivating public workers (Alcazar and others 2006).

Accordingly, in the case of JICA's intervention, we can see the impact of social recognition in two different ways. First, project entities that received good evaluations were more motivated to work efficiently, since they wanted to keep their good record and be recognized as good project entities by the high-level authority (which also may lead to an increase in their budget or individual promotion in the long term). By contrast, project entities that received bad evaluations also had an incentive to work more efficiently since they wanted to avoid social and financial punishment in the short and long term (poorly performing PMTs might face a budget cut and also risk being recognized as inefficient by government officials). From this, we can summarize the social recognition mechanism and draw the following two competing hypotheses:

Hypothesis 3: *A better evaluation leads to higher efficiency in project management.*

Hypothesis 4: *A worse evaluation leads to higher efficiency in project management.*

Mediation Mechanism

The third mechanism involves the presence of the UNDP. Initially, JICA asked the UNDP to assist in its work with Iraqi officials, owing to security risks in the country. According to interviews we conducted in June 2012, the presence of the UNDP seems to have had two positive impacts on the work efficiency of project entities. First, we observed that since UNDP officials could move more easily across the country, the introduction of UNDP-facilitated project management proved to increase efficiency—it is only natural that face-to-face interactions would result in more efficient project management. Second, since Iraqi officials consider the UNDP to be a neutral third party, the Iraqi officials seemed to have franker conversations with UNDP officials, leading to early detection of problems and more efficient project management.

Brown and Ayres (1994) argue that a neutral third party can mitigate inefficiency caused by miscommunication between two parties if the third party can directly observe each party's behavior and disclose it to both groups. Indeed, as a neutral party, the UNDP is well placed to have access to both parties' information and to use it to solve miscommunication. However, the involvement of the UNDP can be a double-edged sword since Iraqi officials may end up relying on the UNDP more than on JICA, leading to an adverse coordination problem among the three organizations, or the amount of work may increase, as Iraqi officials have to work for both the UNDP and JICA. From this, we can derive two competing hypotheses in terms of the presence of the UNDP:

Hypothesis 5: *The presence of a third party leads to higher efficiency in project management.*

Hypothesis 6: *The presence of a third party leads to lower efficiency in project management.*

Research Design

The most challenging task for evaluating these hypotheses is that we do not have appropriate counterfactuals to estimate the impact of JICA's intervention on the effectiveness of the Iraqi government. We thus believe that potential endogeneity issues arise from omitted variables, and some variables certainly lead to bias in our estimates. For instance, we suspect motivation is an endogenous variable: more-motivated project entities should result in both better evaluation and higher efficiency, leading to a biased estimator.

With this caveat in mind, we first compare a treatment group and a control group for each hypothesis. More specifically, for each hypothesis, we create a quasi-treatment group with the best three PMTs and a quasi-control group with the worst three PMTs. For instance, to assess the information-mechanism hypotheses, we pick three PMTs that have received most interactions and three other PMTs that have received fewest interactions and compare the effectiveness of their work.

Next, although the data limitation does not allow us to assess all the hypotheses, we employ a regression analysis to corroborate the exercise. The regression analysis employs panel data to minimize the potential bias owing to omitted characteristics, and we do include a number of important control variables such as motivation to help us isolate the main mechanism discussed in the chapter. The unit of panel-data analysis is project-year with an observational period between 2010 and 2012.

Data

We employ the data that JICA and the UNDP collected. Our main dependent variable—and the way we operationalize effectiveness—is submission delay. The variable measures how long, on average, each PMT takes to finish its requirement in a given year. More specifically, each PMT is supposed to submit a report every month, and we note the difference between the expected submission date and the actual submission date. We employ an annual average time lapse between expected submission dates and actual dates each year.

To test the first two hypotheses (quantity versus quality in the information mechanism), we first employ the frequency variable, coding how often JICA and UNDP officials have contact with each PMT. To collect the data, we conducted a survey and asked each official, "On average, how often do you work with the PMT that you are in charge of in a month's time?" The response is given on a five-point scale, a higher value indicating more frequent communication. Next, to measure the quality of interactions, we employ the amount of feedback JICA gives Iraqi officials as a proxy (the feedback variable). More specifically, we count how many items JICA corrected on reports submitted by Iraqi officials. We expect that the more feedback a PMT receives, the more efficient it becomes over time.

Turning to the second set of hypotheses (positive versus negative feedback in the social recognition mechanism), we employ the "ranking" variable, flagging which PMT receives positive or negative recognition by the high-level authority. We expect that either higher or lower ranked PMTs achieve more efficient work performance.

Finally, to test the third set of hypotheses (UNDP versus not-UNDP in the mediation mechanism), we use a dummy variable that codes 1 if UNDP is involved in a PMT's projector, 0 if they are not. Here, we expect that the presence of UNDP leads to more or less efficient work performance.

To minimize the danger that our results could suffer from omitted variable bias, the regression analysis includes a set of control variables plausibly associated with both the dependent and independent variables: motivation, measuring whether a PMT is more motivated for the work; and project scale, measuring variation in project scale among PMTs. Though it is difficult to measure motivations, we use how well each PMT is organized as a proxy for whether a PMT is committed to the project, what we call organizational motivation. We expect that if a PMT is well designed in the first place, it means that the overseeing ministry for the PMT is more motivated for the project and the PMT thus has to be motivated as well. We also use a time dummy variable to control for temporal dependence. Finally, we use a one-year lag of our dependent variable. This way, we believe we can estimate the effects of independent variables on subsequent efficiency increases in the Iraqi government. The following equation summarizes our basic specification:

$$\Delta Submission\ delay_{it} = \alpha + \beta_1 Feedback_{it-1} + \beta_2 Ranking_{it-1}$$
$$+ \beta_3 Motivation_{it-1} + \beta_4 Project\ scale_{it-1} + \beta_5 Fixed\ effects_{it-1} + \varepsilon_i$$

Table 3-2 shows the summary statistics of variables used for the analyses.

TABLE 3-2. Summary Statistics

Variable	Observations	Mean	Standard deviation	Minimum	Maximum
Submission delay	24	−0.340	5.59	−19.00	9.45
Frequency	15	3.217	0.89	1.50	4.75
Feedback	36	3.205	1.99	0.67	7.33
Ranking	24	6.500	3.53	1.00	12.00
Motivation	27	4.000	2.16	0.00	6.00
ln (planned disbursement)	22	21.309	1.29	19.13	23.66

Results

First, we report our counterfactual analyses by using the data with a format of project-month.[8] Figure 3-5 compares PMTs that have more frequent contacts with JICA and the UNDP with the counterparts that have less frequent interactions. The figure shows that there is no significant difference between the high-contact group and the low-contact group in terms of submission rate, indicating that the impact of frequent contact is not substantial.

Turning to the quality of information, figure 3-6 compares PMTs that have more feedback with those that have less feedback from JICA and the UNDP. We can see that those that have received less feedback are generally more likely to submit required documents on time than those who have received more feedback, suggesting that giving feedback is indeed detrimental to work effectiveness of Iraqi officials.

Figure 3-7 compares PMTs that received the best evaluation in 2011 with those that received the worst evaluation in 2011. The figure demonstrates that the project entities that received a good evaluation are generally more likely to sustain a high level of work effectiveness except in the month of July.

Finally, although the monthly data are not available, we attempt to evaluate the mediation hypotheses by comparing PMTs that work with the UNDP with those that do not. Specifically, we use average number of days taken by JICA to review bidding documents submitted by each

8. We removed two projects from the analyses as outliers because they skew the results.

FIGURE 3-5. Frequency of Interaction with Donor, 2012

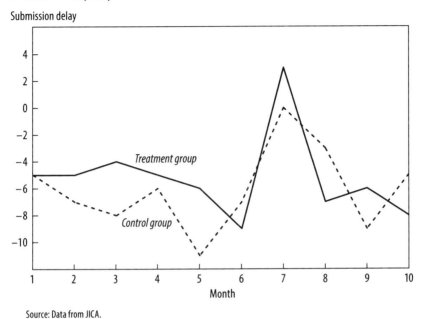

Source: Data from JICA.

FIGURE 3-6. Effect of Feedback on Timely Submission of Documents, 2012

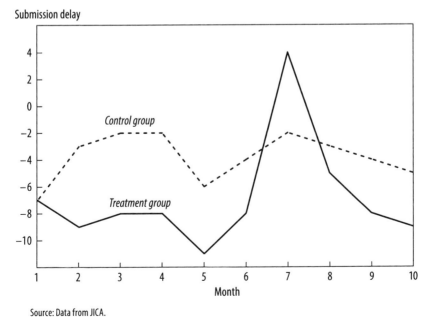

Source: Data from JICA.

FIGURE 3-7. Effect of Social Recognition on Efficiency, 2012

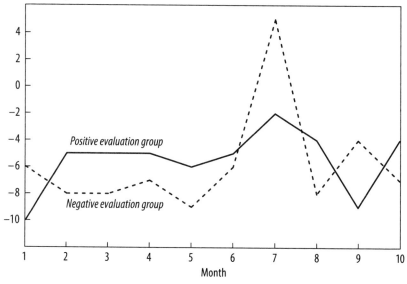

Source: Data from JICA.

PMT. According to the data, whereas the PMTs that worked with the UNDP improved their work effectiveness by about fifteen days, the PMTs working without the UNDP slowed down the process by thirty-four days.[9]

In sum, we have so far found that the quality of interaction may be more important than the quantity of communications, and positive evaluation is more effective than negative evaluation. Yet since it is a bivariate analysis and focuses on a trend only in 2012, we suspect that the analysis cannot detect a longer-term impact of the JICA interventions on the effectiveness of Iraqi officials' work. For example, it may be that those who receive less feedback work better now because they might have received more feedback intensively over the previous years. Similarly, it may be that a positive evaluation is more effective because those who received a positive evaluation in 2011 might have received a

9. We used the following review processes for the analysis: bidding document review and bidding evaluation review.

TABLE 3-3. Regression Analysis[a]

Variables	Submission delay	
	(1)	(2)
Frequency	2.623	
	(3.064)	
Feedback	1.950	2.352***
	(3.515)	(0.741)
Ranking	−0.728	−0.087
	(0.988)	(0.270)
Motivation	−0.007	0.295
	(1.356)	(0.269)
ln (planned disbursement)	0.780	0.517***
	(2.729)	(0.116)
Constant	−22.239	1.507
	(72.395)	(11.198)
Observations	8	17
R-squared	0.577	0.791
Controls	Y	Y
Time-series	N	Y

a. Robust standard errors in parentheses
***$p < 0.01$, **$p < 0.05$, *$p < 0.1$

negative evaluation in previous years and therefore might have worked to gain their reputation.

To address this concern, we next conduct a time-series analysis. Although the data cover only a three-year period, we anticipate detecting a more general impact of the JICA projects on the work effectiveness of Iraqi officials. The empirical results in table 3-3 display the estimated coefficient of the regression analyses. Owing to lack of available variables, we could employ the feedback and ranking variables among the explanatory variables of interest but not the frequency and UNDP variables. As for our dependent variable, we used the same variable of submission delay as in the previous analysis. Furthermore, the analysis suffers from a small sample size ($N = 17$). As for the model specifications, model 1 uses a cross-sectional analysis with control variables such as motivation to see whether we can replicate the previous bivariate analysis. Model 2 employs a time-series analysis with the same control variables as model 1.[10]

Model 1 shows that, controlling for other variables, the feedback variable has a positive sign instead of a negative sign, as found by the previous bivariate analysis. This is confirmed by a time-series analysis in model 2. Model 2 shows that, all else equal, the feedback variable is statistically significant and has a positive impact on submission. This is consistent with hypothesis 2, suggesting that those who receive more feedback are in general more likely to increase their work effectiveness. If we combine these findings with those reported in figure 3-6, we can infer that PMTs that have received more feedback will improve their work effectiveness and become less dependent on JICA or the UNDP over time.

As for the ranking variable, model 1 and model 2 both report a negative sign, which is consistent with hypothesis 4, but the significance level is not sufficient to reject the null hypothesis in the time-series analysis. Although we need to wait to make a final judgment until we collect more data, the analysis suggests that those who receive a negative evaluation in the previous year may be more likely to improve their work effectiveness.

Conclusion

Although we still need to do a follow-up analysis with more data, we believe that the findings of this research suggest an important lesson for postconflict or fragile states on effective implementation of large-scale aid and governance projects. Countries in transition often go through periods of upheaval and weak governance, and Iraq is a prime example. Donors may hesitate to implement large-scale projects in postconflict or postrevolution situations because of security concerns and underdeveloped bureaucratic capacity of recipient states. Nonetheless, by using the successful case of JICA projects in Iraq, this chapter shows that large-scale projects can work in a postconflict society and increase recipient officials' capacity to implement aid effectively. This suggests

10. The analyses are clustered by PMTs, and the time-series analysis uses a random-effect model.

that donors should not withdraw their support in difficult postconflict situations. Given that this is the time when donor engagement is most crucial, the JICA example offers three ways to manage aid in such circumstances.

In this chapter, we propose three baseline mechanisms—an information mechanism, a social recognition mechanism, and a mediation mechanism—to explain the positive impact on project effectiveness in a postconflict society. Drawing on previous studies, we have derived six testable hypotheses from the three mechanisms.

Three findings emerge from empirical tests of these six hypotheses. First, project entities that received more feedback from JICA and the UNDP tended to improve their work effectiveness over time, while the number of interactions or communications may not be as important an indicator as the quality of interactions. This suggests that the quality of donor intervention leads to more positive results than the quantity of intervention. Second, the more negative evaluations a project entity has received in the past year, the more likely is its work effectiveness to increase. These results imply that the social recognition mechanism works better for those who receive negative evaluations than for those who receive positive evaluations. In other words, PMTs work more effectively when they receive "bad" social recognition. Third, because we could not conduct a panel-data analysis for the mediation mechanism, the empirical result for the UNDP involvement should be interpreted as largely descriptive. Yet since we cannot reasonably find alternative explanations for the positive results of the PMTs with the UNDP, and those who work with the UNDP should have had more difficulty in conducting their projects in the first place, we believe that the presence of the UNDP increased work effectiveness and the conclusion will not change even with multivariate analysis.

In sum, our research suggests that donors may be able to increase the work effectiveness to a level able to support large-scale projects even in a postconflict country if they are committed to interacting with local officials and giving detailed comments on how they can facilitate their projects on their own; if a local high-level authority monitors local officials' work and creates a culture where poorly performing officials are not allowed to continue work; if a third-party international organization facilitates communication between the donor and the recipient; or under a combination of the three.

References

Alcazar, Lorena, and others. 2006. "Why Are Teachers Absent? Probing Service Delivery in Peruvian Primary Schools." *International Journal of Educational Research* 45, no. 3: 117–36.

Barling, Julian, A. Gail Rogers, and E. Kevin Kelloway. 2001. "Behind Closed Doors: In-Home Workers' Experience of Sexual Harassment and Workplace Violence." *Journal of Occupational Health Psychology* 6, no. 3: 255–69.

Brown, Jennifer Gerarda, and Ian Ayres. 1994. "Economic Rationales for Mediation." *Virginia Law Review* 80, no. 2: 323–402.

Burnside, Craig, and David Dollar. 2000. "Aid, Policies, and Growth." *American Economic Review* 90, no. 4: 847–68.

Clist, Paul, and Oliver Morrissey. 2011. "Aid and Tax Revenue: Signs of a Positive Effect since the 1980s." *Journal of International Development* 23, no. 2: 165–80.

Collier, Paul, and David Dollar. 2002. "Aid Allocation and Poverty Reduction." *European Economic Review* 46, no. 8: 1475–500.

Collier, Paul, and Anke Hoeffler. 2004. "Aid, Policy, and Growth in Post-Conflict Societies." *European Economic Review* 48, no. 5: 1125–45.

Dalgaard, Carl-Johan, Henrik Hansen, and Finn Tarp. 2004. "On the Empirics of Foreign Aid and Growth." *Economic Journal* 114, no. 496: 191–216.

Duflo, Esther, Pascaline Dupas, and Michael Kremer. 2011. "Peer Effects, Pupil-Teacher Ratios, and Teacher Incentives: Evidence from a Randomized Evaluation in Kenya." *American Economic Review* 101, no. 5: 1739–74.

Easterly, William, Ross Levine, and David Roodman. 2004. "Aid, Policies, and Growth: Comment." *American Economic Review* 94, no. 3: 774–79.

Epstein, Gil S., and Ira N. Gang. 2009. "Good Governance and Good Aid Allocation." *Journal of Development Economics* 89, no. 1: 12–18.

Fernandez, Sergio, and Hal G. Rainey. 2006. "Managing Successful Organizational Change in the Public Sector." *Public Administration Review* 66, no. 2: 1–25.

Flores, Thomas E., and Irfan Nooruddin. 2009. "Financing the Peace: Evaluating World Bank Post-Conflict Assistance Programs." *Review of International Organizations* 4, no. 1: 1–27.

Hanushek, Eric A., and Ludger Woessmann. 2007. "The Role of Education Quality for Economic Growth." Policy Research Working Paper 4122. Washington: World Bank.

Kang, Soenjou, and James Meernik. 2005. "Civil War Destruction and the Prospects for Economic Growth." *Journal of Politics* 67, no. 1: 88–109.

Kosack, Stephen. 2003. "Effective Aid: How Democracy Allows Development Aid to Improve the Quality of Life." *World Development* 31, no. 1: 1–22.

Marshall, Monty G., Keith Jaggers, and Ted Robert Gurr. 2011. *Polity IV Project: Dataset Users' Manual.* Vienna, Va.: Center for Systemic Peace.

Ng, Pak Tee. 2008. "Educational Reform in Singapore: From Quantity to Quality." *Educational Research for Policy and Practice* 7, no. 1: 5–15.

Rondinelli, Dennis A., and John D. Montgomery. 2005. "Regime Change and Nation Building: Can Donors Restore Governance in Post-Conflict States?" *Public Administration and Development* 25, no. 1: 15–23.

Santiso, Carlos. 2001. "Good Governance and Aid Effectiveness: The World Bank and Conditionality." *Georgetown Public Policy Review* 7, no. 1: 1–22.

Tirole, Jean. 1996. "A Theory of Collective Reputations (with Applications to the Persistence of Corruption and to Firm Quality)." *Review of Economic Studies* 63, no. 1: 1–22.

Walter, Barbara. 2004. "Does Conflict Beget Conflict? Explaining Recurrent Civil War." *Journal of Peace Research* 41, no. 3: 371–88.

World Bank. 2011. *Worldwide Governance Indicators*. Washington: World Bank.

4

How to Fill the Implementation Gap for Inclusive Growth: Case Studies Covering Urban Transportation Sector Development in Egypt

HIDEKI MATSUNAGA and MAYADA MAGDY

Since January 2011 Egypt has been going through a turbulent period, two regimes having been toppled by mass protests. Social injustice, a widening gap between rich and poor, and widespread corruption are considered to be the major reasons that protesters took to the streets. Poor infrastructure and deteriorating public services, characterized by frequent power cuts, chronic traffic in Cairo, and piles of garbage on the street, are said to have exacerbated public discontent with the governments of Presidents Mubarak and Morsi. Decades-long low-level investment has resulted in underdevelopment of infrastructure and public services compared with many other emerging economies. In both the business community and the public sector, a great deal of energy and resources are poured into formulating strategy, while too little effort is diverted to the implementation of that strategy. This lack of strategy implementation has led to low rates of public investment, poor infrastructure, and deteriorating public services.

This does not mean that the Egyptian government has not made any effort to improve the situation. On the contrary, to solve these problems, many strategies and plans have been formulated, and numerous projects, programs, and policy reforms have been proposed. According to research conducted by the Japan International Cooperation Agency (JICA), there were at least forty-one existing plans and strategies in various forms as of 2012.[1] In many cases there are too many overlapping strategies, and very few have been implemented to any significant degree.

The presidential election in May 2014 saw Abdel-Fattah el-Sissi, a former military leader, elected by an overwhelming majority vote. Within months of his inauguration, the new administration took a number of major reforms such as the reduction of fuel subsidies and the implementation of the Suez Canal–widening project. For some, expectations are rising that the new leadership has a strong commitment to bringing real change to the country. However, the challenges for the leaders will be how to make the machinery of government work to implement changes and strategies. Public sector management and institutional reform is indispensable for the success of the new government, and much will hinge on reforming implementation.

Bridging the Gap between What to Do and How to Do

The challenge of bridging the gap between strategy and implementation is not unique to Egypt, and while there has been a good deal of research on policy planning, there has been much less on implementation. Still, the research contained in this chapter indicates that Egypt is one of the typical countries suffering from a low implementation rate of plans, owing to the huge implementation gap that exists in the system of the country. The implementation gap is the difference between goals and outputs on paper and how they are carried out in practice. In other words, the implementation gap covers the discrepancies between prescriptions and what happens on the ground.

This chapter identifies key reform areas that would be necessary to bridge the implementation gap in Egypt, based on case studies exploring the barriers to implementation of plans and strategies for urban transport development. Some public sector reform agendas seem to be common among countries, yet no one size fits all, and each country's experience should be studied to understand the local conditions in order to provide relevant recommendations.

---

1. See Sakamoto (2013).

Public Investment Trends in Egypt

If you were to visit today one of the capital cities among emerging economies after a twenty-year absence, you would be astonished by the drastic change that had taken place. There are more high-rise buildings, more highways, and new public transportation systems. In Cairo, however, the city landscape has changed little in the past two decades, and you might be left with a very different impression. Yes, there are more shopping malls and real estate development in the outskirts of the city, but compared with many emerging economies, such changes are hardly drastic. Egypt has experienced declining levels of public investment over the past several decades.

Level of Public Investment in Egypt

There are extensive studies on the impact of public investment on growth. One study shows that public investment has positive effects on growth and that no country has sustained rapid growth without also keeping up substantial rates of public investment—in infrastructure, education, and health. Far from crowding out investment, this spending crowds it in.[2] The International Monetary Fund's 2014 *World Economic Outlook* notes that increased investment in public infrastructure raises output in both the short and long term.[3]

Loayza and Odawara conducted detailed analysis on infrastructure development.[4] They conclude that in the past fifteen years, infrastructure in Egypt has suffered a substantial decline, which may be at odds with the country's goal of raising economic growth. This decline in public investment, however, has not been offset by a rise in private investment.

Figure 4-1 clearly demonstrates a declining trend in investment in Egypt over the past thirty years. Figure 4-2 illustrates this trend for Egypt and for India, Indonesia, and Thailand, countries with similar socioeconomic conditions. As figure 4-2 shows, Egypt witnessed a comparable investment level until the early 1990s, after which the level dropped below that of these other countries.

2. See Commission on Growth and Development (2008).
3. International Monetary Fund (2014b).
4. Loayza and Odawara (2010).

FIGURE 4-1. Egypt's Investment and Savings, 1980–2013

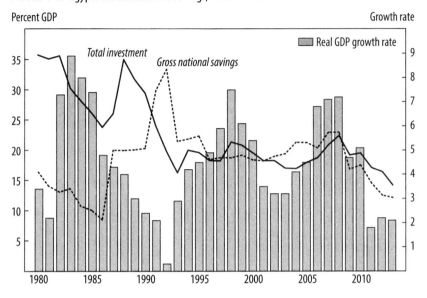

Source: International Monetary Fund, *World Economic Outlook* database, April 2014.

FIGURE 4-2. Investment Share of GDP, Egypt, India, Indonesia, Thailand, 1980–2012

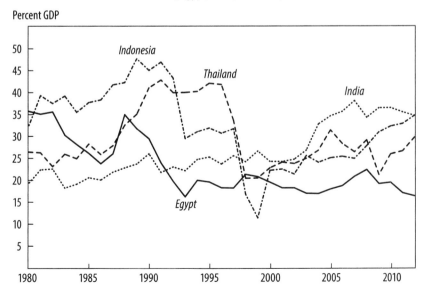

Source: International Monetary Fund, *World Economic Outlook* database, April 2014.

FIGURE 4-3. Public Investment Trend, Egypt, 1982–2012[a]

Percent GDP

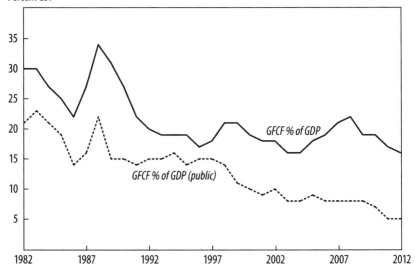

Source: World Development Indicators, World Bank.
a. We chose to use the data of gross fixed capital formation from the World Development Indicators for two reasons: they cover a longer period of time to enable comparison; and they are more indicative than other data sources since they account for the investments by public sector companies in Egypt, which occupy a significant share of public investment.

Public investment in Egypt has been experiencing a declining share of GDP over the past twenty years, shrinking from more than 20 percent in 1988 to less than half of that figure in 2008 (figure 4-3). This is mainly attributable to a large fiscal deficit and high social spending, which came at the expense of a shrinking investment budget. In addition, some issues of public investment management and implementation capacity have undermined the efficiency and effectiveness of public spending, as subsequent sections of this chapter show.

Over the past twenty years, the private investment share of GDP either declined or remained the same. Between 1988 and 2008, it maintained a similar share of GDP (around 12 percent) and thus did not compensate for the decline in public investment.

Over the past thirty years, Egypt has been experiencing a quite volatile trend of real GDP growth, as shown in figure 4-1. There were high growth rates around the late 1990s and accelerated growth, at an average of around 7 percent, from 2006 to 2008. But Egypt has not seen a sustained trend of high growth. The average growth rate during the past thirty years was around 4. 5 percent, 1 to 2 percent less than other emerging economies such as Thailand, Indonesia, and India and much lower than the country's potential.

Public Perceptions

Rapid GDP growth during 2006–10 made GDP per capita grow at rapid rates. However, as figure 2-1 in chapter 2 indicates, it was not accompanied by an increase in positive perceptions among people regarding the impact of growth on their well-being. Opinion polls showed that the share of those describing themselves as thriving (defined as a combination of their current and future expectations of economic well-being) fell from 25 percent in 2007 to 12 percent in 2010, despite steady growth in per capita GDP.[5] In addition, the discrepancy between the rich and the poor has widened: only the richest Egyptians rated their lives better in 2010 than in 2009.

One reason why public sentiment may have declined was the collapse in satisfaction with public services.[6] One opinion poll showed that satisfaction with the public transportation system in Egypt fell by 30 percent between 2009 and 2010, and public perceptions of other public services also worsened. This poll needs to be interpreted with caution since public services do not typically deteriorate in such a short period of time, and the worsening perception must have been exacerbated by other factors. But it is worth noting that the public's satisfaction was in rapid decline until right before the revolution. The new government needs to pay due attention to the people's perceptions of their well-being.

International Experience of Implementing Public Investment Programs

While there are many studies that explain the positive impact of public investment on growth, some counterarguments cast doubt on the efficiency of public investment. Of course, not all spending on public investment leads to positive results, and weakness in public investment

5. See Kharas and others (2012).
6. See Kharas and others (2012).

management has resulted in inadequate returns to both public and private investment in many cases. The International Monetary Fund has noted that a substantial scaling up of public investment in a weak institutional environment runs the risk of potentially undermining its growth benefit as well as its prospects for fiscal and debt sustainability.[7]

Managing public investment matters a great deal. The World Bank has conducted ample research in this area, assessing how public investment management (PIM) works in different countries, and has contributed to expanding knowledge on how to boost implementation and how to efficiently and effectively manage public investment to realize the intended development outcomes. One study by Lursen and Myers and another by Petrie conducted gap analyses of PIM in several countries to identify potential areas for reform.[8] Both studies found gaps in PIM along the implementation cycle in many countries, starting with strategic planning and budgetary inconsistencies, weak linkages with sector policies and poor appraisal processes in the planning phase, procurement problems, and weak monitoring and reporting. They provide a good reference for best practices for improving PIM.

To develop some quantitative method of assessing PIM, Dabla-Norris and others developed the public investment management index.[9]

The index provides a useful indicator of the degree of efficiency in the implementation of public investments along the implementation cycle, starting with strategic planning and appraisal, followed by project selection and budgeting, then project implementation, and finally evaluation and audit. The authors studied the process of PIM in seventy-one low- and middle-income countries, including Egypt.[10] In the budgeting and implementation stages, in particular, they evaluated aspects that can cause implementation gaps such as poor integration between project selection and budgeting, interrupted budget execution and disbursement, inefficient procurement processes, and weak monitoring and internal control.

In general, Dabla-Norris and others found that low-income countries have weaker public investment management than middle-income

7. Dabla-Norris and others (2011).
8. Lursen and Myers (2009) and Petrie (2010).
9. Dabla-Norris and others (2011).
10. Dabla-Norris and others (2011).

countries, albeit with some exceptions. In Egypt's case, on a scale from 0 to 4, where 4 represents better public investment management, it achieved only 1.43, below the average score of 1.68 and lower than the scores of other countries with similar socioeconomic conditions such as Indonesia, the Philippines, and Thailand (1.47, 1.85, and 2.87 respectively). Detailed sub-index scores reveal that the weakest processes in Egypt's public investment management are those pertaining to budgeting and implementation, which scored only 1.2, highlighting the need for improvement in these areas.

As denoted by the public investment management index, Egypt is very weak in budgeting and implementation. Weak public investment is usually a result of weak governance. According to the World Bank's World Governance Indicators, which capture, among other aspects, the capacity of government institutions to effectively formulate and implement policies, Egypt scored 25.4 in the government effectiveness index (on a scale from 0 to 100) in 2012, which compares unfavorably with countries in the region and with those of a similar income group (scoring around 50 points). Even if we take 2010 as the year of comparison, thus excluding the period of political and economic instability in Egypt, the country still scores lower. Ineffective governance and public investment management in general undermine growth and are the main causes of the implementation gap.

Analytical Framework for the Implementation Cycle and Implementation Gap

The real challenge for governments and policymakers is not to formulate a convincing strategy but to effectively implement their plans, whether they involve specific project recommendations or policy reforms. Projects require tangible resources such as financial, physical, and human resources for successful implementation, while policy reforms rely on less tangible resources such as leadership and constituency building. Since developing countries are often thought to suffer from shortages in financial and human resources, policy reforms are considered easier to effect than project implementation. But as later chapters in this volume show, policy reform is often more difficult than project implementation.

So what are the common impediments to implementation? How can strategies move from good intentions to real change on the ground?

The Implementation Cycle

There is no definitive theory of implementation, nor any single commonly accepted framework; yet many studies divide the process of implementation into several phases, albeit in many cases using different terms to describe the implementation cycle.

The plan-do-see cycle and the plan-do-check-action cycle are the simplest methods used to describe an implementation cycle. The plan-do-see cycle divides the process into three major phases, each phase consisting of several actions: planning (direction setting, strategy formulation, and planning), doing (resource mobilization, organizational setting, and action); and seeing (monitoring and evaluation), with the aim of continuously improving the process (see figure 4-4).

The Asia Pacific Community of Practice on Managing for Development Results identifies five components in the public sector implementation cycle: planning, budgeting, implementation, monitoring, and evaluation. Similarly, the Center for Effective Services defines four phases in the process: exploring and preparing, planning and resourcing, implementation and operationalization, and business as usual—the point at which the policy becomes fully integrated into the system.[11]

As these examples show, whatever the description of the implementation cycle, the implementation phase lies in the middle of process, preceded by the planning phase and followed by monitoring and evaluation (in practice, the lines of separation between these phases are not necessarily defined clearly). The cycle must remain dynamic, given that any unforeseen events may require adjustments to earlier phases or those undertaken in parallel. For example, the planning phase may be revisited as a result of experimentation in the implementation phase, while continuous monitoring and evaluation should identify potential improvements to the planning and implementation phases.[12]

11. Asia Pacific COP-MFDR (2011); Center for Effective Services (2012).
12. See Meyers and others (2012).

FIGURE 4-4. The Plan-Do-See Cycle

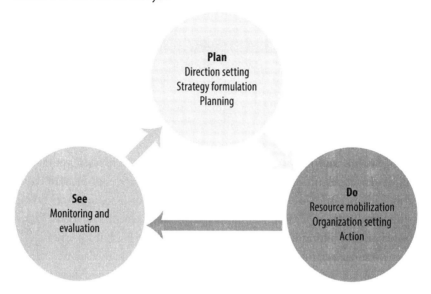

Analysis Based on the Implementation Cycle and Implementation Gap

In this chapter, we use the implementation cycle described in figure 4-5 as our analytical framework.[13] Such a framework helps to identify the required tasks to implement projects and policy reforms and is also useful to assess systemic weaknesses in the implementation cycle.

It is possible to identify several factors that hinder policy implementation and lead to implementation gaps. Implementation gaps exist within each phase of the implementation cycle, as well as between phases. Brynard lists five common variables that affect the implementation process (the "five Cs"): the policy content itself, in the sense of its expected impact on people and how it would influence their reaction; context, particularly the institutional context and state of relations within the organization and among all organizations involved; commitment to implementation, which is usually influenced by other variables; capacity of the public sector to deliver policy changes, whether

13. This implementation cycle is formulated based on a cycle proposed by Brinkerhoff and Crosby in their book *Managing Policy Reform* (Brinkerhoff and Crosby 2002).

FIGURE 4-5. Task-Based Policy Implementation Cycle

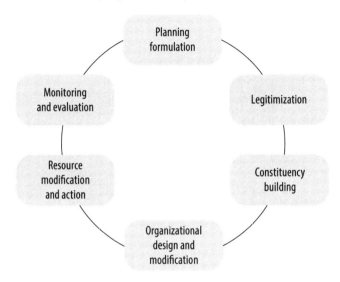

Source: Brinkerhoff and Crosby (2002, p. 32).

they relate to human, financial, or technological capacity, and including nontangible aspects such as leadership and motivation; and clients and coalitions, referring to interest groups and the need to carefully consider the potential stakeholders affected by the policy.[14]

Drawing on the proposed analytical framework presented in figure 4-5, we then use gap analysis to identify key challenges in the implementation process in Egypt. Using urban transport development as a case study, a comparative analysis is made with several Asian cities. Based on these analyses, we present a broader assessment of how the Egyptian public sector institutions may hinder implementation and lead to implementation gaps, and we provide policy recommendations to address these issues.

The Implementation Gap in Urban Transport Development in Egypt

One sector that suffers from an implementation gap in Egypt is the transportation sector, especially urban transportation in Cairo. As

14. Brynard (2005).

most residents and visitors would likely attest, traffic in Cairo is chaotic and unbearable. Traffic congestion is among the heaviest of all large cities in the world, and it is getting worse every year, at great cost to Egypt in terms of time wasted, fuel, air pollution and its accompanying health problems, accidents, and loss of economic productivity.

The Importance of Urban Transportation for Development in Egypt

As in other countries, the urban transportation sector plays a pivotal role in accelerating socioeconomic development in Egypt. Urban transportation is important for linking sectors of production, consumption, and supply of raw materials and is a key to employment generation, poverty reduction, and vulnerable groups' access to the city for economic or social services.

Urban transportation touches and affects the lives of the more than 20 percent of Egypt's population who live in Greater Cairo, as well as the people who commute daily to the city for business and income generation, health care, or education. Without easy access to the city, the living conditions of these people would deteriorate. Ministry of Planning data show that the transportation sector accounts for 4 percent of Egypt's GDP and 6.8 percent of its employment.

In addition, congestion leads to huge economic loss in Egypt, most of it from the time and fuel wasted in traffic, which the World Bank estimates at 50 billion Egyptian pounds (around US$6.5 billion), representing around 3.5 percent of GDP and making Egypt the metropolis with the largest such loss.[15] There are also significant dangers to health caused by pollution as well as deaths caused by traffic accidents, at least 1,000 annually.[16]

Faced with these problems, the government officials in the transport sector interviewed for this chapter recognize the problems facing the sector, as well as corrective steps that need to be taken. The officials note that the urban transportation sector has been the subject of an abundance of strategies and studies, but few have yielded any significant results on the ground.

An urban transport development master plan (the Cairo Regional Area Transportation Study, or CREATS), formulated with the support

---

15. World Bank (2014).
16. See World Bank (2012).

of JICA in 2002, estimates that, without any effort to improve the traffic situation in Egypt beyond committed projects under its fifth five-year plan (2002–07), travel speeds would decline from 19 kilometers an hour, on average, to 11.6 kilometers an hour by 2022, and the average commuting time by car between home and work would increase from 37 minutes to 100 minutes.[17] Worryingly, according to the latest update to this study by the Egyptian Ministry of Transport, the trip speed is expected to drastically worsen to reach 5 kilometers an hour and the trip time to a staggering 240 minutes by 2022 if nothing is done to improve the situation. These alarming findings have caused officials to consider why so little has been done to improve urban traffic and how the implementation gap in the Egypt's urban transportation sector can be filled.

Master Plan for Urban Transport Development in Egypt

Cairo is not the only city suffering from traffic congestion. Many large cities around the world are facing similar challenges. These cities are also adopting a range of measures in attempts to improve their respective conditions. Urban transportation development is a complex issue because so many stakeholders are involved at both central and local levels as well as various social, economic, and cultural factors. Experiences elsewhere in the world have shown that some countermeasures turn out to be effective, while some have had less impact than expected. In the case of Cairo, however, besides the ongoing construction of a subway system, a large problem lies in the fact that few measures have been undertaken, either in capital investment in infrastructure or in policy reform.

This is clearly illustrated through an analysis of CREATS. The study was divided into two phases: phase 1 required the formulation of a transport master plan, which was completed in November 2002, and phase 2 called for feasibility studies of selected priority projects in the master plan. These studies were completed in October 2003.

While planning the methodologies of CREATS, all previous master plans were reviewed and the need to involve more stakeholders was

17. Cairo Regional Area Transportation Study (2002).

identified as a priority in order to make the master plan more comprehensive and implementable (see box 4-1 for key features of CREATS).[18] So substantial efforts were made to make the planning process more inclusive in formulating CREATS.

Sometimes, plans and strategies are not implemented because they were formulated with limited participation, since the sense of ownership for the output is not well shared by stakeholders. Before the revolution, during the Mubarak regime, Egypt produced six five-year plans that set the national policy direction. These plans were drafted inside one section of the Egyptian Ministry of Planning without building consensus among major stakeholders, including each of the ministries responsible for implementation. These national plans were simply concepts on paper that did not call for execution, so Sakamoto has advocated the introduction of inclusive planning to Egypt.[19]

Based on previous lessons, CREATS was designed to secure wider participation among stakeholders. Most of the key stakeholders related to the transportation system in Cairo—the Ministry of Transportation, the Egypt National Institute of Transport (ENIT), the National Authority for Tunnels (NAT), the Egyptian National Railways Authority (ENR), the General Authority for Roads Bridges and Land Transport (GARBLT), the Cairo and Giza Governorates, and others—were involved in the planning process, with three levels of committees being set up to exchange views in an inclusive and effective manner. Civil society and private sector actors were also invited to participate in the discussions. Widespread information-dissemination methodologies were employed by holding a number of workshops and seminars as well as distributing periodic newsletters. Despite these efforts, CREATS did not achieve the desired impact on implementation. The problem of nonimplementation under CREATS lay in the obstacles occurring after the formulation of the plan.

18. Before CREATS, three transport master plan studies for Cairo existed; the first one created under the Transport Planning Authority in 1973 by the International Monetary Fund with French support, the second created in 1989 with JICA support under the Cairo Governorate, and the third created in 1999, with French support, under the National Authority for Tunnels.
19. See chapter 2 in this volume.

BOX 4-1. Key Features of the Cairo Regional Area Transportation Study (CREATS)

Between the late 1990s and early in the new century, JICA provided technical assistance to the Egyptian government to formulate the Greater Cairo Urban Transport Master Plan in two phases. Under the first phase, completed in November 2002, the master plan provided fifty-nine recommendations of projects or programs over a twenty-year period, divided into three groups: short term (2003–07), medium term (2008–12), and long term (2013–22).

Prepared in the belief that additional transport infrastructure alone was insufficient to solve the traffic problem, CREATS called for an integrated set of actions to improve urban transportation, many of which were soft components such as encouraging the connection between transport modals and policies and coordination among transport sector agencies and with other sectors, at the top of which were urban development and land use planning and improving traffic management.

As the figure below shows, five key strategies were proposed, and the achievement of each required infrastructure investment as well as policy and governance reforms.

The study contained recommendations for institutional reform, including the integration and coordination of transport policies and programs for the Greater Cairo metropolitan area. Some traffic management measures were recommended for discouraging car use, such as the

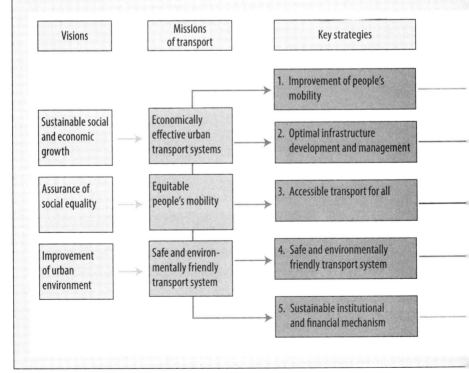

rationalization of fuel prices, road pricing, and parking charges. Other measures were proposed to promote the use of public transport, such as a common ticketing system and priority bus lanes, among others. Most of these were deemed high-priority programs that needed to be undertaken within the short run (2002–07).

As for infrastructure expansion, the plan recommended several projects, chief among which were the extension of metro line No. 2 and the construction of metro line No. 3 from the airport to Nasr City, projects that were already listed in the five-year plan (2002–07); a further extension of metro line No. 2; an extension of line No. 3 and the construction of metro line No. 4; three "super" tram lines of around 53 kilometers; two urban rail corridors linking Cairo with new communities; two new bus lanes and modernization of the bus fleet; and the expansion of selected roads and the introduction of an urban express network.

Phase 2 of CREATS included detailed feasibility studies for five high-priority projects, including a public transport connection between Cairo and new communities in 10th of Ramadan City and 6th of October City, traffic management of major roads in Cairo and Giza, a restructuring of the Cairo Transport Authority, and a new light-rail transit system, referred as Supertram.

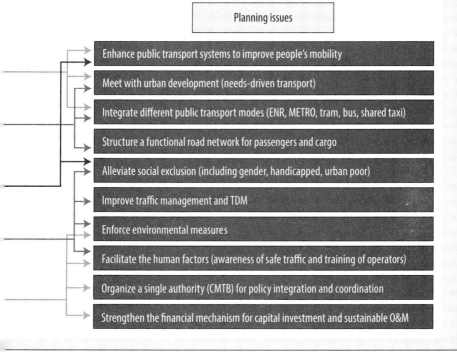

Factors Contributing to the Poor Implementation of CREATS

Our research here tries to identify the reasons behind the poor implementation of urban transportation development and the execution
of recommendations under CREATS, based on interviews with key
policymakers, academics, and public officials in the transport sector.
Through this analysis, we try to identify the root causes of the implementation gap in the urban transportation sector and remedial actions
to address the gap.

Many interviewees claim that CREATS is still relevant and its recommendations could be useful to ease the traffic congestion in Cairo,
if only they were implemented. The following are common factors
described by some of the interviewees as major causes that prevent the
sector from implementing its plans or policy.

Effective Authorization Process

The lack of an effective authorization process for plans and strategies
is identified as a significant factor contributing to the implementation
gap. In case of the five-year plans, article 9 of the Egyptian Planning
Law 70 for year 1973 stipulates that a general framework of the plan is
supposed to be submitted for endorsement by the cabinet and the parliament.[20] At the sectoral and regional levels, in many cases, plans and
strategies are reported to the incumbent ministers who might not be in
position by the time implementation is expected to start. A new minister tends not to have a strong commitment to plans formulated by his
predecessors, so these plans end up gathering dust on bookshelves. One
exception is the energy sector, where long-term strategies are subject
to approval by Egypt's Supreme Energy Council, headed by the prime
minister and made up of key ministers related to the energy sector.

In the case of CREATS, the plan was authorized by a so-called
Higher Committee led by the relevant minister at the time, but both
the minister and the other committee members have since changed and,
while the committee still legally exists, it has not met in many years. As
a result, the legal status of CREATS is unclear, and the commitment of
the government to implementing the plan is weak.

---

20. Government of Egypt (1973).

Coordination of Key Stakeholders

For the implementation of any strategy to succeed, coordination and collaboration from multiple entities is indispensable. Under the Egyptian Ministry of Transport, there are twelve such entities: six service authorities, including ENIT, NAT, GARBLT, and the ENR, and six economic authorities, each of which is in charge of a specific transport subsector or modal.

The coordination problem is not only in vertical coordination within the Ministry of Transport and its affiliated entities, nor only between central and local levels, but also in horizontal coordination among concerned ministries and agencies outside of the Ministry of Transport. In the case of urban transportation, other ministries and agencies such as the Ministry of Housing, the Ministry of the Interior, and the Cairo and Giza Governorates are key stakeholders.

To improve coordination, the Greater Cairo Transportation Regulatory Authority was finally created in 2013 (the decision to establish the agency was taken in 2009). To have such a focal agency among all stakeholders represents a big step forward, but whether it will function effectively remains to be seen, since it currently has only one professional employee. The agency was created as a financially self-sufficient body that is supposed to operate using its own revenue, mainly from license fees to public transportation such as microbuses. This may prove challenging.

A number of other initiatives have been undertaken to improve the planning, coordination, and implementation of transportation plans. The Egyptian Transportation Center of Excellence was another entity created under the Transport Planning Authority and the Ministry of Transport in 2013. This entity was equipped with minimal staff and a small budget, and demarcation between its role and responsibilities and those of the Transport Planning Authority remains unclear. The Transportation Center was eventually dissolved in April 2015 when the director in charge of the entity decided to leave the Ministry of Transport to work in a Gulf country, which commonly happens with many engineers who work for ministries.

Factors Affecting Ministerial Capacity

That the degree of implementation differs across institutions and institutional capacity is a major factor that affects the implementation of policies and projects. Donors sometimes refer to this as absorption capacity, since many institutions in developing countries tend to struggle to implement projects and use allocated donor funds effectively and efficiently. We find it more useful here, however, not to discuss ministerial capacity in general but to identify factors that constrain the institutional capacity of the Ministry of Transport in Egypt.

Leadership is a key factor that affects the capacity of any organization. The Ministry of Transport's frequent changing of ministers has degraded the consistency and continuity of ministry policy. In the three years since the ouster of President Mubarak, there have been seven ministers. The effect of this lack of consistency on policies and priorities for development is one of the most serious issues identified by interviewees. Some interviewees pointed out that one minister expressed interest in the development of the railway system, while the next minister was keen on road development. Since the top-down drive is strong in the Egyptian public system and the technical back office is weaker when ministers change, it is difficult to secure continuity and consistency for the direction of the ministry.

Some interviewees observed that the ministry's involvement in the operation of the transportation system overwhelms the ministry's capacity. Although NAT, GARBLT, and the ENR are quasi-subsidiary organizations of the ministry, in charge of operating each transport modality, the boundary of responsibilities between these subsidiary organizations and the ministry is unclear, often leading to excessive ministerial involvement in operational issues.

Another factor that affects ministerial capacity is the serious shortage of qualified technical staff. This is a common problem not only for the Ministry of Transport but across different ministries. Though the Egyptian public sector employs a huge number of public servants, most of them are administrative staff, and the number of staff with sector-specific technical expertise is insufficient.

The shortage of technical experts on staff often leads to the appointment of outside experts, such as academics, as advisers to the minister. Since most advisers are replaced when ministers leave, it is difficult to accumulate a knowledge base and experience inside the institution. Some interviewees said that this also affects access to information since some of the short-term advisers do not document their work appropriately.

Budget Limitations and Private Sector Participation

Many interviewees claim that budget shortages are the biggest factor preventing the development of the urban transportation infrastructure. Still, since there is a huge need for capital investment in transportation infrastructure, the same could be said for most countries, both developing and developed, which face their own budget constraints.

Even with existing budget limitations, there are still many measures that a country can take. First, a country can improve its selection and prioritization of projects with good sector strategies linked to budgetary commitments, improved cost-benefit analyses, and risk-management strategies. In case of the Egyptian Ministry of Transport, it is not clear which criteria were used in the selection of projects. Some interviewees claimed that officials in charge of budgeting are somehow separated from the planning process so that the priorities in the annual investment plan do not necessarily reflect the sector strategy and priorities.

Second, a country can promote private investment to offset budget constraints, which Egypt has thus far largely failed to do. While the enormous amount of investment and the difficulties in recovering costs in the transportation sector make it difficult to mobilize private sector funding, Egypt is far behind other countries in mobilizing private financial resources for the development of urban transport infrastructure.

Third, poor cost recovery is another factor that affects the availability of financial resources for further investment and undermines the financial soundness of government entities. In theory, users should cover both investment and maintenance costs through fuel prices, tolls, fuel tax, and license fees, but in reality few effective, direct-user charges exist.[21]

The metro tariff remains too low, at 1 Egyptian pound (US$0.14) per ride, far below the rate needed to recover the huge investment costs. Cairo introduced the metro system in 1987, and subsequent extension work has been very slow. This is partly because the existing lines have not contributed sufficiently to offset investment and operating costs, so additional investment decisions tend to be delayed owing to the unavailability of funds. This lack of return on investment can be seen in most transportation subsectors.

21. See Zegras (2006).

Flaws in the Subsidy System

In Egypt, fuel is heavily subsidized, and the prevailing fuel subsidy is hampering the development of the urban transportation system. Vehicle operating costs are a key determinant of modal-choice relationships, and the price of fuel is a major variable in this relationship.[22] So the low price of fuel discourages people from choosing a public transportation option since it costs so little to drive their own cars.

In addition, subsidies place a huge burden on the state budget, accounting for 25 percent of the national budget, and the fuel subsidy constitutes 50 percent of total expenditure on subsidies. It is widely recognized that the fuel subsidy is not an effective mechanism to support the poor since vehicle owners, who tend to be wealthier, benefit most from the subsidized prices. The International Monetary Fund has found that, in Egypt in 2008, the poorest 40 percent of the population received only 3 percent of gasoline subsides.[23] A better mechanism to subsidize the poor requires better targeting, such as through the introduction of a cash transfer system. Better-targeted subsidies would help reduce the burden on the national budget and make more resources available for economic and social development.

Besides being a fiscal burden, subsidies tend to be an ineffective and inefficient policy tool for meeting government objectives. They are regressive, they undermine energy efficiency initiatives, they can reduce investment in the energy sector, and they have negative environmental impacts.[24] The decision by the new government in July 2014 to cut the fuel subsidy and to increase the price of fuel and electricity is both a bold and a welcome step toward mitigating the fiscal burden of subsidies. The reduction of subsidies in Egypt has been considered a third-rail political issue for many years since President Sadat's decision to reduce the food subsidy met with fierce protests in 1977, which eventually made him reverse course. During President Mubarak's reign, fuel subsidies were left largely untouched, adding to the fiscal burden after world oil prices surged. In that sense, the recent decision to cut

22. See Ministry of Transport, Transport Planning Authority, and the Japan International Cooperation Agency (2012).

23. International Monetary Fund (2014a).

24. See International Institute for Sustainable Development (2012).

subsidies should be praised as a first, large step forward. Still, greater reform will be needed in future.

Flaws in the Donor Approach

Donors can be part of the implementation problem. A common criticism of donors is that they tend to overwhelm the recipient government with a multitude of recommendations without setting out a clear implementation plan that takes into consideration the institutional constraints. Some interviewees pointed out that donors need to focus more on improving governance, institutional structure, and human resource development of recipient governments.

Devarajan argues that recommendations made without consideration of the political context of a particular country often fail at the implementation stage.[25] He points out that in Egypt, a major reason for delays in subsidy reform is intervention from politically connected, energy-intensive firms. To implement policy, donors must assess not only the capacity of particular executing agencies but also the political context in which the policy reforms are to be implemented. Devarajan contends that the dissemination of information to the public, especially about the benefits of the change, is an effective mechanism to encourage implementation.

Comparative Analysis with Urban Transportation Development in Other Countries

Egypt is not the only country that suffers from worsening traffic problems; many countries all over the world continue to face difficulties with urban transport development to meet the increasing accessibility needs of growing urban populations. In particular, many emerging economies have been experiencing urbanization in which rapid population increases in metropolitan areas are outstripping expansion in transport infrastructure. Urbanization has brought with it increased congestion, low-quality public transport, and deteriorating air quality and traffic safety. In many countries, slow policy and program implementation has worsened the situation and enlarged the supply-demand gap in the urban transportation sector.

25. Devarajan (2014).

Various attempts have been made by each country to resolve traffic problems. Some measures have been effective, and some passed without much impact, yet useful lessons can be drawn from both successes and failures.

Overview of Urban Transport in Metropolitan Areas in Asia

The Southeast Asian cities of Jakarta, Manila, and Bangkok share socioeconomic characteristics with Cairo, and each is considered to be in the middle stages of development, according to per capita income. They also have high rates of urban density (see table 4-1) and are facing chronic traffic congestion.

The population of the Jakarta metropolitan area in year 2000 was 21.3 million, and it has since increased to almost 28 million (CMEA-JICA 2012). Between 2000 and 2010, the number of cars on the road doubled and the number of motorcycles increased by a factor of 4.6.[26] Consequently, the Indonesian government has implemented many measures to ease congestion. They have expanded the bus network, which is the main mode of transport in Jakarta. Trans Jakarta, the bus rapid-transit system in Jakarta, was set up in 2004 and has expanded to include twelve lines with three more under construction. It is considered the largest such system in the world. In addition, the government is constructing a mass rapid-transit system. Jakarta has also introduced several traffic-demand management (TDM) measures to reduce congestion.

In Manila, there is no metro system. Instead, the city's public transit system centers on an elevated railway called Light Rail Transit. Light Rail Transit was introduced in 1984 and has expanded to four lines. The government has been active in mobilizing private sector investment in the system.

Bangkok was already experiencing severe traffic congestion in the late 1980s, and so it began introducing measures to ease congestion earlier than the other three cities. The city's 1991 strategy (Seventh Plan Urban and Regional Transport) focused on several mega projects, particularly road expansion through the construction of expressways, some of which involved public-private partnerships (PPPs).[27] In 1999 an elevated urban mass-rapid-transit system, Skytrain, began operating.

26. See Kawaguchi and others (2013).
27. See Zegras (2006).

TABLE 4-1. Socioeconomic Data for Cairo and Select Asian Cities

City	Country	Population (1,000s)[a]	Density per km[b]	GDP per capita (current US$)[c]	Transport MP year[d]
Cairo	Egypt	14,900	8,400	3,256	1973, 1989, 1999, 2002
Jakarta	Indonesia	27,550	8,900	3,557	1987, 1990, 2001, 2004
Manila	Philippines	20,750	13,130	2,587	1973, 1985, 1999
Bangkok	Thailand	13,500	5,400	5,480	1979, 1988, 1990

Sources: Demographia World Urban Areas (2014) and World Bank (2012).
a. As of base year (2010).
b. Density is calculated with approximation to the nearest 100th.
c. 2012 current US$, World Bank.
d. Year the Urban Transportation Master Plan was formulated.

A subway line was recently constructed to complement Skytrain, and the government has plans to expand them both to cover the whole city.

Timing of Introduction of Mass Transit System

Several studies indicate that the timing of introducing a mass transit system is a critical decision for successful urban transport management. If the decision is postponed, mass transit systems can be more and more difficult to implement because of complications in acquiring right of way as the economy develops and dependence on private vehicles increases.[28] At the same time, mass transit systems are known to involve high initial investment costs while many developing countries are facing fiscal constraints. Therefore, to strategically consider the investment needs and priorities in the transport sector becomes of utmost importance.

In introducing a metro system in 1987, Cairo was one of the first cities in a developing country to introduce a mass transit system. In the twenty-five years following its creation, the system's three lines have been extended to cover a total of sixty-nine kilometers. Meanwhile, Delhi's metro system, which only came into service in 2002, already has six lines covering 190 kilometers.[29]

The timing for the introduction of metro systems is closely related to the level of socioeconomic development a city has achieved. In the 1980s, it can be said that Cairo was more advanced than these other

28. World Bank (2000).
29. JICA (2011).

Asian cities. So why, despite its early introduction, has the development of Cairo's metro system been so slow compared with that in other large cities in the world? Many interviewees attributed this to budget limitations, but such constraints should be common for most cities. Some pointed out that metro lines have been constructed through soft loans provided by the French government, but since the low tariff makes cost recovery difficult, the government and NAT became hesitant to make further investments because of their repayment obligations.

Others argue that it derives from the institutional capacity of NAT. In the case of Delhi, an executing agency, Delhi Metro Rail Corporation Limited, established in 1995, was a driving force in ensuring the city's metro came into operation on schedule. Both the Delhi Metro and the Cairo Metro No. 4 have been funded by JICA under its soft loan scheme. While lines 1 to 3 of the Delhi metro were, astonishingly, completed without any delay, the development of Cairo Metro No. 4 is facing a further two-year delay, after more than two years following the signing of the loan agreement. An extension to Cairo Metro No. 3 was recently commissioned, but it is said that it has faced six years of delay from the project's original timeline.

Private Sector Participation

Many countries have been trying to mobilize private financing for transportation projects to reduce the burden on the state budget and to promote higher quality and increased efficiency in service provision. In Asian countries, PPPs started to be adopted for transport infrastructure development in the early 1990s, but in Egypt there has been no private sector involvement in urban transport infrastructure development.

The two common schemes applied to PPP-driven transport infrastructure development in Asian countries are build-own-transfer and joint ventures between public and private companies. Many transport infrastructure projects have been built through PPP schemes. Bangkok and Manila have been promoting private sector participation in transport projects since the early 1990s to reduce the burden on their budget and to reduce reliance on foreign loans.

In Manila, a PPP has been used for expressway development and light rail. Joint ventures have been used to develop Metro Manila Skyway and also the Southern Tagalog Arterial Road, the first build-own-transfer project in the Philippines. The first Light Rail Transit line in the early 1980s was financed by relatively expensive borrowing, while the second line was financed through a soft loan from JICA after the failure of the initial trial of build-own-transfer. In the 1990s, the Philippines passed legislation on build-own-transfers to prepare the regulatory framework for private sector participation. Following passage and amendment to the build-own-transfer act, the third Light Rail Transit line—MRT 3—was built and began service in 1999 as a build-lease-transfer project.

In Bangkok, private sector involvement in infrastructure has also centered on expressway development as well as mass urban transit development. The Second Stage Expressway System was built under a build-transfer-operate scheme. Two lines of the Skytrain system and one subway line were built by public-private partnership.

These Asian experiences illustrate the mixture of successes and failures of PPP-led infrastructure development to date. Whether any of them represent success stories is hotly debated. These PPPs certainly succeeded in building up urban transport infrastructure, but many projects have faced financial problems. This is often the case when political calculations are used to inform economic decisionmaking. For example, during the development of the MRT 3 in the Philippines, the government had to guarantee private investors a minimum return on investment to cover any revenue gap. As the government wanted to keep fares low for political reasons, it was left shouldering a huge liability from subsidy payments to the private sector. Bangkok's Second Stage Expressway System was similarly forced to operate using lower toll fares, which affected its profitability. The stock of the Second Stage Expressway System owned by foreign investors was eventually sold to a local construction company.

Traffic Demand Management

Though the developmental impact of introducing a mass transit system is large, the huge investment cost is usually a major impediment to implementation. So, controlling the demand side to match the limitation of supply in infrastructure might be worth considering. Many TDM solutions exist and have been gaining recognition over the past two decades for reducing congestion and decreasing the flow of traffic by reducing the attractiveness of private vehicle use, dispersing demand during peak hours, and using road space more efficiently.

In an attempt to restrict car use during particular areas or hours, Jakarta initiated a so-called three-in-one scheme, which required motorized vehicles entering the city to carry at least three passengers during peak hours to reduce congestion. Manila introduced a color-coding program in 1996, which used number plates to regulate which cars were permitted to drive in the city within certain weekday hours. Other TDM measures such as truck bans and bus priority lanes were introduced. Bangkok has also implemented an intelligent traffic information system, which provides drivers with timely traffic information in order to avoid congestion.[30]

The most effective TDM can be achieved through proper pricing. This could be done through car-licensing fees, parking fees, road pricing, and appropriate fuel cost (without subsidy or with fuel tax). As noted earlier, vehicle operation cost is a key determinant of the modal-choice relationship.

In Jakarta, Manila, and Bangkok, attempts to reduce traffic through proper pricing have always faced intensive debate. For example, Bangkok has tried to introduce some TDM measures such as road pricing, bus priority lanes, and parking restrictions, but these efforts have failed owing to political and institutional constraints.[31] Indonesia's recent efforts to reduce the fuel subsidy have faced large political challenges, but the Philippines successfully removed fuel subsidies in 1998. Such success affects not only demand-side management in the transportation sector but also prices renewable energy more competitively.

The lesson here is that TDM solutions are essential to tackling urban congestion and can be financially less costly than other measures, but to introduce effective TDM solutions can be as challenging as the introduction of a mass transit system, since it requires public acceptance to work. Efficient communication and coordination among concerned agencies and relevant stakeholders are also required.

Land Acquisition and Land Value

Transport infrastructure development, land use, and land development have both positive and negative interrelations. Most cities in both developed and developing countries face land acquisition problems when

30. JICA (2011).
31. JICA (2011).

they are engaged in the development of infrastructure. In developing countries, issues can be more serious, owing to the lack of effective land acquisition laws and proper ways of assessing land value. The delay of land acquisition is often the major cause of delay in the development of infrastructure, particularly for those projects requiring substantial amounts of land.

Many mechanisms and methodologies have been developed to capture the proximity benefits generated from transport facilities on increased land and real estate values and to use such benefits to offset losses from insufficient fare revenues or to reduce reliance on public sector budgets. Land-based financing of infrastructure can be divided into three categories: developer exactions, value capture, and land asset management.[32]

The methodology of land value capture is more complicated than the other two forms of infrastructure financing since to administer the tax system with proper land valuation is not an easy process. In many countries, land asset management—in the form of land sales, one-time development charges, or joint land development with private parties— is far simpler and is being applied. For example in Japan, railway companies have benefited from land development both along rail corridors and the land adjacent to stations. Many developing countries are adopting similar techniques for development of transport infrastructure. In Bangkok, BTS Group Holdings, a public holding company, has been engaged in land development by forming a joint-ventures company with a private company. In Delhi, Delhi Metro Rail Corporation has earned substantial amounts of income from selling land to private investors.[33] In Manila, revenues from commercial development rights for MRT 3 were a large income source for the Manila Rapid Transit Corporation.

In Egypt, a similar exercise has been tried for land development projects on the outskirts of Cairo. The New Urban Communities Authority, a public company under the Ministry of Housing, Utilities, and Urban Development, has been a leading proponent promoting such a scheme. It offers desert land owned by the state to private investors, who then assume responsibilities for the development of on-site and off-site infrastructure in addition to the real estate development. In past exercises, the company has faced a number of legal challenges from investors, and

32. See Peterson (2009).
33. See Singh and Sharma (2012).

the impact on the development of off-site infrastructure still remains to be assessed. But the exercise so far does not seem to have had a strong connection with public transport institutions. This collaboration needs to be strengthened.

Institutional Coordination

As noted in the previous section of this chapter, one of the main weaknesses causing an implementation gap in urban transport development for Cairo relates to a fragmented institutional setup, with weak coordination and communication between the various agencies involved in planning and implementation of transport projects. This institutional barrier hinders and even obstructs any potential effort to approach urban transport planning in an integrated and comprehensive manner, through aligning the individual actions and projects under a clear metropolitan strategy, allocating resources to achieve that goal, and monitoring the implementation. Several emerging countries are suffering from the same institutional deficiencies and lack of communication and coordination. These problems are further exacerbated by limited financial and human resources and unstable political and economic situations.[34] Bangkok, where more than thirty institutions are involved in transport development, faces an even more difficult situation than Egypt, and yet the city has somehow managed to develop its infrastructure since the early 1990s. Manila faced similar hurdles until planners formed in 1995 the Metropolitan Manila Development Authority, an agency that plans, monitors, and coordinates urban development of several cities located in metropolitan Manila.[35]

In 2004, with the support of JICA, the Indonesian government conducted the Study on Integrated Transportation Master Plan for Jabodetabek for the Jakarta metropolitan area.[36] This plan experienced a low implementation rate in its first few years of operation, and the traffic situation greatly worsened.[37] Part of the blame for this implementation gap was the lack of a focal institution to manage the planning, coordination, implementation, monitoring, and evaluation of proposed projects from a holistic metropolitan view. As a result, the government

34. See Kawaguchi and others (2013).
35. See Mandri-Perrott (2010).
36. JICA, BAPPENAS, and Republic of Indonesia (2004).
37. See CMEA and JICA (2012).

established the Jabodetabek Transportation Authority at the central government level with the participation of more than fifteen relevant entities to facilitate the implementation process through coordination of activities and to avoid any overlap.[38]

Several other countries, including India, Singapore, and China, have tried to establish focal or lead institutions for managing urban transport development. Kumar and Agarwal (2013) reaffirm the necessity of considering urban transport development in an integrated and comprehensive manner, which requires establishing lead institutions. While their report specifies that there is no uniform setup for such institutions, the authors provide useful lessons from case studies from other countries. Other experiences indicate that the establishment of lead institutions is not easy and takes time, but once established, the institutions can be sustainable if they have sufficient technical and financial capacities, political support, and control of financial resources to help them meet the public's needs. Whether the newly established Greater Cairo Transportation Regulatory Authority functions well remains to be seen, but there are many lessons the agency and the government can learn from other parts of the world.

In addition to institutional matters within the transportation sector, the relationship with central economic institutions such as the Ministry of Finance, the Ministry of Planning, and these sectoral ministries and institutions does affect strategy implementation. For the Asian countries mentioned above, the roles and function of planning institutions have become a target for public sector reform initiatives especially after the Asian financial crisis in 1998, and it is time for Egypt, whose previous restructuring efforts have not brought any result, to reassess and streamline the role and function of central economic institutions.

Bridging the Implementation Gap in Egypt

Some of the issues that we have observed in the urban transportation sector are common for many other sectors and public institutions in Egypt. While implementation capacity differs according to institution and sector, common problems that cause implementation gaps and hamper the implementation of strategy can be observed across many sectors and institutions.

38. See World Bank (2000).

Our assessment of the causes of implementation gaps is, based on our analytical framework, as illustrated in figure 4-5. The causes of gaps can be attributed to the problems within each phase of implementation and between phases. Some problems cut across multiple phases.

Planning and Formulation

In Egypt, much resource and energy is exerted in the first phase of the cycle—the planning part—with far less attention and resources directed to the subsequent phases of implementation cycle. Even so, planning in Egypt still has room for improvement. One improvement would be to make the process more inclusive by involving a wider group of stakeholders, an issue extensively studied by Sakamoto.[39] Another gap in the planning phase is the lack of a detailed implementation plan, which should be formulated after the formulation of strategies.

The planning stage is often considered complete after the goals have been defined and a strategy formulated. But without clarifying in detail how to execute the plan with identified actions, timeline, and concerned stakeholders, many master plans have foundered. These drivers can be consolidated into an execution or implementation plan.

This is closely linked with the capacity as well as ownership of each executing agency. Once they are given clear direction, some institutions will make all efforts to realize strategies, but when the capacity of a particular institution is weak, automatic implementation will not happen. In such a case, some kind of external support, often from donors, is required. We need to be aware, however, that donor assistance without sufficient participation of executing agencies and stakeholders may create dependency. Enhancing a sense of project ownership is key to successful implementation.

The necessity for an implementation plan becomes more acute for national plans than for sectoral plans since the goals and directions set out at the national level tend to be broad and general so that the gap between goals and actions is wider. Our research indicates that the lack of an implementation plan and weak linkages with each executing agency's plans were one reason for the low implementation of past five-year plans in Egypt. This trend continued even after the revolution in 2011. The Ministry of Planning produced a new ten-year national plan

39. See chapter 2 in this volume.

in 2012, only to begin formulating a new plan for 2015–30 before the first was implemented.

Legitimization and Authorization Process

As noted in the analysis of Egyptian urban transportation development, the lack of proper legitimization or authorization process is one factor contributing to the weak commitment of the Egyptian government to implementation. Legitimization and authorization are important for any policy action since they provide momentum and support for implementation, especially when there is a strain on budget resources. If legitimacy is not appropriately secured, stakeholders will not recognize the need to comply with the plan and to work on achieving it. The level at which legitimization is given is a key issue. Legitimization can be divided into the political level, the executive-branch level, and the public level. Each level has its own challenges.

With higher-level legitimization, plans and strategies are recognized as a commitment by the government to full implementation. The question remains which governing body is best suited to provide such legitimization. The cabinet often has insufficient capacity to undertake such a task. Parliament could be a strong legitimization body, but because it is composed of many members representing different vested interests, consensus building would take time, and it would not work practically. As such, a new higher economic authority, such as a national economic council, could be created to legitimize strategies.

Sometimes, legitimization is provided from the top—the president— which definitely drives project implementation, as some mega projects, such as the Suez Canal Corridor Development Project and the Aswan High Dam, show. In these cases, momentum for implementation is not an issue. However, whether these mega development projects deliver benefits to the wider public is a different story. During the Mubarak era, the Toshka Development Project in southern Egypt was one of the highest-priority projects. Yet the project, which is still in progress, is no longer considered successful. One reason for this is that when top-down drive is too strong, projects may move ahead without enough consideration of economic and technical feasibility.

Some countries give more authority over sectoral strategies to central economic agencies such as planning or financial ministries. In Egypt, however, they have almost no authority over sectoral or regional strategies, even while they retain a role in budget allocations. A central planning agency, such as Bappenas in Indonesia or the Planning Commission in India, used to be given greater authority not only for national master plans but also for sectoral or regional plans. Some countries share such authority among several central economic agencies. In Thailand, the National Economic and Social Development Board is functioning effectively as a central planning agency, albeit a less powerful one than those found in Indonesia and India.[40]

In Egypt, the plans and strategies for authorization and legitimization systems at both political and bureaucratic levels need to be reassessed. It is difficult to strike the right balance between these two levels: if the political level is too strong, it may move without considering proper technical and economic assessment, and it can be subject to excessive political intervention, while with only executive-branch-level endorsement, things may not move in a country like Egypt, where decisionmaking is highly top-down.

The third level of authorization is from the public. In addition to acquiring authorization and legitimization from the government, a kind of authorization or support needs to be given by the final beneficiaries, the Egyptian people. In other words, getting buy-in from the public is another key factor for the success of implementation.

Constituency Building and Public Relations

Constituency building can be said to be one of the weakest points in the Egyptian implementation system. Any plan or policy reform needs to be marketed and promoted so as to acquire public support to be implemented successfully. Also, the wider public should be well informed about the potential benefits and drawbacks of projects and reforms. Devarajan (2014) points out that the "why" of policy reform, such as the cost-benefit analysis, should be provided to the general public—the majority of whom are likely to benefit from the reform—to smoothen the implementation process. The lack of a participatory process and sense of involvement was one of the driving forces that took the Egyptian people to the street in 2011 to topple the regime.

Communication is essential to building trust and credibility for the government and to keeping citizens involved, increasing their sense of

40. See Ohno and Shimamura (2007).

ownership, and reducing information asymmetries among stakeholders involved.[41] People will more readily accept the new strategies when they feel they are part of the decisionmaking and implementation process.

The lack of well-functioning constituency-building mechanisms tends to make the Egyptian government make less controversial policy choices. One such example is the lack of a traffic demand-side management. Demand-side management reform requires less money but more support from the public to be effective.

Egypt's decision in July 2014 to reduce subsidies and to increase the prices of fuel and electricity came as a surprise, and this might be a sign that the new government is prepared to depart from the previous propensity for inaction. Judging from the lack of fierce public opposition, the government's efforts to gain support for the decision appear to be working. Some claim that the past three years of debate concerning the International Monetary Fund program might have laid the foundation for better understanding among stakeholders.[42] The capacity to maintain public support for this tough policy decision will continue to be tested, especially given that further subsidy reform will likely be required.

The decision to raise prices is always difficult for governments. In Japan, it took the government more than sixteen years to raise the consumption tax—one of the lowest among both developed and developing countries—and even then by only 3 percent. Egypt has been debating the introduction of a value-added tax since the mid-1990s. And Indonesia has found it difficult to reform its subsidy system. The Philippines, however, successfully reduced fuel subsidies in 1998.

The Philippines' success involved a range of mitigation measures taken by the government, such as weekly meetings with public transportation leaders, nationwide fuel discounts at 300 filling stations, and the adoption of corporate social-responsibility programs among oil companies to better engage with local communities. In addition, smart cards entitling the holders to discounts, and other services were provided to vulnerable groups such as jeepneys, Filipino microbus drivers,

41. See Organization for Economic Cooperation and Development (2010).

42. Following the revolution of January 25, 2011, to fill the increasing fiscal gap, the Egyptian government started negotiations with the International Monetary Fund to receive loan assistance, on condition that the government would implement an economic reform program. The negotiations were never completed, amid strong objections to the reforms.

and tricycle operators. Such public relations efforts helped mitigate the impact of the decision, and the Philippines was spared large-scale public rallies opposing the fuel price increase.[43]

Compared with the Philippines, the Egyptian government's mitigation measures still appear to fall short, though efforts are being made to introduce a cash transfer system. Egypt should learn from the experiences of other countries in putting a constituency-building mechanism in place to advance the reform process.

Organizational Design and Modification

The question of how to make the machinery of government work to implement projects and strategies is not easily answered for many developing countries. Egypt has a huge bureaucratic system with 6.5 million public employees and more than thirty ministers. Its reform challenges are enormous, but reforming public sector management and institutions will be indispensable to achieving inclusive growth and reducing poverty, as well as solving the implementation problem in Egypt. Such reforms will face strong resistance from those who prefer the status quo. Given the size of the challenges, comprehensive reform recommendations are beyond the scope of this chapter, but two key issues merit specific mention, namely coordination and accountability, as key drivers to enhance the implementation capacity of the Egyptian public sector.

How can coordination among public sector institutions be improved? Coordination issues can be multidimensional. There are so many agencies and institutions within the sector and across different ministries, and fragmentation in organizations can hinder the implementation of complex policies and projects that require coordination and cooperation. Egypt suffers from both vertical and horizontal coordination problems owing to the lack of hierarchical structures in the public sector.

For vertical coordination, problems exist at a number of levels: lines of command within ministries from ministers to entry-level staff, between ministries and subordinate executing agencies, and between upstream core economic ministries, such as the Ministry of Finance and the Ministry of Planning, and downstream bodies, including sector ministries and subordinate state institutions. As for horizontal coordination, coordination between ministers of the

---

43. See International Institute for Sustainable Development (2012).

same rank seems to function to some extent, whether through cabinet or committee meetings. But below the level of minister, such as deputy-level interactions, effective coordination mechanisms do not exist since each ministry's chain of command differs, making it difficult to find the right interlocutors.[44]

The lack of a uniform hierarchy in public sector organization is one crucial cause of bottlenecks for coordination among different institutions in Egypt. Since the whole retooling of the organizational structure in the public sector is an extremely challenging task, as a short-term countermeasure the establishment of a focal agency can serve as a solution in a similar way to the Greater Cairo Transportation Regulatory Authority. But again, without proper resource provision and political support to enhance its capacity and its function, such a solution to establish a focal coordinating agency does not work.

Another coordination challenge in Egypt relates to coordination among or with central economic agencies in the implementation process. In the Egyptian context, the central economic agencies are the Ministry of Planning, the Ministry of Finance, the Central Bank, and the Ministry of International Cooperation. Key questions related to this issue include the following: What would be the optimal organizational setup to conduct strategy formulation, budget planning, and budget execution? What should the relationship be between recurrent and capital expenditures? What should the relationship be between central economic agencies and sector ministries and other stakeholders?

Many countries have faced these issues and grappled with central economic agency reform. In many cases, the role and function of planning institutions have become a target for reform initiatives. In Indonesia, after the ouster of Suharto in 1998, there was heated debate around the appropriate planning system to guide the move toward decentralization and prevention of corruption. A new budget law (Law on State Finances, 2003) and a new planning law (Law on the National Development Planning System, 2004) were introduced, restructuring the roles and functions of the Indonesian Ministry of Planning—known as Bappenas—and the Ministry of Finance. More recently, in India, President Narendra Modi is attempting to reform the country's planning commission, a powerful planning agency.

44. See Dimian and al-Mashat (2014).

These changes are partly influenced by the increasing roles and activities of the private sector and a growing perception that traditional planning institutions are relics of an outdated concept of a centrally planned economic model. The reform efforts in Indonesia and India reflect the growing shift to decentralization.

In Egypt, the economic and political contexts are quite different, as the momentum for substantive decentralization is still weak, and private sector activities are not up to the level of other countries. Also, compared with institutions in Indonesia and India, the Egyptian Ministry of Planning is considered to be less powerful. Yet the Ministry of Planning does have authority over the public investment budget, and the public investment ratio has experienced a serious decline over the past thirty years. Furthermore, numerous strategies and master plans, some of which are formulated by the Ministry of Planning, have not been implemented. It is clear that some kind of reform is necessary for the Ministry of Planning and its relations with line ministries and public agencies.

Some interviewees claim that, at least in its budgetary functions, the Ministry of Planning should be merged with the Ministry of Finance. Such a merger has been debated in the past, though it has never come to pass. Amendments to the 1973 planning law are necessary to meet the current needs and changing environment.[45]

While differing political and economic circumstances over time and across countries mean there is no single solution to this issue, it is time for the Egyptian government to reassess the roles and functions of its central economic agencies, in particular the Ministry of Planning, to improve the coordination among public institutions and to enhance the implementation capacity.

Concerning organizational design and modification, a far broader issue relates to increasing accountability. Who will be accountable for implementation? Of course, each executing agency should be accountable for the implementation process in their sector, but self-regulation does not work in many cases in Egypt. There needs to be a mechanism to hold institutions accountable.

---

45. The Ministry of Planning is currently drafting new legislation, but no drastic change to budget responsibility, nor to roles and functions, is included.

One interviewee suggested that huge infrastructure projects require some kind of "stick" for untimely or inadequate implementation, as there had been for Egypt's great historic projects such as the pyramids, the Suez Canal, and the Aswan Dam. Today, such a deterrent might take the form of applying peer pressure to each responsible agency, policymaker, and leader to move toward implementation.

Positive peer pressure will enhance both the performance and accountability of public institutions. Peer pressure can come from two directions: from the top—the president or prime minister—and from the bottom—citizens. How can such a mechanism be put into place in the Egyptian system? This needs to be tackled in a comprehensive manner.

The 2004 World Bank Development Report points out that account-ability takes many different usages and meanings. According to the report, accountability is a set of relationships among service delivery actors with five features: delegation, finance, performance, information about performance, and enforceability.[46] Good delegation (legitimiza-tion) and financing (resource mobilization) mechanisms are important prerequisites to sustaining and improving performance, while access to information about performance (monitoring and evaluation) and enforceability (peer pressure) are also essential.

The importance of a chain of actions in such a cycle is what we are trying to emphasize in this chapter. As far as accountability and peer pressure are concerned, a proper monitoring and evaluation system will be indispensable.

The institutional challenges to the implementation capacity of Egypt's public sector go far beyond the issues of coordination and accountability discussed above. Egypt's public sector has been fiercely protected for a long time, functioning as an absorption mechanism for the labor force without its effectiveness and efficiency ever being suitably tested. As a result, there are too many employees, which rep-resents a huge fiscal burden for the country. Too many ministries exist, and most ministers struggle to execute their work since technical back offices are weak. Moreover, the lack of well-established hierarchical structures hampers proper coordination. For the new government,

46. World Bank (2004).

which seems determined to maintain momentum for change, it is time to consider serious public sector management and institutional reform.

Resource Mobilization and Action

Before resources are mobilized and actions are initiated, policy change tends to be largely a paper exercise, but the resource mobilization task shifts the policy from paper to action.[47] While resources might have quantitative and qualitative constraints, gaps between strategies and resources are also causes of low implementation. Effective use of different kinds of resources, such as financial, human, technical, and physical resources, is essential for effective and efficient implementation.

In the analysis of the urban transport infrastructure, this chapter discusses the issue related to financial resources, often identified as a key factor impacting the implementation gap in developing countries. But financial constraints can be mitigated by a mixture of countermeasures, including better prioritization, improvement of cost recovery, and the introduction of private sector participation.

The analysis can also be extended to issues related to human resources. At 6.5 million employees, public sector employment as a share of population in Egypt is quite high, at a ratio of 1:13 compared with a world average of 1:30 and 1:80 in the case of Japan. The wage bill consumes more than one-quarter of Egypt's annual budget. In addition to its bloated size, the sector lacks a proper development program for staff, further exacerbating the human resource gaps facing the Egyptian bureaucratic system.

Except for the Ministry of Foreign Affairs and the Central Bank, as well as a handful of subsections within ministries, the public sector does not attract high-quality young candidates. Unlike many Asian countries, public sector jobs are generally not considered as elite posts but rather as posts for those who seek job security. This lowers the quality of the ministries and public sector institutions in general. Owing to the lack of capable technocrats, many ministries try to fill higher policymaking posts with temporary senior advisers, often from universities. These advisers are employed for certain periods of time and do not contribute much to the capacity development of ministries.

---

47. See Brinkerhoff and Crosby (2002).

Dimian and al-Mashat (2014) underline human resource development as critical to advancing policymaking and implementation in Egypt, proposing that it should work on two parallel axes: attracting highly qualified candidates to join ministries for policy management and other senior executive positions and developing the technical and managerial capacities of government staff through well-structured, long-term career development strategies.[48] In doing so, the mandate and technical capacity of the Central Agency for Organization and Administration should be reassessed and modernized.[49] Recent decisions in Egypt to place a cap on wages might discourage competent public sector employees to join.

In addition to the capacity gap in human resources, there is also a demographic problem. Owing to the excessive number of employees, many ministries have frozen recruitment, resulting in a distorted demography where most staff are over fifty years of age. In ten years, as current employees retire, this is likely to become a serious issue for ministries that lack younger employees. Equally, on the other hand, such decrease in the number of employees might offer a good opportunity to substantially reform public institutions. This process should be strategically planned and managed.

Monitoring and Evaluation

The lack of an effective and efficient monitoring and evaluation mechanism is a critical weakness in the Egyptian public system. On this, the majority of those interviewed for the research agreed. To increase the impact and quality of public investment and to promote better service delivery to the public, the monitoring and evaluating mechanism needs to be strengthened. This will have a positive impact on the enhancement of institutional capacity and accountability.

In Egypt, the Ministry of Planning, the National Investment Bank, the Central Auditing Organization, and the Center for Project Evaluation and Macroeconomic Analysis in the Ministry of International Cooperation are key agencies responsible for monitoring and evaluating public spending. The last of these undertakes comprehensive evaluation for donor-funded projects and programs. The other institutions

---

48. Dimian and al-Mashat (2014).
49. Dimian and al-Mashat (2014).

are mainly monitoring the spending of the budget or compliance with laws and regulations, not the developmental impact or performance.

Before the revolution, each five-year plan spared one chapter for analysis on the achievement of the previous five-year plan, but most of the analysis focused on how much money had been spent for each item compared with the original budget. Analysis of the performance of the plan was very weak. In the implementation cycle, it is important that lessons be fed back, both successes and failures, into the next cycle of implementation. An effective feedback system does not exist in Egypt.

Some countries such as the Philippines, Indonesia, and Malaysia have been trying to strengthen monitoring and evaluation mechanisms by introducing results-based management and budgeting, such as key performance indicators, for the public sector. Both the Philippines and Indonesia have made significant progress in establishing a results-oriented public sector management and performance-based budgeting mechanism, where linkages between planning and budgeting have been strengthened. Both countries installed a medium-term expenditure framework and set performance indicators to be monitored during implementation. In the case of Indonesia, the president established a special unit to monitor the progress of results and incentivize performance.[50]

Performance-based budgeting is also used in Malaysia. A whole machinery for monitoring and evaluating the implementation of five-year plans has been set up, coordinated by a special agency called the Implementation and Coordination Unit, which reports directly to the prime minister, while many agencies at the federal, state, and district levels involved in monitoring can coordinate through an online system known as the Project Monitoring System II.[51]

Currently in Egypt, the Ministry of Planning is trying to strengthen its monitoring capacity, an initiative that needs more attention and support. The ministry is trying to align individual projects under a specific program as an initial attempt to manage results. However, measuring results should not be an end in itself but rather a means to receiving feedback and improving performance, decisionmaking, and service delivery.

---

50. See Asia Pacific COP-MFDR (2011).
51. See Chia (2009).

Introduction of effective monitoring and evaluation mechanisms may enhance the capacity of public institutions as well as public officials. In a country like Egypt, where the top-down drive is strong, a results-oriented model of monitoring can be a good mechanism for creating peer pressure and incentivizing performance if it is linked with resource allocation.

In Malaysia, key performance indicators were developed to measure the performance of public organizations and civil servants and improve service delivery. Civil servants are required to prepare their targets and indicators, on which their performance is evaluated annually and based on that their salary raise and promotion are determined. At the organizational level, key performance indicators are used to measure the public institution's performance by evaluating efficiency and effectiveness of service delivery, financial productivity, and public satisfaction.[52]

The effectiveness of such a sophisticated system is nevertheless a matter of debate since, by its nature, public sector work is sometimes difficult to quantify. It is important for Egypt to learn from these experiences and to work on strengthening the public sector's capacity and accountability through a rigorous system of monitoring and evaluation.

Implementing Reform in a Transitional Period

In implementing the policy recommendations proposed here, the special circumstances facing Egypt today must be taken into consideration. After experiencing two political upheavals in the past few years, Egypt is still in a transitional period. The economy is still in recovery, and society remains volatile and disconnected from many economic, political, and social activities, particularly young people. This fluid situation might be a good chance for drastic change, but efforts need to be made to avoid creating more chaos. In considering the effective implementation of reform, we raise here a number of issues specific to Egypt's current circumstances.

First, policymakers and leaders need to have a strategic vision of the short-term and long-term actions, goals, and benefits of their development policies and plans. In the short term, it is quite natural that stability will be given the highest priority in policy deliberations. But the long-term future of the country should not be sacrificed in the pursuit

---

52. See Khalid (2010).

of short-term stability if it stifles the reform process. Egypt needs steady evolution, not revolution, with due consideration of both short-term and long-term goals and benefits.

Second, striking a balance between inclusiveness and efficiency is another challenge. As it was indicated by the Gallup opinion poll referenced in figure 2-1 in chapter 2, rapid growth over the previous decade, particularly from 2006 to 2010, did not bring an improvement in the way people viewed their well-being. One of the key factors leading to the revolutions was the sense of exclusion from the decisionmaking and economic development processes. Achieving inclusive growth should be a major goal of the new government. However, with greater inclusiveness come higher costs and slower processes.

Given the bitter experience of two turbulent political transitions, it is true that in the long run, it is better to involve as many stakeholders as possible. But inevitably this would slow the input process. Egypt's current situation is not business as usual, and in some cases it might be more efficient to go ahead with quick decisions and actions, if a clear goal and appropriate methodology can be identified, as was the case with the recent subsidy reform decision. If the government had postponed its decision until parliament was in place, such a drastic decision might have not been taken at all. Such decisions will make some people unhappy and draw criticism from others over their legitimacy, but as long as the long-term benefit is made clear to the people—in other words, inclusiveness in output—it might be justifiable to give efficiency and speed a higher priority. An extreme example of this can be seen in cases of natural disaster or war, in which efficiency and speed take precedence in order to save people's lives. Still, the government should not always use emergencies as justification for such decisions, and every effort must be made to realize benefits to the people after decisions are made.

Third, the new leaders need to tackle the psychological gaps among public officials regarding goals, decisions, and actions. Historically, Egypt has been a country with a highly centralized system in which the top-down decisionmaking drive is very strong. After the revolution in 2011, the propensity for risk aversion was even stronger, leading to delays in decisionmaking in every aspect. Many politicians and high-ranking government officials suspected of corruption were arrested or went into exile, leaving many ministers and technocrats afraid to make decisions and take actions. This risk-averse atmosphere resulted in longer delays to development projects than were the norm during the period preceding political turmoil.

The new president and prime minister seem to recognize the importance of decisive action, but many middle layers of the bureaucracy, as well as some ministers, seem to be still wondering which way to go. Clear messages should be conveyed by leaders that the public officials will be evaluated on their actions, not on inaction based on fear of making mistakes. Public officials need a greater sense of ownership for their decisions and actions. To change such a mindset is not an easy task, but without it things will not improve.

Conclusion

As the new Egyptian government strives to achieve inclusive growth and make the difficult transition to democracy, it needs to tackle diverse challenges on many fronts. It is grappling, on one hand, with the challenges created by instability in the wake of the revolutions and, on the other, with the historic challenges that have plagued Egypt for so many years.

Underlying this research is the simple fact that though Egypt has many master plans and strategies, few of them have ever been implemented. There is no shortage of ideas regarding what to do but not nearly enough attention paid to how to do, the implementation process. The lack of implementation has been affecting the declining trend of public investment. Though rapid GDP growth was achieved during 2006–10, it did not improve the perceptions most people held regarding their livelihood. Infrastructure and public services were deteriorating, and the development process was not inclusive in either inputs or outputs. This was a crucial factor that led people to take to the street to topple the two governments.

Today, the launch of so many initiatives and strategies by the new government is gradually improving the people's perceptions of their well-being and raising their expectations for the future and for change. The government needs to make every effort to deliver on these expectations in the future. To that end, leaders need to make the machinery of government function more effectively and efficiently. Comprehensive public sector management and institutional reform will be indispensable.

This research identifies the areas in which the new government must effect reform, but this needs even wider and deeper analysis in the current Egyptian context. Such reform needs to be tackled as comprehensively as possible, since even if reform is achieved in one phase of the cycle, if gaps in other phases are more fundamental obstacles, the desired result may not be achieved. Egypt is a country with a great history and tremendous resources and potential. Unfortunately, such resources and potential have not been used and realized in the past several decades. With the new leadership in place, now is the time for implementation. The time has come for Egypt to move from revolution to evolution with steady action.

References

Asia Pacific COP-MFDR. 2011. *Framework for Results-Based Public Sector Management and Country Cases.* Asia Pacific Community of Practice on Managing for Development Results.

Brinkerhoff, D., and B. Crosby. 2002. *Managing Policy Reform: Concepts and Tools for Decisionmakers in Developing and Transitional Countries.* Bloomfield, Ill.: Kumarian Press.

Brynard, P. A. 2005. "Policy Implementation: Lessons for Service Delivery." Paper prepared for the Twenty-seventh AAPAM Annual Roundtable Conference. Livingstone, Zambia: African Association for Public Administration and Management.

Cairo Regional Area Transportation Study. 2002. Cairo: Arab Republic of Egypt and Japan International Cooperation Agency.

Center for Effective Services. 2012. *An Introductory Guide to Implementation: Terms, Concepts, and Frameworks.*

Center for International Private Enterprise and Global Integrity. 2012. *Improving Public Governance, Closing the Implementation Gap between Law and Practice.* Washington.

Chia, D. P. M. 2009. "Evaluation of Public Sector Performance: The Malaysian Experience." Paper prepared for the International Conference on Management for Development Results. Sri Lanka Evaluation Association in collaboration with the Ministry of Plan Implementation, Sri Lanka. April 22–23.

Commission on Growth and Development. 2008. *The Growth Report: Strategies for Sustained Growth and Inclusive Development.* Washington: World Bank.

Coordinating Ministry for Economic Affairs of the Republic of Indonesia (CMEA) and Japan International Cooperation Agency (JICA). 2012. *Master Plan for Establishing Metropolitan Priority Area for Investment and Industry in Jabodetabek Area in the Republic of Indonesia.*

Dabla-Norris, E., and others. 2011. "Investing in Public Investment: An Index of Public Investment Efficiency." Working Paper WP/11/37. Washington: International Monetary Fund (February).

Demographia World Urban Areas. 2014. 10th ed. Belleville, Ill.: Demographia.

Devarajan, S. 2014. *It's Not the How, It's the Why*. Future Development blog. Washington: World Bank (http://blogs.worldbank. org/futuredevelopment/ it-s-not-how-it-s-why).

Dimian H., and R. al-Mashat. 2014. *Helping Advance the Economic Policy Management Process in Egypt: Initial Institutional Reforms for the Executive Branch*. New York: Rockefeller Brothers Fund and Japan International Cooperation Agency.

Government of Egypt. 1973. Law No. 70 Regarding the Preparation of the General Plan of the State and Follow Up of Its Execution. *Egyptian Official Gazette*, no. 34 (August 23).

International Institute for Sustainable Development. 2012. *A Forum for South East Asian Policymakers on Fossil-Fuel Subsidy Reform: Challenges and Opportunities*. Manitoba.

International Monetary Fund. 2014a. *Subsidy Reform in the Middle East and North Africa: Recent Progress and Challenges*. CMEA.

———. 2014b. *World Economic Outlook* database. October.

Japan International Cooperation Agency (JICA). 2011. *The Research on a Practical Approach for Urban Transport Planning*.

Japan International Cooperation Agency (JICA), National Development Planning Agency (BAPPENAS), and Republic of Indonesia. 2004. *The Study on Integrated Transportation Master Plan for Jabodetabek*. Jakarta.

Kaufmann, Daniel, Aart Kraay, and Massimo Mastruzzi. 2010. "The Worldwide Governance Indicators: Methodology and Analytical Issues." Policy Research Working Paper 5430. Washington: World Bank.

Kawaguchi, H., and others. 2013. "Cross-Sector Transportation Authority for Jakarta Metropolitan Area." *Proceedings of the Eastern Asia Society for Transportation Studies*, vol. 9. Tokyo: Eastern Asia Society for Transportation Studies.

Khalid, S.-N. A. 2010. *Improving the Service Delivery: A Case Study of a Local Authority in Malaysia Global Business Review*. Thousand Oaks, Calif.: Sage Publications.

Kharas, H., and others. 2012. *After the Spring: Economic Transitions in the Arab World*. Oxford University Press.

KPMG International Cooperative. 2010. *Success and Failure in Urban Transport Infrastructure Project*.

Kumar, A., and O. Agarwal. 2013. *"Institutional Labyrinth": Designing a Way Out for Improving Urban Transport Services; Lessons from Current Practice*. Washington: World Bank.

Loayza, N. V., and A. Odawara. 2010. "Infrastructure and Economic Growth in Egypt." Policy Research Working Paper 5177. Washington: World Bank (January).

Lursen, T., and A. B. Myers. 2009. "Public Investment Management in New EU Member States." Working Paper 161. Washington: World Bank (February).

Mandri-Perrott, C. 2010. *Private Sector Participation in Light Rail: Light Metro Transit Initiatives*. Washington: World Bank.

Meyers, D., and others. 2012. "The Quality Implementation Framework: A Synthesis of Critical Steps in the Implementation Process." Society for Community Research and Action.

Ministry of Transport, Transport Planning Authority, and the Japan International Cooperation Agency. 2012. Misr National Transport Study. 2012. Cairo.

Ohno, I., and M. Shimamura. 2007. *Managing the Development Process and Aid: The East Asian Experience in Building Central Economic Agencies*. GRIPS Development Forum. Tokyo: Graduate Institute for Policy Studies.

Organization for Economic Cooperation and Development. 2010. *Making Reforms Happen: Lessons from OECD Countries*. Paris.

Peterson, G. E. 2009. *Unlocking Land Values to Finance Urban Infrastructure*. Washington: World Bank.

Petrie, M. 2010. "Promoting Public Investment Efficiency: A Synthesis of Country Experiences." Paper prepared for the World Bank Preparatory Workshop, Promoting Public Investment Efficiency Global Lessons and Resources for Strengthening World Bank Support for Client Countries. Washington: World Bank, July 7.

Singh, M., and R. Sharma. 2012. *Financing Options for Transit System through Real Estate: The Case of Rohini Subcity, Delhi*. The Hague, Neth.: Association for European Transport and Contributors.

World Bank. 2000. *Study on Urban Transport Development*. Washington.

———. 2004. *Making Service Work for Poor People*. World Bank Development Report. Washington.

———. 2012. *Cairo Traffic Is Much More Than a Nuisance*. Washington.

———. 2014. *Cairo Traffic Congestion Study*. Washington.

Zegras, C. 2006. "Private Sector Participation in Urban Transport Infrastructure Provision." Module 1c in *Sustainable Transport: A Sourcebook for Policymakers in Developing Cities*. Bonn, Ger.: Federal Ministry for Economic Cooperation and Development.

5

Youth Employment and Economic Transition in Tunisia

MONGI BOUGHZALA

Tunisia has undergone a seismic political shock that led to the collapse of its previous autocratic regime and to the transition to democracy. The ongoing transformation of political, social, and economic institutions gave birth to a more democratic government but the situation remains politically fragile and economically highly uncertain. The demands for decent jobs, justice, and a better and more inclusive government are not yet satisfied, and youth, who have been the main driving force of this historic transformation, are still frustrated and angry.

Transitions to more inclusive political and economic systems take time as countries struggle to build new democratic institutions and develop a culture of dialogue and compromise that is necessary for democracy to succeed. It is also normal that economies stagnate in postrevolutionary periods because investors consider that risks are greater and prefer to wait until the country stabilizes, but prolonged economic stagnation could jeopardize Tunisia's democratic transition. Youth employment remains the biggest challenge for the country and a crucial condition for a successful transition to democracy. This transition would be hard to sustain without the empowerment of youth and their participation in national policymaking and decisionmaking.

The unemployment problem is not new and certainly not specific to the Arab Spring countries, and it has no easy solution. In Tunisia, unemployment has been persistent because the economy has not been creating sufficient jobs for the rapidly growing number of young people, especially young women, joining the working force every year. The problem has been made more difficult by the fact that educated youth expect good jobs and are not satisfied with the low-productivity, low-wage jobs offered by the private informal sector that are easier to find. They would rather queue up for formal and decent (in the International Labor Organization's sense) jobs currently offered primarily by the public sector. The rebellious unemployed youth expect the government to respond to their legitimate demands and to offer them new opportunities.

Indeed, in the short run, the government has to do something about it: responding to youth through a credible employment program is a necessary condition for the success of the democratic transition. However, obviously the government and the public sector cannot provide jobs for all the unemployed and for the ever-increasing youth population. Strategically, in the medium and long run, developing the formal private sector will be the main sustainable way to meet their aspirations and to allow them to participate gradually, but more massively, in the process of economic and political development.

This chapter is about youth unemployment, inequalities, and private sector development as a way to promote inclusive growth and decent job creation.

Youth Unemployment and Inequalities

In Tunisia, unemployment had been persistently high for more than two decades preceding the 2010 revolution and remains high today. Until 2010 the rate was often above 14 percent, and between January 2011 and May 2012, about 200,000 additional jobs were lost and the unemployment rate reached its highest level at 19 percent. By 2014 the economy had recovered partially and this rate diminished but remained high at around 15 percent.

Youth, between fifteen and thirty years old, make up about one-third of the labor force and three-quarters of the unemployed. On average, but with important disparities, their unemployment rate is above 30 percent. This rate is higher for young women and in poorer regions, especially in the west of the country. There is a wide consensus that angry unemployed youth, in a context of regional disparity and increasing corruption and poverty, triggered the popular revolts and led to the fall of the previous dictatorial regime in Tunisia (as in the other

TABLE 5-1. Structure of the Labor Force, by Education Attainment, 1966–2011

Percent

Education level	1966	1975	1984	1994	2001	2006	2011
High	1.2	1.4	3.3	7	10	15	17
Intermediate (high school and vocational)	7.1	12.8	20	29	30	31	38
Low (primary or none)	91.7	85.7	76.8	64	60	54	45

Source: Tunisian Statistical Institute, Labor Surveys, 2001–11, and population censuses, 1966, 1975, 1984, 1994.

Arab Spring countries). This structural unemployment is the outcome of both supply and demand effects, including the inefficient functioning of the labor market.

The Supply Side of the Labor Market

On the supply side, the demographic pressure is high owing to the rapidly increasing size of the labor force, which is expected to continue to increase for the coming decade (2014–23), despite slowing population growth. The annual rate of population growth is nearing 1 percent (1.03 in 2014), while the labor force keeps growing at 2 percent or more, primarily owing to the likely increase of female participation in the labor market. Moreover, the Tunisian labor force is increasingly educated; the number of university graduates has been rising rapidly as a result of the open and free access to higher education. The proportion of the labor force with university degrees was less than 4 percent in 1984 and less than 7 percent in 1994 but jumped to 13 percent in 2004 and to more than 16 percent in 2010, and then to 17 percent in 2011. The proportion of the educated (those with at least secondary or vocational education attainment) in the total labor force was at 55 percent in 2011 (see table 5-1).

While free and open access to education has led to a large stock of human capital, it has come at the expense of the quality of education and training, and this is certainly a major issue. The skills acquired by this growing labor force are not always adequate. Education has not been designed to impart appropriate skills enabling individuals to move up the value chain and to ensure the transition toward a more productive economy.

The Demand Side

On the demand side, the economy's capacity to create jobs, especially good jobs, and attractive opportunities has been weak, well below the expectations of job seekers. Economic growth has not been adequate, and the demand for skilled and educated labor is limited. Investment has been predominantly concentrated in low-value-added, low-wage, labor-intensive activities based on low-level technologies. Consequently, the demand for more-educated, less-experienced youth is the lowest in the labor pool. The demand is even lower for women and for those living in the poorer hinterland region located mainly in the western regions of the country. These regions are poorer in terms of infrastructure, access to international harbors and ports, and human capital availability. Hence they have been the least attractive for investments and entrepreneurial opportunities and have the least diversified productive activities.

Skill mismatch is also an important factor underlying the low level of employment, and Tunisian employers often complain about the lack of employees with the right abilities. However, although skill mismatch is currently an issue, it has been less important as an explanatory factor of unemployment. The weakness in the overall demand for skills is the main factor. Based on data from the Tunisian national employment agency, only a small share of vacancies are hard to fill. For example, 86.7 percent of the vacancies are filled in less than a month, and another 8.2 percent in less than three months. For no more than 5.1 percent of the vacancies, it takes longer than three months to identify the right match (table 5-2). It is also a fact that the majority of enterprises, including large firms, invest very little in training their staff, implying that they can find the skills they need at a lower cost in the marketplace.

The hard-to-fill vacancies are concentrated in a few domains:
—electromechanical engineering
—electromechanical technicians
—computer science engineering
—maintenance
—technical marketing, including e-marketing

There has also always been an issue with seasonal unemployment. This is an important issue but not essential from the perspective of this chapter.

TABLE 5-2. Job Vacancy Duration

Duration (months)	Frequency (percent)	Cumulative percentage
0–1	86.7	86.7
2–3	8.2	94.9
3–9	4.1	99.2
10–28	1.0	100

Source: Agence Nationale de l'Emploi et du Travail Indépendant (ANETI, Tunisia Employment Agency) database and author's calculations.

Labor market regulations (especially those that limit firms' ability to downsize) are restrictive, in spite of revisions of the labor code in 1994 and 1996, which introduced more flexibility for employers. These and other constraints to investments (access to financial resources, for instance) and enterprise creation are a more serious concern and put a significant limitation on labor demand (see World Bank, *Doing Business in Tunisia* 2012, 2013, and 2015). As a result, enforcement of labor laws and regulations is very weak. Only large firms respect them, while a sizable informal sector widely escapes regulation and leaves employees with little protection.

Therefore, revising the current regulations, including reaching a more appropriate balance between flexibility and protection of workers' rights, is a major challenge for the current and coming governments and for a successful economic and political transition.

Unemployment by Education Level

Educated youth are asking for better and more decent jobs. Yet in the current situation the higher the education level, the lower the probability for a young person to find a job. The unemployment rate increases with higher education levels and is highest for those with university degrees. Across the labor force, the unemployment rate for university graduates was above 22 percent in 2014 and above 30 percent for young university graduates (table 5-3). The number of the unemployed with university degrees was close to 220,000 in 2014, out of around 600,000 unemployed in total.

However, there are even larger numbers of unemployed young people with a secondary education (more than 300,000). Although their unemployment rate is lower than those with higher education, they are

TABLE 5-3. Evolution of the Unemployment Rate by Education Attainment, 2005–11

Percent

Education attainment	2005	2007	2009	May 2011
None	6.3	4.4	6.1	8.0
Primary	14.3	11.5	10.4	12.4
Secondary	13.3	13.5	14.0	20.6
Higher	14.0	17.2	21.9	22.2

Source: Tunisian Statistical Institute, Labor Survey, 2011.

arguably the most desperate, because they generally can only hope for low-wage informal jobs with very little job security. They are also the most likely to keep protesting if their demands are not heard.

Currently, close to 40 percent of the unemployed wait at least one year before finding a job. On average, the more educated who queue up for formal sector jobs wait much longer (figure 5-1).

Income Distribution Inequality

Several observers state that Tunisia's revolution was a revolt against inequality and injustice. However, the data do not indicate an increase in inequality over time. Over the past four decades the average income (measured by the average household or per capita expenditure) has increased while inequality, measured by the Gini coefficient, continuously and significantly decreased. The poverty rate has also decreased as confirmed by the results released in 2012 by INS (INS 2012) and based on recent calculations using a readjusted poverty line. The headcount poverty rate declined from 32.4 percent in 2000 to 23.3 percent in 2005 and then to 15.5 percent in 2010.

The size of the Tunisian middle class has also increased, especially in the past decade. According to the Brookings Institution's database, the middle class reached more than 40 percent of the total population in 2010; it was 25 percent in 2000, less than 15 percent in 1985, and less than 10 percent in 1970 (figure 5-2).[1] The Tunisian Statistical Institute confirms this result. It finds that the size of the middle class

---

1. The Brookings database defines the middle class as "those households spending between $10 and $100 per person per day in [purchasing power parity] terms."

FIGURE 5-1.   Unemployment Duration, 2010

Percent of total labor force unemployed

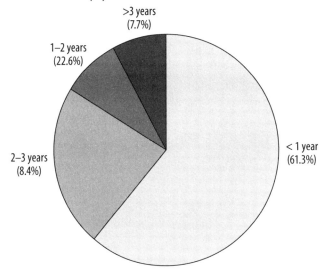

Source: Tunisian Statistical Institute data, Labor Survey, 2010.

FIGURE 5-2.   Income Distribution and the Middle Class (1965–2010)

Middle class as percent of total population

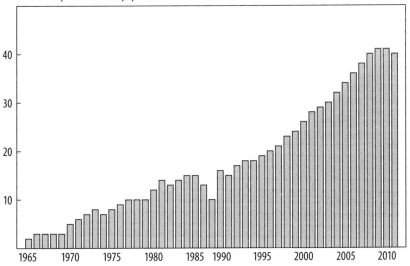

Source: Brookings database.

changed from 70.5 percent in 1995, to 77.6 percent in 2000, and to 81.1 percent in 2005.

If poverty and inequality have decreased overall, what then triggered the Tunisian revolution? Lack of opportunities for youth seems to have been a key driver. As shown earlier, youth face high unemployment, and those who do find jobs usually end up with low-wage informal sector jobs. Poor governance is another important driver. Tunisia ranks low in corruption control and in the area of voice and accountability. That politically connected groups (including relatives of the first family) were able to increase their wealth because of special privileges, while thousands of educated youth were unemployed or forced to accept informal work, fueled popular anger and frustration. Feeling excluded from the economic life of their country, young people also were politically excluded. Lack of democratic rights and institutions allowing them to voice their opinions left youth with revolution as the only option.

Regional and Gender Inequality

Despite the overall decrease in income inequality unemployed youth, especially those from the hinterland poor regions, have ample reasons for revolting. All indicators confirm that regional disparities have been large and persistent: unemployment, income level, and poverty by region show that the western regions are poorer and provide many fewer opportunities to the population and to youth, who have the hardest time finding a job or starting a business. Per capita income (expenditure) in the wealthiest region, the Tunis region, has been around twice that of the poorest regions, which alternate between the northwestern and center-western regions (table 5-4), and the poverty rate is three times higher in the poorest region (table 5-5).

Unemployment rates and duration of unemployment are higher for youth and particularly for women in the poorer regions. Women in particular are the least fortunate. More generally, unemployment, poverty, and lack of opportunities are much higher in the west and the south of the country, including in the Sidi Bouzid and Kasserine area and for women. For instance, the unemployment rate is 22.5 percent in the governorate of Kasserine, and 24 percent in Jendouba and Siliana, compared with 13 percent at the national level. Gafsa (20.1 percent), Sidi Bouzid, Kébili, and Jendouba (24.5 percent) have the highest unemployment rates for university graduates (compared with the national average

TABLE 5-4. Evolution of Per Capita Expenditure, by Region, 1980–2010

	1980	1985	1990	1995	2000	2005	2010
Tunis district	403	725	1,007	1,289	1,761	2,390	3,228
Northeast	239	450	760	958	1,190	1,613	2,113
Northwest	169	284	501	677	1,103	1,416	1,613
Center-west	168	324	502	586	909	1,138	1,496
Center-east	255	544	806	1,275	1,594	1,826	2,693
South	235	382	570	728	1,066	1,700	2,060
National average	248	471	716	966	1,329	1,820	2,360

Source: Tunisian Statistical Institute, Household Expenditure and Budget Surveys, 1980–2010.

TABLE 5-5. Evolution of the Poverty Rate, by Region, 2000–10

Percent

	Poverty			Extreme poverty		
Area	2000	2005	2010	2000	2005	2010
Tunisia total	32.4	23.3	15.5	12.0	7.6	4.6
Large cities	21.5	15.4	9.0	4.3	2.2	1.3
Medium-size cities	32.5	22.1	14.0	10.5	6.5	2.9
Rural	40.4	31.5	22.6	19.1	13.4	9.2
Tunis district	21.0	14.6	9.1	4.3	2.3	1.1
Northeast	32.1	21.6	10.3	10.5	5.4	1.8
Northwest	35.3	26.9	25.7	12.1	8.9	8.8
Center-east	21.4	12.6	8.0	6.4	2.6	1.6
Center-west	49.3	46.5	32.3	25.5	23.2	14.3
Southeast	44.3	29.0	17.9	17.5	9.6	4.9
Southwest	47.8	33.2	21.5	21.7	12.1	6.4

Source: Tunisian Statistical Institute, "Mesure de la pauvreté et des inégalités en Tunisie 2000–10" (www.ins.tn).

of 23 percent) (figure 5-3). Most of these regions remain highly dependent on agriculture, which provides mostly seasonal, low-skill, and
low-wage employment and is not attractive for youth. Unemployment
and poverty strengthened the sentiment of exclusion and discrimination among the populations of the poorer regions, who have developed
a strong belief that their situation is caused by a biased public policy and regional distribution of public investments. Public investments
were indeed concentrated in the coastal regions, and consequently few

FIGURE 5-3. Unemployment Rate, by Governorates, 2007

Percent

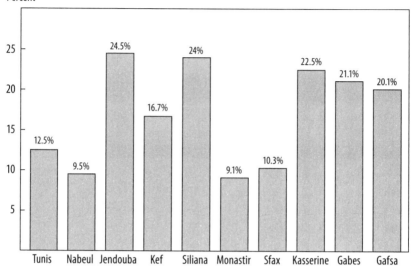

Source: Tunisian Statistical Institute data, Labor Survey, 2007.

private investments are located in these regions. Their populations continue to strongly voice their anger and to demand a fairer distribution
of public investments. Combating unemployment in these regions will
require long-term structural reforms to improve productivity and to
facilitate the creation of new innovative enterprises.

The Gender Bias

Gender bias is a serious concern in Tunisia. Although access to schools
at all levels is equally available for males and females, the numbers of
female students have surpassed those of males. More than 60 percent
of university graduates are females, but the rate of female participation
in the labor force (27 percent in 2011) remains much lower than men's
(70 percent). The unemployment rate for females is also much higher
(nearly twice as high and 19 percent before the revolution). And when
employed, women often receive lower pay.

This bias is stronger for female university graduates, whose unemployment rate across the country (32 percent) is double that for male
university graduates (16 percent). In many regions, the unemployment

TABLE 5-6. Tunisia: World Bank Doing Business Indicators Ranking, 2011 and 2012

	2011	2012	Change
Overall ranking	46	40	−6
Topic ranking			
Starting a business	56	46	−10
Dealing with construction permits	86	85	−1
Getting electricity	45	46	+1
Registering property	65	60	−5
Getting credit	98	96	−2
Protecting investors	46	44	−2
Paying taxes	64	61	−3
Trading across borders	32	31	−1
Enforcing contracts	76	78	+2
Resolving insolvency	38	37	−1

Source: World Bank, *Doing Business*, 2012.

rate for female graduates is above 50 percent. More generally, fewer opportunities are open to women because their mobility is more restricted because of the social constraints and responsibilities imposed on them. They are more likely to accept low- or lower-wage jobs as long as they can stay near home.

Private Sector Development

Despite the relatively good ranking of Tunisia in the World Bank's *Doing Business* report (40th of 183 countries in 2011) (table 5-6), the domestic private sector development remains below expectations. Over the past two decades, Tunisia has undertaken important reforms, including administrative and fiscal changes, and provided incentives for enterprise creation (the investment incentives Law 93-120 passed in 1993), which attracted substantial amounts of foreign direct investment. Despite all these performances, reforms, and actions, Tunisia's private investment remained relatively small—around 15 percent of GDP and less than 60 percent of total investments. The uncertainty and instability following the revolution has depressed private investments further.

Moreover, there has been a significant gap between rules and facts, leaving room for deals, abuses, lack of transparency, and corruption. The business environment (table 5-6) has been plagued by corruption and many other imperfections and uncertainties and has not been conducive to substantial investment and enterprise creation, especially small and medium enterprises (SMEs).

A key economic challenge for Tunisia today is to improve the business environment to increase investments and to create more and better businesses able to create more attractive employment opportunities for youth. Private investments remain modest quantitatively and at the bottom level of the technological scale. In most sectors, even the most competitive firms were clearly unable to move up the value chain or to improve their productivity fast enough. They have not succeeded in switching from labor-intensive, low-wage activities to more capital- and skill-intensive ones.

The aim of this section is to analyze past trends in enterprise development in Tunisia in order to try to understand why private sector development has been below expectations. It is also a preliminary step toward designing a new strategy in favor of more rapid development and better opportunities for youth.

In the literature dealing with private sector development, many people, especially at the World Bank (Ramsden 2011), argue that the best way to create opportunities for youth is to focus on small and medium enterprises. The pro-SME advocates argue that SMEs not only enhance competition and entrepreneurship because they are easier to establish than large enterprises, but also are more productive and can boost employment and alleviate poverty more effectively than larger firms because they are presumably more labor intensive. Advocates also argue that SMEs can create better-quality and more-stable jobs. However, this view is challenged by many skeptics (for example, Schmitter 1974), who emphasize the benefits of large firms, which allow for economies of scale, create even better and more-stable jobs, and are likely to be more competitive in the international marketplace with more exports. The most reasonable view is that, for any given economy, the optimal enterprise structure should include and combine all sizes of businesses and that the proportion of SMEs will depend on many variables, mainly the country's endowment of land, labor, and capital, its technological capacities, and its trade policies.

TABLE 5-7. Distribution of Employment between Public and Private Sectors

Thousands of persons

Sector	2006	2007	2008	2009	2010	2011
Public	677.9	684.9	687.0	692.9	693.4	695.6
Private	2327.0	2400.2	2468.4	2506.0	2584.0	2444.2
Total	3004.9	3085.1	3155.4	3198.9	3277.4	3139.8

Source: Tunisian Statistical Institute, data provided directly to author.

The Role of SMEs

How have SMEs performed in Tunisia, and to what extent do they confirm pro-SMEs arguments? In Tunisia, we define large enterprises as those employing 200 persons or more and SMEs as those employing between 10 and 200.

The Tunisian economy is predominantly private. Although some of the largest and most important enterprises of the country remain state owned, the size of the public sector—including the state-owned enterprises and the government—has been rather modest and stable for the past decade (table 5-7). The share of employment in the public sector was 22 percent in 2011, corresponding to a little less than 700,000 persons as indicated in table 5-7, and GDP was around 25 percent based on the author's calculations and INS data. The public sector's role is still dominant only in three specific sectors: energy and utilities (100 percent of total employment), banking and mining, and, significant but less important, community services and communications. Agriculture, manufacturing, construction, and trade are all predominantly private as well as business services, transport and communications, and tourism. Most of the private sector enterprises are small or micro family-owned enterprises (table 5-7).

Informal Sector

The informal sector, consisting mainly of small businesses (micro enterprises), is actually the largest and the fastest growing at a 5.1 percent annual rate, compared with 2.1 percent for larger enterprises. Exhibiting a great deal of heterogeneity, micro enterprises are the least structured of businesses and the most volatile and uncertain, and they generate mostly low-quality, informal jobs. Based on the most recent national micro enterprise survey conducted in 2007, 98 percent employ no more than two persons, and 87 percent employ only one individual (the employer).[2] Total employment of the informal micro enterprise sector is little more than 500,000 people, 80 percent of whom are men. This is about 16 percent of the country's total workforce and includes only about 5 percent of wage-earning employees, often making a little less than the minimum legal wage (slightly less than 250 Tunisian dinars [TND] a month in 2007) and without any social security. Female employees earn 30 percent less than male employees (TND 182 for women and TND 262 for men in 2007). Even within this micro enterprise category, wage is positively correlated with the size of the enterprise.

The remainder of the informal sector workforce is predominantly self-employed persons whose average income is more than twice the average wage but with a wide variation. Some 80 percent have a primary or secondary education, and 10 percent have a higher education. Micro enterprises cover a large spectrum of activities but are concentrated in food, retail commerce, construction, transportation, and automobile repair (table 5-8). Micro firms have limited access to formal financing, which covers less than 10 percent of their investment; they are mainly self-financed (close to 90 percent of investments). They also have limited access to new technologies. Only a minority (less than 10 percent) have access to the Internet. Their rate of survival is rather low as indicated by table 5-9, which shows that the older these firms are the smaller is the number of people they employ. Therefore, it is no surprise that their productivity is lower and that they are not attractive for educated youth looking for employment—unless they are themselves the entrepreneurs.

Nevertheless, as in many other countries, SMEs are actually the backbone of the Tunisian private sector. Although their number is just 2.5 percent of the total number of firms, they generate about one-third of total employment and account for 43 percent of salaried employees. Yet the environment in which they operate is not always conducive to their growth and development, mainly because of the regulatory framework, fiscal treatment, worker-employer qualification and attitude, and access to finance. Actually, SMEs form an extremely heterogeneous set. The small enterprises (with 10 to 50 employees), which are by far the

---

2. "Enquête sur les Micro Entreprises en 2007," Tunisian Statistical Institute.

TABLE 5-8. Micro Enterprises, by Activity and Sector, 2007

Number of micro enterprises

Division	Sector	Females	Males	Total
14	Other extractive industries	11	379	389
15	Food	2,460	16,235	18,695
17	Textiles	1,463	834	2,297
18	Clothing and fur	6,685	4,059	10,744
19	Leather and shoes	929	3,239	4,168
20	Carpentry	186	10,105	10,291
22	Publishing, printing, and copying	711	2,141	2,852
24	Chemical	197	717	914
25	Plastics	51	138	189
26	Nonmetallic mineral products manufacturing	260	4,156	4,416
27	Metallurgical		468	468
28	Metalwork	54	12,078	12,132
29	Machinery and equipment production	6	581	587
31	Electrical machinery and equipment production	8	573	581
32	Radio, television, and communication equipment	10	131	141
33	Medical, precision, optical instruments, and watches production	156	317	473
34	Auto production		107	107
35	Manufacturing of other materials in the transport industry	39	613	652
36	Furniture manufacturing; other industries	189	6,849	7,038
37	Recycling	265	347	612
41	Water resource management	2	25	27
45	Construction	181	11,966	12,147
50	Auto business and repair	288	23,655	23,943
51	Wholesale	435	13,205	13,640
52	Retail business and repair of household goods	40,491	130,483	170,974
55	Hotels and restaurants	4,702	38,835	43,537
60	Ground transportation	1,710	66,410	68,120
61	Maritime transportation		28	28
63	Transportation auxiliary services	217	758	975
64	Telecommunication and postal services	5,821	7,383	13,204
66	Insurance	61	72	133
67	Financial and insurance auxiliaries	220	279	499
70	Real estate	358	1,426	1,784
71	Dry hire (rentals without operators)	1,572	2,012	3,584
72	Information technology	1,341	2,159	3,500
74	Business-oriented services	7,560	11,051	18,611
80	Education	5,114	3,743	8,857
85	Health and social services	10,403	5,115	15,518
90	Sanitation, roads, and waste management	30	531	561
92	Recreational, cultural, and sports activities	618	3,507	4,125
93	Personal services	9,544	16,214	25,758
Total		104,347	402,924	507,271

Source: Tunisian Statistical Institute, "Enquête sur les Micro Entreprises en 2007."

TABLE 5-9. Employment, by Size and Age of Enterprise, 1996–2010

Age of enterprise (years in business)	Number of employees										Total	Share
	1	2	3–4	5–9	10–49	49–50	50–99	100–199	200–999	≥1,000		
1	37,843	2,773	1,697	1,543	1,269	1,676	1,354	1,012	1,785	74	51,026	3.72
2	33,123	3,789	3,456	3,839	3,437	5,027	4,364	4,197	7,203	2,333	70,767	5.16
3	29,763	3,766	3,518	4,145	3,683	5,788	5,178	5,995	9,080	3,731	74,647	5.44
4	27,058	3,588	3,371	4,066	3,756	5,807	5,596	6,547	10,745	4,922	75,456	5.50
5	24,757	3,385	3,139	3,958	3,518	5,498	5,080	6,248	9,796	4,794	70,173	5.12
6	22,742	3,213	2,969	3,752	3,554	5,260	5,034	6,393	8,751	3,148	64,813	4.73
7	20,828	3,033	2,868	3,592	3,456	5,012	4,987	6,064	9,092	3,101	62,044	4.52
8	19,102	2,917	2,685	3,420	3,350	4,882	4,958	6,494	8,432	2,632	58,871	4.29
9	17,319	2,728	2,558	3,249	3,185	4,676	4,758	6,195	8,822	2,801	56,290	4.10
10	15,598	2,506	2,430	3,067	3,008	4,417	4,406	6,137	8,492	2,204	52,264	3.81
11–15	57,612	10,958	10,318	12,624	12,641	18,243	17,652	24,096	40,619	7,788	212,551	15.50
16–20	32,379	7,860	7,869	8,849	8,799	13,621	13,430	17,728	34,325	9,045	153,906	11.22
21–30	27,506	7,477	8,241	9,375	9,483	15,570	16,173	23,334	53,567	31,639	202,365	14.75
≥30	8,229	2,586	2,880	3,949	4,303	7,474	10,135	16,875	49,627	60,360	166,419	12.13
Total	373,858	60,579	57,999	69,427	67,453	102,950	103,105	137,314	260,334	138,573	1,371,592	
Share	27.26	4.42	4.23	5.06	4.92	7.51	7.52	10.01	18.98	10.10		

Source: Tunisian Statistical Institute data, annual average, provided directly to the author.

TABLE 5-10. Firm Size and Employment Distributions, 1996–2010

Firm size (number of workers)	Number of firms	Percent of firms	Number of jobs	Percent of employment	Percent firms cumulative	Percent employment cumulative
1	344,684	83.30	345,753	28.18	83.30	28.18
2	29,318	7.46	56,290	4.76	90.76	32.94
3–4	16,505	4.07	53,696	4.44	94.83	37.38
5–9	10,223	2.52	64,010	5.29	97.35	42.67
10–19	4,657	1.15	61,661	5.12	98.50	47.79
20–49	3,077	0.77	94,056	7.83	99.27	55.62
50–99	1,362	0.34	95,241	7.92	99.61	63.54
100–199	898	0.23	126,078	10.55	99.84	74.09
200–999	636	0.16	228,812	18.93	100.00	93.02
1,000 or more	51	0.01	86,874	6.98	100.00	100.00
Total	405,843		1,191,822		100.00	100.00

Source: Ministry of Planning and Regional Development, based on the yearly Firm Survey data, annual average, provided directly to the author.

majority among SMEs, are likely to be closer to the informal sector and keep many informal features, in particular in their human resources management, while the larger category behaves more like modern and formal enterprises. The larger the size, the closer they are to formality. Since half of the Tunisian SMEs are really small and employ fewer than 20 persons, and one-quarter employ between 20 and 50 persons, informality is widespread among SMEs. In 2010 only 2,613 enterprises out of 11,242 SMEs employed between 50 and 200 persons each and qualified as medium enterprises and, presumably, fully formal enterprises.

Altogether, smaller SMEs (employing fewer than 50 persons) account for 75 percent of the total number of SMEs and less than 20 percent of wage-earning employment, much less than the larger SMEs, which provide 25 percent. Comparatively, fewer than 1,000 large firms provide more than 40 percent of wage-earning employment, and if large firms are combined with larger SMEs (50 workers or more), they still comprise fewer than 2,500 enterprises but offer 66 percent of private sector jobs (around 650,000 out of a total of nearly one million), which are also the most stable occupations. This means that larger firms create relatively more jobs, which challenges the idea that SMEs are best at creating jobs (table 5-10).

TABLE 5-11. Average Productivity, by Firm Size, 2006[a]

Number of employees	LnMean	LnMedian
10–19	18.14	18.03
20–19	18.04	17.98
50–99	17.94	17.91
100–199	17.82	17.79
200–999	17.62	17.65
1,000 or more	17.28	17.48

Source: Ministry of Planning and Regional Development, provided directly to the author.
a. Productivity measured at Ln(productivity/employee).

However, in terms of productivity, medium-size private firms in Tunisia outperform (table 5-11) and create more value added than large firms. On average, medium firms are more capital intensive than the large private firms, and they consequently generate more value added. This reflects the higher concentration in Tunisia of large private firms in highly labor-intensive activities such as textiles and clothing, whereas the medium firms are in more diversified activities. Medium-size private firms are more productive and more capital intensive than the large ones, but this situation is specific and may be reversed as the structure is changing.

Indeed, the highest proportion of large firms have been in textiles and clothing, but this proportion is decreasing while the share of the electric and electronic (EEI) manufacturing sector, which is more capital and skill intensive and where productivity is higher, is increasing. In 2005, out of a total number of large manufacturing firms, 202 were in textiles and clothing and 55 in EEI; in 2010 the number of firms in textiles and clothing dropped to 171, those of EEI firms rose to 79. The value added by a worker in the EEI sector is equal to TND 45,840 and is much higher than the manufacturing average, which is TND 26,840. Growth in the EEI sector has been the fastest in terms of employment and more so in terms of production and value added (table 5-12). Its value added almost doubled in real terms between 2005 and 2010, compared with an overall growth of 38 percent in the productive (enterprise) sector. This trend is likely to continue and may even accelerate if a new and more appropriate industrial policy is introduced.

TABLE 5-12. Value Added in Medium-Size Firms, by Sector, 2006–10

Millions of constant Tunisian dinars

	2006	2007	2008	2009	2010
Agriculture	4,143.8	4,281.4	4,280.8	4,737.6	4,420.7
Manufacturing	6,766.8	7,935.5	8,656.6	9,879.8	10,301.9
Food industries	1,173.8	1,303.0	1,430.1	1,608.5	1,701.5
Tobacco	58.4	60.5	65.5	73.6	79.6
Textile, clothing and leather	1,737.2	1,950.8	2,051.1	1,911.0	2,066.1
Other manufacturing industries	806.4	835.2	891.0	936.1	1,029.9
Oil refinery	132.4	415.8	296.0	827.4	250.1
Chemical industries	637.8	701.6	758.2	1,283.7	1,199.4
Construction materials	633.1	694.1	755.1	794.5	856.5
Electric and electronic industries	1,587.6	1,974.5	2,409.5	2,445.0	3,118.8
Other industries	4,505.9	5,702.9	5,944.5	7,432.8	6,756.9
Petroleum and natural gas	1,691.5	2,678.6	2,700.5	3,762.7	2,911.1
Mines	252.2	294.2	320.1	621.8	471.9
Electricity and gas	398.8	412.0	526.2	518.1	575.5
Water	156.1	155.9	161.1	176.2	186.2
Construction	2,007.4	2,162.2	2,236.6	2,354.0	2,612.2
Services	18,407.6	20,044.2	21,898.6	23,080.1	25,459.4
Maintenance and repair	172.2	180.7	196.0	204.3	218.2
Commerce	3,545.3	3,802.7	4,057.2	4,217.7	4,787.7
Hotels and restaurants	2,350.5	2,508.0	2,736.3	2,764.7	3,045.2
Transportation	3,490.2	3,815.9	4,330.9	4,673.1	4,943.5
Mailing and telecommunication	1,898.9	2,026.5	2,261.1	2,554.2	2,891.1
Financial services	1,549.1	1,969.3	2,226.9	2,355.1	2,212.8
Other services	5,401.3	5,741.1	6,090.2	6,310.9	7,360.9
Total merchandise sector	33,195.6	37,164.6	39,863.8	44,144.7	46,023.3

Source: Tunisian Statistical Institute, National Accounts 2011.

Exports and Foreign Direct Investment

Large firms contribute much more to exports than SMEs, about 75 percent. Medium firms export 22 percent of total exports, while small and micro firms contribute less than 3 percent. This distribution is not unexpected, since micro and small private firms are concentrated, both in terms of number of enterprises and of employment, in commerce, business services, land transportation, construction, and manufacturing of products that usually do not comply with international export standards.

In Tunisia, there is a distinct category of exporting firms, the offshore firms, of which an important proportion are small and medium enterprises. Offshore firms are those firms that have to export most of their output;[3] they are also called fully exporting firms. These firms are granted generous fiscal incentives based on the investment incentives code. There are nearly 2,000 offshore enterprises, approximately 50 percent of which are small, 30 percent medium, and fewer than 20 percent large. The fact is that the small exporting firms are numerous, but their volume of exports is small.

This particular dual structure of the Tunisian private sector is the outcome of investment incentives instituted by the December 1993 Investment Code, which gives specific incentives that primarily target investments in exported commodities and also incentivizes investments in favor of regional development. This code was amended several times to provide more ad hoc support to other specific private investment, especially SMEs investments. It allows for general and specific incentives:

General incentives: Reinvested earnings are tax deductible to a limit of 35 percent of net individual and company taxable income. In addition, all imported equipment that does not have a domestically produced equivalent is taxed at a lower 10 percent rate. This incentive has now lost most of its impact since equipment imported from the European Union is admitted freely as a result of the Tunisian–European Union Free Trade Agreement.

Export-specific incentives: Export-only firms are granted a virtual tax holiday, which includes a tax break on personal income tax for ten years followed by a 50 percent income tax rate afterward.

Regional development investments: Relatively poor regions benefit from the same income tax holiday as export-only firms and a set of subsidies regarding, for instance, the investment cost and the infrastructure construction.

---

3. They are also allowed to market up to 30 percent of their produce in the local market, but under certain conditions and after paying custom duties.

Agriculture is also granted substantial and specific tax and financial incentives, which have arguably produced a substantial impact on exports but a limited impact on total private investment, be it onshore, offshore, or through foreign direct investment. Private investment growth has been slower than expected, and the trend for foreign direct investment, excluding privatization and energy investments, has overall been rather modest and in the low-productivity sectors.

Previous studies have shown that tax incentives are minor determinants for foreign direct investments and that they matter only for footloose mobile investments, such as the investments undertaken in the textile and clothing sector, which have been so far the most important in the Tunisian case.

In the future, Tunisia aims to encourage and attract better, more skill-intensive, and higher-value-added investments. To reach this objective, fiscal incentives are not sufficient. They need to be complemented by policies that enhance the availability of financial resources, improved infrastructure, and lower labor costs. At the same time, reforms are needed to streamline regulations and improve the quality of institutions that deal with the business environment.

SMEs Financing and the Soundness of the Banking Sector

Small and medium-size enterprises, in particular, are more constrained by the financial factor. They do not have easy access to finance that allows for sustainable growth. Access to bank credit is not equally open to them: large industrial conglomerates and offshore enterprises have easier access. Small businesses, as already mentioned, rely more on short-term debt and on self-financing.

Banks insist on the use of real estate collateral to secure loans they grant to their clients, which is also required by Tunisian law. This sort of rule is not specific to Tunisia, but in the Tunisian context, not only does this law tend to make access to financial resources almost impossible for a large proportion of investors, especially SMEs, but it also does not effectively guarantee creditor rights. It may take many years to recover this type of collateral and a long time before a court of law can authorize the sale of real estate and allow the bank to recapture its capital. It may take even longer for such decisions to be implemented. This indicates to what extent the judiciary system has been inefficient and yet to be upgraded.

The Tunisian banking system is fragile and not well prepared to respond to the financial needs of SMEs, especially the smaller ones. Banks continue to suffer from a high proportion of nonperforming loans, a low level of provisioning, and a very high exposure to vulnerable and risky sectors, mainly in tourism. Several government-sponsored programs were designed to provide more funds to micro enterprises and SMEs, but the size of these programs remains small compared with total investment needs.

For instance, the Solidarity Bank, a fully operational bank with a national network, specializes in providing small loans mainly to micro firms. Obviously, this single bank cannot satisfy all the needs of the micro firms. The Industrial Fund is a national government fund whose aim is to promote SMEs, with a priority to specific regions of the country. During the 1970s and 1980s, this fund financed some 1,700 enterprises (one-fourth of all industrial projects), and public banks had to allocate a share of their resources to this program. However, because only 50 percent of the SMEs repaid their loans and the requirement on the banks was lifted, the fund became less active during the 1990s until it was redesigned to support job creation by providing venture capital. Under the new scheme, the Industrial Fund operates through venture capital firms during the project implementation, rather than funds being immediately granted, to strengthen supervision and monitoring of the entrepreneur's activities.

The Tunisian experience confirms that access to financial resources is an important constraint for SMEs but that financing is not the only problem. Small and medium-size enterprises are actually heterogeneous. The informality of a large part of the SMEs is perhaps a more important constraint on their development; it implies that they are unable to provide reliable and standardized information about their performance and their assets, that they have limited access to technology, public infrastructure, and markets, and that they are unable to attract workers with the right skills. Consequently, they look riskier and less profitable for banks. Informality is itself an outcome of the regulatory system (fiscal, labor laws, customs and administrative procedures, and the judiciary) and of the quality of the institutions in charge of enforcing the regulations. Weak and corrupt institutions combined with complex and inappropriate regulations make the cost of formality high compared with the cost of informality.

Therefore, if the purpose is to qualify SMEs for access to finance and to help them grow faster, it is crucial to undertake major structural reforms with the aim of increasing productivity and creating good quality jobs. Is the Arab Spring revolution making this type of reform possible?

The Arab Spring and After

So far in Tunisia little has been done to respond to youth expectations and regional imbalance and to institute strategic reforms. For a long time, decisionmakers and political bodies have concentrated more on political and electoral issues than economic challenges.

Yet a pattern emerges and allows for some reasonable predictions. There is still hope for consolidating democracy and engaging in inclusive development projects with more transparency, rule of law, political competition, and accountability. Although Tunisia faces a number of challenges in its current political and economic context, it has a unique opportunity to free the economy from the bottlenecks and red tape that previously impeded its development. It can establish major reforms that tackle the issues raised in this chapter in order to create a climate conducive to more private initiative and rapid and inclusive economic development.

Youth, especially angry and unemployed youth and those who have been ignored and least integrated, remain a powerful driving force and a source of hope. The situation has not stabilized, and the only conceivable pathway to a stable state and a sustained democratic and pluralistic transition is contingent on putting the country on an inclusive growth path. Otherwise, unrest will persist. Convergence toward such a stable state requires effective leadership, political cohesion, institutional development, and also a new and innovative participative and inclusive economic strategy focusing on the aspirations of youth and allowing for their participation.

To this end, there is a need to combine private sector development with new roles for the state. Those roles would include an appropriate industrial policy, macroeconomic stability, and wise and equitable public spending and investment, economic integration, and capacity development through a radical reform of the education system.

Some sort of socioeconomic pact that is acceptable to different segments of the population based on a compromise among the major groups in society is also necessary. This compromise would be first between business interests and the expectations of the working class and other politically aware groups in society. This means improving the business environment and building confidence for investors and also satisfying workers and the demands of those calling for more social justice. An agreement needs to be reached between employer associations and trade unions recognizing each other's rights. This agenda should be incorporated in the programs of the emerging political formations.

References

African Development Bank. 2012. "Political Transitions and New Socioeconomic Bargains in North Africa." Economic Brief. ORNA & ORNB. Abidjan, Côte d'Ivoire (www.afdb.org).

Institut National de la Statistique (INS). 2012. Mesure de la Pauvreté, des inégalités et de la polarisation en Tunisie 2000–2010. Joint INS, African Development Bank and World Bank publication. Tunis, Tunisia.

Javdan, Milad. 2011. "Economic Crisis, Political Repression, and Geopolitics in the Middle East," April 15 (www.e-ir.info/2011/04/15/economic-crisis-political-repression-and-geopolitics-in-the-middle-east).

Panitch, Leo. 1980. "Recent Theorizations of Corporatism: Reflections on a Growth Industry." *British Journal of Sociology* 31, no. 2 (Junc): 160.

Ramsden, Neil. 2011. "What's a Trillion Dollars among Friends? Counting SMEs and Their Demand for Financing." Washington: World Bank.

Richards, Alan, and John Waterbury. 1990. *A Political Economy of the Middle East: State, Class, and Development.* Boulder, Colo.: Westview Press.

Rocha, Roberto, Subika Farazi, Rania Khouri, and Douglas Pearce. 2011. "The Status of Bank Lending to SMEs in the Middle East and North Africa Region." Policy Research Working Paper, Results of a Joint Survey of the Union of Arab Bank and the World Bank, March.

Schmitter, Phillipe. 1974. "Still the Century of Corporatism?" *Review of Politics* 36, no. 1 (January): 85–131.

Tessler, Marc. 2011. "What Do Ordinary Arab Citizens in the Arab World Want: Secular Democracy or Democracy with Islam?" Arab Barometer (www.arabbarometer.org/).

Weidig, Dörte. 2011. "SME Lending: Larger Microloans or Smaller Corporate Loans? Where Is the Business Case?" European Fund for South East Europe (EFSE) Annual Meeting, June. Dörte Weidig, managing director, International Projekt consult (IPC), Holger Wiefel, senior bank adviser, IPC, Nataša Ginolas, SME expert, IPC (PowerPoint presentation) (www.efse.lu/media/pdfs/presentations/annual-meetings/2011/workshops/efse-annual-meeting-2011_workshop_sme-lending.pdf).

6

The Role of Micro and Small Enterprises in Egypt's Economic Transition

HAFEZ GHANEM

The success of Egypt's transition to democracy will depend crucially on the ability of the democratically elected leadership to develop and implement a new economic vision that responds to the aspirations of the millions of youth who have so far been marginalized. Growth in the future needs to be much more inclusive than in the past. Therefore, encouraging youth entrepreneurship and the development of small businesses has to be central to any new growth strategy.

While past economic policies (especially starting in 2004) achieved high growth and poverty reduction, they failed to be inclusive, as they left millions of Egyptians trapped in lower-middle-class status, living on $2 to $4 a day, and provided few opportunities for youth who felt economically and socially excluded. There was an increasing sense that the system was unfair, which explains the strong demands for social justice. Inclusive growth could be achieved by shifting away from a system of crony capitalism that favored large and established enterprises to one that focused on developing small businesses and on creating more opportunities for young men and women.

Political Economy Background: Bumpy Transition and Deteriorating Economy

Supporting small businesses and young entrepreneurs makes political sense. Egypt's economic situation has declined sharply during the transition, and the young people who started the revolution may soon become disillusioned. There is a need to show that things have changed and that the dream of the young for a more prosperous and just future is achievable. Resumption of growth is necessary, but if the benefits of growth continue to accrue to the lucky few, youth will be even further disillusioned. An economic program focused on developing small businesses and young entrepreneurs would demonstrate that things have really changed and could be one way to revive hope and mobilize energies in support of the nascent democracy.

The Egyptian revolution of January 25, 2011, was started by youth calling for freedom, dignity, and better living standards. The demonstrators in Tahrir Square shouted, "Bread, liberty, and social justice." The revolution had a political goal to build a more open and democratic society, to achieve liberty, as well as an economic goal of high and inclusive growth, to achieve bread and social justice. The two goals are linked. Transitions to democracy take time, as they involve building new institutions and changing cultures. If they are not supported by a growing economy that creates opportunities and better living standards, they risk failure and a reversion to autocratic rule—or, worse, the rise of extremist and xenophobic forces to power. At the same time, inclusive growth requires broad participation by all stakeholders in society, which is easier to achieve in open and more democratic systems.

Egypt's political transition has been bumpy, reflecting a power struggle between three groups: a military leadership that wielded tremendous power and appeared hesitant about the democratic transition; well-organized Islamist parties that are themselves divided between moderates who support democracy and hard-liners who want to establish a theocratic state; and liberal democrats who are disorganized and divided into a large number of small political parties—most of which have limited popular support. The final round of the presidential elections ended up being a contest between the two most powerful and best-organized groups: the military and moderate Islamists. President Mohamed Morsi's election and his subsequent replacement of all the top military leadership marked a clear victory for the moderate Islamists and provided some hope for a successful democratic transition.

But the road ahead is long, with many obstacles on the way. There are still significant forces among the Islamists and the military that are not supportive of a Western-style democracy. The debate over the new constitution, and the accompanying civil unrest, demonstrated the extent to which the country is polarized between Islamists and liberals. The low participation rate at the December 2012 constitutional referendum, and the fact that the majority of people in Cairo (Egypt's capital and by far largest city, as well as its commercial and cultural center) voted against it, indicate that the debate over Egypt's identity is probably not over. Compromises, which are made difficult by the lack of a democratic culture, still need to be reached to ensure future stability. Egypt's judiciary, press, and political parties (all key institutions for a democracy) continue to be weak.

During the period between February 2011 and December 2012, political issues and questions of national identity took center stage, and the economy was not a priority. The result has been quite negative. The young revolutionaries' demands for dignity and better jobs have yet to be met. In fact, the employment situation has worsened. Investment (both foreign and domestic) fell sharply, tourism came to a standstill, and capital fled the country. The rate of GDP growth fell from more than 5 percent in 2010 to less than 2 percent in 2011, and as a result, officially measured unemployment rose from about 9 percent to more than 12 percent.

The country's financial situation deteriorated rapidly, and ordinary Egyptians felt the pinch in fuel shortages and electricity blackouts. The government deficit, which was already high before the revolution, ballooned to 10 percent of GDP in 2011 and nearly 12 percent in 2012. Accordingly, the public debt rose to nearly 80 percent of GDP, with a large increase in government borrowing from the domestic banking system. The government has been paying about 16 percent interest on its short-term treasury bills, sucking liquidity from the financial system and crowding out private investment. Meanwhile, foreign reserves, which stood at $36 billion in 2010 (covering about seven months' imports), fell to $15 billion in 2012 (slightly less than three months' imports). The situation would have been even worse if other countries in the region (Qatar, Saudi Arabia, Turkey, and Algeria) had not provided exceptional financial support.

A continued economic deterioration would probably have political repercussions and would risk losing the few democratic gains achieved by the revolution so far. Stabilizing the macroeconomy is an obvious priority. Egypt had reached agreement on a program with the International Monetary Fund (IMF) in 2011, but it had to be postponed as the unrest surrounding the adoption of the new constitution made it impossible for the government to implement much-needed (but politically difficult) decisions on subsidies and tax increases. When an agreement with the IMF is finally approved, Egypt will have increased access to foreign financing from bilateral and multilateral donors. It could therefore start implementing a growth and job creation strategy to meet the aspirations of the youth who triggered the revolution.

The new economic program needs to be responsive to the revolution's demands for social justice. This would mean modernizing and expanding Egypt's social security and safety net systems. It would also mean adopting a new, more inclusive growth model that ensures greater opportunities for youth. In the past, governments supported youth by expanding employment in the public sector, but this is no longer sustainable. New opportunities will need to be created by a growing and dynamic private sector, in which small businesses play a key role.

Prerevolution Economic Developments: High Growth and High Discontent

During the period leading to the January 25, 2011, revolution, the Egyptian economy appeared to be doing well. A 2009 World Bank evaluation report states that "between fiscal 1999 and 2007 the Arab Republic of Egypt's economic performance improved substantially. This was particularly true after 2004, following improvements in economic management, structural reforms, and correction of the exchange rate."[1] Table 6-1 suggests that this positive evaluation of the country's economic performance (one year before the start of the revolution) was warranted. The gross domestic product was growing at 4–7 percent a year (supported by high foreign and domestic investment), the current account was under control, and foreign reserves were high. Moreover, this strong performance continued even during the global financial crisis. In 2009 and 2010 the economy was growing at a healthy 5 percent and had reserves equivalent to seven months' imports despite a decline in foreign direct investment and some deterioration in the current account balance. At 11–12 percent, inflation was high by international standards but still within the Central Bank's comfort zone.

---

1. Independent Evaluation Group (2009).

TABLE 6-1. Selected Macroeconomic Indicators, Egypt, 2000–10

Percent of GDP, except as indicated

Year	Current account balance	Foreign direct investment, net inflows	GDP annual growth	GDP per capita annual growth	Gross fixed capital formation	Total reserves in months of imports
2000	−1	1	5	3	19	7
2001	0	1	4	2	18	7
2002	1	1	2	0	18	8
2003	5	0	3	1	16	9
2004	5	2	4	2	16	7
2005	2	6	4	3	18	7
2006	2	9	7	5	19	7
2007	0	9	7	5	21	7
2008	−1	6	7	5	22	6
2009	−2	4	5	3	19	7
2010	−2	3	5	3	19	7

Source: World Development Indicators, World Bank.

Strong growth performance was achieved with what appeared to be virtually no change in income distribution (table 6-2). The Gini coefficient remained stable at around 30–33 percent, which indicates a more equal distribution of income than that in many other developing countries. For example, Gini coefficients were about 55 percent for Brazil, 52 percent for Chile, 46 percent for Malaysia and 63 percent for South Africa.[2] Table 6-2 also shows that, as would be expected from a stable Gini coefficient, the distribution of national income across quintiles has remained quite stable, with the lowest quintile receiving about 9 percent of income and the highest receiving about 40 percent. Doing the same calculations with deciles instead of quintiles does not change the result. The lowest deciles' share has been stable at around 4 percent and the highest deciles' share has been stable at around 27 percent.

Most poverty indicators also showed some improvement (table 6-3). Poverty at $1.25 a day was cut by half, from 4 percent of the population in 1991 to 2 percent in 1996, but remained stable at that level till 2008.

2. World Bank estimates.

TABLE 6-2. Evolution of Inequality, Egypt, Various Years

Percent, except as indicated

Year	Gini index	Income share held by lowest 20 percent	Income share held by second lowest 20 percent	Income share held by third lowest 20 percent	Income share held by fourth lowest 20 percent	Income share held by highest 20 percent
1990	32	9	12	16	21	41
1995	30	10	13	16	21	40
1999	33	9	12	16	21	42
2004	32	9	13	16	21	41
2008	31	9	13	16	21	40

Source: World Development Indicators, World Bank.

And poverty at $2.50 a day was cut from 44 and 46 percent of the population, in 1990 and 1995, to 36 and then 32 percent in 2004 and 2008. On the other hand, poverty rates using the national poverty line (a little less than $2 a day) increased from 17 percent in 2000 to 22 percent in 2008. With the benefit of hindsight, this should have raised concern. Nevertheless, most observers focused on strong growth, relative macroeconomic stability, and declining poverty according to the standard $2.50 in terms of the purchasing power parity (PPP) poverty line. The data seemed to indicate that Egypt was well on its way to becoming a development success story.

Good policies were credited for Egypt's economic performance. Economic reforms started in 1996 with some trade reforms, price liberalization, and selected privatizations and accelerated in 2004, when a new reformist government took office. The government set out to further deepen the reforms by accelerating privatization and reducing tax rates and trade tariffs while simplifying the tax and trade regimes and adopting more business-friendly policy and regulatory frameworks. This program was associated with a rapid increase in foreign direct investment flows and a further acceleration of GDP growth, which led the IMF's 2010 staff report on the article 4 consultation with Egypt to state that "the post-2004 reform agenda has started to pay dividends." Also in 2010 the World Bank identified Egypt as one of the top reformers in its *Doing Business* report, and the World Economic Forum moved Egypt up eleven places in its *Global Competitiveness* report.

TABLE 6-3. Evolution of Poverty, Egypt, Various Years

Percent, except as indicated

Year	Headcount ratio at PPP $1.25 a day	Headcount ratio at PPP $2.50 a day	Headcount ratio at national poverty line	Population (millions)
1990	4	44	n.a.	58
1995	2	46	19	63
1999	2	37	17	68
2004	2	36	20	74
2008	2	32	22	78

Source: World Development Indicators, World Bank.

Yet Egyptians were bitterly complaining about inequality and poverty, and visitors commonly commented on the shocking difference between ostentatious wealth in Cairo's gated communities and the squalor of its shanty towns. The proportion of Egyptians who responded positively to a Gallup poll question on whether they were thriving fell from 29 percent in 2005 to 11 percent in 2010, even as per capita GDP increased by nearly 34 percent over the same time period.[3] And in January 2011, millions of Egyptians were demonstrating in the streets, and a few weeks later Mubarak's regime fell.

What went wrong? The answer to this question could help the new Egyptian leadership define its economic program to avoid past mistakes and support inclusive growth and democratic development. While highlighting aspects of good performance, many observers mentioned signs of weaknesses in the Egyptian reform program under the Mubarak regime, namely, poverty and inequality, youth exclusion, and corruption. The director general of the World Bank's Evaluation Department stated in his foreword to the 2009 evaluation report that future World Bank work in Egypt should focus on "the persistent issue of poverty and inequality." The IMF's 2010 staff report on the article 4 consultation

3. Gallup classifies respondents worldwide as "thriving," "suffering," or "struggling" based on how they rate their current and future lives on the Cantril Self-Anchoring Striving ladder scale, with steps numbered from 0 to 10. GDP per capita (PPP) estimates are from the International Monetary Fund's *World Economic Outlook* database.

pointed out that "Transparency International cites accountability and transparency, and weakness in the legal/regulatory system as key reasons for Egypt remaining 111th of 180 countries in its Corruption Perception Index." While acknowledging that an Egyptian economic revival started in 2004 and had led to a marked improvement in the labor market, Assaad and Barsoum (2007) state that "youth continues to be a most disadvantaged group in terms of higher rates of unemployment, lower earnings and limited job security and stability, with the majority of new entrants finding jobs within the informal economy."

How Did the 2004 Reforms Affect the Middle Class?

A possible explanation for the rising discontent in Egypt is that the 2004 reforms increased the gulf between a struggling middle class and the elite. This could also explain why the revolution was led by educated youth who originate in the middle class. Such an explanation is consistent with recent literature; for instance, Diwan (2012), which emphasizes the important role that the Arab middle class plays in determining political regimes, as well as work carried out by Homi Kharas at the Brookings Institution that stresses the importance of the middle class in economic development.

There are many ways of defining the Egyptian middle class. I start by following Banerjee and Duflo (2008) in defining the middle class as those living on more than $2 a day but less than $10 a day. Table 6-4 shows the distribution of the population among different consumption groups, and table 6-5 shows the number of people in each of those groups. The two tables point out three important facts. First, according to this definition the Egyptian middle class is huge; it represents 83 percent of the population or 65 million people. Second, more than two-thirds of this middle class (44 million people or 56 percent of the total population) live on less than $4 a day. Popular culture in Egypt depicts the middle class as families in which at least one member is a public employee. According to the Banerjee and Duflo (2008) definition this is apparently not true. The vast numbers of middle-class families who live on $2–4 a day work in small enterprises, mostly in the informal sector. Third, the reforms of 2004 do not appear to have helped the middle class. In spite of the increase in average income, the structure of the middle class remained basically unchanged between 2004 and 2008,

TABLE 6-4. Distribution of Population, by Average Daily Earnings

Percent

Year	Less than $2 a day	$2–4 a day	$4–6 a day	$6–8 a day	$8–10 a day	$10–12 a day	$12–14 a day	More than $14 a day
2008	14.61	56.04	19.80	5.25	1.92	0.88	0.48	1.02
2004	17.56	54.44	18.30	5.17	1.97	0.93	0.51	1.12
1999	18.42	54.47	17.54	5.05	1.95	0.94	0.51	1.12
1995	25.21	54.40	13.53	3.62	1.38	0.67	0.37	0.82
1990	26.72	50.11	14.76	4.37	1.74	0.84	0.47	0.99

Source: Author calculations using World Bank's PovCalNet tool.

TABLE 6-5. Distribution of Population, by Average Daily Earnings

Millions of people

Year	Less than $2 a day	$2–4 a day	$4–6 a day	$6–8 a day	$8–10 a day	$10–12 a day	$12–14 a day	More than $14 a day
2008	11.44	43.89	15.51	4.11	1.50	0.69	0.38	0.80
2004	12.79	39.65	13.33	3.77	1.43	0.68	0.37	0.82
1999	12.24	36.20	11.66	3.36	1.30	0.62	0.34	0.74
1995	15.65	33.76	8.40	2.25	0.86	0.42	0.23	0.51
1990	15.19	28.48	8.39	2.48	0.99	0.48	0.27	0.56

Source: Author's calculations using the World Bank's PovCalNet tool.

with more than two-thirds in the $2–4-a-day income group. It is also noteworthy that the number of people living on more than $10 a day (and hence defined as upper class) has remained constant over those four years at about 1.9 million, and their proportion of the population declined slightly from 2.6 to 2.4 percent.

The above discussion could explain why the majority of Egyptians were discontented in spite of economic growth. Vast numbers were trapped in lower-middle-class status, close to the poverty line. They saw the small number of rich benefit from the economic reforms while they remained, for all intents and purposes, poor. This failure to raise the standards of living for the lower middle class distinguishes Egypt's economic performance from that of successful developing countries. The World Bank publishes data on poverty using a $5 poverty line.

TABLE 6-6. Headcount Index at $5-a-Day Poverty Line

Percent

Year	Brazil	Chile	China	Malaysia	South Africa	Egypt
1990	64	45	99	46	70	87
1995	51	36	96	45	72	89
1999	52	33	93	..	72	85
2004	47	24	80	48	66	85
2008	36	19	72	25	62	85

Source: World Development Indicators, World Bank.

Tables 6-6 and 6-7 present the headcount index and the number of poor using this measure for Egypt and five comparator countries. In Egypt the percentage of people living on less than $5 a day has been stagnant, at 85 percent, between 2000 and 2008, while their absolute number increased from 57 to 66 million. During the same period Brazil, Chile, China, Malaysia, and South Africa succeeded in reducing the proportion and absolute number of people living on less than $5 a day (although South Africa to a lesser extent than the others).

Does the above conclusion change if a different definition of the middle class is used? To respond to this question I use a definition developed by Homi Kharas at Brookings. According to this definition, the middle class consists of

> those households that have a certain amount of discretionary income that goes beyond the necessities of life to include consumer durables, quality education and health care, housing, vacations and other leisure pursuits. This group is differentiated from the poor in that they have choices over what they consume. They are differentiated from the rich in that their choices are constrained by their budget; they are price and quality sensitive.

According to this definition, middle-class households are those that spend between $10 and $100 per person per day.

Applying the Kharas definition to the World Bank's household survey data, which is presented in the preceding tables, would yield a very small middle class in Egypt (roughly only 2 percent of the population).

TABLE 6-7. Number of Poor at $5-a-Day Poverty Line

Millions

Year	Brazil	Chile	China	Malaysia	South Africa	Egypt
1990	92	7	1,125	9	26	49
1995	84	5	1,172	9	28	55
1999	89	4	1,171	n.a.	32	57
2004	91	5	1,044	12	31	62
2008	72	3	949	7	30	66

Source: World Development Indicators, World Bank.

However, users of this definition typically apply it to the private consumption data obtained from the national accounts that consistently yield a much higher figure for average consumption than the household surveys. Hence I use the data for the global middle class that is available at Brookings. According to those estimates the Egyptian middle class has grown from 12 percent of the population in 2000 to 22 percent in 2010, which appears to be a positive development. However, this expansion was not sufficient to reduce the absolute number of people living below the middle-class level (hence poor according to this definition). This number increased from 60 million in 2000 to 63 million in 2010.

Therefore, it seems that the different data sets and definitions point out a similar conclusion. From 1990 to 2008, the number of people who were poor or lower middle class continued to increase in spite of the economic reforms and the rapid growth. The vast majority of Egyptians did not benefit from the growth that occurred over the ten years immediately preceding the revolution. Of course it is always possible to argue that given enough time growth would have trickled down, and the poor would have ultimately benefited. But this argument tends to ignore political realities.

Weak Governance and Youth Exclusion

Poor governance, high corruption, and crony capitalism probably added to Egyptians' sense of unfairness. As shown in table 6-8, Egypt ranked in the bottom half of all countries on corruption control in

2010. Among the five comparators, only China has a similar ranking. Egypt's record on corruption control is far below that of Chile, Brazil, Malaysia, and South Africa. Corruption was (and probably still is) pervasive, ranging from small payments to traffic police to huge sums in return for access to government contracts.

Khatri, Tsang, and Begley (2006), while analyzing East Asia, argue that cronyism is a special type of corruption and that certain cultures are more prone to it than others. A system of crony capitalism is probably consistent with Egyptian culture, where loyalty to friends and family is highly valued. In some sense it may also have been consistent with rapid (although noninclusive) growth. Richter and Steiner (2008) describe how this system worked in the tourism sector, where the government sold land to private (mostly Egyptian) investors at $1 a meter and then declared it tourism development land, which made its value increase by 10,000 percent. The private buyers were then able to use the land as collateral to get loans from banks that were thousands of times higher than their original investment. This system led to a rapid growth in tourism revenue, which rose by about 592 percent between 1991 and 2005, outperforming all other sectors of the economy. However, this growth mostly benefited the well-connected elite (who appropriated the initial rent from the land purchase) and increased the sense of inequity. The majority of Egyptians who live on $2–4 a day were simply left behind.

Table 6-8 also shows that Egypt scored poorly on government effectiveness. The middle class (especially those who live on less than $5 a day) are highly dependent on government services: health, education, transport, and security. They suffered from the continual deterioration of those services. Children going to public schools need to pay their own teachers for private tuition in order to pass exams, and patients in government hospitals often need to pay bribes to get service. In 2010 a Cairo taxi driver described to me the relationship between Egyptians and their state as follows: "If a 'baltagy' (violent criminal) goes to a police station he is treated with respect because they are afraid of him. If a rich man goes he will also be treated with respect but he must pay. But if a 'normal honest' citizen goes he is bullied and humiliated." This state of affairs could also explain why most Egyptians felt alienated despite the economic growth.

TABLE 6-8. Selected Governance Indicators, 2010

Percentile rank

Indicator	Egypt	Brazil	Chile	China	Malaysia	South Africa
Control of corruption	34	60	91	33	61	61
Government effectiveness	40	57	84	60	82	65
Rule of law	52	55	88	45	65	58
Voice and accountability	13	64	82	5	31	65

Source: Worldwide Governance Indicators.

Young people, who represent about one-quarter of the population, felt particularly excluded. They did not participate in the social and political life of their country. Table 6-8 shows that Egypt scored far below all other comparators except China on voice and accountability. Assaad and Barsoum (2007) describe the constraints faced by young men and women on expressing themselves and the controls placed on student activities by the security apparatus. The result was that most young people refrained from any civic activities or volunteer work. They felt that their voices could not be heard. Most activist youth joined Islamist movements which, according to Bayat (1998), provided them with an alternative moral and cultural community. Islamist organizations also provided youth with services, such as libraries and sports facilities, that the public sector was unable to deliver.

Youth also suffered from economic exclusion, which can be best illustrated by examining labor market outcomes. Table 6-9 shows that youth unemployment is higher in Egypt than in any of the comparator countries except South Africa. The Egyptian public sector has traditionally provided jobs to the large numbers of graduates entering the labor market each year; currently about 850,000 young people enter the labor market annually, and 70 percent of them have completed at least secondary education.[4] This changed with the economic reforms that aimed at controlling government spending and rationalizing the public sector; given the high fiscal deficit and overemployment in the public sector it is unlikely that this sector will be able to absorb many new graduates. As a result, it has become increasingly hard for young

4. See Assaad and Barsoum (2007).

TABLE 6-9. Youth Unemployment, Aged Fifteen to Twenty-Four, 1998 and 2008
Percent

Year	1998	2008	Share of youth in population
Brazil	17	15	20.0
Chile	15	20	17.2
China	n.a.	n.a.	15.9
Malaysia	9	11	18.3
South Africa	45	47	20.5
Egypt	23	25	22.3

Source: Data from World Bank, World Development Indicators, and United Nations Population Statistics.

people to find jobs, and youth with secondary education or above represent about 95 percent of the unemployed in Egypt. The problem is particularly acute for young women, who are 3.8 times more likely to be unemployed than young men. Of the young men and women who do find jobs, only 28 percent find formal sector jobs—18 percent in the public sector and 10 percent in the formal private sector. The vast majority, 72 percent, end up working in the informal micro and small enterprise (MSE) sector, often as unpaid family workers. Among those who are paid, many have no labor contract, no job security, and no social benefits.

The Egyptian MSE Sector

What is this small enterprise sector that provides jobs for nearly three-quarters of new entrants to the labor market and is a major source of livelihood for the poor and middle class? I use a simple enterprise classification system, widely accepted in Egypt, which is based on number of employees. According to this classification, micro enterprises are defined as those that employ fewer than 10 workers, small enterprises employ 10–49 workers, medium enterprises employ 50–99 workers, and large enterprises employ 100 or more workers. According to a 2006 establishment census by the Central Agency for Public Mobilization and Statistics (quoted in el-Mahdi 2012), the Egyptian labor force is estimated at about 20.1 million workers, with about 7 million working for the public sector and the remainder divided nearly

TABLE 6-10. Overview of MSE Sector, Youth Entrepreneurs, Egypt, 2011

	Average assets (LE)	Average employment (number of workers)	Entrepreneur education (years of formal education)
Total	30,147	2.2	8.4
Youth (15–24) entrepreneur	16,809	2.3	10.3
Youth and female entrepreneur	18,368	2.4	11.2

Source: Author's calculations from the 2003 Economic Research Forum survey.

evenly between agriculture and the nonagriculture private sector. There are 2.5 million nonagricultural private enterprises in Egypt, employing 7.3 million workers. Small and micro enterprises (with fewer than 50 workers each) represent nearly 99 percent of total private enterprises and about 80 percent of total employment (5.8 million workers). Furthermore, of those 5.8 million workers, 88 percent are employed by micro enterprises, with 72 percent employed in enterprises with 1–4 workers and 16 percent in enterprises with 5–9 workers. The remaining 18 percent are employed by small enterprises that employ 10–49 workers. This relative importance of small and micro enterprises for employment generation is not unique to Egypt. For example, Ozar, Ozartan, and Irfanoglu (2008) and Samitowska (2011) show similar results for Turkey and Poland, respectively.

In view of their dominant position in the Egyptian labor market, this chapter focuses on the micro and small enterprise sector. I use two data sources: an MSE survey carried out by the Economic Research Forum (ERF) in 2003 covering 4,957 enterprises, and a survey of 3,000 enterprises carried out in 2010 and 2011 and reviewed by el-Mahdi (2012) in a background paper to the Brookings project on Arab economies. Whenever possible, I base my results on the more recent survey. However, the 2003 survey is larger and covers more questions.

The vast majority of MSEs in Egypt are very small, with average assets valued at 30,000 Egyptian pounds (LE) (some US$5,000) and average employment of 2.2 workers (see table 6-10). The average age of the owner or manager of an enterprise is 40.3 years, with an average education level of 8.4 years of formal schooling. Women entrepreneurs head about 10.5 percent of enterprises. About 12 percent of entrepreneurs are young, between the ages of fifteen and twenty-four.

TABLE 6-11. Distribution of MSEs, by Gender and Age of Entrepreneur, Egypt, 2011
Percent

Age	Male	Female	Total
< 18 years	0.2	0.8	0.2
18 to < 21 years	2.0	4.1	2.2
21 to < 25 years	7.4	9.6	7.6
25 to < 30 years	12.9	13.0	12.9
30 to < 40 years	27.2	21.2	26.6
40 years or more	50.4	51.3	50.5
Total	100.0	100.0	100.0

Source: El-Mahdi 2012.

Enterprises headed by youth tend to have fewer assets (nearly half as many) than the average. Another important feature of young entrepreneurs is that they tend to be better educated than older colleagues, with an average education of 10.3 years. In fact, the simple correlation coefficient between age and years of education for the whole sample is –0.33. Some 15.4 percent of young entrepreneurs are women. They tend to be better educated than their male counterparts, and their enterprises tend to be slightly bigger.

Table 6-11 shows the age structure of entrepreneurs from the 2011 survey. Youth, defined as less than twenty-five years old, represent only 10 percent of the sample (slightly less than in the 2003 survey). However, table 6-11 also shows that if we extend the definition of youth to include all of those less than thirty years old, then young entrepreneurs would represent about 23 percent of total entrepreneurs.

Young people's share of employment in MSEs is much higher than their share in ownership. Using data from the 2003 ERF survey I estimate that those in the fifteen-to-twenty-four-year-old age group represent 37 percent of total MSE employment. If we define youth as being less than thirty years old, this share rises to more than 50 percent. Women's employment in MSEs remains low at only 11.4 percent, as those enterprises are not considered safe for female workers. Half of the women working in MSEs (50.1 percent in the ERF 2003 sample) are less than twenty-five years old. Wages are low; the average wage for male workers in the 2011 survey is $3.70 a day and that for a female

TABLE 6-12. Distribution of MSEs, by Economic Activity, Egypt, 2011

Activity	Frequency	Percent
Trade	1,806	60.2
Services and maintenance	886	29.5
Manufacturing	308	10.3
Total	3,000	100.0

Source: El-Mahdi 2012.

worker is $2.60 a day. Slightly more than half (50.5 percent in the 2003 ERF survey) of employees have a work contract, which shows the precarious nature of employment in this sector.

Egyptian MSEs are mostly family businesses that provide simple services to the household sector. Data from the 2003 ERF survey indicate that 63.5 percent of MSE employees are related to the owner or manager, which supports the view that this sector is dominated by family businesses. As shown in table 6-12, some 60 percent of MSEs work in trade. These are small retailers and wholesalers who sell food products, clothes, furniture, plastics, and building materials. About 30 percent operate in the services sector, including transportation and distribution, laundry, cafes, restaurants, and hotels. Only 10 percent of enterprises are in manufacturing, including food processing, wood and furniture, ceramics, building materials, and some electrical and engineering workshops. In response to a question about their main clients, 90 percent of enterprises mention households, 8 percent sell to other firms or home-based workers, and 2 percent sell to government or public enterprises. Thus it is evident that little subcontracting is taking place. More than 99 percent of MSEs sell mainly to local markets, with few selling in the national market (within Egypt). Only 0.3 percent of enterprises sell to the export market.

Peattie (1987, 851) states that the concept of an informal sector is "utterly fuzzy," and this seems to be the case in Egypt, where most MSEs operate in a gray zone between formality and informality. To be considered formal, an Egyptian enterprise needs to have a business license, be registered as a commercial or industrial establishment, obtain a tax card, and keep regular accounts. Noncompliance with one or more of those four official procedures would make the enterprise

TABLE 6-13. MSE Compliance with Official Procedures, Egypt, 2011

Percent

Procedure	Compliance
Business license	66.4
Commercial or industrial registration	70.1
Tax card	73.1
Keeping regular accounts	28.4

Source: El-Mahdi 2012.

count as informal. Table 6-13 shows the status of compliance in the 2011 sample. Only 21.6 percent of enterprises comply with all four procedures and are therefore considered formal. On the other extreme, 18.4 percent do not comply with any procedure and therefore operate completely informally. The remaining 60 percent of enterprises comply with one or more (45 percent of the total comply with three of the four) of the procedures and are officially considered informal, but in fact seem to be at least partially formal. The one procedure that is least complied with is (unsurprisingly) that of maintaining regular accounts and presenting them to the tax department (see table 6-13). The degree of formality is positively correlated with the size of the enterprise and the education level of its owner; urban-based enterprises tend to be more formal than rural-based ones. Similar results on the relationship between formality and firm size and the characteristics of the entrepreneur were found by Jackle and Li (2006) for Peru.

Micro and small enterprises have low capital-labor ratios and tend to use simple traditional technologies. The average capital-labor ratio calculated from the 2003 survey is around LE 10,000 (about US$1,600) and LE 14,000 (about US$2,300) from the 2011 survey. The surveys asked entrepreneurs about the type of technology they use, including the choice between traditional, modern, and up-to-date. Among the manufacturing enterprises, 68 percent stated that they use traditional technology, while 30 percent use modern technology, and only 2 percent use up-to-date technology. In services the shares were 71 percent traditional, 27 percent modern, and 2 percent up-to-date; while the shares in the trade sector were 80 percent, 19 percent, and 1 percent, respectively. On the other hand, 30 percent of entrepreneurs stated that they introduced innovations to their services and products to meet

TABLE 6-14. Source of Initial Funding to MSEs, Egypt, 2003

Percent of total

Source	All entrepreneurs	Young entrepreneurs
Formal loan	2.3	1.4
Informal loan	2.9	2.2
Individual savings	68.6	73.7
Inheritance	20.2	18.7
Other	6.0	4.0

Source: Author's calculations from the 2003 Economic Research Forum survey.

changing market needs. A 2008 survey on innovation covered 3,000 manufacturing and services enterprises. It found that 19 percent of enterprises had technological innovation activities, with manufacturing firms and larger firms being more likely to innovate. About 90 percent of innovations were produced within the firm, and only 10 percent were produced in collaboration with domestic or foreign partners.

Constraints Facing MSEs

When asked why they did not use modern technology, more than half of the entrepreneurs stated that they could not afford the expense. Table 6-14 shows sources of funding for MSE start-ups. It indicates that only 2.3 percent of entrepreneurs were able to get a formal loan to start their business, and 2.9 percent obtained an informal loan. Access to financing at start-up is even more difficult for youth, as only 1.4 percent of them were able to get a formal loan and 2.2 percent obtained an informal loan. Most entrepreneurs (68.6 percent of total and 73.7 percent of youth) relied on their own savings to start their business. Inheritance is also an important source of financing, with 20.2 percent of entrepreneurs (18.7 percent of youth) stating that they used money they had inherited to start their business.

Access to infrastructure and public services is an important factor affecting the performance of all enterprises, but particularly small ones that do not have the resources to invest in alternatives to publicly provided infrastructure. Table 6-15 presents the proportion of entrepreneurs who answered no in response to questions about access to different types of infrastructure. A surprising finding here is the high

TABLE 6-15. Lack of Access to Infrastructure

	All entrepreneurs	Young entrepreneurs
Water	59.4	57.2
Electricity	6.7	5.7
Telephone	71.9	73.0
Sewage	68.1	67.2
Roads	10.8	9.9
Transport of workers	96.6	97.1
Transport of goods	94.8	95.4

Source: Data as reported in the 2003 Economic Research Forum survey. Author's calculations.

proportion that do not have access to landline telephones (71.9 percent of the total and 73 percent of youth). However, it is not clear how serious this is at a time of increasing access to mobile phones. Public transport for people and goods appears as a major problem for MSEs, with some 95 percent of them stating that they do not have access to those services. The same is true for water and sewage, as 59.4 percent of respondents stated that they had no access to water and 68.1 percent had no access to sewage. There does not appear to be a significant difference between young entrepreneurs and the rest of the sample in terms of access to infrastructure and public services.

Two-thirds of small entrepreneurs identified taxation (tax rates as well as tax administration) as a key constraint facing their business development (table 6-16). This is consistent with the earlier finding that the vast majority of small firms did not comply with the requirement to file their accounts with the tax department. It is commonplace for businesspersons all over the world to complain about taxes. Nevertheless, the loud complaints (based on 2003 data) and massive noncompliance (based on 2011 data) may be an indication that a review of tax policies affecting small businesses is warranted. About 61 percent (64 percent of youth) entrepreneurs mentioned licensing and registration as key constraints. This is surprising, since in the 2003 survey about 70 percent of respondents reported having complied with those requirements. From 2004 to 2010 the government, as part of its economic reform program, embarked on a massive deregulation and simplification effort. Hence this conclusion could be based on data from an earlier period. However, el-Mahdi (2012) states that the deregulation and simplification effort

TABLE 6-16. Major Constraints to Small Business

Percent of entrepreneurs saying it is a major constraint

	All entrepreneurs	Young entrepreneurs
Securing capital	64.6	62.1
Licensing and registration	61.3	64.0
Labor law	32.3	35.7
Labor inspection	44.9	49.2
Tax rates	68.6	66.7
Customs duties	5.8	5.8
Tax administration	65.0	63.0

Source: Data as reported in the 2003 Economic Research Forum survey. Author's calculations.

does not seem to have affected the MSE sector, based on a 2011 survey. Hence there may be two explanations for this result: the entrepreneurs may be ill informed and unaware of the changes, or the deregulation and simplification measures are not being applied by a bureaucracy that is keen to protect possible sources of rents.

Table 6-16 also shows that lack of financing is seen as a major constraint by nearly 65 percent of entrepreneurs (62 percent of youth). More detailed data on access to credit is presented in table 6-17, which shows that only 5 percent of entrepreneurs said that they have had any access to credit, and of those, 47.9 percent (57.1 percent of youth) received that credit from family, friends, or business associates. Banks provided 35.6 percent of credit to MSEs, while the Social Fund for Development and nongovernmental organizations (NGOs) provided 9.2 and 7.3 percent, respectively. The table also shows that young entrepreneurs have much less access to credit from banks and the Social Fund for Development than older ones.

The surveys indicate a significant level of dissatisfaction with government policies affecting small businesses. Entrepreneurs claim that the regulatory framework (licensing, registration, and so on) is a hindrance, that it costs significant time and money, that taxation is high and cumbersome, and that they have little access to basic infrastructure and to credit. Very few seem to have benefited from targeted interventions such as credit from the social fund or special training programs. Hence there seems to be a good case for a review of policies and programs affecting small enterprises in Egypt.

TABLE 6-17. Availability of Credit to Small Businesses
Percent of respondents

	All entrepreneurs	Young entrepreneurs
Access to credit	5.3	4.8
Source of credit		
Friends and family	47.9	57.1
Bank	35.6	28.6
Social Fund for Development	9.2	3.6
NGO	7.3	10.7

Source: Data as reported in the 2003 Economic Research Forum survey. Author's calculations.

Policy Implications

It is important that Egyptian policymakers and international donors recognize that past noninclusive growth patterns, together with a system of crony capitalism, can at least partly explain popular dissatisfaction with the Mubarak regime and the ensuing revolution. Many observers still claim that the revolution was about political rather than economic rights. This would imply that the new government just needs to continue implementing past economic policies and return to past growth patterns. The democratic reforms would ensure increased transparency, participation, and accountability—and hence decreased corruption. This argument is appealing, but it is not consistent with the political economy analysis presented here. Democracy, transparency, participation, and accountability are certainly key popular demands, and they are also necessary steps to achieving inclusive and sustainable growth. But they are not enough. The youth who started the revolution are asking for a change in their economic situation, and they are probably not willing to wait until the benefits of growth trickle down to reach them.

Government needs to develop a new growth strategy—one in which small business and youth entrepreneurship play a key role—that responds to the revolution's demand for bread and social justice. Donors also need to adjust their portfolios to reflect the new political realities. Failure to do so could lead to more disillusionment and cynicism and could ultimately jeopardize the transition to democracy.

The objective of government policy and donor interventions should not be simply to support the growth of the existing MSE sector. It should also aim to transform it by raising its productivity and its linkages to domestic and international markets. Finding low-wage jobs in MSEs for the 850,000 young people who enter the labor market each year so that they increase the ranks of those living on $2–4 a day will not solve Egypt's social problems. The objective should be to support the modernization of the sector so that it can become more dynamic, providing better living standards for young entrepreneurs and decent jobs for new entrants to the labor market. A possible model for the Egyptian MSE sector would be the sectors in Europe and Japan where MSEs lead in innovation, often operate in clusters, and have strong links to larger firms as well as to national and international markets. The key short-term challenge is to create more opportunities for youth who currently suffer from social and economic exclusion. Young women who are discouraged and drop out of the labor market pose a special problem, because increasingly families need two earners to ensure a decent living for parents and children.

Government cannot provide all of the solutions on its own. Past government interventions to support the MSE sector in Egypt and elsewhere have often proved to be ineffective (for example, deregulation and simplification after 2004 does not appear to have encouraged more enterprises to become formal) and even harmful at times (for example, Hill 2001 describes how some of the subsidized credit schemes in Indonesia hurt rather than helped the sector by limiting access). It is important that a new MSE development strategy be devised based on a broad consultation with owners and workers as well as with students who will soon be looking for jobs. Large firms could also contribute to the debate with the aim of increasing interfirm linkages and subcontracting. This would be an excellent opportunity to demonstrate the benefits from Egypt's new open and democratic political system. For decades Egypt's youth have felt that their voice was not being heard, which left them cynical and disheartened. Now could be the right time to engage youth in a broad national debate about their future and their country's development path.

Nongovernmental organizations play a significant role in supporting MSEs. They provide about 10 percent of all credit to the sector, from their own resources as well as from their work as delivery agents for the Social Fund for Development. They also are in a good position to provide technical and marketing support and to help organize broad consultations with relevant stakeholders. Government can help develop NGOs by passing a new law regulating their activities and simplifying procedures for their registration and operations (see Kharas and Abdou 2012). The NGO sector could also provide opportunities for young men and women interested in engaging in the civic lives of their communities and participating in social development and the fight against poverty.

Egypt could benefit from the experience of other countries in MSE development. For example, Hill (2001) reviewed two successful MSE experiences from Indonesia: the Bali garment industry and the Jepara furniture manufacturing cluster. He concludes that four factors were crucial to their success: the existence of some basic industrial competence in a specific field; a conducive macroeconomic environment, including a competitive exchange rate; reasonably good physical infrastructure; and the injection of technical design and marketing expertise that links small producers to new ideas and major markets.

The surveys of Egyptian MSEs discussed in this chapter demonstrate that there is basic competence in several fields, such as tourism and the hospitality industry, textiles, food processing, ceramics, furniture, and, more recently, information and communication technology. The surveys also show that physical infrastructure, especially roads and electricity, do not appear to be the main constraint for MSE development. Hence it seems that, at least in the short run, the Egyptian government, with support from its international partners, needs to focus on providing a conducive macroeconomic environment and on developing a few targeted programs to encourage small enterprises and young entrepreneurs to obtain business and technical expertise, as well as better linkages to markets.

Conducive Macroeconomic Environment

A conducive macroeconomic environment for small business implies a stable economy, a competitive exchange rate, policy and regulatory frameworks that encourage MSEs, and efficient noncorrupt institutions. Egypt's agreement with the IMF to support its stabilization program is an important step that needs to be finalized as soon as possible. An agreement with the IMF will provide Egypt with access to an

TABLE 6-18. Evolution of the Exchange Rate, Egypt and the United States, 2004–12
Percent

	2004	2005	2006	2007	2008	2009	2010	2011	2012-Q2
Egypt consumer price index	95.4	100	107.6	117.7	139.2	156.6	173.1	190.5	203.2
U.S. consumer price index	96.7	100	103.2	106.2	110.2	109.9	111.7	115.2	117.7
LE/USD exchange rate	6.2	5.8	5.7	5.6	5.4	5.5	5.6	5.9	6.0
Nominal exchange rate index	107.2	100	99.2	97.5	94.0	95.9	97.3	102.7	104.3
Real exchange rate index	108.8	100	95.1	88.0	74.7	67.7	62.7	62.1	60.4

Source: International Financial Statistics, IMF, and author's calculations.

increased level of external financing from the IMF itself as well as from other donors who link their assistance to a credible macro framework. It would also provide an encouraging signal to foreign and domestic investors and help restore confidence in the Egyptian economy. Therefore, the agreement is important for small businesses. However, stabilizing the economy also involves taking politically difficult decisions, especially on fuel subsidies, which consume 6–7 percent of GDP, and the taxation of some consumer goods.

Efforts to stabilize the economy need to be accompanied by strong public information campaigns and measures to protect the most vulnerable (Vagliasindi 2012). Indonesia was able to reduce fuel subsidies in 2006 after it launched a public information campaign that clearly identified the benefits of the reform and the compensatory social measures that would accompany it. Similarly, Ghana launched a study on fuel subsidies in 2004. The study's steering committee included a large number of stakeholders (government officials, academics, company representatives, and so on). In 2005 the government used the study to launch a public information campaign that included a description of the social mitigation measures, and it was able to peacefully increase fuel prices by 50 percent.

A competitive real exchange rate encourages the development of MSEs. In that sense the depreciation of the Egyptian pound that accelerated in December 2011 is welcome, but it is probably still not sufficient. Table 6-18 presents the evolution, from 2004 to the second quarter of 2012, of Egypt's consumer price index (CPI), the U.S. CPI, the exchange rate of the Egyptian pound to the U.S. dollar, the nominal exchange rate expressed as an index, and an index of the real exchange rate that is defined here as the nominal LE/USD exchange rate index adjusted for the differential CPI inflation between the two countries. There are many other definitions of the real exchange rate, but I stick here to this definition because it provides the simplest way of demonstrating that Egypt's real exchange rate has been appreciating over the whole period and has continued to appreciate since the revolution.

Using other definitions would not change the result. Inflation was much higher in Egypt than in the United States over the period 2004–10 (just before the revolution), and the Egyptian CPI increased by 81.2 percent while the U.S. CPI increased by only 15.5 percent over those six years. The Egyptian pound relative to the U.S. dollar also appreciated, moving from LE 6.2/USD 1 in 2004 to LE 5.6/USD 1 in 2010. As a result, the real exchange rate appreciated by about 42 percent. The Egyptian pound depreciated after the revolution from LE 5.6/USD 1 in 2010 to LE 6.0/USD 1 in the second quarter of 2012. However, this depreciation was not enough to offset the inflation differential between the two countries, and the real exchange rate appreciated by an additional 3.7 percent. In its 2010 report on the article 4 consultation with Egypt, the IMF states that "the real effective exchange rate appreciated by over 25 percent since the benchmark period for the last exchange rate assessment (end-2007) and now appears somewhat overvalued under each of the standard metrics."[5] If the real exchange rate was somewhat overvalued when growth was strong and the country had external reserves covering seven months' imports, it is probably safe to assume that today it is grossly overvalued.

A review of the policy and regulatory frameworks affecting MSEs is needed. There is a high level of noncompliance with tax laws and regulations, which raises the question of whether they should be revised and simplified to encourage more enterprises to become formal. Government may wish to consider providing tax incentives for small businesses and for young entrepreneurs. Businesses continue to complain about the regulatory framework in spite of the recent simplification. It may be necessary to take another look at the processes affecting small enterprises, in consultation with entrepreneurs. Government should also consider policies to encourage foreign investors to partner with Egyptian MSEs to provide technical design and marketing expertise.

5. IMF (2010, p. 17).

In the case of the garment industry in Bali, the Indonesian government reduced the minimum level of foreign investment from $1 million to $250,000 to encourage small foreign investors to partner with local MSEs, bringing in their technical know-how and market access.

Good tax laws and simple regulations will only be effective if their implementation is not marred by abuse and corruption. Hence efforts to fight corruption and to professionalize the civil service could have a positive impact on MSE development. Fighting corruption is an important goal of the revolution, and since February 2011 there have been more than 6,000 corruption investigations and several high-profile incriminations (African Development Bank and others 2012). While this may send a signal that corruption will not be tolerated, it is not an effective way of ending the type of corruption that hampers the work of MSEs. Government needs to partner with civil society, the press, and business owners to bring about greater transparency and hold civil servants accountable. During its transition, Indonesia created the Partnership for Governance Reform, bringing together government and civil society to lead the fight against corruption.

Targeted Interventions to Support MSEs and Young Entrepreneurs

Reforms to macroeconomic environment need to be complemented by programs and projects that directly target MSEs. Direct interventions by government and donors to support MSEs could include strengthening the Social Fund for Development, support to some pilot MSE clusters, and programs for entrepreneurship development.

The government has designated the Social Fund for Development as the apex institution for the expansion and development of the MSE sector. However, the fund also has another mission, which is to develop safety nets and labor-intensive public works programs. Both missions are important, but they are quite different. There is a risk of their getting confused. For example, the fund could be supporting some MSEs that have a small chance for development as part of its social protection function. It seems, therefore, that there is a need to sharply separate the two roles either by breaking up the fund into two institutions (which may imply a loss of some economies of scale) or by organizational changes within the fund to ensure separate accountabilities.

Developing small businesses is a long-term objective that should be protected as much as possible from shifts in short-term political priorities. An independent review of the fund carried out in 2011 recommended that its independence from political intervention be ensured. It is important to implement those recommendations and to strengthen the governance of the fund in a way that ensures that small entrepreneurs, especially youth and women, have a voice in its operations and strategies.

Strengthening the capacity of fund staff is also a priority, and it is particularly needed in two areas. First, the fund needs to have the capacity to analyze policies affecting MSEs and propose action. Fund staff should play an important advocacy role, ensuring that the interests of MSEs are taken into account in policy deliberations. They are well placed to play this role since all of the important economic ministers are members of the Social Fund for Development's board of directors. Second, priority should be given to strengthening the fund's business development and nonfinancial services. Like most social funds around the world, the fund's focus has been on providing financing, usually through NGOs or commercial banks. But financing alone cannot transform Egypt's MSE sector. There is a need for business training, technology transfer, and access to markets. Naturally, the Social Fund for Development itself should not directly provide those services; rather, it should work with private providers. However, few staff are equipped for this type of activity.

The Social Fund for Development is considering some pilot projects to develop MSE clusters. It is looking at possible clusters for furniture manufacturing in Damietta and in Upper Egypt and at a petrochemicals cluster in Suez. Cluster development could be a useful activity, provided that it is based on an existing local competence. Initially, the fund could focus on supporting local MSEs to better connect with one another, modernize, and link to national and international markets. For such an endeavor to succeed, it would be important to partner with a private enterprise that can provide the technical support and market access. Bringing in a foreign partner would be particularly useful for export-oriented activities. Mobilizing donor support for those types of projects should not be difficult.

A key challenge to the implementation of the vision presented in this chapter is that young Egyptians are not prepared for a life of entrepreneurship and risk taking. Egypt has an antiquated education system that has been geared to produce civil servants and does not provide graduates with the skills needed to survive in a twentieth-century marketplace. Educated youth in Egypt do not have the skills or the inclination to start their own businesses. They prefer the security of a public sector job, even if it implies a long period of unemployment as they wait for a job opening. The obvious solution to this problem is to reform and modernize the education system. This is clearly an important developmental priority, but it will take time to implement and will not affect the millions of youth who are currently in the labor market. The Social Fund for Development could develop entrepreneurship programs to provide skills to youth and help them start their own businesses. It has a track record of projects and programs that target women entrepreneurs that could be further expanded, and new programs that specifically target youth and new graduates could be developed.

The above are some policy directions, and possible priorities for intervention, that may warrant further exploration by government and its development partners. A successful modernization and expansion of Egypt's MSE sector would be an important component of an economic program that aims at achieving inclusive growth. A comprehensive strategy for the sector, taking into account the new political and social realities, needs to be developed through a consultative process that includes all stakeholders.

References

Abu Elmagd, M., N. El Oraby, and R. Pillay. 2011. "Social Fund for Development: An Independent, Forward Looking Review." Cairo: Social Fund for Development.

African Development Bank and others. 2012. "Egypt." In *African Economic Outlook 2012: Promoting Youth Employment*. Paris: OECD.

Assaad, R., and G. Barsoum. 2007. "Youth Exclusion in Egypt: In Search of Second Chances." Wolfensohn Center for Development, Brookings.

Banerjee, A., and E. Duflo. 2008. "What Is Middle Class about the Middle Class around the World?" *Journal of Economic Perspectives* 22, no. 2: 3–28.

Bayat, A. 1998. "Revolution without Movement, Movement without Revolution: Comparing Islamic Activism in Iran and Egypt." *Studies in Society and History* 40, no. 1: 136–69.

Diwan, I. 2012. "Understanding Revolution in the Middle East: The Central Role of the Middle Class." Working Paper 726. Cairo: Economic Research Forum.

El-Mahdi, A. 2012. "Improving Opportunities of the Micro and Small Enterprises in Egypt." Brookings.

Hill, H. 2001. "Small and Medium Enterprises in Indonesia: Old Policy Challenges for a New Administration." *Asian Survey* 41, no. 2: 248–70.

Independent Evaluation Group. 2009. *Egypt: Positive Results from Knowledge Sharing and Modest Lending; An IEG Country Assistance Evaluation, 1999–2007.* Washington: World Bank.

International Monetary Fund. 2010. *Arab Republic of Egypt Article IV Consultation: Staff Report.* Washington.

Jackle, A., and C. Lee. 2006. "Firm Dynamics and Institutional Participation: A Case Study of the Informality of Micro Enterprises in Peru." *Economic Development and Cultural Change* 54, no. 4: 557–78.

Kharas, H. 2010. "The Emerging Middle Class in Developing Countries." Working Paper 285, OECD Development Center.

Kharas, H., and E. Abdou. 2012. "Regulatory Reforms Necessary for an Inclusive Growth Model in Egypt." Global Views, Brookings (November).

Khatri, N., E. Tsang, and T. Begley. 2006. "Cronyism: A Cross Cultural Analysis." *Journal of International Business Studies* 37: 61–75.

Ozar, S., G. Ozartan, and Z. Irfanoglu. 2008. "Micro and Small Enterprise Growth in Turkey: Under the Shadow of Financial Crisis." *Developing Economies* 46 (December): 331–62.

Peattie, Lisa. 1987. "An Idea in Good Currency and How It Grew: The Informal Sector." *World Development* 15 (July): 851–60.

Richter T., and C. Steiner. 2008. "Politics, Economics, and Tourism Development in Egypt: Insights into the Sectoral Transformations of a Neo-Patrimonial, Rentier State." *Third World Quarterly* 29, no. 5: 939–59.

Samitowska, W. 2011. "Barriers to the Development of Entrepreneurship Demonstrated by Micro, Small, and Medium Enterprises in Poland." *Economics and Sociology* 4, no. 2: 42–49.

Vagliasindi, M. 2012. "Implementing Energy Subsidy Reforms: An Overview of Key Policy Issues." Policy Research Working Paper 6122. Washington: World Bank.

World Bank. 2009. *Egypt: Positive Results from Knowledge Sharing and Limited Lending; An IEG Country Assistance Evaluation.* Washington.

7

Jordan: The Geopolitical Service Provider

EMMANUEL COMOLET

Jordan has been, for at least sixty years, a pivot country in the Middle East. Its proximity to Israel, Egypt, the West Bank, Syria, Lebanon, Saudi Arabia, and Iraq makes it a puzzle of influences and populations, especially since the creation of Jordan was already a response to a sense of geopolitical balance in the region. Since then, the country has been using its position on the international scene to trade geopolitical services. Consequently, its economy depends on various external flows and suffers from a lack of domestic resources, most notably in energy and water. These obstacles have led the leadership of the country to value and leverage its central position in the Middle East in order to support its economic development and maintain its regime.

Contrary to numerous countries in the Arab world, Jordan has not recently gone through massive demonstrations designed to topple its head of state.[1] So far, the king has weathered the Arab revolutions and the earth-shattering political movements sweeping many of its neighboring states in the past couple of years. This stability, in the eye of the cyclone, has enabled the country to cash in on the geopolitical services it supports while remaining on the edge of instability.

Indeed, the absence of a strong social movement does not mean that the frailties that appeared in other countries are missing in Jordan. The demographic trajectory, labor force participation, and place of women and young people in the labor market resemble those of other Arab countries affected by popular movements.

---

1. International Crisis Group (2012).

The macro tensions affecting Jordan from 2011 to 2014 primarily had to do with the energy shock caused by sabotages performed on the pipeline coming from Egypt. The consequences on Jordan's current account, on the fiscal balance, and on the public debt have been tremendous, with Jordan seeking and obtaining support from the International Monetary Fund (IMF) in 2012. Meanwhile, in the background, the situation of the labor market remains gloomy, and challenges for the stability and development of the kingdom abound. It appears that, in the wake of the Syrian civil war, Jordan retains its classical geopolitical service-provider mantle: the country still exports influence and to some extent works, and now that it is hosting thousands of refugees, it is not clear how its fragile domestic market will respond.

A Brief History of the Kingdom of Jordan

The Emirate of Transjordan became the Hashemite Kingdom of Jordan in 1946, when Jordan gained independence from the British mandate authorities. But the presence of British troops on Jordanian ground until March 1948[2] appeared to restrict the country's independence. A new treaty, which enabled the United Kingdom to use two air bases and maintain right-of-passage for its troops, sealed a military and political alliance between the two nations. The savviness of the king led to the peaceful independence of the kingdom while allowing good relations with its former colonizer. King Abdullah also asserted his power through the support of a strong army and the Bedouins.

During the 1948 war, Jordan occupied the West Bank, which voted to remain part of the kingdom in a 1950 referendum. The Jordanian parliament approved the union of the two sides of the Jordan River in one state, under the sovereignty of Abdullah. After the assassination of Abdullah by a Palestinian and amid domestic turmoil, King Hussein asserted his power. For instance, he created a national consultative council composed of only Transjordanians (who could be of Palestinian origin). The various links that the crown had established within the country's numerous groups have enabled the continuity of power of the

---

2. According to article 5 of the treaty signed on March 22, 1946, by Jordan and the United Kingdom, as a measure of collective self-defense.

royal family since then, but those were testing times for the stability of the kingdom.

Jordan saw an opportunity to sever ties with the United Kingdom during the Suez crisis in 1956. The treaty between the two countries was repealed, and British troops left the country. The Syrian army, present on Jordanian ground, threatened the kingdom, and the U.S. Navy was ready to intervene if necessary. Jordan then broke ties with Syria and Egypt, even though at the same time its Arab federation with King Hussein's cousin, King Faisal II of Iraq, was failing; this time the United Kingdom was acting as a security insurance by sending parachutists to Amman. Jordan and the United States grew closer in the following years, and the relations of the kingdom with Egypt improved. In the meantime, the country's domestic turmoil was intensifying, and Jordan retracted its support from the Palestine Liberation Organization.

Jordan had signed a defense treaty with Egypt just before the 1967 war, but this did not prevent the loss of the West Bank to the Israeli army, a humiliating defeat for the Jordanian forces. The morale of Palestinians in Jordan remained low after this, particularly for the last waves that arrived (200,000 people), who struggled to integrate into the economic and political spheres of the country. In addition, by losing the West Bank, Jordan lost its most resource-rich land.

The years 1970 and 1971 were the peak of the war between the Jordanian government and some maximalist Palestinian organizations. The government won this conflict with the support of the United States, leading to a rupture between the Palestinians and the Hashemite kingdom. Also, Iraq and Syria closed their borders and Syria, Algeria, and Libya ended their diplomatic relations with Jordan.

The kingdom was then Jordanized, minimizing the political responsibilities of West Bankers, and the king abandoned any claim on the West Bank. At this time, Jordan's relations with Syria had its ups and downs, and Jordan sided with Iraq in its war against Iran, while Syria supported Iran. During those years Jordan's military cooperation with the United States remained important, though U.S. support for Israel was problematic for Jordan.

Eventually, in 1988, King Hussein severed administrative and legal ties with the West Bank and tried to deepen relations with many Arab states (for example, Iraq and Egypt). Reluctantly, the king supported

Saddam Hussein in the Gulf war and paid a steep price for it (Saudi Arabia closed its borders with Jordan, for instance). However, the country was slowly democratized by the king, and, combined with his support for Iraq, the head of state's popularity grew. Jordanian cohesion came to revolve around the king, as is still the case. The economic situation worsened, however. Jordan was highly dependent on Iraq, and Jordan had to rely on structural adjustment programs backed by the International Monetary Fund, the World Bank, and the United States.

Since the signing of the 1994 peace agreement with Israel, the two states are no longer belligerent, and Jordan expects to collect some peace dividends. Financial support—through different channels and modes from the United States, the European Union, Japan, and the World Bank—has enabled the country's economy to rebound and remain afloat. In addition, many countries of the Arab Gulf continue to aid Jordan.

This short history of Jordan shows how, politically, the country has skillfully managed its environment by using its position as an opportunity to build alliances with countries from every angle. The external financial flows it receives suggest that Jordan needs the support of all sorts of actors and has to maintain excellent relations with both the countries of the peninsula and international donors to survive.

Among the external flows, the historical importance of both official development assistance and the size of remittances is clear, and it has been a cornerstone of Jordan's economy since its independence (see figure 7-1). Remittances come from emigrants who probably had not found enough opportunities in the local labor market and so sought better situations abroad. Besides trading geopolitical services, it seems that Jordan has been trading workers as well. Considering the importance of the labor market environment in the Arab revolutions since 2011, this labor effect is an element worth considering as Jordan faces economic challenges similar to those of other neighbor economies in the Middle East and North Africa region.

The Demographic Story

The population of Jordan has skyrocketed since its independence. It has multiplied more than twelvefold in sixty years thanks to both its natural increase and the inflows of population, a result of various periods

FIGURE 7-1. External Flows Received by Jordan, 1973–2013

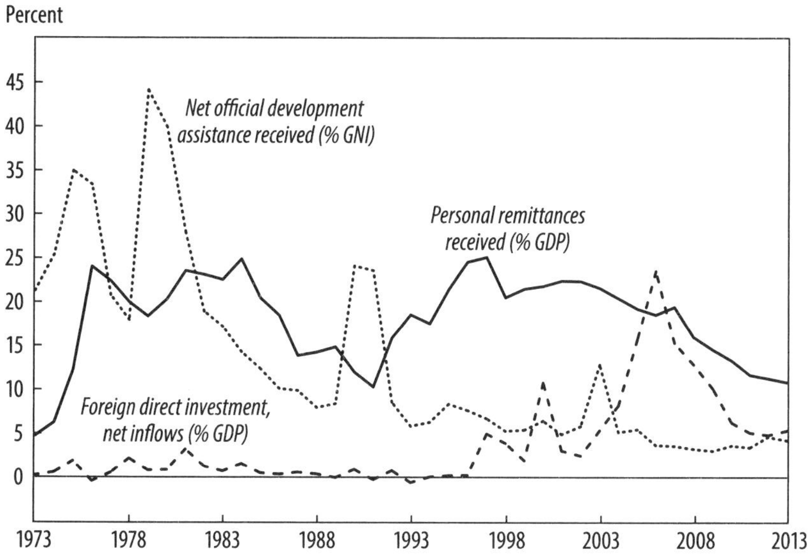

Percent

Source: World Development Indicators, World Bank.

of regional turmoil.[3] From less than half a million people in 1950, Jordan's population rose to nearly 6.5 million in 2012 and is projected to keep growing substantially in the near future.

If the pace of population growth has slowed down from what it was in the 1950s and 1960s, the demographic transition seems to have come to a halt.[4] Jordan's population growth rate is now below 3 percent, and although the fertility rate has decreased from a high of 8.0 children per woman in 1960 to 3.7 in 2010 the decrease has indeed stalled (table 7-1).[5] In terms of population and demographic trends, the country faces other challenges than Tunisia (which has a fertility rate of 2 children per woman and a growth rate around 1 percent) or Egypt or Morocco (which have rates already below 3 children per woman and around a 1.5 percent growth rate). It appears unlikely that Jordan will soon reach the replacement level threshold of 2.1 children per woman.

3. Economic Research Forum and Institut de la Méditerranée (2005).
4. Cetorelli and Leone (2012).
5. Courbage (2011).

TABLE 7-1. Evolution of Jordan's Population Growth Rate and Fertility, 1950–2020

Period	Population growth rate (percent)	Total fertility rate (children/woman)
1950–60	6.830	7.380
1960–70	6.215	8.000
1970–80	3.210	7.585
1980–90	3.870	6.535
1990–2000	3.505	4.715
2000–10	3.030	3.745
2010–20	2.255	3.125

Source: United Nations Population Division.

In addition to this population growth, the Syrian crisis has prompted more than 600,000 refugees to move to Jordan since 2011 (some accounts put it above 1 million).[6] This inflow will have a formidable economic impact in the short and medium term for the country.[7] The arrival of what amounts to almost 10 percent of the population in a three-year span will undoubtedly alter the labor market and the country as a whole. To some extent, Jordan is already a mosaic of populations and a political puzzle.

Estimates put the share of people in Jordan with Palestinian origin (as opposed to East Bankers, also called Transjordanians) at between 50 and 70 percent.[8] The immigration from the West Bank has had a lasting impact, with immigrants coming after 1948 and 1967 granted citizenship, and others arriving in 1991 and 2003 after fleeing Iraq (or Kuwait) during the two Iraqi wars. The civil war known as Black September, in 1970 and 1971, strongly divided West and East Bankers by stigmatizing Jordanians of Palestinian origin, leaving an important rift between the two in the economic activity of the country. This rift is not to be overstated, but it bears monitoring as testing times can bring some tension back.[9]

---

6. Jordan has installed refugee camps for Syrian refugees, as it has for Palestinians, while Lebanon, for instance, has not.
7. Their presence is visible in Amman, particularly in the informal sector for now.
8. See Zahran (2012); El Muhtaseb (2013).
9. Human Rights Watch (2010).

The shape and speed of growth of the Jordanian population are such that, depending on the way the demographic dividend evolves, the growth of the labor force could be either an asset or a burden to the economic and social development of the country. The extent of the consequences of the Syrian crisis on Jordan is unknown at this time, but it will be tremendous and will probably reshape the country's equilibrium.

The Working-Age Population and the Workers

The proportion of the very young population in Jordan (under fifteen years old) has been declining since the early 1980s, when it reached almost 50 percent of the population. This demographic remains the bulk of the population but is now closer to one-third, which implies that the greatest labor-oriented challenges are currently related to the large percentage of young adults. People under the age of twenty-five still represent 55 percent of the country, and the working-age population is above 60 percent. At the same time, the number of young people is still growing in absolute terms, and the need for the economy to create opportunities will only increase. Jobs are and will still be needed at a high rate.

Given the continued increase of Jordan's working-age population, the country's dependency ratio has been steadily decreasing since the early 1980s.[10] Appropriately handled and embraced, this trend could be a good opportunity for Jordan. If well exploited, it can yield demographic dividends (for example, when dependents are few compared with a booming working population). The output produced by such an economy could dramatically increase productivity gains. Ill used, a low dependency ratio can burden a country when opportunities are lacking and people are out of work at an age when work is a necessity and an aspiration. It can lead to tensions or vicious circles of inactivity.

Handling the labor force and the rapid growth of young adults is undoubtedly one of the country's main challenges. Helping provide jobs and opportunities will remain a core mission for public policies in a country such as Jordan.

---

10. Ratio of population aged birth to fourteen and sixty-five and older per 100 population fifteen to sixty-four.

FIGURE 7-2. Jordan's Working-Age Population, 2012

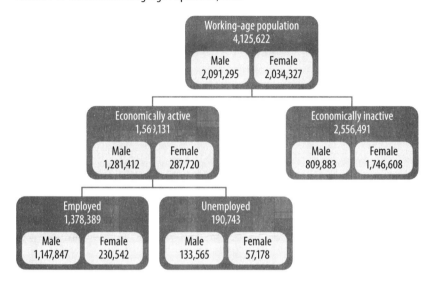

Source: Author's calculation based on Department of Statistics data.

Who Is Working?

The working-age population of Jordan is currently above 4 million (figure 7-2).[11] However, economically active people represented only around 40 percent of this population in 2012 (a figure relatively stable over the past two decades).[12] This implies that approximately 60 percent of working-age people do not even look for a job. This number includes students who normally finish their secondary education at eighteen and retirees (many segments of the public sector enable early retirement). Hence when considering the number of people actually working (excluding the unemployed and economically inactive), only 1.4 million people support a population of 6.5 million. The picture this paints differs greatly from the raw dependency ratio of Jordan and hints at the possibility of increasing the wealth of the country.

11. The International Labor Organization and the Department of Statistics (DOS) of Jordan consider people above fifteen as the working-age population, while the World Development Indicators (WDI) only includes people between fifteen and sixty-four. The former is used except if noted otherwise.

12. The World Bank's World Development Indicators has labor participation at 41, while Jordan's Department of Statistics has it at 39 percent for the year 2011.

FIGURE 7-3. Labor Force Participation in Jordan, 1990–2011

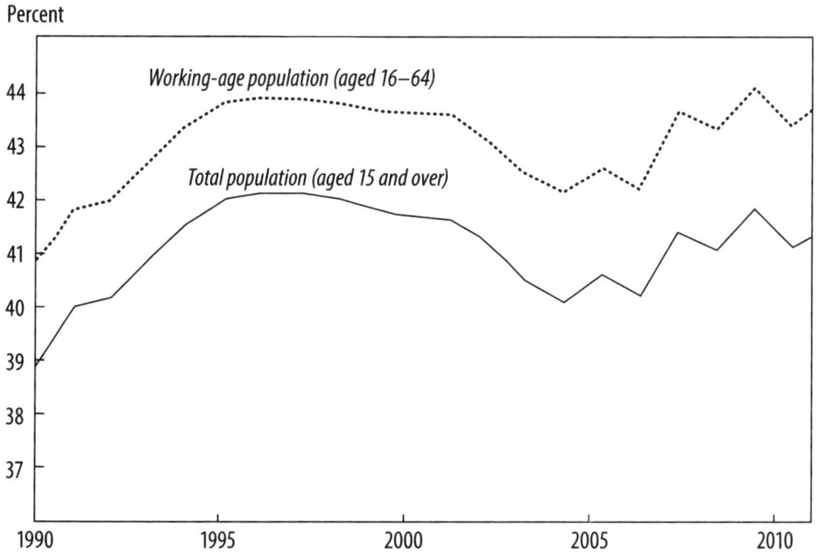

Percent

Source: World Development Indicators, World Bank.

Labor force participation has not been increasing over the medium term (Ahamad 2010). After plateauing in the late 1990s, it had shrunk by 2 percent by 2005 and since then has been regaining ground (figure 7-3). The participation rate for people above the age of fifteen years is estimated at 41.5 percent by the World Bank, a level that is very close to what it was twenty years ago.

Since it compares so poorly with other countries or regions, the Jordanian economy faces the challenge of improving the participation rate of the active workforce. Jordan's youth participation in the labor force is lower than the average in Middle East and North African countries and below the rates of both Asia and sub-Saharan Africa (figure 7-4). This is a major weakness for Jordan, even more so than for most other countries in the region. That it has been able to reach its current level of wealth (Jordan is an upper-middle-income country) does not hide the weakness of the labor participation, which hinders any potential for long-term development, especially in the absence of natural resources.

Therefore, aside from people who are not of working age, economic inactivity and unemployment characterize the bulk of the population. Though the dependency ratio appears to be very favorable, in truth the

FIGURE 7-4. Comparison of International Labor Force Participation Rates, 1990–2011

Percent of total population above age 15

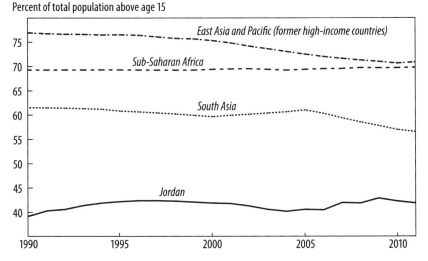

Source: World Development Indicators, World Bank.

ratio of those working in Jordan to those who are dependent is worrisome (table 7-2). It is not so much the strictly defined working-age
population but the population actually working and producing that
matters for Jordan. As mentioned above, this ratio is close to 22 percent, meaning that on average one person supports more than four.
Studying the inactive population can give a sense of who is out of the
workforce, besides young children.

Who Is Inactive?

The inactive population (that is, out of the labor force) is overwhelmingly made up of women. There are more than twice as many inactive
women as inactive men. It is striking that 60 percent of the inactive
population is made up of women with more than a high school diploma,[13] and more than a quarter are men with the same level of education. Thirty percent of the inactive are students, a share that partially
explains the level of the inactivity rate for the whole country; the population is young and there are still numerous students.

Also, when looking at inactivity by education level, one notes a decreasing inactivity as the level of education rises, except in the case of men at

13. Ministry of Labor (2010).

TABLE 7-2. Age Distribution of Population in Jordan, 1950–2010

Year	0–14		15–64		64+		15–24		Total	Total dependency ratio
	1,000s	Percent	1,000s	Percent	1,000s	Percent	1,000s	Percent	1,000s	
1950	205	46	222	49	22	5	78	17	449	102.2
1955	286	44	331	51	29	5	125	19	646	95.4
1960	386	43	465	52	38	4	178	20	889	91.2
1965	503	45	574	51	42	4	214	19	1,120	94.9
1970	759	46	842	51	54	3	298	18	1,655	96.6
1975	937	47	987	50	61	3	344	17	1,985	101.1
1980	1,117	49	1,090	48	73	3	447	20	2,281	109.2
1985	1,311	47	1,372	49	100	4	569	20	2,783	102.8
1990	1,552	46	1,696	50	111	3	737	22	3,358	98.1
1995	1,757	41	2,433	56	130	3	962	22	4,320	77.6
2000	1,877	39	2,742	58	149	3	1,045	22	4,767	73.9
2005	1,986	38	3,087	59	167	3	1,103	21	5,239	69.7
2010	2,265	35	3,971	62	219	3	1,279	20	6,455	62.6

Source: United Nations Population Division.

the bachelor's degree level; generally, more-educated people participate in the labor force. Nonetheless, the percentage of women with a bachelor's degree who are out of the workforce is twice that of men. Women with an intermediate diploma are five times more likely to be out of the workforce (Majcher-Teleon and Slimène 2009). The bulk of inactive people remain those with a lower education, though, in particular children and young adults who have not completed their education (table 7-3).

A Detour by Immigration and Emigration

The picture of the labor market in Jordan would not be complete without looking at foreign workers in Jordan as well as Jordanian workers abroad, since immigration and emigration are important factors in the dynamics of Jordan.[14] The actual figure for foreign workers in Jordan is unknown, but estimates put it between 400,000 and 500,000 people. The Jordanian Ministry of Labor announced that there were

14. For a detailed description of these groups using the panel data of 2010, see Wahba (2012).

TABLE 7-3. Inactive Population, by Gender and Education Level, 2012

Percent

	Men	Women	Total
Total	31.68	68.32	100
Illiterate	2.25	7.83	10.08
Literate	29.43	60.49	89.92
Less than secondary	18.41	37.02	55.43
Secondary	7.70	13.22	20.92
Intermediate diploma	1.02	5.39	6.41
Bachelor's and above	2.29	4.86	7.15

Source: Author's calculation based on Department of Statistics data.

235,000 legal foreign workers at the end of 2012 (down from 335,000 in 2009), two-thirds of them Egyptian; and there are between 150,000 and 250,000 undocumented workers.[15] Overall, they represent roughly one-third of the working population of Jordan. The main characteristics of foreign workers are that they are almost all in the private sector, are mostly low-skilled, and are more likely to work in the informal sector. In short, it seems that they perform jobs Jordanians do not fill, and the economy is heavily dependent on their role in the agricultural and service sectors (Mryyan 2012).

Jordan's emigrants are highly educated. Sixty percent have a university degree, and the large majority of them were employed before leaving, particularly in the private sector. They tend to remain in the private sector abroad. They are also numerous. The Migration Policy Center estimates that there were close to 350,000 Jordanian migrants in 2009, 140,000 in oil-producing countries and close to 70,000 in the United States. The first Gulf war from 1990 to 1992 and the economic crisis of 2008 have led to some return migration (11 percent of the households have some return migrants); nonetheless, migrants remain better educated than those returning and those who stayed, and are an important element of the political economy of the country.

Overall, the number of Jordanian workers abroad could exceed 500,000, equivalent to approximately one-third of Jordan's domestic

15. International Labour Organization (2012).

labor force.[16] A third of those migrants left in the two years before the survey, and 80 percent had visited Jordan in the previous two years.[17] Wahba (2012) finds that 38 percent of Jordanian migrants in Arab countries had professional occupations, the same proportion working in sales and services in Europe and North America.

The size and the level of the Jordanian emigrant group show how, in the absence of opportunities for well-educated nationals, emigration is a way to get jobs better suited to their skills and demands and with often higher wages. It is possible that a high proportion of emigrants are Palestinian, since they are mobile and often well educated.

The value of remittances (at least 12 percent of Jordan's gross domestic product) shows the importance of workers abroad for the country's financing (Saif and El-Rayyes 2009). It seems that emigration serves as a safety valve for Jordanians, offering openings when the domestic job market is blocked up and allowing them to send remittances to help relatives. Wahba (2012) also notes that remittances are mostly sent to households with female heads (half of them above the age of forty), with 3.3 percent of Jordan households receiving some remittance in 2010. It is then likely that men are working abroad and sending remittances back to Jordan.

However, there is no formula for renationalizing jobs in Jordan in the short term. Unskilled jobs occupied by foreigners are often a result of the lack of enthusiasm by Jordanians for these jobs, which they probably have the skills to fill. On the other side of the spectrum, there is a lack of opportunity for skilled Jordanians and a relative brain drain hampering the endogenous growth of the country. Finding a way to have Jordanian emigrants contribute to the domestic economy, besides remittances, is a topic that should be high on the agenda of the government even though it has no easy solution.

Labor Force, Job Creation, and Unemployment

The dynamic of unemployment results from the difference between the growth of the labor force and the net number of jobs created. The matching of the demand for jobs and available offers determines the

16. According to Mryyan (2012).
17. Wahba (2012).

TABLE 7-4. Labor Force Growth, Jordan, by Gender, 1990–2011

	Total			Women			Men		
	Total in labor force	Labor force growth		Women in labor force	Labor force growth		Men in labor force	Labor force growth	
Year		Number	Percent		Number	Percent		Number	Percent
1990	663,272			71,031			592,242		
1991	777,486	114,214	17.22	84,525	13,494	19.00	692,961	100,719	17.01
1992	842,023	64,537	8.30	97,829	13,304	15.74	744,194	51,233	7.39
1993	917,163	75,140	8.92	110,930	13,100	13.39	806,234	62,040	8.34
1994	988,526	71,362	7.78	124,199	13,270	11.96	864,326	58,093	7.21
1995	1,045,166	56,641	5.73	137,166	12,966	10.44	908,000	43,674	5.05
1996	1,089,579	44,413	4.25	145,352	8,186	5.97	944,227	36,227	3.99
1997	1,129,223	39,644	3.64	153,568	8,216	5.65	975,654	31,427	3.33
1998	1,164,876	35,654	3.16	159,342	5,774	3.76	1,005,534	29,880	3.06
1999	1,183,243	18,366	1.58	164,624	5,281	3.31	1,018,619	13,085	1.30
2000	1,212,988	29,745	2.51	172,682	8,059	4.90	1,040,306	21,686	2.13
2001	1,244,332	31,344	2.58	174,152	1,469	0.85	1,070,181	29,875	2.87
2002	1,267,107	22,775	1.83	188,842	14,690	8.44	1,078,265	8,085	0.76
2003	1,282,239	15,132	1.19	180,126	−8,717	−4.62	1,102,114	23,849	2.21
2004	1,307,927	25,688	2.00	170,596	−9,530	−5.29	1,137,331	35,218	3.20
2005	1,364,267	56,340	4.31	197,581	26,986	15.82	1,166,686	29,355	2.58
2006	1,393,811	29,544	2.17	209,386	11,805	5.97	1,184,425	17,739	1.52
2007	1,481,499	87,687	6.29	261,737	52,351	25.00	1,219,761	35,336	2.98
2008	1,517,472	35,974	2.43	263,011	1,274	0.49	1,254,461	34,700	2.84
2009	1,591,950	74,478	4.91	286,319	23,308	8.86	1,305,631	51,170	4.08
2010	1,613,065	21,115	1.33	293,365	7,046	2.46	1,319,700	14,070	1.08
2011	1,677,855	64,790	4.02	308,453	15,088	5.14	1,369,402	49,702	3.77

Source: Ecowin, World Development Indicators, World Bank.

capacity of the economy to fulfill the aspirations of would-be workers. Data for Jordan are difficult to come by and are not always consistent, but such data that exist are instructive in this regard.

The Growth of the Labor Force

According to the World Bank, the labor force of Jordan was the fastest growing in the world between 1990 and 2003. In a little more than twenty years, the size of the labor force grew by a factor of 2.5 (table 7-4). The volatility of the labor force growth—that is, the year-to-year inconsistency in its growth rates—is to be noted, especially in the past ten years, showing that there are more than mechanical trends at work; the population entering and leaving the labor force is rather stable year in and year out, but it seems that people choose to enter or not depending on the year, which explains why rates of labor force growth vary so much. There are even years with a negative number of entries for women.

The labor force growth rate only captures those entering the job market, but if everyone were participating in the workforce, Jordan would need to create approximately 100,000 jobs a year for the next few years to accommodate the number of people who need to enter the workforce. Matching this potential demand is probably the greatest challenge yet for the Jordanian economy. Recent figures of net jobs created do not suggest that the economic growth required for such job creation is likely in Jordan.[18]

Net Jobs Created in Recent Years

Between 2007 and 2011, there have been between 50,000 and 75,000 jobs created each year (table 7-5). This performance is impressive and actually surpasses the growth of the labor force shown above. If Jordan's economy could consistently maintain this high level of job growth, it could alleviate pressure on job markets. In comparison, Assaad estimates the net number of jobs created between 2005 and 2009 at only 35,000 to 45,000 a year.[19]

The data on net jobs created in Jordan reveal that the private sector has accounted for approximately two-thirds of those jobs in recent years,

18. The World Bank has calculated that the elasticity of employment to growth has dramatically shrunk from 1.16 in the 1990s to 0.53 in the the following decade (World Bank 2008).

19. Assaad (2012).

TABLE 7-5. Net Jobs Created Annually, Jordan, by Gender, 2007–11

	2007	2008	2009	2010	2011
Total	70,356	69,092	76,316	62,813	52,888
Men	50,688	51,124	49,714	39,336	36,062
Women	19,668	17,968	26,602	23,477	16,826

Source: Department of Statistics data.

TABLE 7-6. Net Jobs Created Annually, Jordan, by Sector, 2007–11

	2007		2008		2009		2010		2011	
Sector	Number	Percent	Number	Percent	Number	Percent	Number	Percent	Number	Percent
Total	70,356	100	69,092	100	76,316	100	62,813	100	52,888	100
Public	22,230	31.6	26,820	38.8	26,760	35.1	18,402	29.3	18,248	34.5
Private	47,427	67.4	41,893	60.7	49,168	64.5	44,044	70.1	34,088	64.4

Source: Department of Statistics.

while the public sector has accounted for a third of total employment (table 7-6). The formal private wage sector represents one-fifth of employment; the informal private wage, one-fourth; and self-employment, less than one-fifth.[20] Assaad (2012) also studied the long-term changes in the structure of the job market and notes that Jordan managed to substitute formal private sector employment for government employment while avoiding informalization (government hiring has dropped since the 1980s and only went up again at the beginning of this century).

The mismatch between net jobs created and the expectations of the labor force leads to unemployment. This is particularly true in a country with a good education record, where the demand of highly skilled workers hardly finds appropriate answers (Saif and El Rayyes 2009). It is important to keep in mind that unemployment figures only capture people actively looking for jobs; numerous people have been discouraged and no longer look, and so do not appear in the data.

20. Assaad (2012).

TABLE 7-7. Unemployment Rate, Jordan, by Gender, 1983–2011

Percent unemployed

	Total	Women	Men
1983	4.80	22.80	6.60
1986	12.40	22.30	13.30
1987	13.60	25.40	14.80
1993	18.10	30.00	19.70
1995	12.10	29.90	14.60
1996	12.00	24.30	13.70
2001	15.10	19.70	15.80
2002	15.60	19.60	16.20
2003	14.70	19.70	15.40
2004	11.80	16.50	12.40
2007	10.20	25.90	13.10
2008	10.10	24.30	12.70
2009	10.30	24.10	12.90
2010	10.40	21.70	12.50
2011	11.00	21.20	12.90

Source: Data from World Development Indicators, World Bank.

Unemployment

According to Jordanian authorities, unemployment has been fairly stable at less than 13 percent since 2008. It has slowly been trending downward over this past decade, but contrary to data from the World Bank's World Development Indicators, Jordanian data suggest that the impact of the 2008 crisis is almost nonexistent. The level of unemployment remains high, especially since it adds up to an already large inactive population, but it does not appear to be significantly worsening in the short term (table 7-7).

The unemployed population is 70 percent men and is overwhelmingly young (under the age of thirty-nine), with less than 10 percent of the unemployed being over forty (table 7-8). Nonetheless, there is an important difference between men and women, since almost 50 percent of unemployed men are under twenty-four while 50 percent of unemployed women are between twenty-five and thirty-nine; the bulk of unemployed men are younger than the bulk of unemployed women. A possible reason for this could be that men enter the workforce at a

TABLE 7-8. Unemployment, Jordan, by Gender and Age, 2012
Percent

Major age groups	Gender		
	Total	Men	Women
15–24	48.8	49.7	46.7
25–39	41.3	37.5	50.4
40+	9.9	12.9	2.9

Source: Department of Statistics data.

TABLE 7-9. Unemployment, Jordan, by Gender and Education Level, 2012
Percent

Education level	Gender		
	Total	Men	Women
Illiterate	0.9	1.3	0.1
Less than secondary	44.4	60.3	7.3
Secondary	8.2	10.0	3.8
Intermediate diploma	9.5	5.4	19.1
Bachelor's and above	37.0	23	69.6

Source: Department of Statistics data.

younger age than women, while many women remain inactive after they finish school.

The data also show that the percentage of educated people in unemployment is staggeringly high in Jordan, in line with what is observed elsewhere in the region. Indeed, graduates with bachelor's degrees represent 37 percent of the total unemployed, and an astonishing 70 percent of unemployed women (table 7-9). Ninety percent of unemployed women have more than a secondary education, but only 30 percent of men do. Thus for men, the largest contribution to unemployment figures comes from the uneducated. The unemployment field really seems two-tiered: educated women and less-educated men.

The Jordanian economy seems to have been creating jobs at a decent pace, but it still misses the mark if it wants to include all the new members of the labor force. While unemployment remains fairly stable, the pace of job creation should probably be doubled to try to increase the rate of participation in order to include new entrants. Also, the high level of unemployment for men and for highly skilled women can only have deterrent effects on the economic development of the country. The focus of policies on young and skilled people remains necessary; the efforts made to improve education have been successful, but the labor market remains to be translated into a dynamic one, especially for women.

Women: More Educated, More Inactive, More Unemployed

As previously mentioned, the labor participation rate in Jordan is low, even by regional standards—and especially for women (United Nations Development Program 2011). Jordan has the fifth lowest female labor participation rate in the world (only Algeria, Iraq, Syria, and the West Bank trail within a percent).[21]

Women make up only a small portion of Jordan's working population; less than 20 percent of the total workforce is made up of women, and only 16 percent of Jordanian women participate in the workforce (table 7-10). This structural element of the Jordanian economy is of concern as it basically excludes women from the economic and productive process. It has undoubtedly some roots in the cultural background of the country, as the list of the countries with the lowest women's participation illustrates. It is also to be noted that labor participation for men above the age of fifteen has been decreasing since the late 1980s, a development that bears attention because it reflects very poorly on the overall prospects of the Jordanian economy.

The perceived increase in women's labor force participation could be the result of a change in the sample used by the Jordanian Department of Statistics to measure the labor force participation in 2007,[22] with the level measured being at a different "equilibrium" before and after but remaining relatively stagnant before and since 2007. It probably means that the level of women's participation is indeed stable and close to 15 percent today. It should also be noted that the share of women in the labor force rose in the early 1990s, showing a slight change in the willingness of women to participate in the labor force.

21. Assaad and Amer (2008).
22. As shown by Assaad, Hendy, and Yassine (2012).

TABLE 7-10. Labor Force Participation Rates, Jordan, 1990–2011
Percent

Year	Total labor force	Women in the labor force[a]	Women's labor participation rate[b]	Men's labor participation rate[c]
1990	663,272	10.7	8.9	65.3
1991	777,486	10.9	9.3	67.0
1992	842,023	11.6	10.0	66.6
1993	917,163	12.1	10.6	67.5
1994	988,526	12.6	11.2	68.1
1995	1,045,166	13.1	11.8	68.5
1996	1,089,579	13.3	12.0	68.7
1997	1,129,223	13.6	12.2	68.7
1998	1,164,876	13.7	12.2	68.7
1999	1,183,243	13.9	12.3	68.4
2000	1,212,988	14.2	12.5	68.2
2001	1,244,332	14.0	12.2	68.4
2002	1,267,107	14.9	12.8	67.1
2003	1,282,239	14.0	11.8	66.9
2004	1,307,927	13.0	10.8	67.0
2005	1,364,267	14.5	12.1	66.9
2006	1,393,811	15.0	12.4	65.9
2007	1,481,499	17.7	15.0	66.0
2008	1,517,472	17.3	14.6	65.8
2009	1,591,950	18.0	15.4	66.6
2010	1,613,065	18.2	15.3	65.4
2011	1,677,855	18.4	15.6	65.9

Source: World Development Indicators, World Bank.
a. Share of total labor force.
b. Share of female population aged fifteen or older.
c. Share of male population aged fifteen or older.

To be more precise, the labor force participation rate of women by age suggests that, until their late twenties, women's participation increases, but contrary to men, it then decreases (figure 7-5). The contrast is striking since almost all men are part of the workforce between twenty-five and forty. It means that from the beginning of their work lives, women lag behind men in the job market (in terms of experience and date of entry).

There are at least two ways to look at the fact that women are lagging in the labor market: using a contemporary analysis that primarily

FIGURE 7-5. Labor Force Participation Rate in Jordan, by Gender and Age, 2013

Percent participating

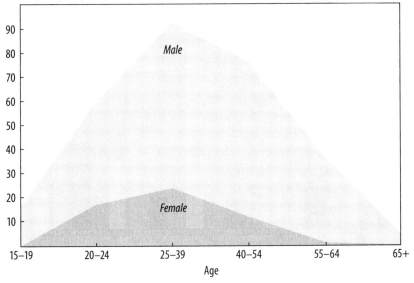

Source: ILOSTAT database.

examines marital status and education levels and using a study over the medium term to see patterns, as Assaad, Hendy, and Yassine (2012) did. Data from 2012 and early 2013 do not change the conclusions they made.

Indeed, participation in the labor market dramatically increases for women with diplomas: in 2012, less than 6 percent of women with less than a secondary education participated in the workforce, while 31 percent and 57 percent of women with an intermediate diploma and at least a bachelor's degree, respectively, participated. For men, the added value of an intermediate diploma or higher degrees is important, but even illiterate men participate in the workforce at more than 20 percent. Assaad, Hendy, and Yassine (2012) state that the ability of more-educated women to get jobs in the government, or in the private sector to a lesser extent, is the reason for the discrepancy between education levels. Only for women with a bachelor's degree or more is the economic activity above 50 percent, while it is almost marginal for any woman with at best a secondary education.

TABLE 7-11. Economic Status, Jordan, by Gender and Education, 2012
Percent

Gender and education level	Economically active			Not economically active	Unemployment rate
	Total	Employed	Unemployed		
Total	38	33.4	4.6	62	12.2
Illiterate	6.8	6.2	0.6	93.2	9.3
Less than secondary	34.8	30.9	3.9	65.2	11.2
Secondary	25.4	23.2	2.2	74.6	8.6
Intermediate diploma	50.7	45.2	5.5	49.3	10.8
Bachelor's and above	70.8	59.6	11.2	29.2	15.9
Men					
Total	61.3	54.9	6.4	38.7	10.4
Illiterate	21.9	19.6	2.3	78.1	10.4
Less than secondary	60.4	53.6	6.8	39.6	11.2
Secondary	45.2	41.4	3.7	54.8	8.3
Intermediate diploma	80.3	74.9	5.4	19.7	6.8
Bachelor's and above	82.6	73.5	9.1	17.4	11.0
Women					
Total	14.1	11.3	2.8	85.9	19.9
Illiterate	1.3	1.3	0	98.7	2.1
Less than secondary	3.8	3.4	0.4	96.2	11.0
Secondary	5.6	5.0	0.6	94.4	11
Intermediate diploma	30.9	25.4	5.5	69.1	17.8
Bachelor's and above	57.1	43.4	13.7	42.9	24.0

Source: [pls provide source]

However, women's unemployment rate rises systematically with education, more strongly than for men (for whom the correlation is weaker). While there is almost no unemployment for women with low qualifications, the share of jobless women with secondary education and above who are in the labor force is very large (table 7-11).

Many authors emphasize that marriage[23] seems to push women to drop out of the workforce (the opposite is true for men). Whatever their level of education may be, married women are indeed less present in

23. And childbearing, most probably.

TABLE 7-12. Distribution of Working-Age Population, by Gender, Employment Status, and Marital Status, Jordan, 2010

Percent

Gender	Below secondary			Secondary and above			University and higher			Total		
	Never married	Ever married	Total	Never married	Ever married	Total	Never married	Ever married	Total	Never married	Ever married	Total
Women												
Employed	7	5	5	15	12	13	53	43	46	15	12	13
Unemployed	2	1	1	7	2	4	26	8	14	6	2	4
Out of labor force	92	95	94	78	85	82	21	50	40	78	86	83
Men												
Employed	42	80	61	41	84	64	72	85	80	45	82	65
Unemployed	10	5	7	6	4	5	16	3	8	10	4	7
Out of labor force	48	15	32	53	13	31	12	12	12	45	14	29

Source: Assaad, Hendy, and Yassine (2012).

the labor force.[24] This trend is particularly true for educated women. Half of the married women are out of the labor market, while only 21 percent of unmarried women are (table 7-12). This pattern holds true to a lesser extent for women with a secondary degree, while the difference for less-educated women is marginal. Moreover, the group of women with the highest unemployment rate is made of unmarried, educated women, 26 percent of whom are unemployed.

In comparison, men are more active when married, except for those with higher degrees (for those with higher degrees, there is no variation in employment between the married and unmarried). However, for men too, the educated unmarried are the most unemployed group as a share of the population. Also, unmarried people are more unemployed than married ones, probably because they need to be in the labor force to support themselves.

24. As shown by Al Salamat, Mryyan, and Raddad (2007).

TABLE 7-13. Top Ten Economic Activities for Women above Age Fifteen, Jordan, 2012
Percent

Economic activity	Jordan	Rural	Urban
Education	41.8	47.9	40.6
Human health and social work activities	14.3	15.4	14.1
Public administration and defense; compulsory social security	12.1	17.7	11.1
Manufacturing	6.4	5.9	6.5
Wholesale and retail trade; repair of motor vehicles and motorcycles	5.5	3.4	5.9
Financial and insurance activities	3.2	0.7	3.6
Professional, scientific, and technical activities	3.0	0.9	3.4
Other service activities	2.8	1.6	3.1
Activities of households as employers; undifferentiated goods— and services—producing activities of households for own use	2.5	0.6	2.8
Information and communication	1.9	0.4	2.2

Source: Department of Statistics, Employment and Unemployment Survey.

Education is the main economic activity for women (more than 40 percent of working women are employed in that sector).[25] The health and public administration sectors follow, with just under 15 percent of women working in these sectors in 2012. This illustrates the fact that besides the public sector, there are few economic activities where women are present (table 7-13).

Assaad, Hendy, and Yassine (2012) use the panel data gathered in 2010 to study the dynamics of female employment over the past forty years. They find that "women new entrants were much more reliant on government jobs in the 1970s and 1980s than their men counterparts" (over 60 percent of women relied on public sector jobs until 1985). The share of working women who were in the government sector then fell to 25 percent in the 1990s and rose to 30 percent in the years of this century. Women faced the possibility of fewer government jobs, and new hiring primarily benefited men. The job status of women subsequently became more precarious because they had to take either informal wage employment or temporary jobs. Studying the trajectories of young women entering the labor market, Assaad, Hendy, and Yassine (2012) confirm that many women drop out of the workforce in their

25. According to Mryyan (n.d.).

first ten years, especially women with less family-friendly jobs (that is, outside of the government). The only mobility appears to be from formal private jobs to government jobs.

Labor opportunities for educated women are declining since the environment of private sector employment is not as family friendly,[26] and the public sector has a somewhat diminished capacity to absorb young graduates.[27] This trend is a development worth following in light of the tighter margin for public jobs: the public budget is very much constrained, which means that job openings will have to come from the private sector. The need for private sector dynamism should be the driving force of the labor market. Even if they are overall better educated, women's economic activity remains weak, and their unemployment rate is systematically higher than men's. They are either inactive, unemployed, or work in formal employment.[28] Encouraging the private sector to employ women is therefore another important challenge for Jordan.

Young Jordanians: How to Enter the Labor Force?

The balance of the young population (under thirty) has recently shifted toward young adults, with their overall share of the population having decreased at a slower pace than that of young children. Almost two-thirds of the population remains under thirty, with a little less than 50 percent under twenty. This shift creates tremendous pressure on the economy to provide jobs now and in the short term, especially since the improvements of school enrollment and education attainment have been remarkable (see tables 7-14 and 7-15).[29]

Despite a changed environment, younger educated generations continue to expect interesting and high-level jobs, though first jobs of a precarious and informal nature are becoming more common while more secure public jobs have been harder to get.[30] This is an important

26. As shown by Darwazeh and others (2007).
27. Assaad, Hendy, and Yassine (2012).
28. Compare Amer (2012).
29. Mryyan (n.d.). According to the World Development Indicators, the gross enrollment ratio is the total enrollment in primary, secondary, and tertiary education, regardless of age, expressed as a percentage of the population of official primary education age. The ratio can exceed 100 percent owing to the inclusion of overage and underage students because of early or late school entrance and grade repetition.
30. Assaad (2012).

TABLE 7-14. Population as Share of Total Population, by Age Cohort, 2000–12

Percent

Year	Years of age					
	0–4	5–9	10–14	15–19	20–24	25–29
2000	13.30	13.90	12.60	12.30	10.30	8.10
2002	12.00	13.10	12.50	12.50	10.90	8.00
2004	12.00	12.40	12.80	12.20	10.70	7.80
2006	11.70	12.20	12.90	12.00	10.30	7.90
2008	12.20	12.00	12.60	11.10	9.90	7.90
2010	12.50	12.00	11.90	11.40	9.70	7.70
2012	12.10	12.00	11.40	11.10	9.30	7.50

Source: Department of Statistics, Employment Survey.

TABLE 7-15. School Enrollment, Jordan, 1971–2010[a]

Percent

Year	Primary	Secondary	Tertiary
1971	102.67	47.15	3.06
1980	107.64	77.43	14.80
1990	101.48	76.09	20.41
2000	97.96	84.23	28.32
2010	91.99	86.93	37.74

Source: World Development Indicators, World Bank.

a. According to the World Development Indicators, the gross enrollment ratio is the total enrollment in primary, secondary, and tertiary education, regardless of age, expressed as a percentage of the population of official primary education age. The ratio can exceed 100 percent owing to the inclusion of overage and underage students because of early or late school entrance and grade repetition.

development, since public employment had been the goal of qualified young graduates—especially Transjordanians—as part of the social contract with the state. The rupture of this kind of tacit social contract appears to have been an important factor in the contestations in some Maghreb countries, and Jordan has yet to experience this backlash. In short, the public sector will not be able to absorb highly educated Jordanians in bulk anymore; they will not be able to follow their elders' career paths and will have to look for other kinds of opportunities.

It is interesting to note that women outnumber men in school by more than 3 percent. A little less than 60 percent of women between

TABLE 7-16. Economic Activity of Young People, Age Fifteen to Twenty-Four, Jordan, 2011

Percent

	Men	Women
Currently enrolled students	54.48	58.05
Employed	28.20	4.60
Unemployed	9.50	4.40
Economically active	37.70	9.00
Economically inactive	62.30	91.00

Source: Department of Statistics data.

fifteen and twenty-four are enrolled in school. However, this fact does not explain the discrepancy in economic activity, with men being four times more active than women. The share of young women neither active nor employed dwarfs the share of young men, a development that is undoubtedly harming the economy (table 7-16). This statistic confirms the fact that women stay away from any economic activity at a rate that is considerable—only 9 percent of women ages fifteen to twenty-four are economically active.

For young women working, it seems that they are mostly employed when they have a higher degree of education, while men with a lower education are prevalent in the workforce (table 7-17). Among the young workforce, women with higher education are more likely to be employed than men with a similar degree or less-educated women. This suggests that some women are selecting out of participation in the working world. In general, women with little education opt out of the labor force altogether, while those with at least a high school education give it a try.

According to Assaad, the "share of formal private employment in the employment of new entrants to the Jordanian labor market has more than tripled from 10–12 percent in the mid-1980s to 36–38 percent in 2010."[31] Indeed, after unemployment, the most prevalent sector entered after school is formal private employment, both for men and women.[32] It is an encouraging fact, since growth of the formal private sector is the best way for the country to economically and socially develop over the long term.

31. Assaad (2012, p. 3).
32. According to data gathered by Amer (2012).

TABLE 7-17. Distribution of First Employment Status after School, by Education Level and Gender, Jordan, 2010

	Men				Women			
Status	Less than secondary	Second-ary	Post-secondary and university	Total	Less than secondary	Second-ary	Post-secondary and university	Total
Public	11.6	21.7	22.1	15.6	0.2	1.5	10.9	4.1
Private, formal	12.4	16.2	29.9	17.2	1.6	3.9	18.5	7.8
Private, informal	31.9	18.8	9.8	24.6	2.8	2.9	3.8	3.2
Employer or self-employed	1.9	1.8	3.1	2.2	0	0.4	0.1	0.1
Unpaid worker	6.3	3	2.2	4.8	0.3	0	0.6	0.4
Unemployed	27.8	31.7	31.1	29.2	4.4	5.3	29.6	13.2
Out of labor force	8.2	6.8	1.9	6.5	90.7	86	36.5	71.4
Total		100	100	100	100	100	100	100

Source: Amer (2012).

The mismatch between young graduates and jobs available should be investigated in more detail. However, the increasing importance of private employment after school is interesting for the future, since the private sector has to take over some of the public sector's traditional role as the main prospect for young Jordanians. Nonetheless, the 35 percent of young men and 85 percent of young women who are either inactive or unemployed after schooling cannot be overlooked. The gap between men and women is already very wide for young people, and only young qualified women try to bridge it.

Conclusion and Policy Recommendations

The Syrian crisis has exacerbated long-standing issues for Jordan. Jordan has welcomed migrants from many different areas since its independence and remains diverse, but the country's economy is fragile and needs external support. The arrival of numerous refugees is probably going to dramatically alter the economic environment of Jordan and its labor market dynamics. The changes could also severely impact the political equilibrium between Transjordanians and West Bankers. Hence Jordan continues to try to financially and politically leverage its position in the Middle East as a buffer zone, even more in times of regional turmoil.

Even though Jordan has managed to avoid the informalization of Egypt, for instance, the current situation is only conducive to a deterioration of the job market situation. However, it is also an opportunity for Jordan to create endogenous development since the main exports of Jordan (skilled workers and geopolitical influence) are highly volatile.

Support of International Donors to Keep the Economy Afloat

Jordan is at the center of the storm including countries in the Arab peninsula, between political upheavals in Egypt and Syria, a resurgent civil war in Iraq, and the Israeli-Palestinian standstill. Even though Jordan has so far weathered the storm, and the collateral effects, remarkably and has proven its resiliency, the international support it receives is as necessary as ever to avoid its downfall. Jordan has received various types of much-needed financial aid since early 2011. For instance, Gulf Cooperation Council members have agreed to fund up to $5 billion in projects over five years but have faced difficulty implementing them since the funds are often earmarked toward mega projects that might take a long time to implement.[33] Europe, France, and the United States have also been channeling bilateral and multilateral funds to help the Jordanian economy. An International Monetary Fund program has helped Jordan remain economically stable since 2012, with macroeconomic conditions that do not allow the country much flexibility in its fiscal policy. Central as it is, politically speaking, Jordan will try to continue gathering as much support as it can from Europe, the United States, Japan, and the Gulf Cooperation Council. Overall, the macroeconomic imbalances are such that international donors must remain committed to the stability of Jordan by supporting it. Smaller or medium-size projects would serve both purposes of improving the infrastructure and compensating for the low level of economic activity. This would also help the economy prepare for better days.

33. The GDP of Jordan was approximately $30 billion in 2012, according to the World Development Indicators of the World Bank Data.

Tightly Manage the Balance between Transjordanians and West Bankers

As the budget constraints reappear as an important element in the political economy of Jordan, the government and international donors have to acknowledge different ways to deal with the longtime balance between Transjordanians and West Bankers. The division of labor between public jobs for Transjordanians and private sector activities for West Bankers does not seem sustainable with the public job glut Jordanians face. The implicit social contract that has held that public sector jobs will be available for educated Transjordanians will slowly evolve, as Transjordanians look for more private sector jobs. In the meantime, the West Bankers' demands to be part of the public policymaking could be growing. Intriguingly, Transjordanians might be the first to be discontent because of the changes in their expectations and aspirations, with the number of public jobs available shrinking. Also, the number of Jordanians of Palestinian origin means that the value of the assets they own is tightly linked to that of Palestine,[34] which means that any economic or political problem in Jordan could potentially have dramatic consequences for Palestine.

Support Economic Sectors Conducive to the Employment of Women and Graduates and the Return of Skilled Migrants

Active labor market policies have been implemented on an upward trend, but according to a 2012 evaluation by the World Bank, wage subsidies and soft skills do not seem to have had "large impacts on generating sustained employment for young, relatively educated women in Jordan." The wage subsidy helped graduates gain work experience, and training for soft skills ameliorated "positive thinking and mental health," but sixteen months after the experiment there were no lasting impacts on employment (World Bank 2012).

The low number of jobs being created means that Jordan needs to find niches to create some traction; its skilled workforce and emigrants could thrive in sectors such as information and communications technology, financial services, or pharmaceutical products. The government

34. Reiter (2004).

TABLE 7-18. Education Level of Employed Youth, Jordan, 2012

Percent

	Illiterate	Less than secondary	Secondary	Intermediate diploma	Bachelor's and above
Total	0.63	65.91	11.65	6.01	15.80
Men	0.62	72.49	12.29	4.03	10.59
Women	0.67	18.62	7.66	19.81	53.22

Source: Department of Statistics, Employment and Unemployment Survey.

could implement incentive schemes to build competitive sectors in those areas.[35] So far, it seems that poorly educated Jordanians enter the workforce mostly because they have to, while educated people prefer to wait and see.

Social protection programs that help with childcare and motherhood could be improved—since public jobs with comfortable benefits are increasingly scarce—to better engage women in the job market outside the government. There is much room for improvement in the economic inclusion of women, with better incentives for companies and individuals. Since younger women are more educated than men, their relative exclusion is a tremendous loss for Jordan (table 7-18).

Alter Expectations

Matching young people's expectations and skills with potential jobs or exciting challenges remains elusive, which means that expectations have to be altered. The improvements in the general levels of education among Jordanians needs some counterpart in the job market, otherwise it will continue to lead to the brain drain Jordan has been experiencing. A young booming population is usually creative and entrepreneurial, and it can yield demographic dividends. The government and international donors could further encourage the development of economic niches in the private sector with ad hoc incentives to attract skilled Jordanians off the waiting list for public jobs. The mindset will need

35. The qualified industrial zones have not given traction to the rest of the economy and also employ many foreign workers.

to evolve, which can only happen in the long run through incremental changes. But altering the expectations of Jordanian graduates is paramount when it comes to changing the political economy of the country and enabling a future economic takeoff. Also, the prejudice against women is detrimental to the well-being of Jordan; including women and supporting their participation in the labor force would benefit Jordan socially, politically, and economically.

References

Ahamad, B. 2010. "The Outlook for Employment by Occupation for Jordan." Amman, Jordan: National Center for Human Resources Development, Almanar Project.

Al Salamat, M., N. Mryyan, and K. Raddad. 2007. "New Entrants to Jordanian Labor Market." Amman, Jordan: National Center for Human Resources Development, Almanar Project.

Amer, M. 2012. "The School-to-Work Transition of Jordanian Youth." Working Paper 686. Cairo, Egypt: Economic Research Forum.

Assaad, R. 2012. "The Structure and Evolution of Employment in Jordan." Working Paper 674. Cairo, Egypt: Economic Research Forum.

Assaad, R., and M. Amer. 2008. "Labor Market Conditions in Jordan, 1995–2006: An Analysis of Microdata Sources." Amman, Jordan: National Center for Human Resources Development, Almanar Project.

Assaad, R., R. Hendy, and C. Yassine. 2012. "Gender and the Jordanian Labor Market." Working Paper 701. Cairo, Egypt: Economic Research Forum.

Cetorelli, V., and T. Leone. 2012. "Is Fertility Stalling in Jordan?" *Demographic Research* 26, no. 13: 293–318.

Courbage, Y. 2011. "Population Changes and Perspectives for Arab South Mediterranean Countries." In *IEMed Mediterranean Yearbook 2011*. Barcelona, Spain: IEMed (www.iemed.org/observatori-en/arees-danalisi/documents/anuari/med.2011/canvis-i-perspectives-de-la-poblacio-dels-paisos-arabs-del-sud-de-la-mediterrania-l2019any-2011.

Darwazeh, N., and others. 2007. "Factors Affecting Women's Participation in the Private Sector in Jordan." Amman, Jordan: National Center for Human Resources Development, Almanar Project.

Economic Research Forum and Institut de la Méditerranée. 2005. "Jordan Country Profile: The Road Ahead for Jordan." Marseille, France: Forum Euroméditerranéen des Instituts de Sciences Économiques.

El Muhtaseb, L. 2013. "Jordan's East Banker–Palestinian Schism." Oslo, Norway: Norwegian Peacebuilding Resource Center Expert Analysis.

Human Rights Watch. 2010. "Stateless Again: Palestinian-Origin Jordanians Deprived of Their Nationality." New York.

International Crisis Group. 2012. *Popular Protest in North Africa and the Middle East (IX): Dallying with Reform in a Divided Jordan.* Middle East Report 118. Brussels, Belgium.

International Labour Organization. 2012. *Jordan's National Employment Strategy, 2011–20.* Geneva, Switzerland.

Majcher-Teleon, A., and O. Slimène. 2009. "Women and Work in Jordan: Case Study of Tourism and ICT Sectors." Working paper. Turin, Italy: European Training Foundation.

Ministry of Labor. 2010. *National Employment Strategy, 2011–20.* Amman, Jordan.

Mryyan, N. 2012. "Demographics, Labor Force Participation, and Unemployment in Jordan." Working Paper 670. Cairo, Egypt: Economic Research Forum.

Mryyan, N. n.d. "Labor Market Functioning: The Case of Jordan." Turin, Italy: European Training Foundation.

Reiter, Y. 2004. "The Palestinian-Transjordanian Rift: Economic Might and Political Power in Jordan." *Middle East Journal* 58, no. 1: 72–92.

Saif, I., and T. El-Rayyes. 2009. "Labour Markets Performance and Migration Flows in Jordan." National Background Paper. Florence, Italy: Robert Schuman Center for Advanced Studies.

United Nations Development Program and Ministry of Planning and International Cooperation. 2011. *Jordanian Human Development Report: Jordan Small Business and Human Development.* Amman, Jordan.

Wahba, J. 2012. "Immigration, Emigration, and the Labor Market in Jordan." Working Paper 671. Cairo, Egypt: Economic Research Forum.

World Bank. 2008. "Hashemite Kingdom of Jordan: Resolving Jordan's Labor Market Paradox of Concurrent Economic Growth and High Unemployment." Economic and Social Development Unit of the Middle East Department, Middle East and North Africa Region. Washington.

———. 2012. "Soft Skills or Hard Cash: The Impact of Training and Wage Subsidy Programs on Female Youth Employment in Jordan." Policy Research Working Paper 6141. Washington.

Zahran, M. 2012. "Jordan Is Palestinian." *Middle East Quarterly* 19, no. 1: 3–12.

8

The Opportunities for and Challenges to Female Labor Force Participation in Morocco

YUKO MORIKAWA

In the Middle East and North Africa (MENA) region, women remain an untapped resource. They constitute 49 percent of the total population, including more than half of the university students in some countries, yet they make up just 28 percent of the labor force (World Bank 2004). Morocco is no exception: women make up 50 percent of the population[1] and 47 percent of tertiary education enrollment[2] but only 26 percent of the labor force.[3] Furthermore, the female labor force participation (FLFP) rate in Morocco declined from 30 percent to 26 percent between 1999 and 2010.[4] Indeed, the FLFP rate in the MENA region is the lowest in the world (figure 8-1). It is important to understand the mechanisms behind the low female participation rate, as higher FLFP rates could lead to higher economic growth in the region. For instance, according to a report by the World Bank, if FLFP rates were increased to predicted levels calculated from various demographic and economic factors, average household earnings would increase by 25 percent, which would allow many of those households to achieve middle-class status (World Bank 2004).

Many researchers have conducted studies on the relationship between gender inequality and economic development. Seguino (2000)

1. ILO Database, 2012.
2. World Bank World Development Indicators Database, "Ratio of Female to Male Tertiary Enrollment (89.1%), 2010."
3. ILO Database, 2012.
4. World Bank World Development Indicators Database, 1999–2010.

FIGURE 8-1. Female Labor Force Participation Rate, Ages 16–64

Percent

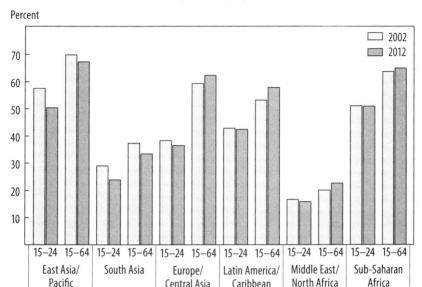

Source: World Bank, World Development Indicators.

makes the rather provocative claim that in semi-industrialized economies, gender inequality actually promotes economic growth through
enhanced investment. Here, gender inequality concerned the difference
in wage levels of women and men, which translated into higher profitability on investments using low-wage female labor. Although we can
find similar arguments by Erturk and Çağatay (1995), Schober and
Winter-Ebmer (2011) make a counterargument that gender inequality
in wages is not related to higher economic growth; rather, the impact
of gender inequality is negative for growth. In these attempts to explain
the relationship between economic development and gender equality,
it is important to distinguish the two directions of causality: whether
economic development brings about gender equality, or gender equality brings about economic development. According to Duflo (2011),
although we find evidence supporting both directions of causality, we
need to consider policy options, acknowledging that neither economic
development nor women's empowerment is "the magic bullet" for realizing economic development and gender equality.

A recent report by the IMF shows a U-shaped relationship between
GDP per capita and FLFP rate across countries (figure 8-2). Comparing

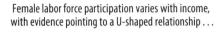

FIGURE 8-2. Comparison of Female Labor Force Participation across Countries, 1980 and 2010

Female labor force participation varies with income,   . . . with cross-sectional points
with evidence pointing to a U-shaped relationship . . .   shifting upwards over time.

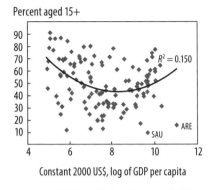
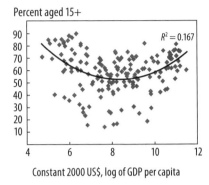

Source: IMF, *Women, Work and the Economy* (2013).
SAU = Saudi Arabia; ARE = United Arab Emirates.

the data sets for 1980 and 2010, we find that the average FLFP rate shifted upward over the period. When we look at the same indicators in 2010 while focusing on some of the MENA countries, it is clear that these countries are not in line with the dominant U-shape relationship of FLFP rate and GDP per capita but remain at the bottom of the graph because of the low FLFP rates (figure 8-3).

World Bank data (2004) indicate that the prevailing pattern of economic development in MENA—namely a large proportion of public sector jobs, strong government controls, and inward-looking trade policies—has kept the FLFP rate low in the region. Comparing MENA and East Asia, Klasen and Lamanna (2008) claim that gender gaps in employment explain a larger share of the growth differences between these two regions, suggesting that MENA countries are held back by their low FLFP rates. So why is the FLFP rate so low in Morocco and other MENA countries? What is necessary to achieve higher female labor force participation? Drawing on existing literature and statistics, this chapter examines three approaches to understanding FLFP in Morocco. The first approach considers the role played by social institutions, such as the legal framework (World Bank 2014e). The second approach explores supply-side factors, such as sociocultural norms and demographic and household-related characteristics (World Bank 2004; Haghighat 2005). The third approach assesses the impact of

FIGURE 8-3. Female Labor Force Participation across Individual Countries, 2010

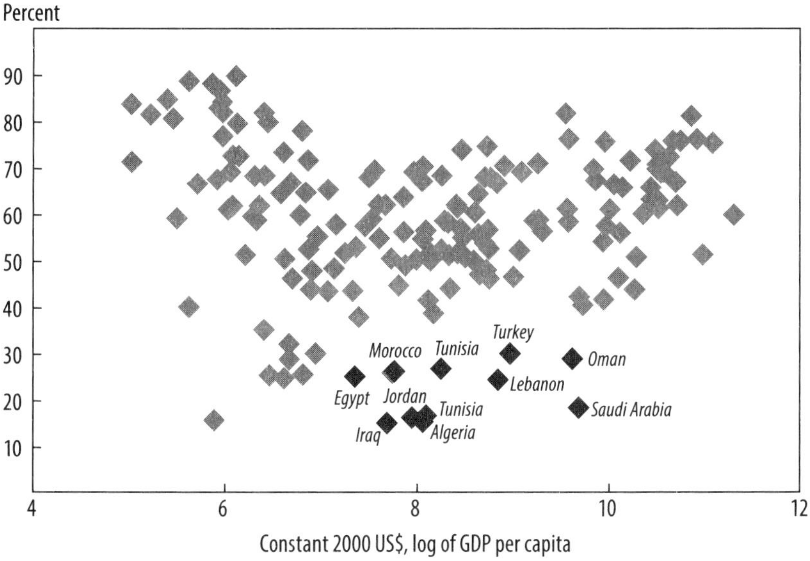

Percent

Source: World Bank, World Development Indicators.

demand-side factors on FLFP, using both macro-level analysis focusing on aggregated demand, represented by the unemployment rate, and micro-level analysis of demand from firms or other employers. Building on the analysis, the chapter proposes policy measures to enhance female participation in the Moroccan labor market. Since FLFP rates differ greatly between urban and rural areas, as rural women are engaged mainly in agricultural activities, this chapter focuses on urban women.

Social Institutions and FLFP

The World Bank report "Women, Business and the Law 2014" indicates that the MENA region had the second-highest proportion of legal restrictions on women in 1960 and the highest proportion today (World Bank 2014), which might partly explain the low participation of women in MENA societies. For example, a husband's unilateral right of divorce and a wife's legal obligation to obey her husband may create an additional barrier to women's entry into the labor force (World Bank 2004). At the same time, Rauch and Kostyshak (2009) note that MENA's Arab countries have laws that prohibit labor discrimination in the workplace, arguing that the lower level of FLFP has to stem from de facto discrimination rather than from de jure discrimination. This seems to be especially applicable to Morocco. Branisa, Ziegler, and Klasen (2010) calculate the social institution and gender index (SIGI) by considering a country's family code, civil liberties, the physical autonomy of citizens, traditional preferences for male offspring, and property ownership rights. Morocco is ranked 43 among over 100 non-OECD countries, the second-highest ranking for a MENA country after Tunisia. In fact, in 2004 significant reforms to the Moroccan family law, Moudawana, led to a rise in the minimum marriage age for women from 15 to 18, placed a family under the joint responsibility of both spouses, and eliminated a woman's legal obligation to obey her husband (Deiana 2009). However, there remain issues regarding enforcement, as some judges have circumvented the law while others are still unfamiliar with the amendments.[5] In 2012, roughly 10 percent of the marriages recorded in Morocco involved a girl under the age of 18, permitted under articles 20 and 21 of Moudawana, which allow family judges to authorize the marriage of minors. Even though the articles require well-substantiated arguments to justify such marriages, more than 90 percent of requests are authorized.[6] By removing legal restrictions on women, including those that are implicit, the society would be better prepared for working women.

Supply-Side Factors and FLFP

Among supply-side factors impacting FLFP, H'madoun (2010) indicates that religion is a key determinant, with Muslim and Hindu women having significantly lower participation than those of other religious backgrounds. The question of religion was further investigated by Hayo and Caris (2013), who concluded that traditional identity and perception of

5. Aida Alami, "Gender Inequality in Morocco Continues, Despite Amendments to Family Law," *New York Times,* March 16, 2014 (www.nytimes.com/2014/03/17/world/africa/gender-inequality-in-morocco-continues-despite-amendments-to-family-law.html).

6. S. Raiss, "Mariage des mineurs au Maroc: Entre amendement et abrogation des textes des loi," *Au Fait Maroc,* December 10, 2012; HREA, *The Moroccan Family Code (Moudawana) of February 4, 2004* (www.hrea.org/moudawana.html) http://www.aufaitmaroc.com/maroc/societe/2012/12/10/entre-amendement-et-abrogation-des-textes-de-loi_200918.html on June 23.

family roles was a more meaningful explanation than religious identity. Carvalho (2010) points out peer effects, proposing a model of social influence in which agents care about the opinions of other members of their community. In Amman, Jordan, Chamlou, Musi, and Ahmed (2011) find that traditional social norms, measured by the attitude of household members toward working women, reduce female labor participation. As for Morocco, World Bank (2012) reports that more than 30 percent of young women face obstacles to working because their husband will not allow it and 23 percent claim that their parents will not allow it. Also, 11 percent point to social norms as obstacles. These figures imply that sociocultural norms are a strong determinant of young female labor participation in Morocco.

With regard to demographic and household-related factors, Chamlou, Musi, and Ahmed (2011) argue that women with postsecondary education are more likely to participate, based on the data collected in Amman. In the case of Pakistan, Kiani (2009) shows that education and household expenditures have positive but insignificant impacts on FLFP, whereas household income has a negative impact. Here, higher expenditures have a positive impact as female members would be expected to contribute financially in order to afford the expenditures, while household income has negative impact because high-income households have less need for their female members to work. According to a World Bank report on Yemen published in 2014, unmarried women in urban areas are more likely to participate in the workforce than married women or women in rural areas. This suggests that norms about women's role outside the home may be more strictly enforced after marriage and in a more conservative, rural society (World Bank 2014). In Morocco's case, Taamouti and Ziroili (2010) examine the relationship between individual factors and FLFP, concluding that for urban women education is the main determinant of labor market participation.

Major Labor Indicators in Morocco

According to official figures published by the Moroccan High Commission of Planning (HCP), the proportion of the employed, unemployed, and inactive populations varies depending on sex and region. As shown in figure 8-4, a large percentage of women, especially in urban areas, is categorized as "inactive," which includes students going to school and those who are out of school and not working. Unemployment here is

FIGURE 8-4. Portion of Population Inactive, Unemployed, and Employed

Percent

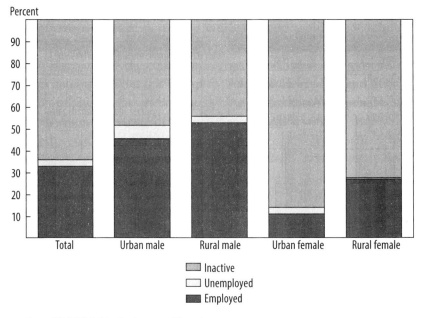

Source: HCP (2013), Activity, Employment and Unemployment.

dcfined as those who are unemployed and looking for a job. The proportion of unemployed is in general very low, while it is practically zero
for rural women. It is important to note that in these figures, employment is defined in its larger sense, including part-time and irregular
jobs. Even with this broad definition, only 10 percent of urban women
are working. Considering recent developments in secondary education
for urban girls, this figure remains quite low.

The HCP data reveal a number of challenges:

Youth are disproportionately unemployed. The unemployment rate
for youth ages 15 to 24 years is more than double (19.3 percent) the
national level (9.2 percent). This is important given that youth made
up almost 20 percent of the total population in 2010.[7] According to
World Bank estimates, youth aged 15–29 make up 30 percent of the
total population and 40 percent of the active population between the
ages of 15 and 64 (World Bank 2012).

7. United Nations, Department of Economic and Social Affairs, Population
Division, "World Population Prospects: The 2012 Revision" (2013).

FIGURE 8-5. Net Enrollment Rate, Primary Education, 2008–13

Percent

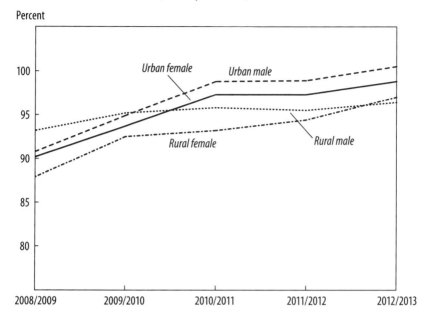

Source: Ministry of National Education, Morocco.

There is a big gap between youth and the older population in their engagement in the labor market, especially for men. More than 70 percent of older urban males (ages 25 and older) but only 24 percent of young urban males (ages 15–24) are working. A similar gap exists in rural areas, where 85 percent of the older age group but only 54 percent of the younger group are actively working. The gap looks smaller with regard to females, since the proportion of active women among them is much lower. Among urban women, 6 percent of youth and 16 percent of the older age group are employed. The proportion of active rural women is generally higher than the proportion of urban women, as they are engaged in family agricultural activities.

In urban areas girls are enrolled in lower-secondary education as much as boys are, but there remains a gap between urban and rural areas in enrollment of girls. As for the primary education enrollment rate, Morocco has made great progress, especially among rural girls. As shown in figure 8-5, the net enrollment rate for primary education had reached more than 95 percent across all categories by 2012. However, a sharp contrast shows up between urban and rural areas

FIGURE 8-6. Net Enrollment Rate, Lower Secondary Education, 2008–13

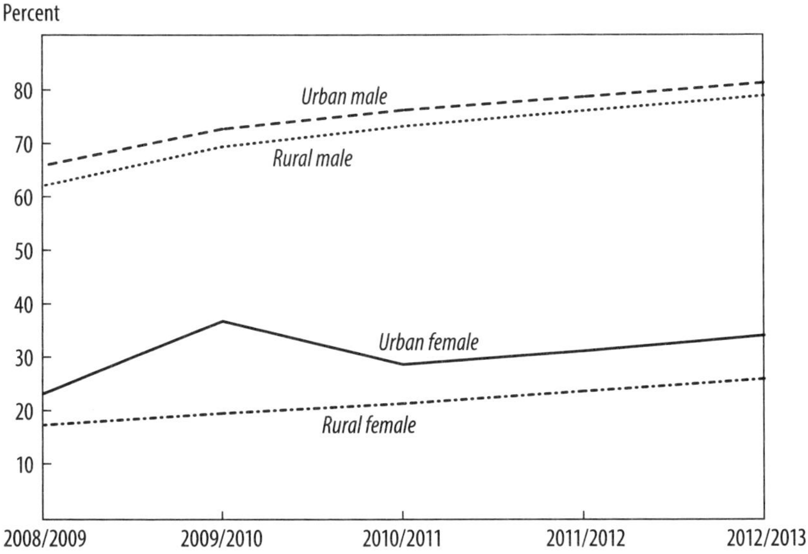

Percent

Source: Ministry of National Education, Morocco.

regarding enrollment in lower-secondary education. As shown in figure 8-6, the net enrollment rate in lower-secondary education is around 80 percent for urban boys as well as urban girls, while the rate is much lower (34 percent) for rural boys and even lower (26 percent) for rural girls. Among urban residents, we see that educational attainment up to the lower-secondary-education level is almost equal for boys and girls.

Opportunity cost of low FLFP. Because the Moroccan government and families are investing in education and urban girls' enrollment in lower-secondary education closely matches that of urban boys, there is a huge opportunity cost if educated women work much less than their male peers. In addition, according to an OECD report, boys performed better than girls in mathematics in only thirty-seven of the sixty-five countries and economies that participated in PISA 2012, and between 2000 and 2012 the gender gap in reading performance—favoring girls— widened in eleven countries (OECD 2012). The results indicate that both boys and girls in all countries can succeed in all these subjects tested by PISA, highlighting the cost that MENA societies, including Morocco, are paying by not fully realizing the potential of educated females.

Realities Faced by Moroccan Young Women

As we saw in the literature review, there are several supply-side factors impacting female participation in the labor market, such as social norms, education, and household income. We focus here on data on the urban female population, which shows the lowest rate of labor force participation across categories, and describe the realities in which women live. In particular, the data demonstrate that despite the higher level of education that women are now attaining, traditional norms are still playing a role in decisionmaking; the data also suggest what changes might enhance women's participation in the labor market. It is important to establish career paths for educated young women that conform with social norms in order to promote further educational attainment for girls. If higher education fails to lead to higher returns through employment, rational calculation would discourage people from investing more in education.

The World Bank conducted a household and youth survey in 2009–10 in which data were collected from 2,883 young people (ages 15–29) to better understand their circumstances (World Bank 2012). I first review findings from the survey with regard to youth labor participation and then analyze urban female decisionmaking regarding labor participation. I conclude with some policy recommendations to enhance the participation of urban women in the labor market.

Review of the Findings from World Bank Survey

The World Bank survey produced some important findings with regard to youth labor participation:

Young females are even more discouraged than young males in finding jobs. Figure 8-7 shows the proportion of the population employed, unemployed, or out of the labor force among youth (15–29) who are not enrolled in school. Looking at the population currently out of the labor force, a higher percentage of young females are demotivated (19 percent) in their search for work than young males (15.5 percent). While a majority (53.5 percent) of urban young females are out of the labor force because of family reasons or other constraints, almost 20 percent are out of the labor force because they are discouraged.

Nonparticipation among young females declines with higher education. Figure 8-8 shows that higher educational attainment leads to

FIGURE 8-7. Labor Force Participation Status among Youth, Aged 15 to 29, Not in School

Percent

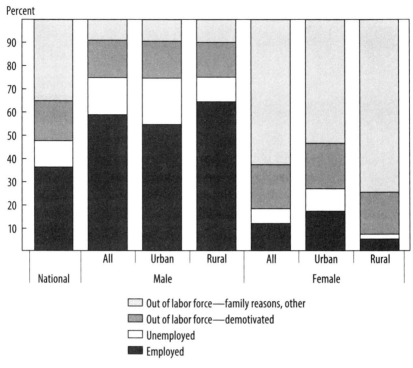

Source: World Bank (2010); Morocco Household and Youth Survey, 2009–10.

higher participation in the labor force among women. The share of youth not attending school and not participating in the labor market decreases from 93 percent among those with only a primary education to 81 percent for those with a lower-secondary education and to 62 per-cent for those with a secondary education. Only 37 percent of young females with a tertiary education are out of the labor force. Among males, the share of nonparticipating youth is relatively stable, rang-ing between 20 percent and 27 percent for all education levels. Young women who have completed higher education have a higher probability of participating in the labor market.

Informal employment is widespread, but not among young urban females. Youth tend to be engaged in informal employment, with nei-ther job contracts nor social security. Figure 8-9 shows that the share of employment without contracts is overwhelmingly high for rural areas (almost 100 percent for women and 94 percent for men) as well as for

FIGURE 8-8. Share of Youth Not in School and out of the Labor Force

Percent

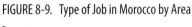

Source: Morocco Household and Youth Survey, 2009–10.

FIGURE 8-9. Type of Job in Morocco by Area

Percent

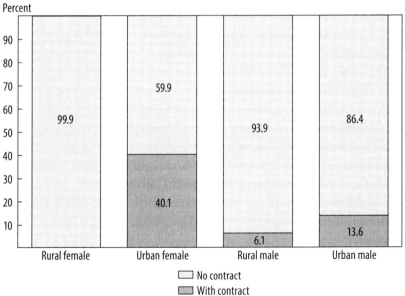

Source: World Bank (2010); Morocco Household and Youth Survey, 2009–10.

FIGURE 8-10. Reason for Not Expecting/Willing to Work among Young Urban Females, Ages 15–29, in Morocco

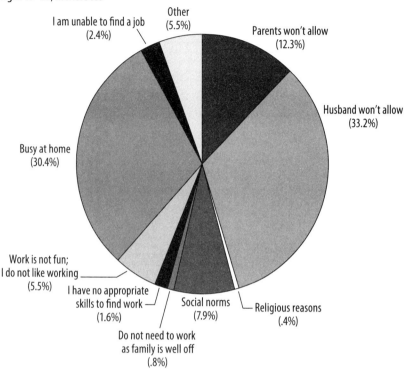

Source: World Bank (2010); Morocco Household and Youth Survey, 2009–10.

urban men (86 percent). However, the share is much lower—around 60 percent—for urban women, while 40 percent of them are working with contracts. Thus, the informality of employment may be a factor impacting urban female labor force participation.

Urban Female Youth and Labor Participation

Using World Bank (2012) data, this section analyzes urban female decisionmaking on labor participation and nonparticipation.

Social norms are a strong reason for not participating. Figure 8-10 shows the reasons given by young females who are either currently in school but not expecting to work afterward or are already out of school and not willing to work. Family opposition constitutes more than 45 percent, while 30 percent of respondents said that they are busy at home.

FIGURE 8-11. Comparison of Reasons for Not Expecting/Willing to Work among Urban Females by Education Level

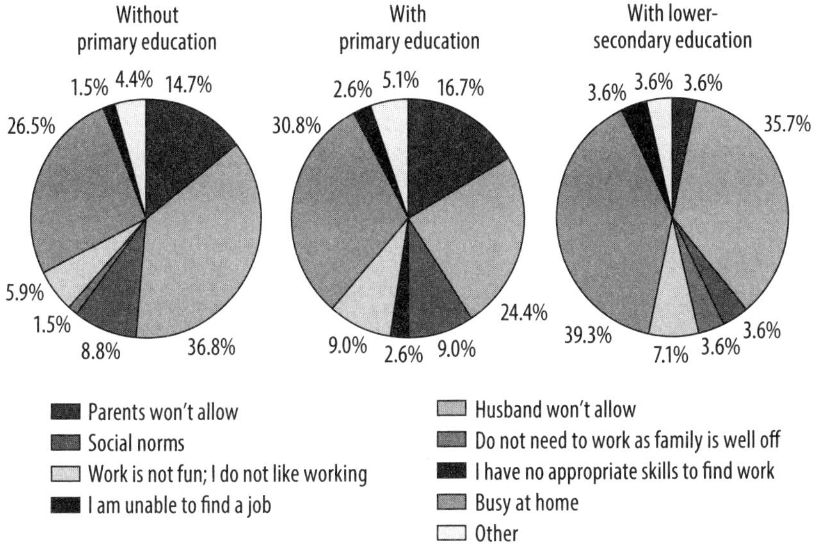

Without primary education

1.5% 4.4% 14.7%
26.5%
5.9%
1.5%
8.8%   36.8%

With primary education

2.6% 5.1% 16.7%
30.8%
24.4%
9.0% 2.6% 9.0%

With lower-secondary education

3.6% 3.6% 3.6%
35.7%
39.3%
7.1% 3.6% 3.6%

■ Parents won't allow   ☐ Husband won't allow
■ Social norms   ▨ Do not need to work as family is well off
☐ Work is not fun; I do not like working   ■ I have no appropriate skills to find work
■ I am unable to find a job   ▨ Busy at home
                                   ☐ Other

Source: World Bank (2010); Morocco Household and Youth Survey, 2009–10.

We saw previously that the nonparticipation rate decreased with higher education levels for young women. Multiple factors could explain the decrease. Given that more than 45 percent of urban females indicated family opposition as a reason for nonparticipation, we can expect that family opposition becomes less dominant when female family members are more educated. However, looking at the reason for not expecting or being willing to work by education level (figure 8-11), we see similar results for different education levels, with some variation. Family opposition remains a major reason in each education level, while for those with a lower-secondary education, the opposition seems to come mainly from male spouses. However, this interpretation should be treated carefully, as the number of observations for those with a lower-secondary education is limited to twenty-eight, while the number is sixty-eight for those without primary education and seventy-eight for those with primary education.

Social norm reasons become less dominant among urban females with higher education, but they might be busier at home. Assuming that family opposition is related to societal norms, we can consider family opposition, religious reasons, and social norms as one category representing sociocultural norms. The share of this category among reasons declines with higher education. The share is 61 percent for those without a primary education, 52 percent for those with a primary education, and 46 percent for those with a lower-secondary education. Interestingly, the "busy at home" reason constitutes 26 percent of reasons given by females with the lowest education level, 31 percent by those with a primary education, and 39 percent by those with a lower-secondary education. It is impossible to draw a conclusion from the existing data as the number of observations is limited. However, we might able to interpret this result as an expression of the transitional status of educated women, who are facing a growing expectation for them to contribute financially through work but also ongoing sociocultural barriers keeping them at home, as indicated in figure 8-12.

The unemployed are especially discouraged. By surveying urban women who were available for work but unemployed (defined as those who did not work in the last seven days) and all participants who were not searching for a job, researchers tried to determine why these groups were not searching for work. Among unemployed youth, the main reason that they were not searching for a job is that they believed that there were no jobs (figure 8-12). The data show a difference between women and men who believe that there are no jobs and those who are tired of looking for work, which is the second-biggest reason for both genders. Among urban females, a majority of the unemployed (55 percent) indicated that they believed that there were no jobs so they were not searching for a job while less than 14 percent were tired of looking for a job. Among urban males, the perception is different: 40 percent believed that there were no jobs while more than 31 percent were getting out of labor market because they were tired of looking for a job. In each case, the number of people who thought that they did not have enough training or education to find a job is relatively small, just 5.5 percent for urban females and 6.7 percent for urban males.

Education and job searching are related among urban female students, while the unemployment rate is high among secondary and tertiary education graduates. When all participants, regardless of their current status, were asked why they were not searching for work, the main reason among urban females was that they did not have enough training or education (30 percent), as shown in figure 8-13. Considering

FIGURE 8-12. Reason Given by Moroccans for Not Searching for Work

Urban male

1.7% 0.8% 8.4%
0.8%
0.8%
0.8%
6.7%
4.2%
0.8%
1.7%
3.4%
39.5%
31.1%

Urban female

0.7% 0.7% 6.2%
0.7% 2.8%
2.1%
4.8%
0.7%
5.5%
2.1%
1.4%
0.7%
3.4%
55.2%
13.8%

■ Believe there are no jobs
▦ Do not know an effective way to look for a job
▢ Waiting for government/public sector recruitment
▤ Do not have enough training or education
▨ Family responsibilities
▨ Lack of personal contacts
■ I do not need to work

▢ Tired of looking for work
▨ Employers prefer to recruit women
■ No suitable jobs
▨ No time to search
▢ Opposition by a family member
▨ Already found work which will start later
▨ Other

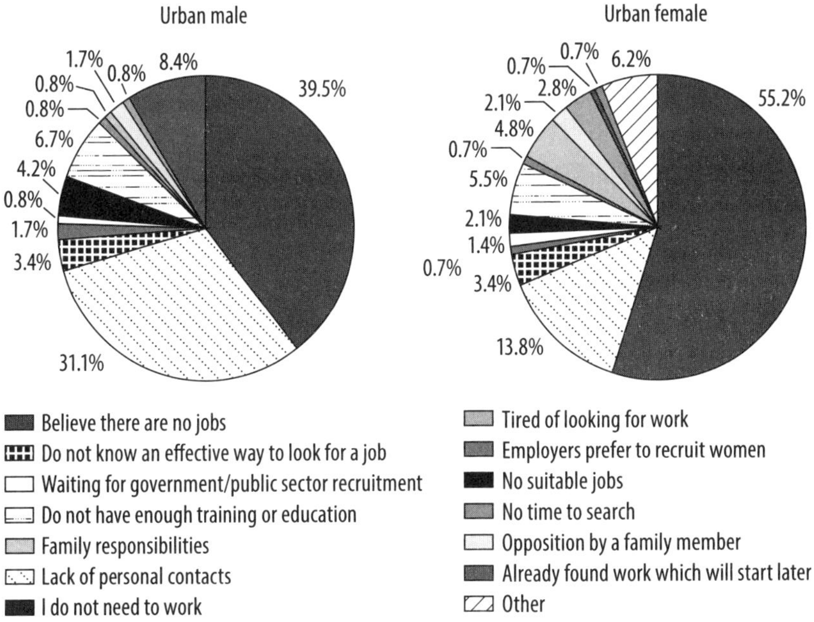

Source: World Bank (2010); Morocco Household and Youth Survey, 2009–10.

the small portion of unemployed youth who indicated insufficient training or education as their primary reason for not searching for work,
this larger share among all participants can be explained by the larger
presence of students among the sample (254 students among 595 urban
females). Thus, when we subdivide into students and non-students, we
find that urban young women who were out of school did not suggest that insufficient training or education was the reason why they
were not searching for a job. Rather, they had family responsibilities
or faced family opposition to their search for work. At the same time,
the high percentage of students who answered that they did not have
enough training or education might imply that they expected that getting more training or education would better prepare them for future
job searching. This corresponds to the drop in the nonparticipation rate
for urban women who have achieved higher educational attainment.
However, in Morocco, higher education does not necessarily lead to a
higher employment rate, even in urban areas. Figure 8-14 shows that
the unemployment rate is higher for those with a secondary education

FIGURE 8-13.   Reason Given by Young Urban Females for Not Searching for a Job in Morocco

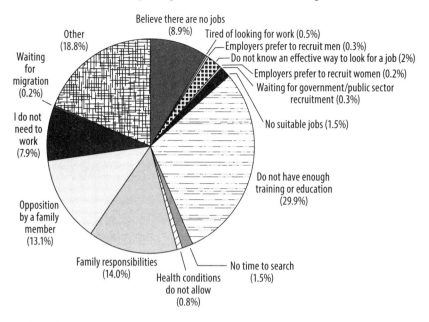

Source: World Bank (2010); Morocco Household and Youth Survey, 2009–10.

FIGURE 8-14.   Unemployment Rates in Morocco by Education Level

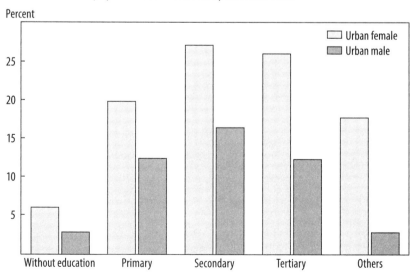

Source: HCP, *Activity, Employment and Unemployment,* 2012.

FIGURE 8-15. Job Preference among Urban Youth in Morocco

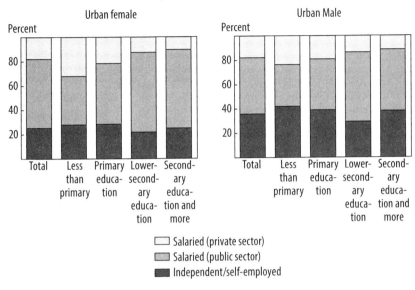

Source: World Bank (2010); Morocco Household and Youth Survey, 2009–10.

(27 percent for women and 17 percent for men) than for those with a primary education (20 percent for women and 13 percent for men). Even among those with a tertiary education, the unemployment rate remains high—26 percent for females and 12 percent for males. Although participation in the labor market is greater among those who have completed higher education, employment is far from guaranteed.

Public sector jobs are preferred for their stability by those with a higher education. As shown in figure 8-15, urban females and males both prefer salaried public sector jobs upon completion of higher education. Correspondingly, there is decreasing interest in salaried private sector jobs among better-educated females and males, with 13 percent of lower-secondary-education female graduates interested, 10 percent of high school or tertiary-education female graduates interested, and 14 percent (lower-secondary graduates) and 11 percent (high school or tertiary graduates) of males interested. The result implies that private salaried jobs are less attractive for those with higher education, even though Morocco's manufacturing sector is believed to have had some success in increasing female participation in the salaried private sector (World Bank 2004). Quality and stable salaried jobs in the private sector need to be promoted for those productive youth to be more engaged in private sector development.

Women, especially those with a secondary education or higher, have a stronger preference for public salaried work than men. Indeed, 65 percent of urban females who, at a minimum, have graduated from high school prefer to find work in the public sector, while the percentage is only 50 percent for their urban male peers. The difference shows up mainly in the preference for independent work or self-employment among individuals possessing more than a high school education (some 25 percent of urban females and 38 percent of urban males). Among urban females, there seems to be a stronger preference for job security over greater independence as a worker. The reason for their preference for salaried work, both public and private, is largely explained by the greater security that these jobs provide. Given the fact that the majority of respondents preferring salaried work prefer public sector jobs, they must find more job security in public sector employment.

Comparison of Values

To better understand the rationale behind the youth responses shown above, it is helpful to look at the values underlying Moroccan society. The World Values Survey, which consists of nationally representative surveys conducted in almost 100 countries that focus on human beliefs and values, enables comparisons across countries by using a uniform questionnaire. The following section offers some comparisons between Morocco, Jordan, Malaysia, Chile, and Japan. Jordan was chosen because it shares similarities with Morocco, Malaysia because it is an Asian Muslim-majority country,[8] Chile because it is an example of a fast-growing country in Latin America, and Japan because it is a non-Muslim country with a "traditional" value set.

Men are perceived as the main income earners. Perceptions on gender roles vary across countries. In Jordan, Morocco, and Malaysia, majorities agreed with the statement "When jobs are scarce, men should have more right to a job than women," while a majority of the sample in Chile disagreed, and almost half of the sample in Japan answered

8. Malaysia's Muslim population is estimated at around 61 percent of the total population.

FIGURE 8-16. When Jobs Are Scarce, Men Should Have More Right to a Job than Women

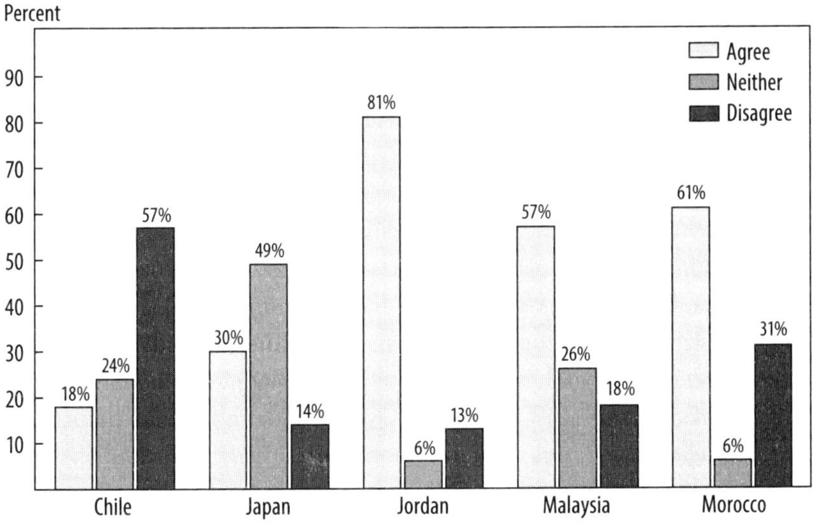

Percent

Source: World Value Survey, 2010–14.

"Neither (agreed nor disagreed)." This would seem to confirm that a majority of people in Jordan, Morocco, or Malaysia believe that male employment should be prioritized, perhaps because they think that men are likely to be the main income earners in a family (figure 8-16).

Values relating to working women and housewives differ. When asked generally about the relationship between work and women, respondents in all five countries valued the independence that women enjoy when they have a job, with half of the samples agreeing with the statement "Having a job is the best way for a woman to be an independent person." Less than 30 percent of the sample disagreed with the statement, even in Morocco and Jordan (figure 8-17).

However, the samples reacted differently to statements associating women with their role as mothers. To the statement representing "traditional" values, "When a mother works for pay, the children suffer," 57 percent of the sample in Jordan strongly agreed, whereas in Malaysia 57 percent of the sample disagreed and 23 percent strongly disagreed (figure 8-18). Although people in Chile felt least strongly among the five countries about a man's right to employment, the proportion of people either disagreeing or strongly disagreeing with the traditional values statement was higher in Malaysia than in Chile. It seems that

FIGURE 8-17. Having a Job Is the Best Way for a Woman to Be an Independent Person

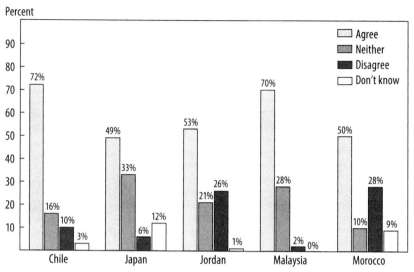

Source: World Value Survey, 2010–14.

in Malaysia, the role of a mother is not undermined by the fact that she is working. Comparing Morocco to Jordan, Moroccan values were more moderate, with 25 percent of the sample strongly agreeing with the statement, while 39 percent agreed and a total of 26 percent either disagreed or strongly disagreed. An interesting case is Japan, in which almost half (48 percent) of the sample disagreed while one-third of the sample said that they didn't know, possibly reflecting conflicts of values among individuals.

Except for Japan, similar results show up regarding the statement on the value of being a housewife. People in Jordan and Morocco responded positively to the statement "Being a housewife is just as fulfilling as working for pay," while people in Malaysia and Chile show more diverse values, with slightly more opposition. In the case of Japan, a majority of the sample agreed with the statement, in contrast to their disagreement with the statement about the negative image of working mothers.

Looking at the attitudes across the five countries, we would say that, in general, people agree with the notion that women become more independent when they have a job. However, when women become mothers, there are two types of countries: those that value the "formal" work of mothers as much as their "informal" work at home and those that

FIGURE 8-18. When a Mother Works for Pay, the Children Suffer

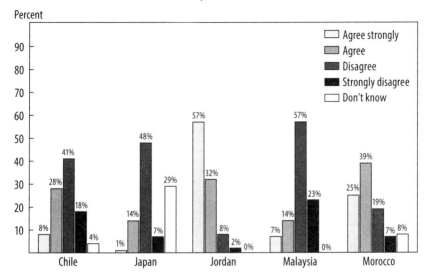

Source: World Value Survey, 2010–14.

perceive "formal" work by mothers negatively because they assume that children suffer as a result of it. In the latter type of country, including Morocco and Jordan, the role of housewives is highly valued, which could lead young women to internalize that view and lead more of them to become housewives unless other factors come into play.

Values concerning women's education and their success in work differ. To the statement "University education is more important for a boy than for a girl," more than 70 percent of the sample population in three of the five countries disagreed (including strong disagreement) (figure 8-19). In Morocco, nearly 40 percent of the sample strongly disagreed, indicating the importance that Moroccans put on tertiary education for girls. This level of disagreement is the highest among the five countries. Taken together with the previous results, this might imply that Moroccans have different values with respect to young women before marriage and married women, particularly those with children.

When asked about the potential performance of women at work, majorities in Jordan and in Morocco agreed with the statement "On the whole, men make better business executives than women do." Similar results can be seen regarding men and women as political leaders. In Chile, about 70 percent of the sample disagreed or strongly disagreed.

FIGURE 8-19. University Education Is More Important for a Boy than for a Girl

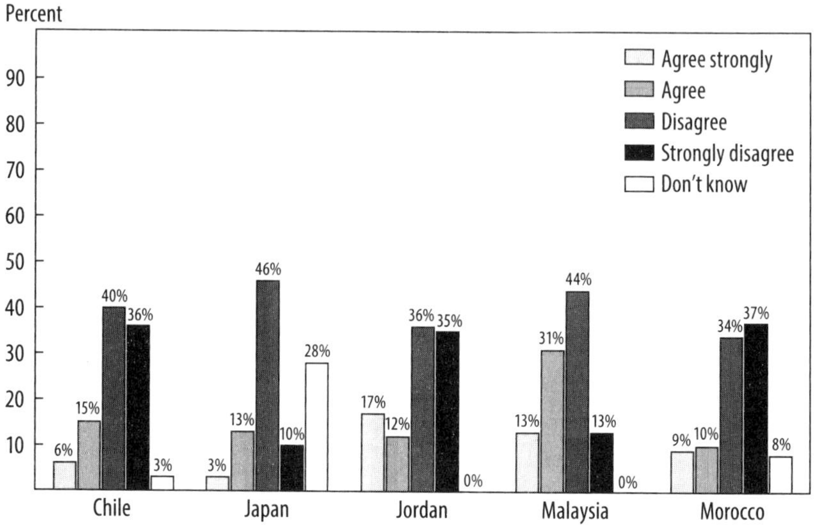

Percent

Source: World Value Survey, 2010–14.

Interestingly, in Malaysia, where working mothers are encouraged, 14 percent strongly agreed with the statement and 45 percent agreed, while only 36 percent disagreed. In Malaysia, mothers seem to feel less guilty when they work, but that does not mean that female potential is recognized as much as that of men.

Policy Suggestions

Based on the above analysis, urban females in Morocco have higher expectations of participating in the labor market when they are more educated. At the same time, because of greater job security, those females want public sector employment, which is becoming scarce for new entrants. Looking at attitudes across different societies, we see that values such as university education for girls and women's independence through employment are highly regarded by Moroccans, as much as they are in other countries. However, when it comes to women with children, they tend to prioritize the role of mother over the role of worker. A pilot case in Jordan shows that an intervention through vocational training was more effective in rural communities than in an urban, heterogeneous environment. In urban areas, the job retention rate was only 20 percent after the intervention. Major constraints result from transportation challenges, wage levels, marriage, type of job, and cultural issues.[9]

It would be interesting to look at Malaysia to help determine the factors that lead people to believe in the value of working mothers. Although there might be a question of which—reality or belief—comes first, in either case such a case study would provide insights for Morocco regarding, for example, the importance of childcare facilities or various forms of help from relatives in rearing children.

A possible approach by the government is to promote decent work in the private sector. Improving the quality of private sector jobs in terms of job security and working environment would lower the physical and sociocultural hurdles for urban women to work in the private sector, thus enhancing female participation in the labor market. Creating decent jobs in the private sector is even more crucial given that the public sector is no longer able to absorb all the new entrants seeking higher-quality work. These industry-related aspects will be examined in the following part of the chapter.

Demand-Side Factors and FLFP

The third approach uses demand-side factors to explain the low female labor force participation rate. This approach includes both macro-level analysis focusing on aggregated demand, represented by the unemployment rate, and micro-level analysis of demand from firms.

Overview of Industry-Related Factors

Before addressing the question of female participation, I present several findings from a recent report by the World Bank on job creation in the MENA region (World Bank. 2014b). First, GDP growth over the last two decades was driven by demographic change rather than labor productivity. Private sector job creation was too weak to absorb the fast-growing labor force. Second, the fundamentals of job creation in the MENA region are similar to those in other regions: young firms and more productive firms create more jobs. In the MENA region, however, low firm turnover (firm entry and exit) and slow productivity growth limit the pool of young firms and more productive firms and ultimately

---

9. The pilot case and its findings were shared by Mayyada Abu Jaber.

reduce job creation. That is because of a combination of slow within-firm productivity growth and misallocation of labor and capital across firms. Third, various policies across MENA countries limit competition and undermine firm turnover, productivity growth, and job creation. Using Morocco as one case, the report shows that several dimensions of the business environment—such as tax administration, corruption, and the cost of finance—impact employment growth and disproportionately affect young firms. Finally, the report provides direct evidence that policies in MENA countries have often been captured by a few politically connected firms. This has led to a policy environment that creates privileges rather than a level playing field and undermines private sector growth and job creation (World Bank 2014). These factors lie behind the high unemployment rate among youth in MENA countries.

To return to the question of FLFP, the relationship between the unemployment rate and FLFP can be interpreted in two ways. When weak economic performance fails to generate a level of employment sufficient to absorb new entrants into the labor market, it is likely to result in lower FLFP, since employers prefer to hire men because they believe that male income is more important to families (World Bank 2004). For instance, the International Labor Organization (ILO 2012) reports that in North Africa, the female youth unemployment rate increased by 9.1 percentage points in the aftermath of the economic crisis but by only 3.1 percentage points for young males. Yet comparison of the relationship between unemployment and female labor force participation in OECD countries and MENA countries indicates that in the long term, a healthy economy with higher female participation in the labor force is also more likely to enjoy lower unemployment (World Bank 2004).

In terms of micro-level analysis of demand-side factors, Fakih and Ghazalian (2013) find that firm-related factors, mainly private foreign ownership and exporting activities, have positive implications for FLFP rates in MENA's manufacturing sector. Similar results are found in Egypt, where foreign-owned firms are more likely to employ women than their domestic counterparts. In addition, large firms are much more likely than small- and medium-size firms to employ women, and the textile sector is the most likely of all sectors to employ women (World Bank 2013).

We know that the low FLFP rate represents a large opportunity cost for MENA societies, where even young males are having difficulty getting decent private sector work. Also, industrial policies in these countries sometimes hinder healthy competition among firms and therefore result in fewer jobs than might be expected. What industrial policies are being pursued in Morocco to spur job creation and promote higher FLFP? In the following sections, the chapter takes a closer look at the tourism sector in the services industry and at the manufacturing industry. It examines strategies set by the government of Morocco for tourism (Vision 2020) and for the manufacturing industry (Emergence Plan) and their impact on job creation. It is noteworthy that neither strategy makes explicit reference to issues affecting or policies promoting FLFP.

Tourism as a Job-Creating Industry: From "Vision 2010" to "Vision 2020"

According to the ILO, the tourism industry is one of the fastest-growing sectors of the global economy, accounting for more than one-third of total global services trade (ILO 2011). It is estimated that by 2022, employment in tourism will account for 328 million jobs worldwide, equivalent to nearly one in ten jobs in the global workforce (ILO 2013). The high intensity of labor within the industry makes it a significant source of employment and places it among the world's top creators of jobs that require varying degrees of skills and allow for quick entry into the workforce by youth, women, and migrant workers (ILO 2011). Tourism's ability to generate employment not only in the formal but also in the informal sector has been cited as one of its key advantages for developing countries (Elkan 1975; deKadt 1979; Sinclair 1998). Sinclair (1998) also points out that empirical studies have revealed the relatively skill-intensive nature of tourism employment. This requires more detailed study, as a more recent analysis indicates a high proportion of low-skilled, domestic worker–type jobs that are open to female workers in the sector (ILO 2013). Another important point is that the tourism industry has a significant multiplier effect on employment in other sectors. With regard to the sectoral supply chain, one job in the core tourism industry indirectly generates roughly 1.5 additional jobs in the related economy (Goldin 2010; Bolwell and Weinz 2008).

With regard to gender in tourism-related employment, a United Nations Environment and Development UK (UNED–UK) study estimated that, on average, 46 percent of the tourism workforce was female in 2002 (UNED 2002). At the same time, many companies in the tourism sector are small and often family-owned enterprises, and the mix of paid work and domestic work among women is unclear, which makes it difficult to distinguish between formal and informal employment (ILO 2013). In terms of income disparity, there is a significant income gap between male and female workers in the sector, with females earning less than males, which might be due to more managerial posts being occupied by men (ILO 2013). The ILO notes that education and vocational training are key requisites for the operational effectiveness of the sector (ILO 2011). Whether the required training is to be provided by the government or by employers, the sector needs qualified employees to improve its quality.

Overview of the Tourism Sector Strategy

In Morocco, the tourism sector plays a big role in the economy. In 2010, it represented 7.5 percent of GDP, 6.6 percent of the working population, and almost 15 percent of revenue in the balance of payments. In 2001, recognizing the industry's importance, the government of Morocco published a ten-year strategic plan for the tourism sector entitled Vision 2010. Over the course of Vision 2010, the sector grew rapidly despite the global economic downturn. According to the Ministry of Tourism, the number of international tourists to the country more than doubled, from 4.4 million in 2001 to 9.3 million in 2010, with average annual growth of 8.7 percent. That growth made tourism the biggest source of foreign currency for the country, surpassing remittances from Moroccans living abroad. The amount of direct employment in the sector also increased substantially, by 40 percent, to 450,000 jobs, making it the second-biggest source of employment after agriculture. The development of human capital was among the pillars of Vision 2010. Collaboration between the Ministry of Tourism, vocational training offices, and private stakeholders resulted in training for 12,300 people in 2010, up from only 2,000 in 2001.

Building on the success of Vision 2010, the government set up Vision 2020, showing its commitment to the tourism sector as one of the driving forces of the economic, social, and cultural development of the country. The goal of Vision 2020 is to double the size of the tourism sector. In addition to its goals relating to increasing accommodation capacity and the number of international and domestic tourists, the plan aims to generate 470,000 new direct positions, creating a total of almost 1 million jobs by 2020. The strategy argues for the need to train 130,000 young people and to make the industry more attractive for younger job seekers. In order to overcome these challenges, plans are being made to create new schools specializing in tourism and hotel management.

From 2012 to 2013, the actively employed population in Morocco increased by 157,000 (HCP 2013). If the strategy is successful, it will create an average of 47,000 new positions each year, nearly one-third of the number of new entrants in the active population. This number becomes more significant when we take into account the associated indirect employment opportunities, which have previously equated to 1.5 indirect positions for every direct position.

According to the National Confederation of Tourism of Morocco (CNT), the proportion of female workers in the Moroccan tourism sector, 25.9 percent, is relatively low[10]—lower than the average of the global tourism sector, which is 46 percent. Recognizing that the low rate of female labor participation is not particularly sector specific, the CNT indicates that it also reflects a widespread disparity between men and women in Morocco. Consequently, the CNT proposes taking affirmative action to enhance female participation in the tourism sector, such as by providing increased access to education and employment. The CNT asserts that under the current strategy, gender issues are neither prioritized nor systematically integrated into the strategy. In order to distribute job creation in the tourism sector equitably, steps to mitigate gender disparities should be incorporated into the planning, implementation, and evaluation stages of the process.

Policy Suggestions

It is clear that the tourism sector has great potential for job creation in Morocco. More effort should be made to measure female labor participation in the tourism sector. In a report on Moroccan women and the labor market prepared by HCP, the services industry is treated as one category, without a more detailed analysis of its subsectors (HCP 2013). In addition, while it might be technically difficult to quantify the tourism sector's effects on indirect employment, efforts should be made to measure its broader impact and multiplier effects. Since the tourism sector is the country's second-largest employer, gender issues should be factored into Vision 2020's planning, implementation, and evaluation

10. CNT (www.tourismapost.com/femmes-tourisme-encore-peu-nombreuses/).

processes in order to fully realize the potential of the female labor force in Morocco.

Manufacturing as a Strategic Industry: Emergence Plan

According to a Ministry of Economy and Finance report on employment in Morocco's manufacturing sector, the gross job destruction rate was stable from 1986 to 2003, while the gross job creation rate varied significantly (MEF 2006). It implies that labor adjustment by firms has been implemented mainly through job creation, not through job destruction. That is in contrast to developed economies, in which firms adapt to market change by decreasing the number of positions (MEF 2006).

At the same time, the rate of creation of temporary employment in the manufacturing industry is double that of permanent employment. This phenomenon can be explained by rigid labor regulations, which make it difficult for firms to fire workers (MEF 2006). This rigidity of regulations concerning firing is also suggested in Bottini and Gasiorek (2009), which studies the relationship between trade and job reallocation in Morocco. By analyzing the impact of trade openness on the labor market, they found that increased exposure to external markets has a substantially positive impact on job creation. On the other hand, increased openness of domestic markets has a negative impact on job creation, although there is little evidence of an increase in job destruction. This is likely attributable to the strict laws regarding firing workers, which limit the economy's capacity for adjustment.

Another important aspect is technological change, which improves productivity. GDP growth decomposition of Morocco covering 2006–10 shows that the single factor contributing most positively to growth was increased productivity, followed by an increase in the size of the working population. Indeed, changes regarding employment rate had a negative effect on growth (Verme and others 2014).

Bottini and Gasiorek (2009) indicate in their firm-level analysis that Morocco is specializing in unskilled, labor-intensive manufacturing. What is more, firm-level regressions confirm the labor-saving nature of technological change, and an increase in productivity reduces the demand for labor, particularly for unskilled workers. This leaves the government with the challenge of promoting technological change to improve productivity in order to achieve long-term economic growth while trying to maintain current jobs and create new ones in the shorter term.

FIGURE 8-20. Proportion of Permanent Full-Time Female Workers in Manufacturing Firms in Morocco

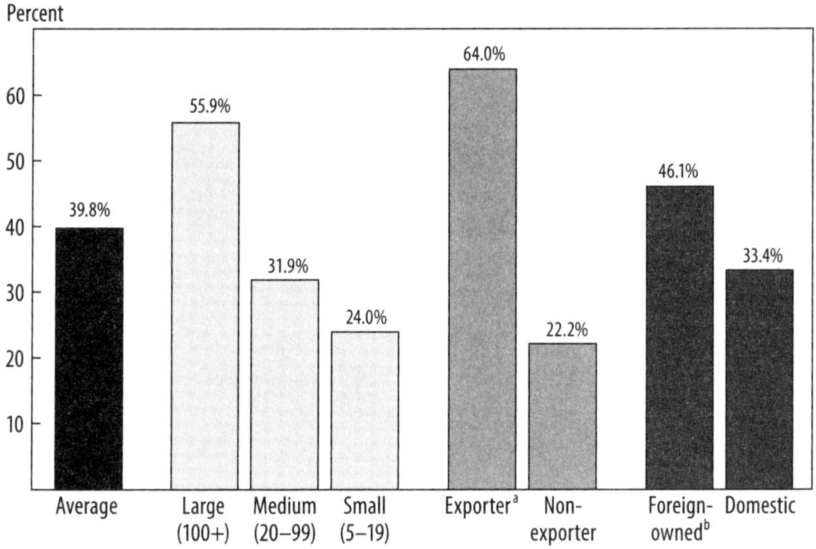

Percent

Source: Enterprise Survey Database on Morocco, 2007.
a. Direct exports are 10 percent or more of sales.
b. Ownership is 10 percent or more foreign.

In terms of female participation, the Enterprise Survey of Morocco shows that in the manufacturing sector, the proportion of female full-time workers in large firms is more than twice as high as that in small firms (figure 8-20). Firms with more than 10 percent foreign ownership have a higher proportion of female workers than domestic firms do. What is most remarkable is the export factor. The proportion of female workers in exporting firms is almost twice as high as that in non-exporting firms.

Overview of the Emergence Plan

The government of Morocco continues to make considerable efforts to develop its industry. In 2005, the government launched the Emergence Strategy, an industrial policy framework later elaborated into the National Pact for Industrial Emergence (the Emergence Plan), covering the period 2009–15. Under this framework, the government has designated six priority sectors and promoted their development. The designated sectors are automobiles, aeronautics, offshoring (of services), electronics, textiles and leather, and food processing. The Plan has five

TABLE 8-1. Profile of Necessary New Positions, 2009–15[a]

Profile	Offshoring	Car industry	Aeronautics	Electronics	Textile and leather	Food industry
Management	1,000	1,500	300	200	300	500
Engineer	3,000	7,000	1,900	1,400	2,000	500
Technician	10,500	29,000	3,000	2,700	5,700	8,500
Operator		32,500	9,800	4,700	24,000	14,500
Administration I	23,500	...	...	...	...	...
Administration II	32,000	...	...	...	...	...
Total	70,000	70,000	15,000	9,000	32,000	24,000

Source: Program-contract 2009–15 for "Emergence Plan."
a. Numbers are approximate.

main pillars: promotion of the six strategic sectors; promotion of the competitiveness of small and medium enterprises; promotion of human resource development for industry; improvement of the business environment; and creation of a Moroccan investment development agency. The Plan, which aims to promote domestic and foreign investment in these sectors, is designed to achieve four goals by 2015: the creation of 220,000 jobs; an increase in industry-related GDP by an additional 50 billion Moroccan dirhams (MAD), which is equivalent to about $5 billion; an increase in export volume by 95 billion MAD ($9.5 billion); and 50 billion MAD ($5 billion) of private investment in industry-related activities. Table 8-1 provides a breakdown by industry of where the new positions are to be added.

Table 8-2 shows the status of job creation at the end of 2012, the Plan's midway point. By adding 111,000 jobs, the Plan has attained roughly half of its overall objective, but with considerable variation across sectors and years. In absolute numbers, the automobile industry created the most new jobs, adding more than 31,200 from 2009 to 2012, followed by offshoring, which created more than 29,600 new positions. These are the two sectors with the biggest job creation targets (70,000 jobs) over the Plan's duration, and these results suggest that the initial prioritization of these sectors has worked to some extent. At the same time, job creation in the offshoring sector has been rather unstable, showing variation across years. What is more problematic is that there were sectors that recorded a net decline in jobs in 2011 and 2012, including electronics

TABLE 8-2.   Midterm Job Creation Results in Six Strategic Sectors

Number of jobs, unless otherwise noted

	Job creation						
	2009	2010	2011	2012	Total	Objective 2009–15	Objectives achieved
Car industry	4,379	8,293	9,149	9,024	31,205	70,000	45%
Aeronautics[a]	1,531	400	694	1,106	3,731	15,000	25%
Offshoring[b]	14,633	4,000	9,555	1,445	29,633	70,000	42%
Electronics	1,748	1,700	−550	−559	2,339	9,000	26%
Textile and leather	6,310	20,014	−4,622	−710	20,992	32,000	66%
Food industry	3,863	12,271	3,343	3,612	23,089	24,000	96%
Total	32,824	46,68	17,569	13,918	110,989	220,000	50%

Source: Bank Al Maghrib, 2012 Annual Report; Government of Morocco, Emergence Plan (www.emergence.gov.ma/Pages/Emergence.aspx, accessed July 7, 2014).
   a. Data of Aeronautics don't include companies for service.
   b. For Offshoring, data concern figures in the exporting location.

and textiles and leather. Although exports grew steadily during those years, job creation remained disappointing. This phenomenon might be because of higher productivity achieved in these sectors or lower demand in the domestic market, offsetting the growth in exports.

To achieve its export target, the Plan needs to be boosted. Table 8-3 shows the increase in exports in the strategic sectors from 2009 to 2012. The increase remains low, at 26.6 billion MAD in total, compared with the target of an additional 95 billion MAD of exports from 2009 to 2015. Although we need to take into consideration the fact that the period 2009–12 coincided with a difficult external environment and the economic crisis in Europe, which is Morocco's main export destination, an achievement rate of 28 percent after three years will make it difficult to realize the target increase of 95 billion MAD by 2015. Still, in 2013, the car industry saw exports hit 31 billion MAD, while aeronautics and electronics exports grew to 8.1 billion MAD and to 7.8 billion MAD, respectively, stimulated by large-scale investment from global companies, such as Renault and Bombardier.[11]

11. Oxford Business Group, "Economic Update Morocco," May 19, 2014 (www.oxfordbusinessgroup.com/economic_updates/maroc-le-secteur-manufacturier-fer-de-lance-des-recettes-%C3%A0-l%E2%80%99exportation#english).

TABLE 8-3. Midterm Results for Exports in Six Strategic Sectors

	Export (billion MAD)			
	2009	2010	2011	2012
Car industry	12.0	18.3	23.4	27.0
Aeronautics[a]	4.1	4.7	5.8	6.4
Offshoring[b]	4.9	6.0	7.1	7.3
Electronics	5.1	6.3	7.1	7.0
Textile and leather	30.7	31.9	34.0	33.3
Food industry	15.5	16.7	15.9	17.9
Total	72.3	83.9	93.3	98.9

Source: Bank Al Maghrib, 2012 Annual Report.
MAD = Moroccan dirhams.
a. Data of Aeronautics don't include companies for service
b. For Offshoring, data concern figures in the exporting location

Overview of Each Sector's Strategy

Offshoring Sector: The implementation of the Emergence Strategy in 2005 went well for the offshoring sector. The sector created more than 20,000 new jobs between 2005 and 2008, while more than 50 firms expressed interest in relocating to the two existing industrial zones—Casanearshore and Rabat Technopolis—within one year. An additional four industrial platforms for offshoring are planned in Fez, Tetouan, Oujda, and Marrakech.

The 2009–15 strategy offers economic incentives over the first three years following a firm's relocation to an industrial zone, such as a tax ceiling of 20 percent on profits for firms making more than 70 percent of their turnover from exports. Eligible firms can also benefit from government subsidies for the training of new and existing employees. The amount of subsidy varies depending on an employee's profile, but it can reach as high as 65,000 MAD.[12]

Car Industry: Describing the car industry as a sector with strong potential, the 2009–15 strategy focuses on the development of manufacturing equipment and on the building of a second assembly plant in Morocco. The first assembly plant operated by Renault was inaugurated

12. Official instruction by Office of the Prime Minister, Circulaire n: 9/2007, May 2007.

in February 2012, with a production capacity of 170,000 cars per year, which had increased to 340,000 cars per year by October 2013. In order to promote further development of the sector, the government set up two industrial zones dedicated to automobile equipment manufacturing, the Tanger Automotive City, located near the Renault plant, and the Kenitra Automotive City. Both of the zones will be developed on 300 hectares and will accommodate about 15,000 jobs by 2015. Wiring, textiles, and plastics are recognized as the country's three naturally strong manufacturing areas, so the strategy places emphasis on promoting higher-value-added manufacturing, particularly in metallurgy, such as stamping, surface treatment, and electronics.

Aeronautics: At the time of launch of the 2009–15 plan, aeronautics was a newly developing sector that included only 60 firms, of which more than 70 percent were less than five years old, and supported around 7,000 jobs. Given that aeronautics is typically closely connected to other advanced technologies and industries, the government chose aeronautics as one of the priority sectors for which it would incentivize investment. It paid off: in 2011, the Canadian aerospace manufacturing company Bombardier decided to establish a $200 million facility in Nouasser, which became operational in 2014 and is expected to employ 850 skilled workers by 2020.[13] The majority of the existing firms were concentrated around Aeropole of Nouasser. The 2009–15 plan doubled the area of the zone to 200 hectares and rebranded it Nouasser Aerospace City.

Electronics: The electronics sector has two categories: electronics for the general public—such as "brown" products (for example, televisions and radios) and "white" products (for example, refrigerators and washing machines)—and specialized electronics, such as embedded electronics for cars and aircraft, medical devices, and industrial electronics. The specialized electronics sector is considered to have especially high potential to advance Moroccan industrialization, as it is labor intensive but requires low levels of capital and technical expertise, while structural changes in industry would allow Morocco to produce more integrated and higher-value-added products over the longer

13. Bombardier press release, September 30, 2013 (www.bombardier.com/en/media-centre/newsList/details.bombardier-aerospace_20130930_bombardieraerospacebreaksgroundonn.bombardiercom.html).

term. The 2009–15 plan identifies three priority subsectors of specialized electronics: mechatronics, industrial electronics, and embedded
electronics for automobile and aeronautical products.

The electronics sector industrial zones are grouped together by spe-
cialization: mechatronics and industrial electronics in the Casablanca
region (40–50 hectares), two zones for automobile-embedded electronics in Tanger and Kenitra (5–10 hectares), a zone for aeronautical
electronics in Nouasser (5–10 hectares), and a cluster of electronics
companies in Mohammedia (40 hectares).

Textiles and Leather Sector: Textiles and leather is the most important manufacturing sector in Moroccan industry, comprising 40 percent
of manufacturing jobs (20,000), 13 percent of GDP (9.6 billion MAD),
and 27 percent of industrial exports. However, the export performance
of the Moroccan textile sector is largely affected by changes to the
EU import quota for Chinese products, as the EU is the main export
destination for Moroccan textiles. This leaves the sector vulnerable, as
the sector's exports go to just a few European countries. In addition,
the textiles and leather sector is composed of small firms (with average turnover of around 15 million MAD), with 60–70 percent of their
turnover relying on subcontracting. The 2009–15 plan aims to stabilize
the industry in this competitive international market while realizing the
sector's full potential through two different initiatives: promotion of
wider coverage of industrial value chains to export more value-added
products to achieve stable export performance;[14] and development of
Morocco's domestic market, for which potential growth is expected
to be as high as 60 percent by 2015. The objective for 2015 is for the
sector to contribute an additional 1 billion MAD to GDP and 32,000
new jobs by 2015.

Food Processing Industry: The food processing industry in Morocco
is important, representing 35 percent of industrial GDP as well as 15–20
percent of industrial companies and formal employment. Recognizing
Morocco's advantages in having a low-cost labor force, available agricultural products, and a good geographic location, the 2009–15 plan
tries to strategically leverage the agricultural sector (Plan Maroc Vert),

---

14. The program contract describes visions such as aggregation of small firms
and development of domestic, flexible procurement of necessary inputs for the
industry.

to increase domestic demand, and to secure stable external demand for "Mediterranean products." By 2015, the impact is estimated to be worth an additional 10 billion MAD to GDP and 24,000 new jobs.

Analysis of Five Strategic Industrial Sectors and Female Participation in Manufacturing

This analysis uses industrial statistics from 2011, made public through the Moroccan Industry Observatory.[15] The statistics contain major indicators, such as turnover, value added, exports, and number of employees by sex. In order to look at the relationship between industrial growth and job creation in the five industrial sectors chosen in the Emergence Plan, the analysis used the following five subsectors: food industry (2-digit code: 15), textiles and leather (adding up three 2-digit codes: 17, 18, and 19),[16] manufacturing of electronic machines and devices (2-digit code: 31), the car industry (2-digit code: 34), and manufacturing of other transport materials (2-digit code: 35) as an approximation for aeronautics.

The textiles and leather sector is a major source of employment, especially for women. The sector's size in terms of turnover and its capacity for employment do not correspond because of the difference in labor intensity in each industry. Among the five sectors, the food industry makes up 23 percent of overall industry turnover while it represents 21 percent of the total industrial employment. Meanwhile, textiles and leather work is more labor intensive, making up 34 percent of the total industrial employment while accounting for only 6 percent of total turnover. Another important feature of the textiles and leather industry is the high proportion of female employees. As shown in figure 8-21, 71 percent of all textiles and leather industry employees are female, which is the highest percentage among the five sectors, followed by 57 percent in electronics and 44 percent in the food industry. The ratio of female employees in the car industry and other transport materials manufacturing is much lower, at 10 percent and 32 percent respectively. According to the Moroccan Industry Observatory, the total ratio of female employees is reported to be as high as 45 percent.

15. "Observatoire Marocain de l'Industrie" (www.omi.gov.ma/Publication/Pages/Industrieenchiffres.aspx).

16. 17: textile industry, 18: clothes and coat industry, and 19: leather and shoes.

FIGURE 8-21. Female Employee Ratio

Number of employees

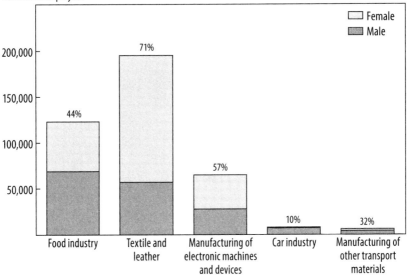

Source: Moroccan Industry Observatory, *Industry in Numbers*, 2011.

There is large variation in productivity and labor costs. When we look at figure 8-22, it becomes clear that the highly labor-intensive textiles and leather industry is relying on a low-cost labor supply, especially from the female labor force, and that it has a low level of productivity. It is likely that its female workers completed no more than a primary education, resulting in their ability to perform only nonskilled or low-skilled labor. The car industry shows the highest productivity, while its employment capacity remains low. However, higher productivity in the car industry can lead to the development of a skilled labor force in Moroccan industry, which is important for its long-term growth. Interestingly, labor costs across the sectors do not vary as much as productivity, although the textiles and leather sector and the electronics sector have the cheapest labor cost and the highest female employee ratio.

Exporting companies play a crucial role. Figure 8-23 indicates the crucial role played by exporting companies in these sectors. Except for the food industry, for which exporting companies represent only 45 percent of total turnover, all the other sectors rely largely on

FIGURE 8-22. Productivity and Cost per Employee

MAD 1,000

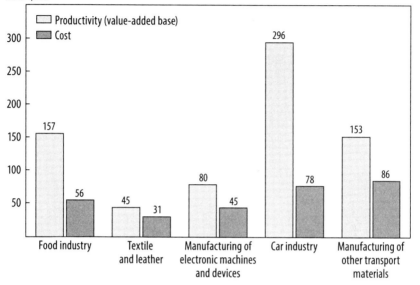

Source: Moroccan Industry Observatory, *Industry in Numbers,* 2011.

FIGURE 8-23. Ratio of Exporting Company

Number of turnovers

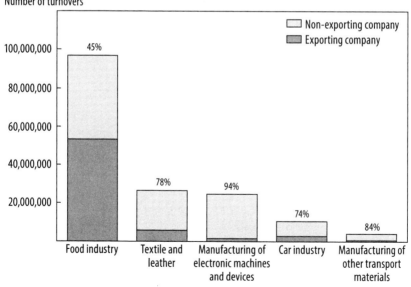

Source: Moroccan Industry Observatory, *Industry in Numbers,* 2011.

FIGURE 8-24. Business Size: Average Turnover per Company

Number of turnovers

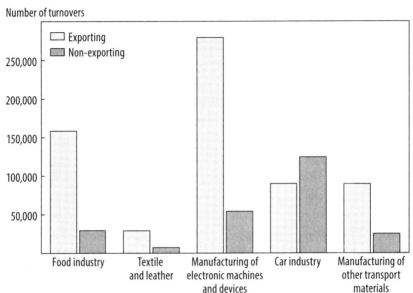

Source: Moroccan Industry Observatory, *Industry in Numbers,* 2011.

exporting companies for their turnover: 78 percent for textiles and leather, 94 percent for electronics, 74 percent for the car industry, and 84 percent for manufacturing of other transport materials. This might be explained in part by the domestic market for each product, which is large for the food industry and much smaller for expensive products such as electronics and cars.

Exporting companies in the electronics sector are the biggest employers. As seen previously, exporting companies play an important role in terms of turnover. Figure 8-24 compares average turnover per company in exporting companies and non-exporting companies. The four sectors excluding the car industry show larger turnover among exporting companies, most remarkably in the food industry and the electronics industry, for which an exporting company's average turnover is five times as big as that of a non-exporting company. There are similar differences when comparing the number of people employed by exporting and non-exporting companies. As indicated in figure 8-25, exporting companies generally employ at least four times as many

FIGURE 8-25. Average Number of Employees per Company

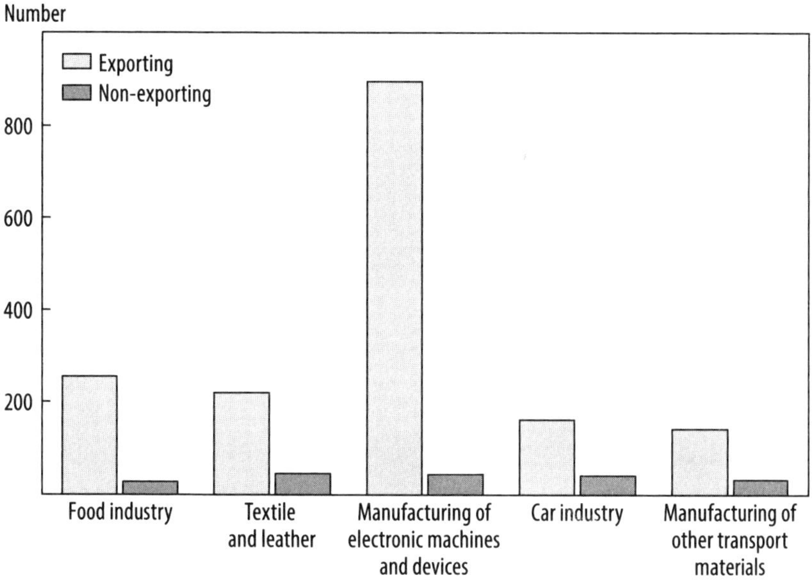

Number

Source: Moroccan Industry Observatory, *Industry in Numbers,* 2011.

people as non-exporting companies and as many as nine times more in the food industry and 20 times more in the electronics industry.

A large number of female workers are employed by exporting companies. Exporting companies employ large numbers of workers, especially female workers, compared with non-exporting companies. Seventy-four percent of workers in exporting companies in the textiles and leather sector are female, while 58 percent of workers in exporting companies in the electronics sector are female (figure 8-26).

Policy Suggestions

In the manufacturing industry, exporting companies in the textiles and leather sector are currently the main employers of female labor. That is because of the labor-intensive nature of the sector, which employs the largest number of workers among the five priority sectors, as well as the low cost of female labor. Indeed, 71 percent of all employees in the sector are female. However, this situation only reinforces existing structural challenges for the female labor force, as it is

FIGURE 8-26. Ratio of Male and Female Employees in Exporting and Non-Exporting Companies

Numer of employees

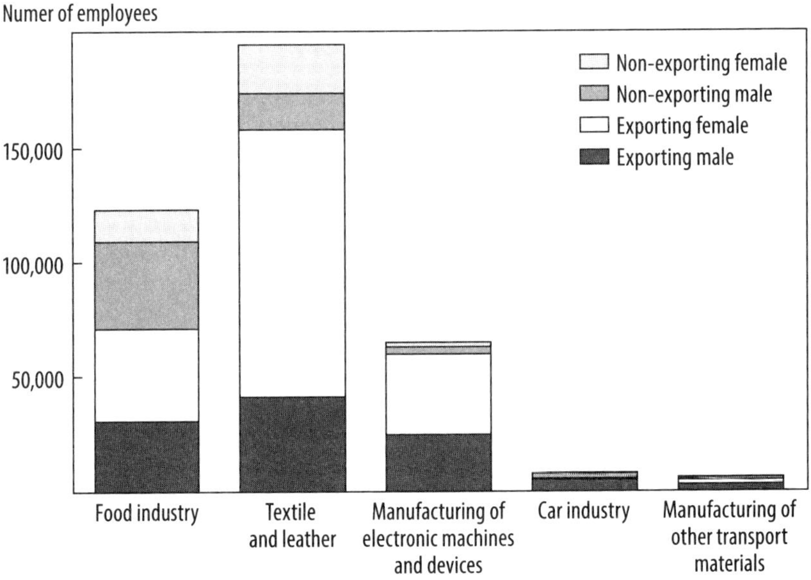

Source: Moroccan Industry Observatory, *Industry in Numbers*, 2011.

difficult for them to advance and develop the skills that could lead to higher wages in the future. The textiles and leather industry mainly uses low-skilled labor.

In order for the economy to tap the underutilized potential of urban educated women, the electronics sector shows promise. The current female employee ratio of the electronics sector is 54 percent, which is already the second-highest among the five priority sectors after the textiles and leather sector. Another characteristic of the electronics sector is the high proportion of exporting companies, which account for 98 percent of total turnover of the sector. It requires more detailed study to determine why exporting companies employ female workers more than non-exporting companies do. In an interview conducted with the management of one of the foreign-owned factories making electronics devices, it was suggested that they see female employees as diligent and precise in their work. According to the management, female workers prefer working for their factory because of the favorable working environment, including the good relations that exist between management and workers. As various products are manufactured in the electronics sector, it provides an opportunity for low-skilled workers to receive training and raise their skill level by working on the production of more complicated products and eventually to work in more complicated sectors, such as the car industry. In parallel, as young firms create more jobs, it would be important to enhance a system with higher firm turnover as a result of healthy competition. In order to stimulate such competition, it is important to level the playing field for all the actors. The government has already succeeded in attracting large-scale factories in the car and aeronautics industries to the country. In order to realize active job creation dynamics using these factories, policies should be carefully chosen to promote small, young, high-quality local firms. It also is in policymakers' interests to give incentives for adherence to regulations among small firms.

Conclusion

The low female labor participation rate in Morocco is hindering the country's full potential for economic development, as shown in the U-shape model (figure 8-3). Since various factors underlie this issue, such as social institutions, societal values, female education levels, and employers' preferences in different industries, it is important to view the issue of female labor force participation through multiple lenses. This chapter considers three components: the role of social institutions, supply-side factors, and demand-side factors.

Through its social institutions, Morocco can increase female participation in the labor market by modernizing its legal framework, particularly as it relates to family law. From the supply side, young females are getting more and more education in urban areas, without necessarily getting jobs. As they face opposition to working from family members, it is necessary to create jobs with decent conditions in both the public and private sectors in order to give more options to those women who see public sector work as the only source of stable employment. Further research might consider in more detail countries such as Malaysia, which shares similar values to Morocco, while having much higher FLFP. On the demand side, private sector growth should be promoted to create more jobs. In addition, as the quality of the working environment is an important factor for female workers, policies to create decent jobs should be prioritized.[17] The tourism sector has strong potential to provide jobs in the future, but female labor participation in tourism needs further study to determine the opportunities and challenges, including the impact on indirect job creation. As for manufacturing, the electronics sector can benefit from tapping the pool of urban educated female workers to advance their product lines. Proper training, together with policies to connect foreign-owned large-scale factories with small local firms, can support skill development. Currently, neither of the two industrial strategies examined in this chapter pay specific attention to female labor force participation. The government needs to recognize the opportunity cost that the economy is paying by not fully using the potential of women and to focus on measures to promote female labor force participation in their strategies.

It is clear that FLFP is a complex issue that requires careful coordination among many stakeholders to fully address all of the challenges. Government leadership, with careful coordination among ministries and agencies, will be indispensable for implementing effective policies to promote FLFP.

References

Achy, Lahcen. (2013). "Structural Transformation and Industrial Policy in Morocco." Working Paper 796. Egypt: Economic Research Forum.

Akerlof, G. A., and R. E. Kranton 2010. *Identity Economics*. Princeton University Press, 2010.

Bandiera, Oriana, and Ashwini Natraj. 2013. *Does Gender Inequality Hinder Development and Economic Growth? Evidence and Policy Implications.* Washington: World Bank.

Bank Al Maghrib. 2012. Annual Report (www.bkam.ma/wps/wcm/connect/ resources/file/ebaed70d3d2840b/DERI-RAPPORTANGLAIS%2002_8_ 2013.pdf?MOD=AJPERES&attachment=true).

———. 2013. Annual Report (www.bkam.ma/wps/wcm/connect/resources/file/ ebb07b0f411cf39/ANNUALREPORt_ENGLISH13.pdf?MOD=AJPERES& attachment=true).

17. According to the ILO, decent work has a multifaceted nature. It includes work that is productive and delivers a fair income; security in the workplace; social protection for families; better prospects for personal development and social integration; freedom for people to express their concerns, organize, and participate in the decisions that affect their lives; and equality of opportunity and treatment for all women and men.

Branisa, Boris, Maria Ziegler, and Stephan Klasen. 2010. *The Institutional Basis of Gender Inequality.* Paper provided by Verein für Socialpolitik, Research Committee Development Economics in its series Proceedings of the German Development Economics Conference, Hannover 2010 with number 16.

Bolwell, O., and W. Weinz. 2008. *Reducing Poverty through Tourism.* Geneva: International Labor Office.

Bottini, Novella, and Michael Gasiorek. 2009. *Trade and Job Reallocation: Evidence for Morocco.* Egypt: Economic Ressearch Forum.

Carvalho, J. P. 2010. "Veiling." Discussion Paper Series. Department of Economics, University of Oxford.

Chamlou, N., S. Musi, and H. Ahmed. 2011. "Understanding the Determinants of Female Labor Force Participation in the Middle East and North Africa Region: The Role of Education and Social Norms in Amman." AlmaLaurea Working Papers No. 31. AlmaLaurea Inter-University Consortium (www2. almalaurea.it/universita/pubblicazioni/wp/pdf/wp31.pdf).

Deiana, Manuela. 2009. "Improving Women's Rights in Morocco: Lights and Shadows of the New Family Code." *International Journal of Interdisciplinary Social Sciences,* vol. 3, no. 11.

deKadt, Emmanuel Jehuda. 1979. *Tourism: Passport to Development? Perspectives on the Social and Cultural Effects of Tourism in Developing Countries.* World Bank and UNESCO. Oxford University Press.

Douidich, M., A. Ezzrari, R. Van der Weide, and P. Verme. 2013. *Estimating Quarterly Poverty Rates Using Labor Force Surveys.* Washington: World Bank.

Duflo, Esther. 2011. "Women's Empowerment and Economic Development." *Journal of Economic Literature* 50, no. 4: 1051–79.

Elkan, W. 1975. "The Relation between Tourism and Employment in Kenya and Tanzania." *Journal of Development Studies* 11, no. 2.

Enterprise Surveys. Washington: World Bank (www.enterprisesurveys.org).

Erturk, K., and N. Çağatay. 1995. "Macro Economic Consequences of Cyclical and Secular Changes in Feminization." *World Development* 23, no. 11 (November).

Fakih, A., and P. L. Ghazalian. 2013. *Female Labour Force Participation in MENA's Manufacturing Sector: The Implications of Firm-Related and National Factors.* IZA Discussion Paper No. 7197. Institute for the Study of Labor (http://ftp.iza.org/dp7197.pdf)

Goldin, Claudia. 1995. "The U-Shaped Female Labor Force Function in Economic Development and Economic History." In T. P. Schultz, *Investment in Women's Human Capital and Economic Development.* University of Chicago Press.

Goldin, I. 2010. *The Economic Case for Tourism.* UNWTO/South Africa International Summit on Tourism, Sport and Mega-Events, February 25, 2010.

H'madoun, M. 2010. *Religion and Labor Force Participation of Women.* Faculty of Applied Economics, University of Antwerp.

Haghighat, Elhum. 2005. "A Comparative Analysis of Neopatriarchy and Female Labor Force Participation in Islamic Countries." *Electronic Journal of Sociology* (www.sociology.org/content/2005/tier1/__islamLaborforce.pdf).

Haut Commissariat au Plan. 2009. Government of Morocco. Enquete Nationale sur le secteur informe.

———. 2012a. Enquete Nationale sur l'emploi.

———. 2012b. La femme marocaine en chiffres.

———. 2013a. Enquete Nationale sur l'emploi.

———. 2013b. Femmes Marocaines et Marché du Travail: Caractéristiques et Evolution.

Hayo, Bernd, and Tobias Caris. 2013. "Female Labour Force Participation in the MENA Region: The Role of Identity." Philipps-Universitaet Marburg.

HCP (Haut Commissariat au Plan, Enquete Nationale sur l'emploi). 2013.

ILO (International Labor Organization). 2011. "World Parliament of Labour Turns 100." *World of Work Magazine* 71.

———. 2012. *Global Employment Trends:* May.

———. 2013. *International Perspectives on Women and Work in Hotels, Catering, and Tourism.*

———. 2014. *Women and Men in the Informal Economy.*

IMF (International Monetary Fund). 2013. *Women, Work, and the Economy.*

Kabeer, Naila, and Luisa Natali. 2013. *Gender Equality and Economic Growth: Is There a Win-Win?* IDS Working Paper 417. Institute of Development Studies.

Kiani, Kausar Adiqa. 2009. "Determinants of Female Labor Force Participation." *Asean Marketing Journal* 1, no. 2.

Klasen, Stephan, and Francesca Lamanna. 2003. *The Impact of Gender Inequality in Education and Employment on Economic Growth in the Middle East and North Africa.* (www.uni-goettingen.de/de/sh/download/d393147d 20889b6084364424cfa64150.pdf/klasenlamanna.pdf).

———. 2008. *The Impact of Gender Inequality in Education and Employment on Economic Growth in Developing Countries: Updates and Extensions* (www.iza.org/conference_files/worldb2008/klasen_s146.pdf).

Rauch, James E., and Scott Kostyshak. 2009. "The Three Arab Worlds." *Journal of Economic Perspectives* 23, no. 3.

Mammen, Kristin, and Christina Paxson. 2000. "Women's Work and Economic Development." *Journal of Economic Perspectives* 14, no. 4.

MEF (Ministry of Economy and Finance, Government of Morocco). 2006. Concentration et persistance des flux bruts de création et de destruction d'emplois du secteur manufacturier.

———. 2011. Secteur du tourisme: Bilan d'étape et analyse prospective.

OECD. 2012. OECD Program for International Student Assessment (PISA) (http://pisa2012.acer.edu.au/).

Pampel, F. C., and K. Tanaka. 1986. "Economic Development and Female Labor Force Participation: A Reconsideration." *Social Forces* 64, no. 3.

Sahar, Nasr. 2010. *Egyptian Women Workers and Entrepreneurs: Maximizing Opportunities in the Economic Sphere*. Washington: World Bank.

Schober, Thomas, and Rudolf Winter-Ebmer. 2011. "Gender Wage Inequality and Economic Growth: Is There Really a Puzzle?—A Comment." *World Development* 39, no. 8, August.

Seguino, Stephanie. 2000. "Gender Inequality and Economic Growth: A Cross-Country Analysis." *World Development* 28, no. 7, July (http://ssrn.com/abstract=252913).

Sinclair, Thea M. 1998. "Tourism and Economic Development: A Survey." *Journal of Development Studies* 34, no. 5.

Taamouti, Mohamed, and Mustapha Ziroili. 2011. *Individual Determinants of Female Labor Participation in Morocco* (www.scss.tcd.ie/John.Haslett/conference/PresentationsForLinda20110930/PapersSubmittedSinceConf/650024.pdf).

Tansel, A. 2001. *Economic Development and Female Labor Force Participation in Turkey: Time-Series Evidence and Cross-Province Estimates*. Economic Research Center, Middle East Technical University (www.erc.metu.edu.tr/menu/series01/0105.pdf).

Thévenon, O. 2013. "Drivers of Female Labour Force Participation in the OECD." OECD Social, Employment, and Migration Working Papers. OECD.

UNDP (United Nations Development Program). 2009. *Development Challenges for the Arab Region*. New York.

UNED [National University of Distance Education]. 2002. "Gender and Tourism: Women's Employment and Participation in Tourism. Summary of UNED–UK's Project Report."

Vella, F. 1994. "Gender Roles and Human Capital Investment." *Economica* 242.

Verme, P., A. G. Barry, J. Guennouni, and M. Taamouti. 2014. "Labor Mobility, Economic Shocks, and Jobless Growth—Evidence from Panel Data in Morocco." Policy Research Working Paper 6795. Washington: World Bank.

World Bank. 2004. *Gender and Development in the Middle East and North Africa: Women in the Public Sphere*. Washington.

———. 2006. *Fostering Higher Growth and Employment in the Kingdom of Morocco*.

———. 2007. *Enterprise Surveys Morocco*.

———. 2012. *Morocco: Promoting Youth Opportunities and Participation*.

———. 2013. *Opening Doors: Gender Equality and Development in the Middle East and North Africa*. 2013.

———. 2014a. *Gender and Development in MENA*.

———. 2014b. *Jobs or Privileges: Unleashing the Employment Potential of the Middle East and North Africa*.

———. 2014c. *Labor Mobility, Economic Shocks, and Jobless Growth: Evidence from Panel Data in Morocco*.

———. 2014d. *The Status of Yemeni Women: From Aspiration to Opportunity*.

———. 2014e. *Women, Business and the Law: 2014 Fact Sheet*.

9

Designing Youth Employment Policies in Egypt

AKIRA MURATA

The design of youth employment policies has become a central issue in the effort to promote urgently needed inclusive growth in Egypt. Developing better economic opportunities for Egypt's youth will help maintain the foundation of a country currently in the midst of a demographic transition. Egypt is experiencing a marked "youth bulge" and is consequently facing high unemployment among its youth, particularly among the highly educated.[1]

Educated Egyptian youth are said to be more likely to apply for or wait for public sector jobs. Indeed, this seems to be the same in other Arab economies, such as Tunisia.[2] The past government-supported practice of expanding youth employment in the public sector is no longer sustainable. More and better economic opportunities for the youth population need to be generated in the private sector by encouraging youth entrepreneurship and the development of micro and small enterprises (MSEs).[3] Inclusive growth could be achieved by shifting youth job preference toward a future growing and dynamic private sector and away from the bloated public sector.

I would like to thank Katherine Kimball, Daniel Allen, and Takayuki Watanabe for editing the final version of this chapter.

1. A youth bulge is a period in which "the age group of youth is far more numerous than for all other age groups combined" (Fuller 2003, p. 2).

2. See Boughzala (2013).

3. See chapter 6 in this volume.

Dynamic Demographic Transition and Slow Economic Transformation in Egypt

A large percentage of Egypt's population is made up of its youth: more than half of the country's population is under the age of twenty-five. According to the World Population Prospects by the United Nations Population Division, the population in Egypt has nearly quadrupled from 1950 to the present, rising from 21.5 million inhabitants to stand currently at over 81.1 million. It is projected to grow by more than 50 percent over the next four decades (see United Nations 2012). The United Nations Population Division projections and estimates of the age structure in Egypt indicate that the proportion of people aged fifteen to twenty-four peaked at 21 percent of the total population in 2005 and has been expected to decline since (see United Nations 2012). The proportion of children under fifteen has already declined significantly, from 40 percent in 1990 to 31.5 percent in 2010. These declines are now reflected in the largest-ever group of youths making its way into the labor market, in both absolute and relative terms (Assaad and Barsoum 2007). The Egypt Labor Market Panel Survey indicates that the number of new entrants into the workforce has more than doubled, from about 400,000 a year in the late 1970s to about 850,000 a year in the early years of this century (Assaad 2007).

In a country with a youth bulge, the dependency ratio declines as the number of working-age people outpaces the number of economically dependent people (typically the very young and elderly). The population dynamics from 1950 to 2010 have changed the age structure of Egypt enormously, with a large increase in youth aged fifteen to twenty-four (see United Nations 2010). If the increase in the number of working-age youth can contribute to productive activities in their societies, the youth bulge will become a demographic dividend or bonus. However, if a large group of youth cannot find good jobs and obtain a satisfactory income, then the youth bulge will become a demographic time bomb as the economically frustrated youth become a potential source of social and political unrest (World Bank 2011).

Some Asian economies have been able to turn the youth bulge into a demographic dividend. Egypt and Indonesia show a similar demographic transition over the decades (see Murata 2014, p. 4). In terms of the share of value added to the economy, these countries have been moving from economies with a high percentage of agricultural activity toward ones with an increasingly large share of manufacturing industries. With respect to employment, Indonesia has been moving from having a high share of employment opportunities in agriculture toward having an increasing share of employment opportunities in both the manufacturing and service sectors (see Murata 2014, p. 5). This has occurred through a dynamic change in Indonesia's economic structure. In terms of total manufacturing output in Indonesia, high-tech's share of manufacturing increased from 11.15 percent in 1970 to 31.21 percent in 2007. The portion of manufacturing jobs in Indonesia also rose from 10.12 percent to 18.68 percent during the same period (see Asian Development Bank 2013). However, this structure has largely stagnated in the case of Egypt. Indeed, dynamic demographic transition and a slow economic transformation in Egypt have fostered unemployment. The youth unemployment situation can be a key measure of a country's success in turning the youth bulge into a demographic dividend.

Youth Unemployment Situations in Egypt

The Middle East and North Africa region faces an urgent need for job creation. To absorb an increasing number of unemployed youth, the region needs to at least double its employment opportunities (International Labor Organization [ILO] 2007). Among African middle-income countries, the ratio of youth to adult unemployment is often higher than in other parts of the world (African Development Bank [AfDB] and others 2012). In Egypt, the youth unemployment rate in 2007 was 25 percent, whereas for adults it was only 4 percent (see ILO 2011).

Intense labor supply pressures lead to youth exclusion; a growing number of youths are relegated to marginal sources of livelihood or to the ranks of the unemployed. Labor force projections show that, despite the slowing growth of the youth population, increasing female participation rates driven by rising education attainment will continue to exert significant pressure on the labor market until 2010, when the growth of the labor force is expected to moderate (Economic Research Forum 2004). However, unemployment and inactivity of the working-age population, particularly women, are still prevalent in the Middle East and North African countries. Nearly three-quarters of working-age women do not participate in the labor force, and women constitute 80 to 90 percent of the region's inactive population (World Bank 2013). The youth population continues to be the most disadvantaged group in terms of higher rates of unemployment, lower earnings, and limited job security and stability, with the majority of new entrants into the employment market finding jobs only within the informal economy (Assaad and Barsoum 2007).

The unemployment rate is high among the youth population in Egypt, especially the highly educated. This is not a new problem. As early as the British mandate, there have been concerns that unemployment among the educated could lead to civil unrest (Williamson 1987). As of 2010, the Egyptian unemployment rate was reportedly 9.7 percent. While overall unemployment rates were not particularly alarming, there was a concentration of unemployment among college-educated youth. Based on the Egypt Labor Force Survey 2010, the youth unemployment rate was estimated to be around 40 percent for those with tertiary education, which is much higher than the rate for those with lower education attainments (World Bank 2013). Close to 87 percent of the unemployed in Egypt are between the ages of fifteen and twenty-nine, and unemployment among Egyptian college graduates is ten times higher than for those who did not go to college (LaGraffe 2012).[4]

With regard to unemployment rates by education attainment and gender, Assaad and Barsoum (2007) observe that university graduates are the only education group whose unemployment rates increased between 1998 and 2006, regardless of their gender. Because, for many of this group, the pay rate in the private sector was still below their reservation wage, they simply stopped seeking employment and were counted among the unemployed.[5] Recently, wage gaps between public and private sectors in Egypt have been increasing owing to the rise of public salaries. In 2011 the average public wages in Egypt were 80 percent more than those in the private sector (see figure 9-1).

The dramatic contraction in government hiring from 1998 to 2006 led to fewer applications for government jobs (Assaad 2007). This was especially true for female technical secondary school graduates,

4. The 24 million Egyptians who are between the ages of fifteen and twenty-nine are referred to in the demographic security field as those of "fighting age" (LaGraffe 2012).

5. The reservation wage is defined as the minimum wage rate at which a worker would accept a job.

FIGURE 9-1.   Egypt: Average Wage Gap between Public and Private Sectors, 1999–2011[a]

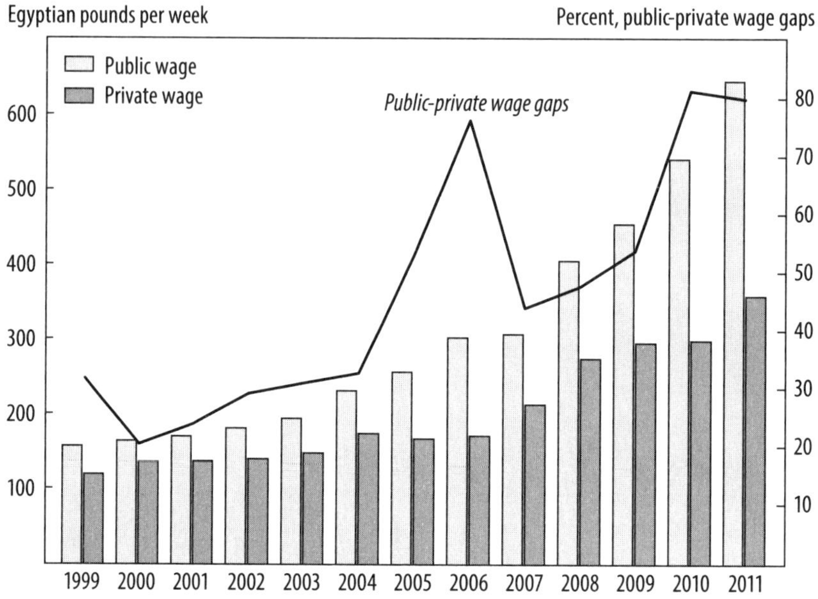

Egyptian pounds per week   Percent, public-private wage gaps

Source: Central Agency for Public Mobilization and Statistics, Cairo.
a. The average wage gaps between public and private sectors were computed as follows:

$$\text{Public-private wage gap} = \left(\frac{\text{Public Wage}}{\text{Private Wage}} - 1 \right) \times 100.$$

whose unemployment rate declined more than any other group, owing to a decrease in labor force participation rather than an increase in employment.

Shortcomings are revealed in both the capacity of the Egyptian economy to create sufficient demand for young labor, and in the capacity of the Egyptian education and training system to produce labor market entrants that meet the requirements of employers (ILO 2007). Despite a growing supply of employees with secondary and tertiary diplomas, employers still face a shortage of staff with the skills and education they require (Akhtar 2010). Assaad and Roudi-Fahimi (2007) note that the slowness of the education systems in the region—including Egypt— to respond to increasingly market-oriented and open economies has resulted in significant mismatches between the skills demanded in the job market and those possessed by new entrants. Most young people in school plan to specialize in the commerce and business administration field (30 percent), the education field (12 percent), or the engineering field (11 percent). This is despite the fact that the occupational clusters associated with these fields appear to be overcrowded, with limited opportunities for employment (ILO 2007).

However, the demand for low-skill work remains high. Seventy-one percent of Egyptian job vacancies, identified in the employer's survey conducted by ILO, were for manual occupations, while only 22 percent of the vacancies were for professional positions. The food-processing industry expects strong growth in demand for labor in the near future, while other industries show no specific prospect for an increase in employment (Japan International Cooperation Agency [JICA] 2012). The mismatch between labor demand and supply combined with the rapidly growing number of new entrants to the labor market leads to a protracted transition from school to work for Egyptian youth.

Inadequacies in the qualification system in Egypt lead firms to hire people through personal connections. According to an attitude survey of university students and companies conducted by the Japan International Cooperation Agency in Cairo and Alexandria in 2012, the highest percentage of respondents cited lack of recommendation as a reason for rejection of a job applicant by companies, accounting for half of the respondents (figure 9-2). Recommendation is a hiring method unique to Egypt, in which a letter of recommendation, rather than the applicant's ability or aptitude, is considered a priority hiring factor by companies. This is because companies have few means to evaluate the applicant's competence in an objective manner, owing to the lack of a formal and comprehensive qualification system that would otherwise demonstrate the skills and competencies of applicants. While the majority of large corporations hire people through examination and interview, MSEs still attach great importance to letters of recommendation or personal connections. As a result, a sizable number of university graduates cannot meet the qualification demand for employment, regardless of their competence or skill (JICA 2012).

Young job seekers need work experience but have fewer opportunities to acquire it. The ability to cite work experience is then the most important characteristic in a successful application for a vacancy for manual or production workers and for professional or managerial employees (see ILO 2007). Egyptian employers face difficulties recruiting qualified workers, as the training system often fails to produce people with the skills that are required to perform the jobs. Enterprises

FIGURE 9-2. Egypt: Major Overall Reasons for Rejection of Job Applications, 2012

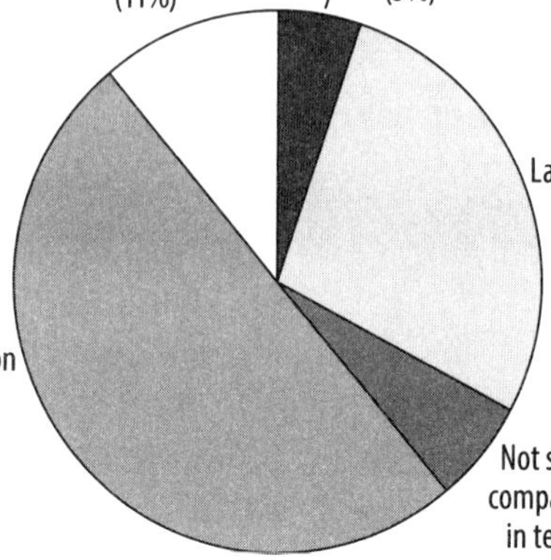

Source: Japan International Cooperation Agency (2012).

are staffed by underqualified workers, who often lack practical experi-ence. But at the same time, formal training after employment is almost entirely lacking, and vocational training opportunities for jobless and unskilled Egyptians are also limited. In an employer survey conducted by the ILO, only 14 percent of employers reported that their employees received training during the previous year, of which 88 percent was on-the-job training. Of these employers, 50 percent reported the train-ing was acquired on equipment at the job site, 62 percent reported the training was provided by an enterprise's staff, and 98 percent indicated the training fees were provided by the enterprise.

School-to-work transition is more difficult for educated youth who pursue highly skilled occupations, while it is easier for their less edu-cated counterparts who engage in low-skill work, such as that in the agricultural sector. The ILO employer survey confirmed that the selec-tion process by employers is more discerning for highly skilled jobs, which helps to explain the more difficult transition of youth who choose to stay in school longer. Unfortunately, the lingering lower demand for higher-skilled workers coincides with a situation in which more and more young people are staying in school and aspiring to higher edu-cation. The ILO survey in Egypt that examined the school-to-work transition found that young Egyptian people, particularly women, face serious difficulties and challenges in finding a career job after leaving school. The study shows that only 17 percent of respondents (those between the ages of fifteen and twenty-nine) had completed the transition from school to a career job, which is defined as a regular job that the worker has no immediate plans to change. One-quarter were still in transition—that is, either unemployed or not yet in a career job—and the rest had not begun their transition because they were still in school or not planning to seek work (ILO 2007).

There are significant gender differences in school-to-work transition. The ILO survey shows that 30 percent of male respondents had completed their transition to a career job and 35 percent were still in transition. In the case of females, only 4 percent had completed their transition, 18 percent were still in transition, and the majority—78 percent—were still inactive. Moreover, according to the Central Agency for Public Mobilization and Statistics in Egypt, while female school enrollment through secondary school exceeds 40 percent, a study on the school-to-work transition shows that only 4 percent of females make the transition from school to career jobs as opposed to 30 percent of males in the same age group (ILO 2007).

An analysis of the 2006 Egypt Labor Market Panel Survey also highlights the gendered nature of school-to-work transition. In 2006, 50 percent of male graduates had found their first job within two years of leaving school, down from three years in 1998. Seventy-five percent found jobs within five years of leaving school in 2006, whereas in 1998 it would have taken nearly eight years for that number to find jobs. The female rates of transition from school to work are much lower and do not exceed 25 percent even after fifteen years. There is no perceptible improvement for women in the transition time from 1998 to 2006 (see Amer 2006; Assaad 2006).

As for a current local labor market perception, most of the Egyptian youth, regardless of gender, expressed a greater feeling of unfairness in the conditions of the labor market for fresh graduates, such as their wage, employment opportunity, job selection process, and workload, compared with their Indonesian counterparts. On the other hand, our survey revealed that in Egypt a greater proportion of female respondents than males felt a sense of unfairness based on gender disparity in wages and job opportunities. The proportion of Egyptian and

FIGURE 9-3. Youth Perceptions of Unfairness in Local Labor Market Conditions, by Country and Gender

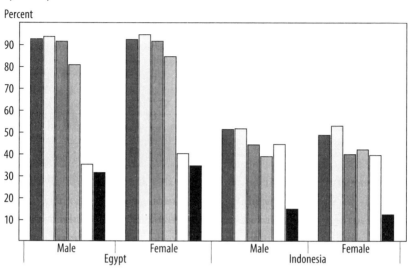

Percent

Source: 2013 JICA Job Preference Survey in Egypt and Indonesia.

Indonesian females who felt an unfair disparity existed was found to be similar (see figure 9-3).

Structurally Distorted Job Preferences for Public Sector Employment

Despite being increasingly better educated, young Egyptian graduates had structurally distorted job preferences for public sector employment and waited in anticipation of such jobs rather than joining the private sector (Amin and others 2012, pp. 5–6). Assaad (2006) argues that the long-standing Egyptian government policy of guaranteeing government employment to upper secondary and university graduates had given households distorted signals about the labor market (Assaad and Barsoum 2007). Because Egypt did not formally abolish the guarantee scheme, which had arranged government jobs for university graduates since the 1950s, young graduates, especially women, continued to aspire to public sector employment (ILO 2007).

In North Africa in general, many young people want a government job. The Gallup World Poll shows that among seven North African countries, Egypt and Tunisia have the largest proportions of youth who prefer government employment to private sector jobs or self-employment. The poll asked young Egyptians which employment sector they would choose if wages and benefits were equal in all sectors. Of the respondents, 53 percent said they preferred government jobs (Silatech 2009).[6] Employment with private business seemed to be less attractive to young people. This mismatch between young people's expectations and the reality of the job market has undoubtedly led to much frustration. This also causes higher youth unemployment as young people hold out for the expected public sector job instead of searching for other work in the private sector.

The growth of public sector employment is already very limited in North African countries. Instead of allowing a continuing focus on the public sector, efforts must be made to help young people develop realistic expectations and to create a strong private sector that is capable of offering attractive jobs (AfDB and others 2012). With regard to public employment, there are a limited number of jobs. However, the private sector could generate more job opportunities for educated youth who still lack skills and experience.

Focusing on job creation at MSEs and poverty alleviation, the Egyptian Social Fund for Development—established in 1991 by presidential decree 189—has grown into a leading institution mobilizing national and international resources to invest in social development (JICA 2011). Further generation of employment opportunities in the private sector will commence when economies become more competitive and start to attract greater foreign direct investment. However, just creating more private sector employment opportunities cannot be a sustainable response to this employment gap, unless job preference among youth is gradually shifted away from the bloated public sector and toward private sector employment.

---

6. This is Gallup's first comprehensive poll of youth in the Arab economies in 2009.

FIGURE 9-4. Egypt, Tunisia, and Indonesia: Wages and Compensation of Public Employees, 1990–2011

Percent of total government expenses

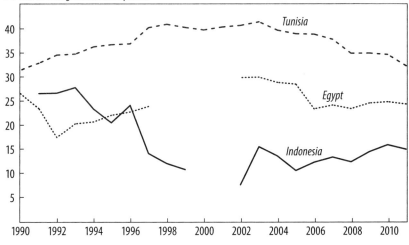

In addition, there is an urgent need for improvement in the high-cost structure of public employment. The percentage shares of wages and compensation of public employees in Egypt and Tunisia have been much higher than those in Indonesia.[7] The current share in Egypt is similar to that of Indonesia in the early 1990s (figure 9-4).

Data

To examine the factors that influence job choice and to look for possible policy options that can improve structurally distorted job preferences among youth in Egypt, the survey responses associated with this chapter were collected from engineering students at ten universities in six cities in Egypt during the period July through October 2013.[8] The

7. Compensation of employees consists of all payments in cash, as well as in kind (such as food and housing), to employees in return for services rendered, and government contributions to social insurance schemes such as social security and pensions that provide benefits to employees.

8. Together with El-Zanaty and Associates, the JICA Research Institute conducted the survey at the following universities in Egypt: Cairo University (Giza); El-Shorouk Academy (Cairo); Faculty of Engineering at Ain Shams University

total number of student respondents was 1,259, consisting of 891 males and 368 females, who were randomly selected from the lists of the student identification numbers. The surveyed universities in Egypt are of different types—five public universities and five private universities, including two private higher technological institutes and one international university—because we assume that the quality of education and curriculum differs among the institution types and this could in turn influence the students' job choices. Similarly, in the Indonesian survey, respondents were randomly chosen among engineering students at eight universities, both public and private, in five cities.[9] There were 1,216 total survey respondents, consisting of 711 males and 505 females. The 2013 JICA job preference survey is composed of the student questionnaire and the university questionnaire. The student questionnaire asks the respondent a wide variety of questions about job preference, student characteristics, family characteristics, lifestyle, motivation for work, perceptions of the local labor market, politics, and risk attitude. The university questionnaire asks for information on the number of students and academic staff and on university curriculum or courses as well as the services they provide for their students.

Almost all respondents show a willingness to work after graduation regardless of their gender, except for those who pursue further education and those who are about to get married. However, it was revealed that most students in both countries are ignorant or have an unduly pessimistic view of the unemployment rate. The unemployment rates for the total labor force and for young people were perceived by the survey respondents to be much higher than the actual rates.

In terms of job preference, figures 9-5 and 9-6 show the first, second, and third most important attributes influencing job choice among

---

(Cairo); Faculty of Engineering at Mansoura University (Mansoura); Faculty of Engineering at Matareya Helwan University (Cairo); Higher Institute for Engineering and Technology in New Damietta (Damietta); Higher Technology Institute in 10th of Ramadan City (6th of October City); Minia University (Minya); Modern University (Cairo); and British University in Egypt (Cairo).

9. Together with the Demographic Institute, Faculty of Economics at University of Indonesia, eight universities were surveyed in Indonesia: University North Sumatra (Medan); Medan Institute of Technology (Medan); University of Indonesia (Jakarta); Bandung Institute of Technology (Bandung); Parahyangan University (Bandung); Ahmad Dahlan University (Yogyakarta); Hassanudin University (Makassar); and Atmajaya University (Makassar).

FIGURE 9-5. Egypt: Important Attributes Influencing Job Choice among Engineering Students, by Gender, 2013

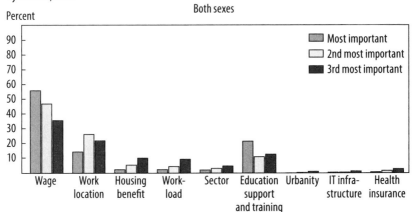

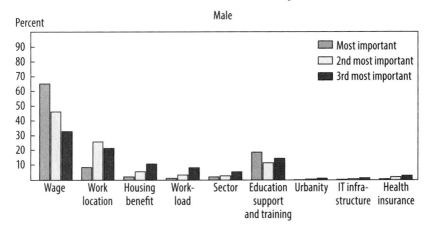

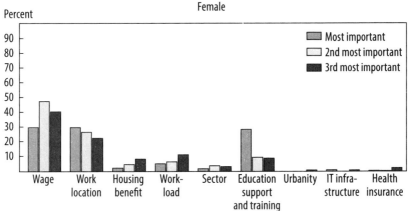

Source: 2013 JICA Student Survey.

FIGURE 9-6. Indonesia: Important Attributes Influencing Job Choice among Engineering Students, by Gender, 2013

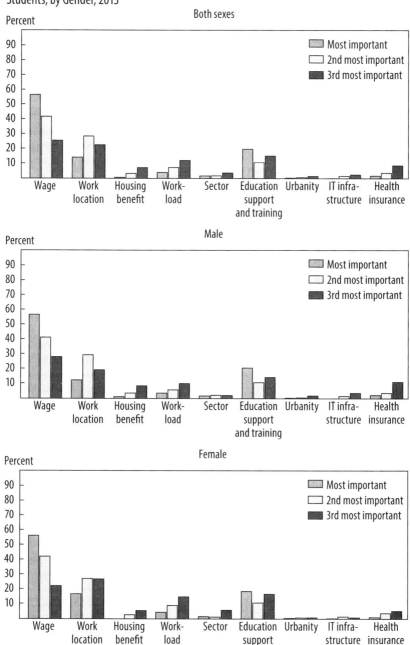

Source: 2013 JICA Student Survey.

FIGURE 9-7. Egypt and Indonesia: Most Important Attributes Influencing Job Choice among Engineering Students, Type of University, 2013

Percent

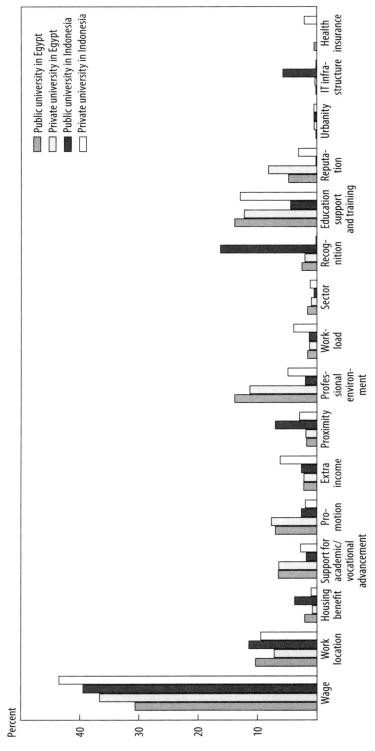

Source: 2013 JICA Student Survey.

engineering students in Egypt and in Indonesia, respectively. It is obvious that wage is one of the most important attributes. Besides wage, education opportunities and the possibility of upgrading qualifications or skills and work location were also important factors. Interestingly, only Egyptian female respondents placed equal importance on these three job attributes (wage, education opportunities, and work location).

Across all types of universities in both countries, wage was found to be as important as job attributes (figure 9-7). Despite their similarity, the differing importance of some attributes was found to depend on students' school type. Students in private schools tend to place more importance on wage compared with those in public schools, regardless of their country. Indonesian students were more likely than Egyptians to choose wage as the most important job attribute. Egyptian students placed a greater emphasis on other attributes such as access to further education, promotion possibilities, and professional environment. Moreover, Indonesian public university students placed especially higher priority on recognition from their supervisor or boss and infrastructure, as measured by Internet or mobile phone connections and electricity supply, whereas a relatively lower priority was placed on the opportunity for education opportunities and the possibility of upgrading qualifications (see figure 9-7).

With regard to work locations, more than 60 percent of Egyptian students preferred to work away from their current location, and this showed strong overseas employment aspiration, mainly owing to the better living conditions abroad (Murata 2014, p. 21). On the other hand, 90 percent of their Indonesian counterparts were willing to move from their current location to pursue better experience, skills, and career, but their ideal destinations are diverse and eclectic, ranging from domestic cities to foreign countries and even "anywhere." Egyptian students show a preference for working in the Arabic-speaking countries of the Middle East such as Saudi Arabia, the United Arab Emirates, and Kuwait. Compared with Egyptians, Indonesians face a more universal language barrier in foreign countries, so their popular destinations include developed countries such as Japan, the United States, Singapore, Germany, and the United Kingdom.

The survey found that university students in both countries do not really consider employment sector as the most important factor when they decide on a job. Most, as noted above, prioritized wage as

FIGURE 9-8. Egypt and Indonesia: Students' Preference on Employment Sector, by Gender and Type of University, 2013

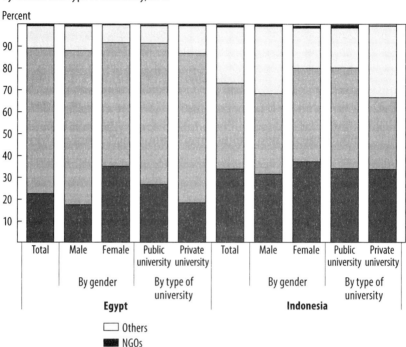

Source: 2013 JICA Job Preference Survey in Egypt and Indonesia.

a deciding factor. However, in reality, students have a general preference for certain sectors they most favor for future employment that
can be derived from the combination of other job attributes such as
wage levels, availability of social benefits, and job security. Contrary to
our expectations, the survey found that Egyptian engineering students
currently have a strong preference for working in the private sector
as compared with their Indonesian counterparts (see figure 9-8). This
preference is stronger among male students. On the other hand, female
respondents still show an interest in public sector jobs. Public university students tend to prefer working in the public sector, while those
at private universities opt for self-employment, household enterprise,
or entrepreneurship. However, each university has its own different

curriculum and set of courses, and therefore caution must be applied when we discuss features of students' job preferences based on types of university. In addition, the location also could influence the preference.

To examine the determinants of a student's choice of employment sector, a multinomial logit regression model was used, taking into consideration features of students (gender, grade-point average, social network aspiration, willingness to take career risks, and intolerance of uncertainty and ambiguity), features of their families (parents' education attainment and business ownership) and location (living within Greater Cairo or not for the survey in Egypt, and living within Java or not for the survey in Indonesia).[10] The findings of this regression model reveal that female respondents in both countries would rather get a job in the public sector, while Egyptian men prefer the private sector and Indonesian men are more likely to seek self-employment, household enterprise, or entrepreneurship. Location near the main labor market (Greater Cairo in Egypt, or Java in Indonesia) was found to decrease the probability of students preferring a job in the public sector. This can be explained by the fact that there is greater variety among employment opportunities in these areas. With regard to parents' education attainment, it was found that if a student's mother completed a master's or doctoral degree, that student is significantly more likely to prefer a job in the private sector in both Egypt and Indonesia. Business ownership by any family member or relative significantly and positively influenced students' preference for self-employment, household enterprise, or entrepreneurship. Students with the willingness to take risks in their career had a higher preference for self-employment and disliked the idea of working in the public sector. Moreover, Egyptian students who are risk averse also had a greater preference for self-employment, probably owing to recent political unrest and thus uncertainty behind public sector jobs.

Factors Influencing Students' Job Preferences

Among other job attributes, wage was found to significantly influence their job choices for engineering students in Egypt and Indonesia (see Murata 2014, p. 25).[11] The effect of the wage level is more pronounced

10. For more detailed results, see Murata (2014, table 4).
11. For more detailed results, see Murata (2014, table 5).

for Egyptian respondents than for their Indonesian counterparts. Among those in Egypt, females identify wages as a greater priority than males, but in Indonesia there were no clear gender differences in the impact of wage on job preferences. Offering education opportunities and the possibility of upgrading qualifications probably attracts job seekers, but its impact gets smaller if they take into account overseas employment as an option. On the other hand, having the opportunities of good information technology (IT) infrastructure and support for health care benefits becomes more important for Egyptian respondents seeking overseas employment. Similarly, housing support from employers is preferred for overseas employment opportunities, but youth seeking jobs domestically seem to prefer to stay with parents, siblings, and relatives, and therefore, they show no interest in this support.

With all other things being equal, household enterprise or self-employment was preferred to wage employment at public and private sectors among students in both countries. In general, men were found to have the greater motivation to work in this sector. This preference might be explained as one of the features of engineering students, as they tend to be ambitious at an early stage in their career and expect to become entrepreneurs in the near future. In terms of job preferences between public and private sectors, wage employment at a private enterprise was significantly preferred to employment in the public sector among Egyptian men, while other students showed a modest preference for working in the public sector (though our findings show no significant difference). Uniquely to Egyptian men, the estimation result reveals that workload does not matter when choosing a job. This means that young males in Egypt are desperately anxious and desire any job, and therefore opting for a light workload does not seem to be an attractive option.

Willingness to Pay (or Receive Lower Wages)

Figures 9-9 and 9-10 show the extent to which young respondents are willing to pay or receive lower wages in exchange for receiving a better job attribute. Figure 9-9 considers a set of job choices with the combinations of job attributes including sectors of employment, whereas figure 9-10 instead takes into account work locations including overseas employment. Our findings reveal that with education support during a

FIGURE 9-9.   Egypt and Indonesia: Willingness-to-Pay Estimates and 95% Confidence Intervals for Job Attributes, including Sectors[a]

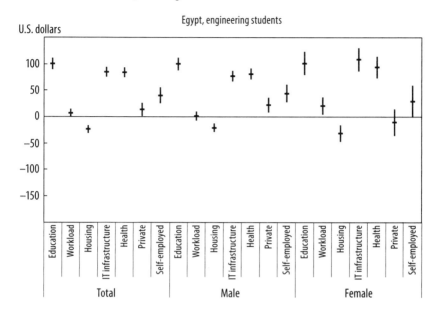

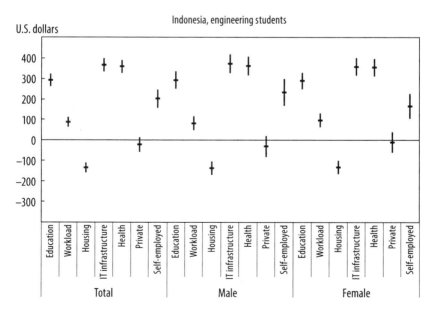

Source: 2013 JICA Job Preference Survey in Egypt and Indonesia.

a. The average exchange rates in the second quarter of 2013 were 6.938 Egyptian pounds per U.S. dollar and 10,664 Indonesia rupiah per U.S. dollar (see International Monetary Fund 2013). The detailed variable definition can be found in the appendix of Murata (2014).

FIGURE 9-10.   Egypt and Indonesia: WTP Estimates and 95% Confidence Intervals for
Job Attributes, including Work Location[a]

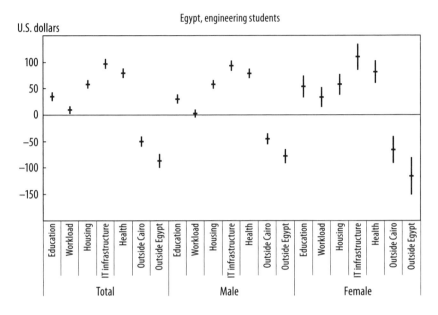

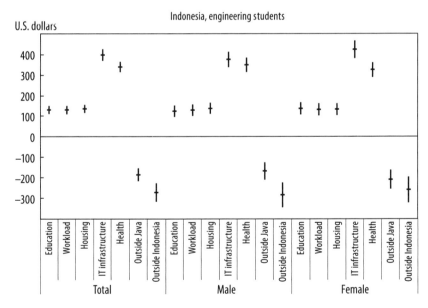

Source: 2013 JICA Job Preference Survey in Egypt and Indonesia.
    a. The average exchange rates in the second quarter of 2013 were 6.938 Egyptian pounds per U.S. dollar and 10,664
Indonesia rupiah per U.S. dollar (see International Monetary Fund 2013). The detailed variable definition can be found in the
appendix of Murata (2014).

contract, a good IT infrastructure, and support for medical insurance, the respondents in both countries are willing to give up a part of their wage for a job. The willingness to pay (WTP) estimates for these job attributes (measured in U.S. dollars) were found to be less important to Egyptian students than to their Indonesian counterparts, which results partly from the differences between the monthly wage levels in Egypt and Indonesia. If a work location was extended overseas, offering support for a decent dwelling also became an attractive option for them, while they then gave lower priority to education support (though it is still positive and significant).

In this study, comparing men with women revealed a gender difference in the importance of job attributes, as measured by the WTP estimates. As figure 9-9 shows, compared with their male counterparts, Egyptian female students attach a higher value to a light workload, good IT infrastructure, and support for health insurance, but they put less value on private sector employment. In terms of gender differences between Indonesian students, it was found that male respondents give greater weight to household enterprise or self-employment than female respondents. There is no gender difference between Indonesian male and female respondents in the WTP estimates for other job attributes used in the analysis. Moreover, figure 9-10 also shows that in addition to light workload and good IT infrastructure, education support was valued more among Egyptian female students than their male counterparts. On the other hand, Egyptian female students are less likely to value overseas employment. In terms of the WTP estimates, figure 9-10 also reveals that Indonesian male and female respondents had similar results. But Indonesian females placed greater value on good IT infrastructure once overseas employment was included as one of the job attributes.

Policy Options to Change Students' Job Preferences

The current potentially biased labor supply situation in Egypt has resulted mainly from the prolonged, structurally distorted job preferences between public and private sectors, particularly among youth. Two policy options might be taken to make private sector jobs more attractive: narrowing sector wage gaps and offering better conditions of job attributes.

FIGURE 9-11. Egypt: Probability of Taking a Job in the Public and Private Sectors, by Wage Gap (with All Else Equal), 2013[a]

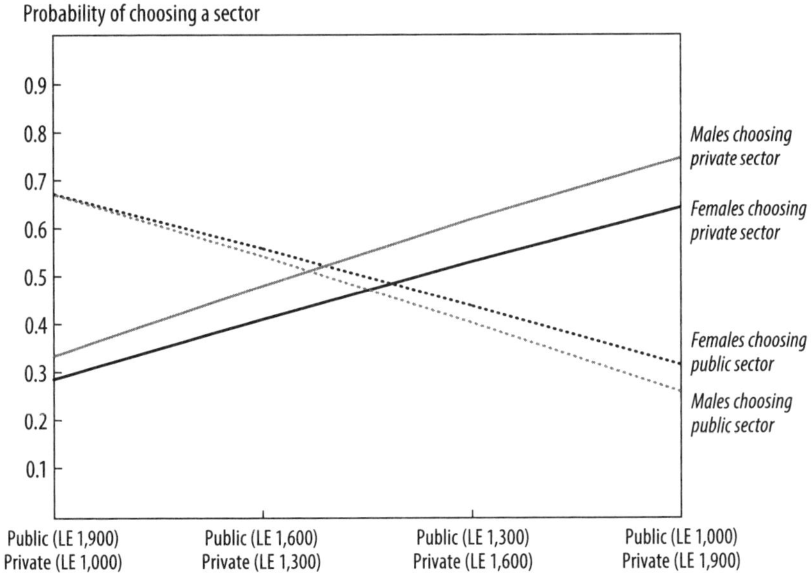

Probability of choosing a sector

Source: 2013 JICA Job Preference Survey in Egypt and Indonesia.
a. LE = livre égyptienne (French for Egyptian pound).

Narrowing Sector Wage Gaps

Figure 9-11 shows the varying probabilities of taking a job in the public and private sectors in Egypt under the different scenarios of sector wage differences. If the public sector monthly wage is 90 percent higher (1,900 Egyptian pounds, equivalent to US$274) than in the private sector (1,000 Egyptian pounds, equivalent to US$144), the probability of taking the public sector job is around 0.67 (or 67 percent) among both males and females, which is more than double the probability of taking a private sector job.[12] However, if the wage gap falls to only 300 Egyptian pounds (equivalent to US$43), the gaps between the probabilities of taking the jobs in public or private sectors narrow to 0.064 (or 6.4 percentage points) for males and 0.150 (or 15.0 percentage points) for females, meaning that its policy impact can be greater among

12. The average exchange rate in the second quarter of 2013 was 6.938 Egyptian pounds per U.S. dollar (see International Monetary Fund 2013).

males. The findings of this study also denote that a 30 percent increase in private sector wages raises the probability of Egyptian males taking such a job by 0.14 (or 14 percentage points) and raises the probability of Egyptian females taking such a job by 0.12 (or 12 percentage points). Thus in the context of the future development of the private sector in Egypt, narrowing the wage gap between public and private sectors really matters. These findings may help us to understand the reason policymakers need to observe local wage settings.

Offering Better Social Benefits and IT Infrastructure

An improvement in nonwage job attributes can also make private sector jobs more attractive than those in the public sector. As an example, here we imagine that an Egyptian student has the opportunity to take a public sector job with a monthly wage of 1,600 Egyptian pounds (equivalent to US$231). The probability of taking such a job is 0.54 (or 54 percent) among males and 0.50 (or 50 percent) among females in our survey in Egypt. With the wage level of 1,000 Egyptian pounds and all other things being equal, their probability of taking a job in the private sector was, on average, 0.334 (or 33.4 percent) for males and 0.285 (or 28.5 percent) for females. Even if a private enterprise offers a light workload, the probability of its being chosen over a public sector job increased by 0.06 (or 6 percentage points) among females, but little for males. Still, the students prefer public sector employment. However, offering better social benefits and IT infrastructure significantly contributes to an increase in job uptake rates. Our findings reveal that these offers could raise the uptake rate of a private sector job the most among males with education support by 0.326 (or 32.6 percentage points), and its rate among females with good IT infrastructure by 0.300 (or 30.0 percentage points). Health insurance support also significantly increases its uptake by around 0.26 (or 26 percentage points), regardless of gender (see figure 9-12).

Conclusion

This study on which this chapter is based sought to address the high youth unemployment rates in Egypt, particularly among the highly educated, driven by a demographic youth bulge. The most obvious findings for policy are that the public-private sector wage differentials must be

FIGURE 9-12.   Egypt: Probability of Taking a Job in the Private Sector If One of the Attributes of a Private Sector Job Improves (with All Else Equal), 2013[a]

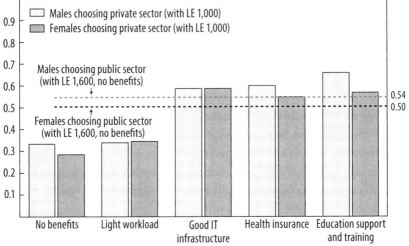

Probability of choosing a sector

Source: 2013 JICA Job Preference Survey in Egypt and Indonesia.
a. LE = livre égyptienne (French for Egyptian pound).

narrowed; better benefits must accompany private sector employment (particularly support for continuing education, upgrading qualifications, and health insurance); and good IT infrastructure matters. Taken together, these steps could significantly contribute to an increase in the rates of private sector employment among young Egyptian job seekers, even in the case of continued high public sector wages. However, these findings are limited to engineering students. Further investigation and experimentation with youth in general is strongly recommended.

References

African Development Bank (AfDB) and others. 2012. "Promoting Youth Employment." In *African Economic Outlook 2012: Promoting Youth Employment*. Paris: OECD Publishing. http://dx.doi.org/10.1787/aeo-2012-en.

Akhtar, S. 2010. *Quality of Education: The Gateway to Employability*. MENA Knowledge and Learning Quick Notes Series, no. 22. Washington: World Bank. March.

Amer, M. 2006. "The Egyptian Youth Labor Market School-to-Work Transition, 1998–2006." Paper prepared for the Egypt Labor Market Panel Survey: Economic Research Forum Dissemination Conference. Cairo. October 30.

Amin, M., R. Assaad, N. al-Baharna, K. Derviş, R. M. Desai, N. S. Dhillon, A. Galal, H. Ghanem, C. Graham, D. Kaufmann, H. Kharas, J. Page, D. Salehi-Isfahani, K. Sierra, and T. M. Yousef. 2012. *After the Spring: Economic Transitions in the Arab World.* Oxford University Press.

Asian Development Bank. 2013. "Key Indicators for Asia and the Pacific, 2013." Mandaluyong City, Philippines.

Assaad, R. 2006. "Employment and Unemployment Dynamics." Paper prepared for the Egypt Labor Market Panel Survey: Economic Research Forum Dissemination Conference. Cairo. October 30.

———. 2007. "Unemployment and Youth Insertion in the Labor Market in Egypt." Working Paper 118. Cairo: Egyptian Center for Economic Studies.

Assaad, R., and G. Barsoum. 2007. "Youth Exclusion in Egypt: In Search of Second Chances." Middle East Youth Initiative Working Paper 2. Wolfensohn Center for Development, Brookings, and Dubai School of Government. September.

Assaad, R., and F. Roudi-Fahimi. 2007. "Youth in the Middle East and North Africa: Demographic Opportunity or Challenge?" Washington: Population Reference Bureau.

Boughzala, M. 2013. "Youth Employment and Economic Transition in Tunisia." Working Paper 57. Global Economy and Development, Brookings.

Economic Research Forum for Arab Countries, Iran, and Turkey. 2004. "Egypt Country Profile: The Road Ahead for Egypt." Femise report. Cairo.

Fuller, G. E. 2003. "The Youth Factor: The New Demographics of the Middle East and the Implications for U.S. Policy." Analysis Paper 3. U.S. Relations with the Islamic World, Brookings (June).

International Labor Organization (ILO). 2007. "School-to-Work Transition: Evidence from Egypt Employment Policy Papers." Geneva: El-Zanaty and Associates.

———. 2011. *Key Indicators of the Labor Market.* 7th ed. Geneva (http://dx. doi.org/10.1787/888932600336).

International Monetary Fund. 2013. *International Financial Statistics* (December). Washington.

Japan International Cooperation Agency (JICA). 2011. "Survey on Assisting the Development of Egyptian Financial Markets for Micro, Small, and Medium Enterprises: General Survey on Bottlenecks for MSME's Access to Finance." Tokyo.

———. 2012. "Data Collection Survey on Human Resource Development in the Industry Sector in the Middle East Region." Tokyo.

LaGraffe, D. 2012. "The Youth Bulge in Egypt: An Intersection of Demographics, Security, and the Arab Spring." *Journal of Strategic Security* 5, no. 2: 65–80. doi: 10.5038/1944-0472.5.2.4

Murata, A. 2014. "Designing Youth Employment Policies in Egypt." Working Paper 68. Global Economy and Development, Brookings (January).

Silatech. 2009. "The Silatech Index: Voices of Young Arabs." Silatech and Gallup Organization (http://dx.doi.org/10.1787/888932600925).

United Nations. 2010. *World Population Prospects: The 2010 Revision.* Geneva: United Nations, Department of Economic and Social Affairs, Population Division.

————. 2012. *World Population Prospects: The 2012 Revision.* Geneva: United Nations, Department of Economic and Social Affairs, Population Division.

Williamson, B. 1987. *Education and Social Change in Egypt.* London: Macmillan.

World Bank. 2011. *World Development Report 2011: Conflict, Security, and Development.* Washington.

————. 2013. *Jobs for Shared Prosperity: Time for Action in the Middle East and North Africa.* Washington.

10

Improving Regional and Rural Development for Inclusive Growth in Egypt

HAFEZ GHANEM

The Egyptian economy needs to start growing again, and the benefits from growth need to be more fairly distributed. Egypt was growing at a healthy rate of 5 to 7 percent during the five-year period before the 2011 revolution. However, as Ghanem (2013) argues, growth was not sufficiently inclusive. The middle class did not benefit enough from growth, and the proportion of Egyptians living on less than $5 a day remained stagnant at about 85 percent. This is quite different from the experience of other emerging economies, such as Brazil and India, where the percentage of poor fell dramatically during high-growth periods. Assaad and Barsoum (2007) show that youth felt particularly excluded as they suffered from a high unemployment rate of about 25 percent, and even those who found jobs usually ended up working in the informal sector, where they typically earned less than $4 a day and had no job security or social benefits.

There is also a spatial dimension to this lack of inclusiveness. About 57 percent of Egypt's population lives in rural areas. Rural poverty is three times higher than urban poverty, and more than 80 percent of the extremely poor live in Upper Egypt, which is home to about half of Egypt's population.

I would like to thank Abdessalam Ould Ahmed for providing excellent comments on an earlier version of this chapter. I have also benefited from participation in the MENA Regional Dialogue on Family Farming organized in Tunis in November 2013 by the UN's Food and Agriculture Organization. I am grateful to dialogue participants—particularly Nora Ourabah Haddad, Benoit Horemans, Noureddine Nasr, and Mohamed Bengoumi—for very useful discussions.

Ghanem and Shaikh (2013) show that Egypt's economic situation deteriorated after the revolution as political instability and a sense of insecurity led to a decline in investment, capital flight, and rising unemployment. By mid-2013, growth was down from 5 percent to about 2 percent, overall unemployment rose from 9 percent to 13.5 percent, and foreign reserves declined so that they barely covered three months' imports. The low international reserves made it more difficult to import, and the prices of many imported necessities, including food, rose rapidly. As usual it is the lower middle class and the poor, especially the rural poor, who suffer most from the slow economy. That is why it is important that Egypt adjust its economic policies and adopt a strategy to achieve inclusive growth.

Several emerging economies (for example, Brazil under President Luiz Inácio Lula da Silva) have succeeded in drastically reducing rural poverty. As described by Da Silva, Del Grossi, and De Franca (2011), economies successful at reducing rural poverty have adopted a three-pronged strategy: supporting institutional reforms that ensure that the rural poor have a greater voice in economic decisionmaking, developing agriculture and agro-processing so as to enhance rural livelihoods, and putting in place targeted social protection programs that mainly consist of cash transfers to the rural poor. This chapter presents an analysis of Egypt's experience in rural and regional development and compares it with international experiences. It argues that reforms along the lines that were adopted in Brazil could help improve rural incomes and reduce regional disparities in Egypt.

Egypt's Agriculture and Rural Space

Egypt has been an agricultural country for millennia, with agricultural and peasant society forming the basis of Egyptian civilization. Even today more than half of the population lives in rural areas. The country's area is about 1 million square kilometers, but 97 percent of it is desert. Therefore, nearly all of the population lives on 3 percent of the land, in the Nile valley south of Cairo (Upper Egypt) and the Nile delta (Lower Egypt). Thus land and water availability are important constraints on agriculture and rural development. Arable land amounts to about 0.05 hectare per person, one of the lowest rates in the world, and water availability is limited to Egypt's quota of Nile water.

Abaab and others (2000) describe Egyptian agriculture as a special case in the Mediterranean region. It is an intensive irrigated agriculture with two or three plantings every year. Rural space in Egypt consists of about 5,000 villages built along the Nile and the cultivated areas around them, which are, in turn, surrounded by desert. The typical agriculture production unit is a small family farm, with about 75 percent of farms being less than one hectare. Family members typically engage in multiple activities: agriculture, animal production, and off-farm employment. Most farm families have cows or water buffalos, with an average of two animals per family. There are few industrial or service activities in rural areas. Hence for people living on small farms, employment typically means wage labor on one of the larger farms nearby.

Historically, Lower Egypt has always been more developed than Upper Egypt. Lower Egypt's proximity to major ports on the Mediterranean has encouraged trade and the export of agriculture products. It has also led to the development of industry. Nearly all of Egypt's textiles industry, which started growing in the mid-nineteenth century, is in Lower Egypt.

Because of the need to centrally manage the country's irrigation system, the Egyptian state has been heavily involved in regulating agriculture since the days of the pharaohs. Starting in the 1950s, the government adopted a strongly interventionist policy and regulatory framework. The state controlled all crop areas, and farmers were not free to plant what they wanted. The rent of agricultural land was also fixed by government. Government controlled all farm-gate prices, which were typically 40 to 60 percent below international prices. By paying farmers a low price for their output, the government could ensure inexpensive food for the urban centers. In a sense, as in most developing countries, the government was implicitly taxing farmers to subsidize city dwellers. This all changed with the deregulation that began in 1986. Now farmers are free to produce what they want and sell it at market prices, and the market for agricultural land has been liberalized.

Large Regional Variations in Poverty and Opportunities

In spite of the deregulation, the incidence of extreme poverty in Egypt for people living in rural areas is still nearly four times that for those in urban areas. Table 10-1 shows the poverty headcount index using

TABLE 10-1. Poverty, Egypt, 2011

Percent of total population

Region	People living under extreme poverty line	People living under lower poverty line	People living under upper poverty line
Urban	2.6	10.6	24.6
Rural	9.6	30.0	52.7
Total	6.7	22.0	41.2

Source: World Bank (2011).

three poverty lines. The line for extreme poverty is defined by the cost of buying sufficient food. That is, the extreme poor are defined here as those who cannot afford to buy a minimum food basket. The table shows that 6.7 percent of the population of Egypt is extremely poor. The figure for urban areas is only 2.6 percent, while that for rural areas is 9.6 percent. That is, nearly one of every ten rural inhabitants in Egypt is extremely poor and food insecure.

Table 10-1 also shows the incidence of poverty using two other poverty lines. The lower poverty line is based on a basket of goods and services that is considered by the government to be the minimum. According to this lower poverty line, 22 percent of Egypt's population is poor, but rural poverty is 30 percent—nearly three times the incidence of poverty in urban areas. The World Bank has developed a high-poverty line to help identify the near-poor. Using this higher-poverty line yields a national headcount index of 41.2 percent and a rural poverty rate of 52.7 percent, about double the urban poverty rate.

Poverty in Egypt also varies by region. In analyzing the incidence of poverty it is useful to divide Egypt into four regions: metropolitan Egypt, which comprises the large cities, especially Cairo and Alexandria; Lower Egypt, which includes the fertile delta region north of Cairo; Upper Egypt, which includes the Nile valley south of Cairo; and the border regions, which include the desert areas along the border with Libya and in the Sinai Peninsula. Each of those regions (except the metropolitan region) is divided into rural areas and urban centers.

Table 10-2 shows that Upper Egypt represents a special problem. It has about 50 percent of the country's population but hosts 83 percent of the extremely poor and 67 percent of the poor. The problem in

TABLE 10-2. Regional Distribution of Poverty, Egypt, 2012

Percent

Region	Extreme poverty	Poor	Near-poor	Share of population
Metropolitan	2.8	4.6	9.1	17.0
Lower Egypt	13.7	27.6	44.7	31.1
Upper Egypt	83.1	67.1	45.0	50.3
Borders	0.4	0.7	1.3	1.5
Total	100	100	100	100

Source: World Bank (2012).

Upper Egypt is especially serious in the rural areas. Urban Upper Egypt has 11.6 percent of Egypt's extremely poor and 11.3 percent of the country's poor. On the other hand, rural Upper Egypt has 71.5 percent of the extremely poor and 55.8 percent of the poor. Lower Egypt has less poverty. About 30 percent of Egypt's population lives in Lower Egypt, and the region is home to 13.7 percent of the country's extreme poor and 27.6 percent of the poor. However, it is important to note that the vast majority of the poor and extremely poor in Lower Egypt also live in rural areas.

Other measures of welfare give similar results. For example, 15 percent of urban women do not receive any prenatal care; in rural areas that figure is 33 percent. Forty-three percent of women in rural Upper Egypt are illiterate compared with 20 percent in urban Upper Egypt. The illiteracy rate for women in rural Lower Egypt is 31 percent.

Table 10-3 shows the human opportunity index (HOI) for rural and urban Egypt. This index was developed at the World Bank based on the idea that outcomes in income and consumption are affected by the opportunities available to people, and particularly children, and that all people should be given an equal opportunity in life. The index measures access to variables that affect a person's economic opportunity, such as education, health care, clean water, non-overcrowded housing, and so on. As can be expected, the aggregate index for urban dwellers (80) is higher than the aggregate index for rural dwellers (70). This implies that the difference in observed income and consumption between urban and rural areas is partly the result of lack of access to some basic services that compromise rural dwellers' life opportunities.

TABLE 10-3. Human Opportunity Index, Egypt, 2009

Variable	Urban	Rural
Primary education	88	85
Secondary education	69	60
School attendance (aged nine to fifteen)	92	87
Water	96	85
Sanitation	74	17
Lighting energy source	100	98
Cooking energy source	99	97
Non-overcrowding	64	55
Telephone	84	64
Assisted birth	93	79
Postnatal care	33	24
Prenatal care	87	73
Immunization	85	85
Non-wasting	74	75
Non-stunting	72	67
Non-underweight	88	82
Aggregate index	80	70

Source: World Bank (2012).

Table 10-3 also presents the various components of the rural and urban HOI scores. As can be expected, urban areas seem to offer better opportunities in nearly every aspect measured by the index. However, the biggest difference seems to be in the area of sanitation services, where the rural index is only 17 compared with an urban index of 74. Both urban and rural areas score poorly in the area of postnatal care, with a score of 33 for urban areas and 24 for rural ones.

The HOI index can be aggregated into four groups describing access to different types of services: education (primary, secondary, and so on); adequate housing (water, sanitation, and so on); early childhood (prenatal and postnatal care, immunization, and so on); and nutrition (wasting, stunting, and so on). Table 10-4 presents those four aggregate HOI scores for the four regions of Egypt. While Upper Egypt lags most in terms of education and adequate housing (particularly access to sanitation), the border areas lag most in terms of early childhood development and nutrition.

TABLE 10-4. Aggregate Human Opportunity Index, Egypt, by Region, 2009

Service	Metropolitan	Lower Egypt	Upper Egypt	Borders
Education	76	78	70	77
Housing	89	77	68	75
Early childhood	77	69	65	55
Nutrition	77	77	75	65

Source: World Bank (2012).

Allocation of Public Investment

Public spending appears to reflect political realities rather than a desire to reduce regional inequalities. As table 10-5 shows, metropolitan areas, with 17 percent of the population, receive nearly 34 percent of public investment, although they have lower poverty rates than the rest of the country. Upper Egypt, with about half the population and the vast majority of the extremely poor—receives only 25 percent of public investment. This probably reflects a desire to keep the big cities relatively satisfied to avoid demonstrations and unrest that could jeopardize political stability. Prioritizing the welfare of relatively well off urban dwellers, and hence neglecting rural areas, is a common phenomenon in developing countries with weak institutions, where the rural poor are unable to participate in economic decisionmaking.

The cross-sector allocation of public investment also appears to need revision. For example, the border areas receive a disproportionate amount of public investment, given their share of population and poverty. Nevertheless, this could have made sense if the investment were directed at early childhood development and nutrition, sectors in which the border areas are lagging. However, as table 10-5 shows, the disproportionate share of public investment in border areas has been directed at the electricity sector rather than health or education. Similarly, there is pressing need for investment in sanitation infrastructure in Upper Egypt, a sector that has been long neglected, and in postnatal care across the whole country.

Problems with the geographic and sectoral allocation of public investment reflect the noninclusive way in which planning is carried out and the lack of a real link between plans and actual expenditures. Sakamoto (2013) analyzes the planning process in Egypt and compares

TABLE 10-5. Distribution of Public Investment in Selected Sectors, Egypt, 2009
Percent

Sector	Total	Electricity	Water	Education	Health
Metropolitan	33.6	6.4	16.9	30.4	32.1
Lower Egypt	30.3	20.0	53.9	35.6	32.4
Upper Egypt	25.6	29.7	20.9	30.2	30.9
Borders	10.4	43.9	8.4	3.9	4.6
Total	100	100	100	100	100

Source: World Bank (2012).

it with good practices in successful economies of East Asia. He argues that a new approach to planning and allocation of public spending is needed. The planning process needs to include representatives of different ministries as well as the private sector and civil society. Beneficiaries of public expenditures, particularly the poor, need to have a voice in the decisionmaking process. There is also a need to better coordinate activities of the various line ministries and to put in place a mechanism that links plans to actual expenditure decisions.

Egypt needs a transparent and inclusive planning system that allows a societal dialogue on economic issues and consensus building around key priorities. The absence of such a system creates an environment where corruption can develop and weak implementation is tolerated. The experiences of Japan, Indonesia, and Malaysia with inclusive planning demonstrate how inclusiveness goes hand in hand with economic growth and poverty reduction. As argued by Sakamoto (2013), Japan's Economic Planning Council, Malaysia's implementation monitoring mechanism, and Indonesia's participatory planning process during its democratic transition are examples that could be adapted to the Egyptian context.

Brazil also provides an example of inclusive planning. When Luis Ignacio Lula da Silva was elected president of Brazil, fighting hunger was one of his top priorities for achieving social justice. Therefore, he created a National Food and Nutritional Security Council, which is a good example of an inclusive economic institution. It had fifty-nine members, seventeen of whom were government representatives and forty-two representatives of civil society, and was chaired by a civil society representative. The council met on the premises of the presidency and made their recommendations directly to President Lula. Because the problem of hunger is intersectoral in nature, the council had a broad membership so that all sectors of the economy were represented. The council was also conceived as a tool to provide voice for those suffering from hunger and to improve cooperation between government and civil society. Under the council and President Lula da Silva, Brazil was extremely successful in eliminating hunger.

Social Protection and Safety Nets

The relatively large numbers of extremely poor people, mostly concentrated in rural Upper Egypt, are not being reached by the existing social safety net system. Egypt's social safety net accounts for a substantial share of public spending but does not have a commensurate impact on poverty and human development. Much of the spending goes to universal fuel subsidies (about 7 percent of GDP), which benefit the rich more than the poor and distort resource allocation.

Bread subsidies cost Egypt about 1.5 percent of GDP. According to the World Bank (2011), in the absence of food subsidies poverty in Egypt would have been significantly higher—31 percent instead of 22 percent. However, the World Bank study also shows that the cost of food subsidies could be greatly reduced if leakages were eliminated and coverage narrowed to those who really need it.

Cash transfers to the poor and vulnerable represent only 0.1 percent of GDP. Those nonsubsidy social safety net programs are largely fragmented, poorly targeted, and limited in scope. Currently, there is no cohesive system that can adequately protect the growing number of the poor, provide mitigation against some of the adverse impacts of economic reform, and be scaled up in times of crisis.

Egypt should consider reforming the fuel subsidies system, improving governance and financial viability of key energy sector actors, replacing untargeted subsidies with an efficient and well-targeted social safety net system, and providing immediate protection to the poor and the vulnerable hard hit by the deteriorating economic conditions and subsidy reforms. The objective should not be to eliminate universal subsidies to reduce overall spending but rather to replace them with more effective mechanisms that target the extremely poor. The net effect on the budget deficit could be zero. Nevertheless, reductions in fuel subsidies will need to be carried out carefully. That 57 percent of the fuel subsidy in Egypt goes to the top two-fifths of the income distribution can be misinterpreted; the vast majority of this group lives on just $4 to $10 a day. Thus most of those two top quintiles should be classified as either middle class or poor but certainly not rich. Moreover, the 57 percent figure implies that 43 percent of the subsidy benefits people who live on less than $4 a day. Therefore, notwithstanding the regressive nature of the subsidy, it seems clear that reducing or eliminating it will hurt the middle class and therefore will be politically difficult to implement.

This is not a new problem. When President Anwar Sadat tried reducing subsidies in Egypt in 1977, there were massive street riots, and he was forced to reverse the decision. President Habib Bourghiba in Tunisia faced the same problem. In 2011 Nigeria tried eliminating fuel subsidies; but, faced with massive protests, the government was compelled to restore them in part. Jordan too faced street riots in 2012 when it lowered fuel subsidies.

A change in the social protection system from untargeted subsidies to targeted social protection would require a broad national dialogue and consensus building. The objective needs to be clearly stated as using the huge resources that are currently channeled to untargeted subsidies in a more efficient way to help the poor.

Some developing countries (including Ghana and Indonesia) have succeeded in reducing energy subsidies and replacing them with better-targeted mechanisms. Egypt can draw important lessons from these experiences. Vagliasindi (2012) studied twenty developing countries and found that they managed to reduce the average cost of energy subsidies in their budgets from 1.8 percent of GDP in 2004 to 1.3 percent in 2010—and that this, in turn, led to both a reduction in energy intensity and increased energy efficiency.

Programs that succeed in reducing energy subsidies have usually included two features: compensatory measures to help the most vulnerable and a strong communications strategy to convince the public of the benefits. In Indonesia, when President Megawati Sukarnoputri tried to implement energy price reforms in 2003, he was met with stiff opposition and had to roll back the program. Three years later President Susilo Bambang Yudhoyono tried again, starting with a public information campaign that clearly identified the benefits of the reform and the new safety net programs for the poor. The people were apparently convinced by the need for the reform and the government's commitment to protect the most vulnerable. He was able to reduce subsidies with little opposition.

In 2004 the government of Ghana launched a study on the impact of fuel subsidies. The study's steering committee included a variety of stakeholders (government officials, academics, company representatives, and the like). By 2005 the government was able to use the committee's report to launch an information effort that subsequently reduced fuel subsidies by 50 percent. The study had detailed social mitigation measures and showed how to minimize backlash in order to achieve its end goal. As a result, the government knew how best to avoid public opposition on the issue and how to communicate its policies to the public. In particular, the government clearly outlined how it plans to use the savings from the reduced fuel subsidies to provide targeted assistance to the poor.

Egypt may consider expanding the use of targeted cash-transfer mechanisms. Those could be region specific, with different programs for Upper Egypt and Lower Egypt, but initially they need to focus on rural areas where nearly all the extremely poor live. Such programs could be conditional or unconditional depending on the region's context. For example, in Upper Egypt, where 44 percent of women are illiterate, cash transfers could be conditioned on girls' school attendance. Alternatively, they could be unconditional, based only on a means-testing system.

Egypt needs to move away from fragmented project-based social protection to a systemized approach. This means using common administrative mechanisms, unique beneficiary identification, common targeting techniques, common monitoring and evaluation systems, and integrated transfer modalities. Naturally, such a system needs to be built up gradually as administrative capacity is being built. A mechanism to avoid leakages and corruption, perhaps through a partnership with civil society, needs to be built into the design of the new system.

Egypt can benefit from Latin America's experience in this area, especially Brazil's Bolsa Familia and Mexico's Progresa-Oportunidades. Bolsa Familia is the largest program of its kind in the world. It covers 26 million families, about 25 percent of the population. The program gives poor families (defined as living on less than $55 a month) a transfer of $13 a month for each vaccinated child attending school up to a maximum of five children. It also provides a transfer of $15 a month for each youth (sixteen to seventeen years old) attending school up to a maximum of two per family. In addition, extremely poor families (defined as living on less than $28 a month) receive a basic unconditional benefit. The money is transferred, preferably to the female head of household, through special debit cards issued by a publicly owned bank.

Mexico's Progresa-Oportunidades was created with the express objective of replacing price subsidies with a cash transfer program. Today it covers about 5 million families, representing 24 percent of Mexico's population and nearly all of the country's extremely poor. It operates in all of the country's thirty-one states with a budget of $2.8 billion. Cash transfers are conditioned on changes in the recipient's behavior. Beneficiaries need to invest in their own nutrition, health, and education. Progress is periodically measured through comprehensive evaluations of programs, operations, and results.

The experience of Latin America shows that direct cash transfers can be used to achieve poverty reduction as well as development objectives. By providing cash to poor families those programs help raise their consumption and get them out of poverty. It is a much more direct method than generalized price subsidies for products that can be consumed by the poor as well as the nonpoor. By making part of the transfer conditional on school attendance or immunization, the programs also encourage investment in human capital and thus help achieve long-term development objectives. There is also some evidence that recipients of cash transfers in rural areas tend to save part of it and use it for investments in productive physical capital.

Many of the cash transfer programs are also used to enhance women's social and economic empowerment. Many studies have shown that transferring money to women instead of men leads to an increase in family welfare, particularly improving children's education, nutrition, and health. By putting cash in the hands of women, programs like Bolsa Familia and Progresa-Oportunidades have improved women's status within the household and enhanced their self-esteem and socioeconomic empowerment.

Developing Agriculture and Agro-Industries

Agriculture is crucial for Egypt's economy and particularly for poor households. It accounts for around 14 percent of GDP, employs 30 percent of the labor force, and is responsible for about 20 percent of total exports. Nearly 40 percent of the poor in Egypt rely directly on agriculture. All of the poor in rural areas are either directly or indirectly affected by agriculture. Therefore, agriculture growth and the resulting growth in the nonfarm rural economy would have significant poverty reduction effects. Development of the agricultural sector would also have strong equalization effects as it reduces the large income gaps between urban and rural areas and between Upper Egypt and the rest of the country.

Extreme land fragmentation is a key feature of Egyptian agriculture. About 40 percent of Egypt's agriculture is divided into parcels of less than 3 *feddans* (about 1.2 hectares). This fragmentation is increasing owing to demographic pressures, inheritance laws that divide the land up among all surviving children, and the lack of a well-functioning land market that allows land purchase to form larger and more economically viable parcels. According to the most recent agricultural census, the area of arable land divided into parcels of less than 3 feddans has increased from 2.3 million feddans in 1980 to 3.0 million in 2000. Increasing fragmentation has two important direct effects. First, about 12 percent of prime agricultural land is being lost in separations and boundaries between very small parcels. Second, average farmer income has stagnated even though productivity and real income per feddan have been rising by about 1.7 percent annually for the past thirty years.

Water availability is a binding constraint for agriculture development and rural poverty reduction. Egypt's rural population has nearly doubled since 1980, while the Nile's water resources are more or less fixed at about 55.5 billion cubic meters a year. The government has tried to increase water availability through the treatment of drainage water for reuse for irrigation and through the greater use of underground water. On the demand side, there are several efforts to improve irrigation facilities and plant water-efficient varieties to reduce average water use. However, the government has resisted introducing cost recovery for irrigation water. Agriculture development and rural poverty reduction in Egypt will depend crucially on the modernization of the water and irrigation systems and the introduction of new crop varieties that require less water.

As described earlier, the agriculture sector has gone through a series of liberalization efforts since the 1990s. These reforms included liberalizing the land market as well as product prices. Moreover, farmers

TABLE 10-6. Land Use of Major Agricultural Products, Egypt, 1980–2007

Percent

Product	1980	1990	2007
Wheat	11.9	16.1	17.9
Maize	17.1	16.2	13.6
Rice	8.7	8.5	11.0
Cotton	11.2	8.5	3.8
Vegetables	9.3	9.2	8.7
Fruits	3.1	7.1	8.4

Source: Ministry of Agriculture and Land Reclamation (2009).

are now free to decide which crops to produce on their land, and they follow market signals. This has led to a change in the structure of Egyptian agriculture. As shown in table 10-6, the area under cotton (traditionally Egypt's largest cash crop and main export) declined from 11.2 percent of the total in 1980 to 3.8 percent in 2007, while the area allocated to wheat production and fruits increased significantly.

The structure of the agricultural labor force has also been changing rapidly. The proportion of young people has increased, reflecting the overall demographic change in Egypt. Moreover there has been a huge increase in the number of university graduates with agriculture degrees. However, according to the Ministry of Agriculture and Land Reclamation (2009) the quality of new graduates has declined significantly. Education institutions are not producing graduates with the types of practical skills demanded by the labor market. The ministry has been trying to remedy this situation by developing special training programs in areas where labor supply is insufficient to meet the demand.

With limited land and water resources, agricultural growth and farmers' incomes depend crucially on increasing yields. Over the past three decades, yields for many crops have increased at fast rates. Wheat yields doubled between 1980 and 2007. Yields for rice increased by 67 percent over the same period, and water consumption per unit was reduced by 25 percent. During the same period maize yields increased by 90 percent, sugar cane yields by 44 percent, tomato yields by 116 percent, and strawberry yields by 673 percent. On the other hand, yields of some major crops—like cotton—remained stagnant, which could explain farmers' decisions to reduce the area under cotton production.

Future growth and rural poverty reduction will require a continued increase in yields through technological enhancement.[1]

Livestock production (including poultry and fisheries) represents 40 percent of the value of total agriculture production in Egypt. Moreover, it is an important source of income for small and landless farmers. Landless farmers own 17 percent of all cows in Egypt, 6 percent of all water buffalos, and 25 percent of all sheep and goats. Moreover, 93 percent of all cows, 86 percent of all buffalos, and 55 percent of all sheep and goats are owned by small producers who own less than ten animals. Demand for livestock products is increasing rapidly as income increases. Therefore, this is a sector that can contribute significantly to rural poverty reduction.[2]

Marketing—whether domestically or for exports—is a serious constraint to agriculture development and increasing farmers' incomes. The majority of smallholders continue to use the traditional marketing system known as *kerala*. Under this system, the crop is sold in the field at a price per feddan. The buyer takes control of the product in the field and handles the harvesting, selection, grading, and transportation. An obvious problem with this system is that it does not allow for much price differentiation to reflect quality. This also means that the farmer gets a lower share of the market value of the product, as the buyer needs to be compensated for harvesting and grading. For example, in the case of many vegetables the farmer's share of the market price is only about 20 percent. As Egypt tries to expand its exports, and as the domestic market becomes more quality sensitive, some buyers are trying to make changes to kerala by introducing some quality criteria.

Weak marketing, storage, and transportation systems also lead to large postharvest losses. The Ministry of Agriculture and Land Reclamation estimates that about 15 percent of all of Egypt's agriculture output is lost after harvest. This is about average for developing countries. However, given the tight water constraint that Egypt is facing and the fact that poor farmers need to make a living out of very small land parcels, every effort needs to be made to limit and reduce this waste.

As shown in table 10-7, agro-industries, which could make an important contribution to value added and employment generation in

1. Ministry of Agriculture and Land Reclamation (2009).
2. Ministry of Agriculture and Land Reclamation (2009).

TABLE 10-7. Industrial Transformation of Agricultural Products, Egypt, 2009

Product	Output (million tons)	Share transformed (%)
Tomatoes	8.6	0.7
Potatoes	2.3	7.8
Other vegetables	9.4	1.8
Fruits	9.8	0.9
Meat and poultry	1.5	0.3
Milk	5.0	25.0

Source: Ministry of Agriculture and Land Reclamation (2009).

rural areas, are not sufficiently developed. Only a small portion of agricultural production goes through any form of transformation, processing, preparation, or preservation. And most of the agro-processing that takes place in Egypt (70 percent, according to Ministry of Agriculture estimates) occurs in the informal sector. Agro-processors in the informal sector do not follow quality or health and safety norms, and they sell their products cheaply in local markets. There are virtually no long-term contractual arrangements between farmers and agro-processors. The processors rely on buying what is available in the market, which may not always fully reflect their needs in terms of quality and quantity.

Although Egyptian agriculture has tremendous export potential, particularly to European and Gulf markets, export growth has been relatively slow and concentrated in a few traditional commodities: raw cotton, rice, citrus fruits, and potatoes. The contribution of nontraditional products in which Egypt has a competitive advantage (including different fruits and vegetables, medicinal plants, cut flowers, and so on) to export growth has been very weak. Export development has been hampered by inadequate transport infrastructure, market information, and quality assurance processes to ensure that health and safety standards are met. Moreover, the vast majority of smallholders do not participate in export activities owing to the lack of contractual arrangements between smallholders and exporters as well as to the lack of attention to quality.

On the positive side, several examples show that, when provided with adequate support, smallholders are able to meet quality standards and sell for export, thus considerably increasing their incomes. Some civil society organizations have been active in this area with good results. The SUN nongovernmental organization (NGO), which was created in 2002 and operates in Upper Egypt, is a good example. This NGO works with smallholders. It organizes them into associations and provides them with technical, managerial, and marketing support. It links smallholders to large producers and exporters through different contractual arrangements and outgrower (contract farming) schemes. In its first five years of operations it signed nearly 900 different contracts with exporters and agro-processors. It also prioritizes women's participation in the program. By 2007 more than 12,500 smallholders had joined SUN associations. They exported nontraditional products worth 85 million Egyptian pounds and estimate that participants' income rose by 60 million pounds.

The challenges facing Egyptian agriculture and rural development, as well as the opportunities, are well known, and the Ministry of Agriculture and Land Reclamation has developed a comprehensive strategy for the sector until the year 2030. The strategy has six objectives: improve rural living standards and reduce poverty; increase the sector's contribution to national food and nutrition security; sustainably use natural resources; enhance land and water productivity; increase the sector's competitiveness in international and national markets; and improve the climate for agricultural investments.

The strategy presents a long-term vision and a large number of actions that need to be taken over the next fifteen to twenty years to achieve it. In today's political environment in Egypt it is important to focus on a few short-term actions that can bring about fairly quick results. Moreover, since smallholder and landless farmers constitute the vast majority of rural dwellers as well as the majority of poor people, policies should target small producers and help them raise their productivity and improve their linkages to national and international markets.

Private investment in rural areas is important for enhancing livelihoods and employment. Receiving land titles is a major constraint, as it can take more than ten years to obtain a title to agricultural land. This discourages investment and makes it difficult to use land as collateral for bank loans. Moreover, investors in both agriculture and agro-industries face complicated procedures and are required to obtain permits and clearances from several different ministries and public entities. The Ministry of Agriculture's strategy includes actions to simplify procedures, encourage investment, and facilitate access to credit.

Those actions could be undertaken quickly and could provide a signal that the government is serious about rural development.

Organizing smallholders, providing them with extension services to increase productivity and improve quality, and linking them with local markets as well as exporters are important ways of raising their incomes and helping them get out of poverty. The SUN example discussed above demonstrates how civil society can play a key role in this area. However, this is just an isolated example, and civil society's role in rural development has been quite limited. As shown by Kharas and Abdou (2012), government has not been encouraging those activities, and the legal framework facing civil society organizations is very constraining. The Ministry of Agriculture's strategy recognizes the importance of developing the activities of rural NGOs and presents proposals on how to achieve that. It argues for new simplified legislation governing all rural NGOs. The ministry is also willing to provide administrative as well as technical support to those organizations and to help link them with agriculture research institutes and universities. Again, those are actions that can be started quickly to achieve early and tangible results.

Producer organizations are a special form of NGO that can play an important role in strengthening the governance system of the agriculture sector, particularly in developing and supporting smallholders. Problems caused by the large number of very small farms can be tackled through the development of strong producer organizations that group farmers together to ensure that their voice is heard in policy discussions and also help enhance access to technology, inputs, and markets. Smallholders' low level of political participation combined with the lack of strong organizations representing them may explain why development strategies and policies tend to be biased in favor of urban activities. Independent and strong producer organizations could play an effective advocacy role and could help lobby politicians to promote the interests of farmers. Producer organizations could also play an important economic role, grouping farmers together to enhance their access to technology and inputs and to improve market access and help them retain a larger share of value added. In fact, civil society organizations are often much better placed than government agencies to deliver extension and technical support to small farmers.

Concluding Remarks and the Role of Development Partners

A strategy to achieve inclusive growth in Egypt cannot ignore the problems caused by regional inequalities and rural poverty. This chapter proposes an approach to dealing with those issues that includes moving to a more inclusive system of planning and budget allocations that would ensure that more resources flow to lagging areas; revising the social safety net system to rely more on cash transfers that are targeted to the poor; and implementing agriculture policies that focus on supporting smallholders and linking them to national and international markets.

Egypt's development partners have a great deal of experience in those areas and could provide important support to achieving inclusive growth through financing and knowledge sharing. The Japan International Cooperation Agency is already supporting a project on inclusive planning in Egypt. Implementation of this project would help improve the allocation of public investment. The World Bank has done extensive work on social safety nets and can support reforms in this area. Several donors are funding agriculture development and could scale up their interventions and focus them on supporting smallholders.

References

Abaab, A., and others. 2000. *Agricultures familiales et développement rural en Méditerranée*. Paris: Editions Karthala.

Assaad, R., and G. Barsoum. 2007. "Youth Exclusion in Egypt: In Search of Second Chances." Middle East Youth Initiative Working Paper. Washington: Wolfensohn Center for Development, Brookings.

Da Silva, J. G., M. Del Grossi, and C. De Franca. 2011. "The Fome Zero (Zero Hunger) Program: The Brazilian Experience." Brasilia, Brazil: Ministry of Agrarian Development.

Ghanem, H. 2013. "The Role of Micro and Small Enterprises in Egypt's Economic Transition." Working Paper 53. Global Economy and Development, Brookings.

Ghanem, H., and S. Shaikh. 2013. "On the Brink: Preventing Economic Collapse and Promoting Inclusive Growth in Egypt and Tunisia." U.S. Relations with the Islamic World, Brookings.

Kharas, H., and E. Abdou. 2012. "Regulatory Reforms Necessary for an Inclusive Growth Model in Egypt." Global Views, Brookings.

Ministry of Agriculture and Land Reclamation. 2009. "Strategy for Sustainable Agricultural Development 2030." Cairo.

Sakamoto, K. 2013. "Efforts to Introduce Inclusive Planning in Egypt." Working Paper 54. Global Economy and Development, Brookings.

Vagliasindi, M. 2012. "Implementing Energy Subsidy Reforms: An Overview of Key Policy Issues." Policy Research Working Paper 6122. Washington: World Bank.

World Bank. 2011. "Poverty in Egypt, 2008–09." Report 60249-EG. Washington.

———. 2012. "Reshaping Egypt's Economic Geography: Domestic Integration as a Development Platform." Report 71249. Washington.

11

Promoting Inclusive Growth in Arab Countries: Regional and Rural Development and Inequality in Tunisia

MONGI BOUGHZALA and MOHAMED TLILI HAMDI

The January 2011 uprising in Tunisia was about jobs and justice for all regions of the country. Although some indicators suggest that overall inequality and poverty have decreased in Tunisia over the last five decades and that the size of the middle class has grown, by 2011 regional disparities and inequality between the rural and the urban areas had become unacceptable. Regional disparities, which have been persistently large in Tunisia, were perceived as a serious injustice. The coastal regions and the rural regions, which are located mostly in the western part of the country, did not receive an equitable share of the benefits of the country's economic growth. Some areas have benefited very little. Youth from the poor rural areas often have to migrate to the cities to look for work, and most of them end up with low-paying and frustrating jobs in the informal sector. The more educated among them feel even more politically and economically excluded because they face a very uncertain outlook and the highest rate of unemployment. Tunisia's poorer regions are predominantly rural and their economies are much less diversified than urban economies. Agriculture remains the main economic sector in these areas, offering only low-productivity and low-pay employment. As a result, the per capita income in these regions is around half that of the wealthiest regions, and the poverty rate is three times higher.

Although Tunisia has made some important progress in building women's rights, gender bias is another serious concern that is more prevalent in rural areas. However, there are many promising statistics. Girls have equal access to schools at all levels and in basically all regions. The absolute number of female students has outgrown that of males, and more than 60 percent of university graduates are females. Yet the rate of female participation in the labor force remains low. While 70 percent of males participated in the country's labor market in 2011, only 26 percent of Tunisian females did so. The female unemployment rate is also much higher—nearly twice the rate for males—and when employed, women often receive lower pay. This bias is strongest for female workers and university graduates living in the poor rural regions in the west of the country. Female participation in agricultural employment is relatively high, but such employment is most often unpaid family work or seasonal work, which is paid the lowest wages in the country.

In the period leading up to the 2011 uprising, these disparities strengthened the sentiments of exclusion, injustice, and discrimination felt among Tunisians from the predominantly rural regions, who strongly believed that their situation was caused mainly by biased policies and unfair regional distribution of public investments. And while the democratization of education had not been successful in ensuring job growth, it was critical in raising the level of awareness about regional disparities and the urban/rural economic gap.

Regional disparities do not, however, mean that Tunisia's rural regions remain totally backward or that nothing has been achieved in the poorer regions. In fact, over the previous five decades various government programs and projects had been implemented in these regions. Dams were built, other infrastructure projects were completed, millions of olive trees were planted, and schools were opened everywhere. But the government effort in the western regions was much less substantive than it was in the rest of the country, and little was done to develop modern nonagricultural economic activities.

Inadequate government investment is not the only factor contributing to Tunisia's rural poverty. The scarcity of natural resources (mainly water), the distribution of land, and limited access to financial resources are among the other important structural economic constraints facing agricultural development. The majority of the rural population is either landless or owns micro farms (defined as less than ten hectares of rather arid land or less than two hectares of irrigated land) and has a limited formal education. Consequently, rural residents have a very limited access to new technologies and financial resources and their productivity is low.

What then is to be done to provide new opportunities for the people of primarily rural regions? What policies and measures will allow them to benefit from faster and more inclusive growth? Those are the questions addressed in this chapter. The answers are based on a study of Tunisians' current circumstances, with a focus on the main barriers to growth in underdeveloped regions in terms of both resources (public and private) and institutions and the people's empowerment. Special attention will be paid to the population, the labor force, infrastructure, financial constraints, and the institutional system. Two regions—called governorates in Tunisia—will be covered in more detail, namely Le Kef in the northwest and Sidi Bouzid in the midwest. We also examine best international practices and the literature on economic development. There is indeed much to be learned from rural and regional development across the world, especially from the experiences of Far East and Southeast Asian countries, notably South Korea and Taiwan.

This chapter proposes alternatives to policies now in place and offers recommendations to boost productivity and income for the rural population in Tunisia's poor regions. We argue that while it is possible, improving productivity in agriculture is only part of the solution. It cannot serve as a complete solution because agriculture by itself cannot ensure a decent livelihood for all of Tunisia's rural population. A strategy based on micro-farming alone cannot be sustained and will not be efficient in the long term, especially for impoverished Tunisians who own small farms or are almost landless. Regional development requires major structural reforms and strategies and comprehensive government-initiated programs operated within a holistic framework that combines public and private interventions. Such programs must integrate public infrastructure, training and capacity development, marketing, financial resources, and institutional reforms. Coordination among all these dimensions is primarily the responsibility of Tunisia's government, though development efforts could surely remain market friendly and include a participatory approach. However, because development programs must efficiently use resources in order to be sustainable and because some regions with limited resources may be unable to operate such programs, it is unlikely—even in the long run—that all areas of Tunisia will be able to provide enough quality employment opportunities to their residents, particularly youth. Inevitably, more rural Tunisians will eventually migrate, either within the same region or between regions. In some cases, migration between regions is likely to remain the main stabilizing mechanism. Politically, this will not be an easy sell, as all of Tunisia's governorates claim that they are entitled to equal shares of government programs.

This study is organized in four sections. The first section is an overview of regional and rural development and disparities in Tunisia that covers population, public investment in education and infrastructure, natural resources, and financial resources. The second section focuses on Tunisia's Le Kef and Sidi Bouzid governorates, addressing specific causes of rural poverty and barriers to development and youth employment. The third section briefly reviews regional and rural development in Asian countries in order to draw lessons relevant to Tunisia. The fourth section presents our conclusions and suggests policy recommendations.

Overview of Regional and Rural Development and Disparities in Tunisia

Development plans were begun in Tunisia shortly after its independence in the early 1960s, but they paid little attention to regional development issues.[1] Later, attempts were made to integrate the geographic and regional dimensions of planning into the development planning process, but those efforts were minimal and inefficient. Moreover, the Tunisian government has always been very centralized and biased in favor of the coastal cities. The eastern regions and cities kept attracting more public investment because for historical reasons—compounded by the lack of democracy—the western regions were politically underrepresented.[2] The strongest lobbies in Tunisia came from the east coast, and they systematically pushed for more investment in their regions while neglecting the others. It took at least twenty years before

1. Tunisia gained independence from France in 1956.
2. For those reasons, see, for instance, Henia (2014).

the first regional development programs were launched and more than thirty years for the government to admit that the benefits of growth were unequally distributed among regions. Starting in the 1980s, some actions were taken, mainly in the form of integrated development programs, but they were not enough to change the main resource allocation mechanisms or significantly reduce the level of inequality. Many institutions were created for the sake of regional development, but none of them could initiate and implement major comprehensive plans for the poor regions.

Unequal Progress and Development

The regional disparities found in Tunisia do not mean that nothing was achieved in the western regions; rather, they reflect the fact that less attention was given to the development of the poor western regions. In accordance with the Lipsetian theory (Lipset 1959), which argues that democracy is "secreted out of dictatorship by economic development," the poorer regions could rebel and demand a more equitable and democratic system only after reaching a certain threshold of development. Substantial progress was actually achieved everywhere. By 2010, in all regions, Tunisia's illiteracy rate dropped to less than 22 percent and around half of the population aged ten years or more had a secondary if not a higher education (table 11-1 and table 11-2). (In contrast, in the early 1960s, when more than 90 percent of the population had little or no education, the illiteracy rate was more than 65 percent.) There was virtually universal access not only to education but also to water, electricity, and basic health care in all urban areas and in a large portion of rural areas, and the transportation and communication infrastructure was also much more developed than in the 1960s. In short, the government invested in all regions but simply invested less in the western ones.

Starting in the 1990s, the Tunisian government showed increased interest in regional development. Development plans and documents from the time show that while cutting regional disparities was a government priority, the public resources allocated to the poorer regions and the strategies adopted to reach the stated goals were insufficient. The distribution of investment remained weighted toward the more powerful regions. Private investment, which depends on the level and quality of public investment, was also much lower in the western regions

TABLE 11-1. Tunisia's Labor Force, by Level of Education, 1966–2011

Percent of total labor force

Education level	1966	1975	1984	1994	2001	2004	2010
Higher	1.2	1.4	3.3	7.0	10.0	7.9	17.0
Secondary (general and vocational)	7.1	12.8	20.0	29.0	30.0	32.0	38.0
Primary	26.2	32.6	34.4	40.1	40.2	37.0	34.9
None	68.0	56.1	46.4	37.2	24.3	23.1	10.1
Total	100.0	100.0	100.0	100.0	100.0	100.0	100.0

Source: Institut National de la Statistique, Labor Surveys, 2001–11; Population Census, 1966, 1975, 1984, 1994.

TABLE 11-2. Labor Force, by Region and Level of Education, Tunisia, 2010

Percent

Region	Higher	Secondary	Primary	None	Total
Grand Tunis	26.7	42.6	26.8	3.7	100.0
Northeast	13.7	37.9	37.7	10.7	100.0
Northwest	12.6	29.7	36.0	21.7	100.0
Kef	12.5	26.7	35.8	25.0	100.0
Mideast	17.7	38.6	36.3	7.2	100.0
Midwest	12.0	28.6	37.9	21.5	100.0
Sidi Bouzid	11.8	27.1	34.9	26.2	100.0
Southeast	19.1	40.0	35.5	5.3	100.0
Southwest	20.5	41.2	31.1	7.1	100.0
Tunisia total	18.2	37.5	34.0	10.1	100.0

Source: Institut National de la Statistique, Labor Survey 2010.

(table 11-3). Investment laws and fiscal incentives offered to attract private investors to Tunisia's poor regions had little effect. The lack of investment was aggravated by the excessive centralization of the government and more generally by the poor business environment. In such an environment, informal and sometimes corrupt institutions emerged to fill the gaps in the rigid and inefficient regulatory system. As a result, by 2010 nearly 90 percent of new enterprises and jobs were created in the major coastal governorates of Tunis, Bizerte, Nabeul, Sousse, Monastir, and Sfax—that is, in the northeast and mideast regions, where 60 percent of Tunisians live. The share of foreign investment in

TABLE 11-3. Distribution of Industrial Activities, Tunisia, by Region, 2011

Region	Enterprises (more than ten employees)		Employment	
	Number	Percent	Number	Percent
Northeast	1,291	22.8	131,407	27.7
Tunis region	1,427	25.1	127,477	26.9
Mideast	2,058	36.4	158,441	33.7
Northwest	275	4.3	16,796	2.5
Midwest	242	4.3	16,982	3.6
Southeast	242	4.3	13,958	2.9
Southwest	126	2.2	8,576	1.8
Total Tunisia	5,661	100	473,637	100

Source: Ministry of Planning and Regional Development, based on Institut National de la Statistique, "Statistiques Issues du Répertoire National des Entreprises," 2011.

these coastal areas is even higher: 95 percent of foreign direct investment is there. Not much was done to break this vicious circle.

Income Inequality and Poverty

As a result of low public and private investment in Tunisia's western regions, income and consumption levels there are significantly lower than in the northeast and mideast regions. Per capita consumption in the poorest region, as shown in table 11-4, the midwest, is 1,138 Tunisian dollars a year—half that of the wealthiest, the Tunis metropolitan region (2,390 Tunisian dollars a year).[3] That is, of course, a key indicator of regional disparity and a determining factor in the observed social unrest and continuous migration to the eastern cities. The northwest and southwest regions are a little better off, mainly because they have already lost a large part of their population to migration. Following a relatively rapid inflow of investment, the southeast has been catching up for the last decade: at 4.7 percent, the southeast had the highest consumption growth rate in Tunisia, where the average is only 2.9 percent.

Not surprisingly, in rural areas average income as measured by consumption is much lower than in urban areas (table 11-5): about half the average of urban areas and less than half that of large cities. Again, this explains why these cities keep attracting waves of migrants from

3. One Tunisian dollar (TND) = 0.6 U.S. dollar (in December 2013).

TABLE 11-4. Per Capita Consumption and Annual Growth Rate, Tunisia, by Region, 2000, 2005, and 2010

Constant 2005 Tunisian dinars

Region	Per capita consumption			Annual growth rate, 2000–10 (%)
	2000	2005	2010	
Grand Tunis	2,000	2,331	2,624	2.8
Northeast	1,320	1,547	1,718	2.7
Northwest	1,127	1,292	1,311	1.5
Mideast	1,707	1,902	2,189	2.5
Midwest	968	1,034	1,212	2.3
Southeast	1,126	1,574	1,787	4.7
Southwest	1,068	1,338	1,507	3.5
Tunisia	1,441	1,696	1,919	2.9

Source: Institut National de la Statistique, Household Consumption Surveys, 2000, 2005, and 2010.

TABLE 11-5. Per Capita Consumption, Tunisia, Urban and Rural

2005 Tunisian dinars

Milieu	Per capita consumption			Annual growth rate, 2000–10 (%)
	2000	2005	2010	
Communal	1,985	2,326	2,516	2.4
Big cities	2,291	2,640	3,005	2.8
Average towns	1,746	2,045	2,124	2.0
Rural	1,048	1,213	1,337	2.5
Total	1,441	1,696	1,919	2.9

Source: Household Consumption Survey 2000, 2005, and 2010.

the west. The west's lower consumption and income levels are correlated with more poverty and unemployment. Poverty rates are much higher in the western regions (table 11-6 and figure 11-1)—averaging 25.9 percent in the northwest—and are highest in the midwest, where the average poverty rate is 32.3 percent. Poverty is also higher in the rural areas (table 11-7), where it is about 50 percent higher than the national average and more than twice the rate seen in large cities (only 9 percent in 2010). However, all poverty rates, including those in the western regions and the rural areas, have notably decreased over the

TABLE 11-6. Poverty Rate, Tunisia, by Region and Year

Percent

	Poverty rate			Extreme poverty rate		
	2000	2005	2010	2000	2005	2010
Grand Tunis	21.0	14.6	9.1	4.3	2.3	1.1
Northeast	32.1	21.6	10.3	10.5	5.4	1.8
Northwest	35.3	26.9	25.7	12.1	8.9	8.8
Mideast	21.4	12.6	8.0	6.4	2.6	1.6
Midwest	49.3	46.5	32.3	25.5	23.2	14.3
Southeast	44.3	29.0	17.9	17.5	9.6	4.9
Southwest	47.8	33.2	21.5	21.7	12.1	6.4

Source: Institut National de la Statistique, Labor Surveys, "Mesure de la pauvreté, des inégalités et de la polarisation en Tunisie 2000–10."

FIGURE 11-1. Poverty Rate, Tunisia, by Region and Year

Percent

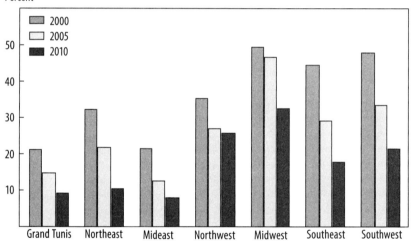

Source: Institut National de la Statistique, "Mesure de la pauvreté, des inégalités et de la polarisation en Tunisie 2000–10."

last five decades, especially between 2000 and 2010. This is consistent with the fact that some efforts were made in these regions but fewer than in the east.

Unemployment also is higher in the western and southern regions and for the more educated (table 11-8). However, unemployment is a problem everywhere for educated youth, especially university

TABLE 11-7. Poverty Rate, Tunisia, by Location and Year[a]

Percent

	Poverty rate			Extreme poverty rate		
	2000	2005	2010	2000	2005	2010
Tunisia	32.4 (0.8)	23.3 (0.7)	15.5 (0.6)	12.0 (0.5)	7.6 (0.4)	4.6 (0.3)
Large cities	21.5 (1.4)	15.4 (1.1)	9.0 (1.0)	4.3 (0.6)	2.2 (0.4)	1.3 (0.3)
Small cities	32.5 (1.3)	22.1 (1.1)	14.0 (0.9)	10.5 (0.8)	6.5 (0.6)	2.9 (0.4)
Rural	40.4 (1.3)	31.5 (2.6)	22.6 (0.6)	19.1 (1.0)	13.4 (0.9)	9.2 (0.8)

Source: Institut National de la Statistique, Labor Surveys, "Mesure de la pauvreté, des inégalités et de la polarisation en Tunisie 2000–10."

a. Number in parentheses is a standard deviation.

TABLE 11-8. Unemployment Rate, Tunisia, by Region and Education Level, 2010

Percent

Region	Total	Higher education	Secondary	Primary	None
Grand Tunis	13.2	14.4	14.5	11.1	4.0
Northeast	11.0	21.9	11.7	8.3	4.4
Kef	12.4	28.0	15.2	10.1	4.9
Northwest	14.4	31.6	17.9	10.6	6.1
Mideast	9.3	19.4	8.1	6.5	4.7
Sidi Bouzid	14.7	40.2	16.9	10.3	7.0
Midwest	16.8	35.4	16.7	8.8	5.0
Southeast	16.8	35.4	16.7	8.8	5.0
Southwest	23.4	41.7	24.0	14.1	8.4
Total Tunisia	13.0	22.9	13.7	9.2	5.7

Source: Institut National de la Statistique, Labor Survey 2010.

graduates. Women are even harder hit, with an unemployment rate about twice that of men—about 50 percent for women with a higher education degree. These figures reflect very few good opportunities in predominantly rural regions. Only occasional or seasonal low-paid jobs are available, often as unsalaried farm workers or employees in the informal sector working under very hard conditions. The next section explores more deeply the potential as well as the work conditions and development issues in the predominantly rural regions of Le Kef and Sidi Bouzid.

Development Challenges and Potential in Two Tunisian Rural Governorates: Le Kef and Sidi Bouzid

What the Le Kef and Sidi Bouzid governorates have in common is that both are heavily dependent on agriculture and have benefited relatively little from Tunisia's development over the past five decades. Neither has been the recipient of any special development effort or major non-agricultural project. They have attracted little private nonagricultural investment, and a significant proportion of their labor force has migrated to other regions because of the lack of employment opportunities. More than half of the population of Le Kef is rural, and it has negative population growth. Of course, as indicated above, the governorates have seen gains in terms of education, poverty reduction, and access to basic services. However, compared with their human and natural potential and with other regions, they have not received their fair share of the progress made in Tunisia.

Sidi Bouzid

Sidi Bouzid is where the Tunisian uprising started in December 2010—and, we argue, not by chance. Sidi Bouzid, which became a separate governorate in 1973, is geographically at the heart of Tunisia (see figure 11-2). Covering approximately 4.3 percent of Tunisia's territory, it hosts about 4.1 percent of the population.[4] More than 70 percent of the population is rural and involved in agricultural activities, and 41 percent of its employed labor force is fully employed in agricultural activities. Sidi Bouzid, part of the midwest region, is situated in a rather arid or semi-arid area. Indeed, its agriculture depends on very volatile and uncertain rainfall. More than half of Sidi Bouzid's agriculture also relies on underground water reserves—the governorate's only treasure, but one that is under threat of overexploitation. Of its 460,000 hectares of cultivated land, around 48,000 hectares (a little more than 10 percent) benefited from an irrigation system in 2012.

4. Sidi Bouzid's historical name is Gammouda.

FIGURE 11-2. Map of Sidi Bouzid Governorate, Tunisia

Fairly Effective Rural Development Programs but Forgotten Youth

It is important to note that modern irrigated agriculture was introduced rather recently in this region; it started in the 1970s and accelerated in the 1980s, ultimately generating an agricultural boom. Sidi Bouzid became a major agricultural center in just a few decades, known especially for its fruits, vegetables (20 percent of total national production), and olive oil. But the benefits of modern irrigation have reached their limit.

Agriculture has always been the main pillar of Sidi Bouzid's economy, but until the 1970s most of its agriculture was based on low-yield cereal production and semi-nomadic sheep herding. Only a few small, settled communities had mastered vegetable growing. Within a few decades, a state-initiated process led to a deep transformation that turned the governorate's semi-nomadic people into peasants and farmers with the skills to engage in intensive irrigated farming. The process had several components. First, the tribally owned land was divided into private lots; this major reform created an incentive for investing in agriculture, which was critical for the emergence of sustainable family farming. The government also built the first water systems based on use of groundwater and deep aquifers and facilitated farmers' access to financial resources and to subsidized agricultural inputs, including seeds and fertilizers. Important public infrastructure projects—roads and electrical and safe water networks—also were completed, to the benefit of all the agricultural community, including the poor.

Private investment was even more substantial. Farmers of small and medium-size plots responded quickly to the state's intervention and then took over. They continued to invest in irrigation facilities even when the state, starting in the early 1990s, slowed down its interventions and stopped or reduced its subsidization of most of the inputs. Thus, almost 90 percent of the total irrigation investment—48,000 hectares of irrigated land—was the outcome of private investment. The total area of irrigated land more than doubled since 1995, increasing from 22,300 hectares in 1995 to 48,800 hectares in 2012. This growth was mainly a private sector achievement, obviously profit driven. The diversified pattern of production—including vegetables, fruits, olives, cattle, milk, and poultry—ensured more stable incomes. Thus, in 2005, Sidi Bouzid had become a major producer of olive oil (9.5 percent of national production), almonds (23.8 percent), melons, tomatoes (8.8 percent), and pomegranates (10 percent), and the governorate saw incomes increase and life conditions and well-being improve significantly in many of its villages and rural areas.

This success story, however, has been only partly, not fully, inclusive. The profits generated and the proven water reserves attracted investors from outside the region, mainly from Sfax, who developed large modern farms concentrated in the most fertile part of Sidi Bouzid. Because these investors transferred their profits back to their home region, the local population benefited very little.[5] When local residents had agreed to sell their land to investors from outside their governorate (who were now perceived as new colonizers), they did not realize that they were making such a bad deal.

5. Sfax is a major industrial city in Tunisia located on the east coast.

Moreover, the growth process did not allow for youth integration, employment, and participation. Income growth and easy access to schooling offered young people a chance to benefit from secondary and tertiary education. They expected that education would be their key to finding better employment in various sectors, either in the region or elsewhere in the country, but for many of them that did not happen. Few employment opportunities were available, and fewer still inside the governorate.

That is not to say that the overall rate of unemployment is much higher in Sidi Bouzid than the national average. The real issue is that unemployment is very high for educated youth, especially those with a tertiary education. In 2010 the average unemployment rate for university graduates in Sidi Bouzid was around 40 percent. It was even higher for young girls and women, many of whom have simply exited the labor market. While there has been a persistent scarcity of seasonal, low-paid farm laborers, low-paid farm work is far below their expectations and to some extent not socially valued. Even those educated young people who are interested in farming and willing to start a farming business often lack the financial resources and own little or no land (water and land resources are quite limited). As a result, young people in Sidi Bouzid typically join a lengthy waiting list for formal—preferably government—jobs.

Consequently, because the likelihood of suitable employment was slim, the educated youth of Sidi Bouzid were and still are frustrated and ready to express their anger by all available means. They are not alone. Similar emotions run through many other comparable parts of the country. In December 2010, those emotions ignited the first sparks of the rebellion, sparks that quickly spread throughout the country and turned into the much more complex revolution in Tunisia and in the rest of the Arab Spring countries.

Natural Resources

The most important natural resources in Sidi Bouzid are water and land.

Water. Water, the most important resource in Sidi Bouzid, is also a significant constraint. The existing but limited water supply inhibits the development of not only agriculture but also other activities considered for future investment and initiatives. This land-locked governorate's

TABLE 11-9. Water Resources in Sidi Bouzid

Type of resource	Resource access points	Amount exploited (million cubic meters per year)	Potential amount (million cubic meters per year)	Rate in use (percent)
Groundwater	10,781 surface wells	81.90	62.00	132
Deep aquifer	750 deep wells	66.76	89.00	72
Rainwater	34 small artificial lakes and dams	60.00	131.00	45
Total		208.66	282.00	73

Source: Direction of Water Resources, CRDA Sidi Bouzid 2011.

underground reserves are its most valuable asset, and its distance from the relatively water-rich region in the north and from the sea means that there are no other reasonable alternatives. There already is evidence that Sidi Bouzid is overexploiting its water and should instead urgently promote water conservation, more efficient irrigation techniques and sustainable cropping patterns. Sidi Bouzid's total water reserves are around 281 million cubic meters a year, a little more than half of which—151 million cubic meters—comes from underground sources.[3] Table 11-9, which is based on current official statistics, indicates that up to 73 percent of deep aquifers are already used up, so there is room for further investment in irrigating more land. In fact, government authorities have said that this statistic (the only statistic available so far) is inaccurate because of the increasing number of farmers who pump from deep aquifers illegally and that no accurate information about the rate of use of the aquifers is available. However, there are indications that the critical overexploitation level has already been reached and that the quality and volume of the water reserves are deteriorating. That is possibly an outcome of the government's more lenient attitude toward Sidi Bouzid—of its willingness to appease the governorate's rebellious population.

Moreover, groundwater is not uniformly distributed over the region; only a few localities are endowed with this resource. The unlucky areas are, of course, even more frustrated.

Land. In aggregate terms, land is less of a constraint on development than water. Even though it is a small governorate, Sidi Bouzid

TABLE 11-10. Distribution of Farm Land in Sidi Bouzid, by Size, 1994–2004

Hectares

Size	0–1	1–2	2–3	3–4	4–5	5–10	10–20	20–50	50–100	≥100	Total
1994											
Farms (1,000s)	2	2.4	3	2.4	2.8	9.0	8.9	4.6	0.8	0.3	36.0
Farms this size (percent)	5.6	6.7	8.3	6.7	7.8	25.0	24.7	12.8	2.2	0.8	100
Farms this size or smaller (percent)	5.6	12.2	20.6	27.2	35.0	60.0	84.7	97.5	99.7	100	
2004											
Farms (1,000s)	2.8	2.5	4.8	2.2	2.7	8.7	7.2	4.9	0.8	0.26	37.1
Farms this size (percent)	7.6	6.7	12.9	5.9	7.2	23.6	19.5	13.3	2.3	0.7	100
Farms this size or smaller (percent)	7.6	14.3	27.2	33.1	40.3	63.9	83.5	96.8	99.3	100	

Source: Ministry of Agriculture, "Enquête sur les structures des exploitations agricoles," 1996 and 2006 editions.

contains a wide variety of land types, including forest. The main issue is the structure of land ownership and distribution (tables 11-10 and 11-11). Of the governorate's farms, 64 percent are very small (less than ten hectares) or micro farms (less than five hectares). Such plots are hardly sustainable unless irrigated. About only 10 percent of these small holdings—an estimated 2,000 holdings—are irrigated and may be viable. Of the 37,000 farmers active in Sidi Bouzid in 2005, only around 10,000 had enough land to continue to farm sustainably, while the remaining 27,000 could not rely on agriculture for their living and are likely to eventually leave unless alternative activities were developed nearby. The majority of those who farm are too poor to survive on their own land, and they own too little land to leave to their children. That suggests that improving the productivity of these small and micro farms, although crucial, will not be sufficient to meet the needs and expectations of the people in Sidi Bouzid. While there is some scope for economic diversification in Sidi Bouzid, it looks rather limited in the coming decade given the governorate's natural

TABLE 11-11. Distribution of Irrigated Land, Sidi Bouzid, by Size of Holding, 2005

Hectares

Size	0–1	1–2	2–3	3–4	4–5	5–10	10–20	20–50	50–100	≥100	Total
Area	175	575	1,316	1,124	1,545	9,412	8,562	8,719	2,825	5,623	39,876
Farms this size (percent)	0.4	1.4	3.3	2.8	3.9	23.6	21.5	21.9	7.1	14.1	100

Source: Ministry of Agriculture, "Enquête sur les structures des exploitations agricoles," 2006.

and human endowments. Therefore, in the long run, massive rural-to-urban and out-of-region migration is expected, regardless of government policy choices.

The privatization of previously tribal land radically changed the incentive structure and greatly contributed to the economic growth of Sidi Bouzid, but the land reform measure is still incomplete. Farmers often remain without formal land titles registering their individual ownership of their land. These farmers often share land with family members or are in the midst of lengthy ongoing disputes over land ownership. As a result, they have difficulty accessing bank financing, which is typically based on mortgages. Government loan facilities previously provided credit to many farmers, but many now hold unpaid loans, which makes it even more difficult for farmers to obtain new bank loans.

Government Services

Farmers also have difficulty accessing new technologies because of the limited extension service offered to them by government agencies and because they have had little schooling and formal training (table 11-12): 85 percent have only a primary education or none. (This is actually true for all farmers across the country.) Ten years ago, 90 percent had very little education, which may indicate a significant change and the beginning of the emergence of a new, more modern agriculture in the region. However, peasants' and farmers' level of education remains low. That is, agricultural activities are unattractive not only to youth but to the working population in general.

This difficulty is aggravated by the poor quality of vocational training and higher education institutions in Sidi Bouzid, which are not

TABLE 11-12. Farmers, Sidi Bouzid, by Education Level, 2005

Percent

Region	Higher	Secondary	Primary	None	Total
Midwest	3.2	13.0	36.3	47.5	100.0
Sidi Bouzid	3.5	12.5	36.5	48.0	100.0
Tunisia Total	3.3	12.8	37.9	46.0	100.0

Source: Ministry of Agriculture, "Enquête sur les structures des exploitations agricoles," 2006.

demand driven, and they are quite disconnected from the region's current and future needs for skills. In addition, the gap between the skills required and existing capacity is enormous. As stated above, graduates of this system try to look for jobs elsewhere, but they often end up waiting at home for uncertain and very unlikely employment opportunities—a state of affairs that has driven them to exasperation.

There also are well-established public service institutions in the region, but they do not seem to respond to the population's expectations. Indeed, the people of Sidi Bouzid have an ambivalent attitude toward these government institutions: they need them, but they also think that they are too bureaucratic, poorly equipped, and inefficient. Citizens widely share the feeling that their region was not equitably treated—that it has received too small a share of government attention and major projects, including infrastructure, health care, and promotion of nonagricultural activities. Thus, many were among the first to join the uprising in January 2011.

The case of Sidi Bouzid also shows that the Tunisian government implemented important agricultural development programs. High growth in the agricultural sector was achieved, better infrastructure was built, and access to education and health services was improved for most of the population, but few opportunities outside the agricultural sector are available for youth, especially the educated. The design of rural development programs has major weaknesses in terms of extension services, land entitlement, water resource sustainability, management, and marketing. As explained later in the chapter, more successful international experiences, for example, in Korea and Taiwan in the 1970s, show that better alternatives are available. Regarding agriculture, improvements in income and productivity consistent with more sustainable use of water and land resources are possible. Yet even there, agriculture has not been able to offer enough opportunities to all rural people. Diversification will be crucial, but it may be slow to materialize given the limited resources in the area. Therefore, a larger and accelerated exodus from Sidi Bouzid is to be expected and should be planned for. After all, regional development does not exclude mobility out of a region to regions with higher potential and growth. As far as Sidi Bouzid is concerned, this prediction is obviously contingent on its current prospects and knowledge about its potential and capacities, which may evolve in the future.

Le Kef

Le Kef, in the northwest of the country on the Algerian border, has more natural resources and more potential than Sidi Bouzid (see figure 11-3). Yet so far it has not performed better, and it has attracted even less investment and attention from the rest of the country and the central government. The only major investment in Le Kef was in a cement factory built in the 1970s. Even the agricultural sector, Le Kef's main economic activity, has hardly evolved since Tunisia's independence. Sixty percent of Le Kef's land continues to be used to grow cereals and raise cattle in very suboptimal conditions. Only 4 percent of the governorate's land—less than 15,000 hectares—is equipped with irrigation and intensive farming facilities.

The population of Le Kef has been decreasing for decades, and because of the exhaustion of its iron mines, its economy has suffered in terms of development and income generation opportunities. Le Kef, more than Sidi Bouzid, was clearly impacted by the Tunisian government's bias against rural areas from 1960 to 1987. At the expense of farmers, low food prices were fixed by the government—mainly for grains and other staple food commodities—in order to protect urban consumers and to control wages. By the end of the 1980s, this policy was partially adjusted and grain prices were increased, but subsidies on agricultural inputs were discontinued. Cereal production has since become relatively profitable but not profitable enough to jump-start a new era of growth and prosperity in the grain-producing regions. Pricing bias is not the

FIGURE 11-3. Map of Le Kef Governorate, Tunisia

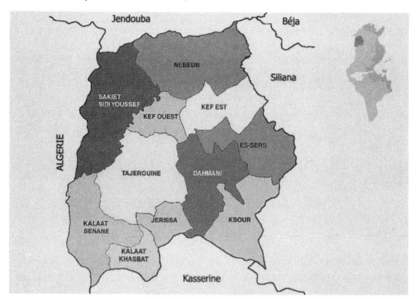

only impediment to growth and development in this part of the country; there are social and institutional constraints related to land distribution and ownership and to access to finance, knowledge, and innovations. Urgent reforms therefore need to be undertaken in all those domains to make development more likely and more inclusive.

Although agriculture is the predominant sector and more than half of the population is rural, Le Kef's economy is more diversified than that of Sidi Bouzid. It includes a larger share of manufacturing enterprises—close to 6 percent of employment is in manufacturing—and a small but promising tourism sector. Even so, no major nonagricultural industry has emerged. The existing private enterprises are predominantly small and micro enterprises with an average size of hardly more than one employee per enterprise.

Poverty is still more concentrated in the rural areas, where a large part of the population is more or less landless and faces meager prospects. It is possible to improve the situation of rural residents and reduce their poverty through better policies, but sooner or later most of them will leave the countryside and migrate to the urban areas in the same governorate or elsewhere to look for more and better opportunities.

TABLE 11-13. Population Growth, Le Kef, 2007–12

	2007	2009	2010	2012
Population	257,573	256,285	256,710	255,454
Rate of growth (percent)	−0.50	−0.50	0.17	−0.49

Source: Institut National de la Statistique, Labor Survey 2007, 2010, and 2012.

FIGURE 11-4. Population Growth, Le Kef, 2006–12

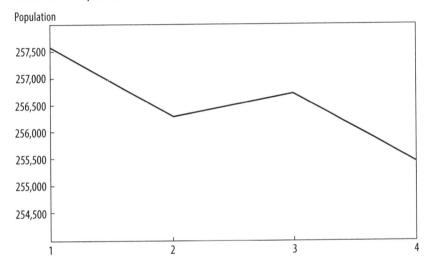

Population

Source: Institut National de la Statistique Labor Survey, 2007, 2010, and 2012.

Population and Labor Force Capacities

Le Kef comprises about 500,000 hectares. It has a population of around 255,000—2.5 percent of Tunisia's total population—but the population is steadily decreasing (table 11-13 and figure 11-4) at half a percent a year because of low fertility and migration to the eastern cities. Migration has been more pronounced in the old mining towns. The share of unskilled labor in Le Kef's labor force remains significantly higher than in most other regions and governorates. Yet, as in Sidi Bouzid and the rest of the country, the people of Le Kef have profited since independence from increasing access to education, health care, and other basic services. Around 40 percent of the population ten years of age or older have at least a secondary education, a share that reflects great progress since the 1960s though much less than in the eastern

TABLE 11-14. Labor Participation and Unemployment, Le Kef, 2007–22

Year	2007	2008	2010	2012
Labor force (1,000s)	94.8	95.0	108.1	104.4
Number of employed (1,000s)	79.0	83.3	94.8	92.3
Unemployment (1,000s)	15.8	11.7	13.3	12.1
Unemployment rate (percent)	16.7	12.4	12.4	12.1

Source: Institut National de la Statistique, obtained directly from INS by request.

TABLE 11-15. Unemployment Rate, Youth and Women, by Education, Le Kef, 2010
Percent

	People with higher education	People with secondary education	Youth (aged 16–29)
Le Kef	28	15.2	30
Le Kef women	38.2	21.1	
Tunisia	22.9	13.7	26.5

Source: Institut National de la Statistique Labor Survey, 2010.

regions. But as in Sidi Bouzid, the vocational training and higher education facilities that were built are of rather low quality and not geared to meeting the region's needs.

In spite of out-migration, Le Kef's labor force is growing, and it is characterized by a remarkably higher rate of participation by women than is average for Tunisia (35 percent for Le Kef and 26 percent for the nation). Indeed, there is a relative shortage of unskilled and seasonal labor in the governorate. Thus—and in a way paradoxically—the unemployment rate is relatively low and even lower than in most of the eastern regions. This is due not only to the persistent exodus from the governorate but also to its larger share of unskilled labor. In Tunisia, unemployment is lower for the unskilled everywhere in the country. However, the lower unemployment rate does not mean that unemployment is not an issue in Le Kef (tables 11-14 and 11-15 and figure 11-5). In fact, it is as important an issue as it is in the other western governorates because it is as high or higher for educated youth and for women. Again, there is a structural and persistent mismatch between the skills and the jobs available. Meanwhile, young unemployed people would rather wait or rebel than accept poorly paid agricultural work. Women

FIGURE 11-5. Decreasing Unemployment, Le Kef, 2007–12

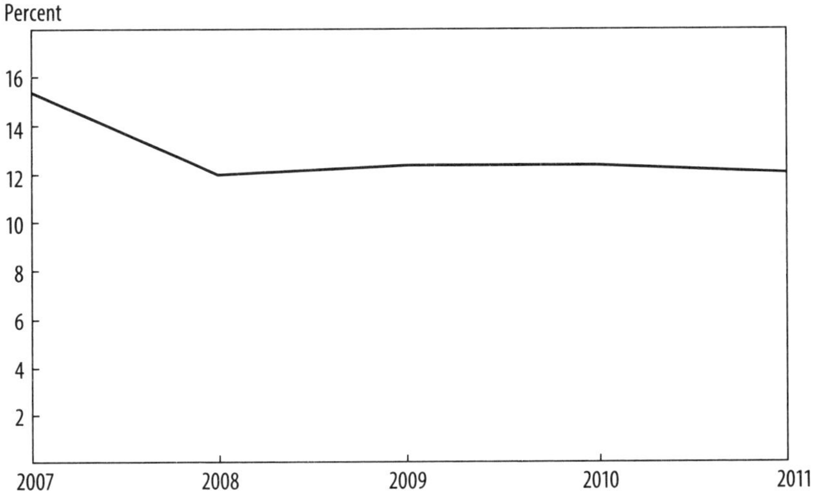

Percent

Source: Institut National de la Statistique Labor Survey 2007, 2010, and 2012.

with limited schooling are the most willing to work as seasonal farm laborers or as family aides. Men, except those with higher education (who would rather wait for a government job), often end up working in the informal sector.

The informal sector is pervasive and currently constitutes at least half of the region's economy. The most problematic part of this sector is that linked to illegal border trade with Algeria, which operates within opaque and corrupt networks that are hard to combat and to reorganize. Although potentially organized trade with Algeria may offer much greater opportunities, the border zones remain among the poorest and most excluded from Tunisia's development process. Overall, people working in the informal sector feel excluded and have no access to certified training and capacity building. Their connections with the illegal organizations are perhaps a form of revenge against a government that has excluded them.

Rural and Agricultural Development in Le Kef

Half of Le Kef's population is rural, and about 40 percent of its employed total labor force works in the agricultural sector. That is to say, the rural population is about 125,000 people; the rural labor force is about 52,000 people; and 40,000 persons work in the agricultural sector. Unlike in Sidi Bouzid, where agriculture is relatively booming, agriculture in Le Kef has evolved very slowly and attracted relatively little investment. The persistence of high poverty in Le Kef's rural areas is due in part to this lack of investment and slow productivity growth. There is underinvestment in all areas, including infrastructure, physical capital, and human capital.

Agriculture in Le Kef also is characterized by low and inadequate use of natural and human resources. The introduction of new and more appropriate crops and technologies has been slow, and one of the main reasons is unequal land distribution. The majority of Le Kef's population is landless or owns only very small farms or micro farms, and the larger farmers have little incentive to innovate and switch to more efficient and sustainable production models (table 11-16). Nevertheless, there is a great potential for development in the agricultural sector, but it will not happen spontaneously. It requires a government master plan (designed through a participatory approach) that integrates various key factors including infrastructure, training, land distribution and property rights, environment, marketing, entrepreneurship, financing, investment, and solutions to farmers' current debt problems. In the long run, the requirements of sustainable development and viable farming should and will lead to a drop in the rural population and the level of employment in the agricultural sector.[6] Accordingly, rural development and agricultural development ought to be linked with the development of other sectors, primarily the industrial and the tourism sectors in the case of Le Kef. Let us clarify this argument.

As mentioned above, about 40,000 people in Le Kef work in agriculture. Based on the Ministry of Agriculture's 2006 survey on the structure of the agricultural sector, only about half of this group are permanently employed in agricultural activities; the other half work as irregular seasonal and occasional workers or as family aides receiving no or little personal income. The 2006 survey finds that such seasonal agricultural work amounts in aggregate to about 173,000 days, indicating that on average, seasonal agriculture workers in Le Kef work

---

6. Obviously, sustainable development has to be profitable for the enterprise, otherwise it would not be pursued. A loss-generating activity would not last and so would not be undertaken.

TABLE 11-16. Distribution of Holdings by Size in Le Kef, 2005

Size of holding (hectares)	Number	Percent	Area (hectares)	Percent
0–1	779	4.3	168	0.04
1–2	1,199	6.6	1,742	0.4
2–3	1,547	8.5	2,754	1.0
3–4	1,540	8.5	5,382	1.4
4–5	1,350	7.4	6,048	1.6
5–10	4,221	23.3	30,309	7.8
10–20	2,903	16.1	40,418	10.5
20–50	2,776	15.9	84,634	21.8
50–100	1,170	6.5	78,886	20.4
100 or more	624	3.5	136,002	35.1
Total	18,110	100.0	387,356	100.0

Source : Ministry of Agriculture, "Enquête sur les structures des exploitations agricoles," 2006.

less than ten days each year as wage earners. They try to survive by cultivating their small farms or micro farms and by relying on multiple sources of volatile income brought in by all household members belonging to the labor force. Overall, underemployment among the rural population is close to 50 percent, indicating that 20,000 jobs need to be created in order to fully employ the rural population. Could those jobs be created within the rural areas? If not, 20,000 additional migrants may have to leave the rural areas of Le Kef.

Some of them may arguably be employed in nonagricultural rural activities, but the possibilities for this type of employment are rather limited. As we discuss later, alternative rural activities exist and there also is real potential in alternative irrigated farming—mainly in fruits and vegetables and dairy production. However, in the long run, farming opportunities are still not enough to accommodate the entire existing rural population. In the medium and long run, agriculture will lose more workers than it can absorb. Rural-to-urban migration will continue and may even accelerate as alternative activities in the urban areas continue to be developed, given that labor mobility is generally driven by the difference in expected return on employment. Therefore the main challenges in the short and medium run are in the timing of the migration process and in finding ways to combat and limit poverty among the poorly employed rural population.

TABLE 11-17. Land Distribution by Farming Mode in Le Kef and Sidi Bouzid, 2005

| | Farming mode | | | | | | | | | | Total |
| | Direct farming | | Rent | | Tenant farming | | Share cropping | | Other modes | | |
	Number	Percent	Number	Percent	Number	Percent	Number	Percent	Number	Percent	Number
Le Kef	33,296	90.9	1,226	3.3	2,090	5.7	0	0.0	37	0.1	36,649
Sidi Bouzid	67,137	99.2	255	0.4	130	0.2	89	0.1	67	0.1	67,678
Total	894,274	94.8	20,683	2.2	19,930	2.1	3,453	0.4	4,554	0.5	942,895

Source: Ministry of Agriculture, "Enquête sur les structures des exploitations agricoles," 2006.

Ideally, radical agrarian reform allowing for the redistribution of land owned by the richest landlords to the poor farmers may provide not only more justice but also a more efficient use of resources. However, politically, this option is not considered. The small fraction of farmers—624 in 2005—who own large estates of 100 or more hectares represent 3 percent of the total number of Le Kef's farmers, yet they control and often misallocate 35 percent of its land. The misallocation of land is not caused by the size of the holdings but by the farmers' behaviors and situations. The rich landlords in this region used to own an even larger share of the cultivated land and to control a rather feudal system. Their property generated large rents, and they did not have to do farm work themselves or directly supervise workers. A large number of the current landlords still have the same rentier and feudal attitude and would rather avoid any direct involvement in farming, preferring instead either to rely on tenants or to rent their land for limited periods of time to farmers who then do not have an incentive to invest in the land and to take important risks. As a result, the land, which often is the best and has the most potential, is locked in a stagnant agrarian mode and is persistently allocated to traditional low-return grain production with little diversification and productivity growth. Table 11-17 shows that in Le Kef, tenant farming and farming on rented land is more frequent than in the rest of the country—and much more so than in Sidi Bouzid. The proportion of rented and of tenant-run farms in Le Kef—3.3 percent and 5.7 percent, respectively—may seem small. In fact, those percentages are substantial because they correspond to the 3 percent of large farms and the 6.5 percent of medium-size farms

FIGURE 11-6. Distribution of Holdings, by Size, 2012

Percent

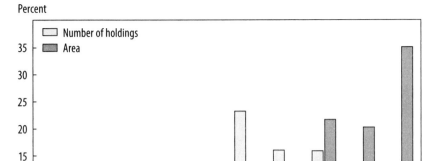

Source: Ministry of Agriculture, "Enquête sur les structures des exploitations agricoles," 2006 edition.

(50 to 100 hectares) that together form 55 percent of total cultivated land in Le Kef (2005 data).

This uneven and inadequate land distribution is aggravated by the very complex issue of land ownership, certified registration, and fragmentation resulting from heritage rules. This is a major issue throughout Tunisia, and it applies to all sizes of holdings and often blocks all access to financial resources and modernization projects. Therefore, while radical agrarian reform comparable to the measures undertaken in Japan and Korea is not on any influential political party's agenda, the country urgently needs measures to ensure and clarify property rights, and create incentives for more direct farming and effective involvement of farmers in the management of their projects. This is important for investment, productivity, and income growth of large holdings and even more important for small and medium ones (figure 11-6).

The Debt Burden

Farmers in Le Kef are burdened by the heaviest total farm debt in the country (table 11-18)—more than 8 percent of the total national agricultural debt—while less than 4 percent of Tunisian farmers are

TABLE 11-18. Agricultural Debt, Le Kef, 2007[a]

Tunisian dinars, 1,000s

	Outstanding debt	Unpaid debt	Contractual interests	Penalty interests	Total debt
Le Kef	16,055	25,643	9,602	15,641	66,941
Total Tunisia	279,533	269,158	100,991	162,199	811,881

Source: Ministry of Agriculture.
a. No more recent data are available, but it is clear that the situation has not improved in Le Kef and in the rest of the country.

in Le Kef.[7] This is another factor hindering investment and access to finance for farmers. The debt has been accumulating for decades, and the government has allowed it to persist instead of using the legal measures available to stop it.

Le Kef's Natural and Cultural Resources

The natural resources found in Le Kef's rural areas are important, diverse, and underexploited or used in suboptimal ways. Le Kef is home to relatively significant water and land resources and proven reserves of phosphates and various raw materials needed for the production of construction materials. There is also a rich cultural heritage and a large number of historical and archeological sites. Agriculture, tourism, manufacturing, and mining are examples of activities that compete for the use of water and land resources. However, most potential nonagricultural jobs probably would materialize in urban areas. The rural population would then have to move to urban areas to take advantage of them.

The southern part of Le Kef is partly sub-arid, receiving around 300 millimeters of rainfall a year, and the northern part is sub-humid, receiving 500 millimeters or more. Winters are cold and sometimes freezing, with regular but modest snowfall, and summers are moderately hot. However, as in the rest of the country, rainfall is highly volatile, making agricultural yields very random, and the volatile weather may have a negative impact on underground water reserves. The area includes farms of various types and varying quality, but often the land is threatened by water and wind erosion (table 11-19). Without protection

---

7. A large part of this outstanding debt is actually long overdue, and it is financially worthless in terms of bank assets.

TABLE 11-19. Water Erosion, Le Kef, 2003

Degree of erosion	Area eroded (hectares)	Area eroded (percent)
Very limited	195,600	38
Average	194,400	38
Strong	118,100	23
Total	508,100	100

Source: Ministry of Agriculture (2003).

TABLE 11-20. Water Resources and Their Use, Le Kef, 2012

Million cubic millimeters

	Potential			Mobilization			Gap		
	1990	2000	2005	1990	2000	2005	1990	2000	2005
Rainwater	275	275	275	84.47	120.12	131.21	190.53	154.88	143.79
Deep aquifers	28.64	42.9	46.8	8.71	12.66	12.76	19.93	30.24	34.04
Groundwater	25.1	25.1	25.09	27.8	25.95	21.98	−2.7	−0.85	3.11
Total	328.74	343	346.89	120.98	158.73	165.95	207.76	184.27	180.94

Source: Kef Regional Agricultural Bureau.

and precautions, the threat may become very serious. In spite of its relatively high capacities and the availability of important water resources in many parts of Le Kef, irrigated farming has been a recent development in this governorate, where 80 percent of the existing 15,000 hectares of irrigated land have been developed only since 1990.

The total estimated water available in Le Kef is 346.8 million cubic millimeters (Mm^3) a year, 35 percent of which is rather underused groundwater and stream water (table 11-20). Given these resources and current know-how, more than 40,000 additional hectares might be irrigated and used for fairly intensive fruit and vegetable production and other labor-intensive activities—a lot compared to what has been achieved so far in terms of intensive irrigated farming.[8] However,

8. This figure (40,000 hectares) is based on the assumption that 3 Mm^3 of water is needed to irrigate 1,000 hectares and that 35 percent of the water resources are not used.

even under the most optimistic assumptions and full use of the area's agricultural potential, while agriculture may allow for the creation of a large number of new jobs, it would be less than the 20,000 jobs needed for full employment of the rural population. The total number would depend on the types of crop and the farming techniques used, which are hard to predict at this stage.

Of the 360,000 hectares of cultivated land, 215,000 hectares are allocated to cereal and cattle production, which traditionally is dependent on rainfall and has become increasingly less labor intensive and more and more mechanized. There are also about 120,000 hectares of grazing land and forest that require even less labor. Moreover, most of the landowners and farmers are men (18,000) who have little formal education (80 percent are illiterate or have only a primary education) and are unlikely to initiate by themselves, without any government intervention, any major transformation in farming modes and techniques and alternative nonagricultural activities.

Development Institutions and the ODESYPANO Experience

Generally speaking, the Tunisian institutional system is excessively centralized and the regional development institutions are managed in a top-down model. The inefficiency of this system is especially obvious in the area of irrigation water management, training and extension services, and marketing of agricultural products.

Over the past decade, the government tried to deal with the key obstacles to the development of the agricultural sector and the improvement of the well-being of the rural population. Special administrative agencies, for example, have been created to deal with some of its specific needs and even to experiment with a less-centralized governance scheme. ODESYPANO, one such agency, was created in 1981 to supervise and implement development projects for selected forested and isolated hilly areas in Tunisia's northwest, including in the governorate of Le Kef.[9]

About 25 percent of Le Kef's land is mountain forest and grazing land, and poverty is pervasive in those areas despite various possibilities for development. Mountain areas also suffer from poor infrastructure

9. ODESYPANO is the abbreviation for the Office de Développement Sylvo-Pastoral du Nord Ouest.

and low educational attainment among the majority of the population, which remains isolated because of the low quality and low density of the roads and utility networks and the high cost of building infrastructure in hilly areas.

ODESYPANO is especially relevant as a rural development institution. Its programs target a population, 95 percent of whom are rural and poor. The agency's mission is to improve the well-being of the targeted population and to serve as an intersectoral coordinating agency. Its activities focus on land protection and the promotion of new, sustainable, income-generating activities, including diversification of agricultural production. It is supposed to adopt an integrated, participatory approach.

Over the three past decades, ODESYPANO has indeed achieved a great deal. As of 2006, it had protected 176,408 hectares of land; created 30 lakes and more than 1,000 reservoirs; built milk-collection facilities, schools, and basic health centers; and laid 2,053 kilometers of country roads. The agency also has provided better access to clean water and electricity and contributed to income growth in the region that it covers, where income has increased on average at an annual 5 percent rate, owing in part to the introduction of new techniques and crops and to better access to inputs and markets. However, the nationwide average growth rate is 5 percent, so it is not totally the outcome of ODESYPANO's efforts. Although ODESYPANO has not been fully empowered—as it should be, according to its mission—it has proved that it can act as a developer and an effective organizer and coordinator close to the people. The village offices and committees that it has established are quite effective in achieving its goals.

However, because its financial resources and real power have been limited, its achievements, although substantial, are well below the needs of the population. Total investments over the 25 years from 1981 to 2005 amounted to 224 million Tunisian dinars (around $150 million, coming mainly from foreign aid), for 260,000 people.[10] That is the equivalent of about 1,000 dinars ($650) per person for 25 years, or $26 per person per year. It was enough to partially alleviate poverty for some of the targeted population but too little to have a significant positive impact on their well-being.

10. In several governates, including Le Kef.

ODESYPANO was not in practice empowered to deal with all the key barriers to rural development, including access to financial resources for the population, registration of and entitlement to land and assets, and illiteracy and lack of effective training. Based on ODESYPANO's data and on our own field investigation, it is clear that little or nothing was done to provide poor peasants with more land, more cattle, and better training. They had no access to bank financing apart from some negligible microcredits. For instance, income and life could be radically improved for a large number of peasants if each were provided with a few dozen sheep (about fifty animals), enough to generate a decent, regular income. That would be feasible if ODESYPANO could guarantee the loans that the farmers need to buy the sheep, but the agency cannot do that because it does not have the financial resources and the power to do it. Development of some major new activities could also make a significant difference for the targeted region. For instance, the region has real potential for tourism but lacks the infrastructure and capital to jump-start the industry. In Taiwan, in contrast, the government promoted the creation of a large number of enterprises in rural areas and many good, off-farm jobs.

ODESYPANO's experience shows that while a partial approach may be beneficial, it is not sufficient. There is a need for a holistic approach integrating all the key factors and dimensions of development (training, institution building, capital accumulation, price and marketing policies, and so forth), which are out of its control. The successful experience of several other countries, especially Asian countries, was more holistic.

Lessons from Other Countries

Alternative approaches and better policies in the area of regional and rural development may be drawn from the experiences—both failures and successes—of other countries. In particular, never before in human history have as many people been saved from poverty and hunger as have been saved recently in China, India, and other Asian countries, such as Vietnam, where the largest rural communities continue to live. (See, for instance, Ravallion and van de Walle 2008.) The reforms undertaken in these countries (Looney 2012; Norel 2005; Peemans 2011; Park 2009) confirm the importance and efficiency of free and private enterprise, including in agriculture, and show how

crucial incentive compatibility and complementarity of private interests and collective (regional or national) targets are. Without incentive
compatibility, objectives would not be reached even if they were technically feasible. In the case of Tunisia, this is important because there
are many inconsistencies between certain government policies—such as
price policies—and objectives regarding agriculture growth. Reforms
should also fit in a comprehensive economic reform program and complement other major policies, including those concerning industry, the
labor market, international trade, the money supply, and the exchange
regime. More specifically, for the rural population and for agricultural
growth, the government should devote sufficient effort to maintaining infrastructure projects such as irrigation systems and roads and
to ensuring reasonable input prices. It should also provide an efficient
and equitable marketing platform for agricultural commodities. These
measures would have a positive impact on production and create an
incentive for farmers and peasants to adopt more efficient technologies
and to respond to the increasing and changing demand for food.

South Korea (hereafter referred to as Korea) and Taiwan have quite
successfully integrated most of these conditions and learned from the
flawed policies that they adopted in the 1960s, which were similar to
Tunisia's current policies. Korea started in the 1960s with a price policy
that was biased against the farming and rural community. The purpose
was to keep food prices (primarily grain prices) low, but that created a
disincentive for higher productivity and growth. Peasants, who remained
very poor, quickly began a mass migration to the cities. In the early
1970s, Korea decided to correct the disequilibrium by launching the
Saemaul Undong Movement (also known as the New Village Movement
or the New Community Movement), a radically different approach with
a positive bias toward the rural population that was consistent with the
export promotion strategy that the country adopted at the same time and
with the continuous improvement of its export sector competitiveness.

However, it was not consistent with Korea's commitment to the World
Trade Organization (WTO) and with its later obligations as a member of the Organization for Economic Cooperation and Development
(OECD). Indeed, ten years later, it had to readjust its rural development
policy in order to comply with its new status. At its current stage of
development, Korea can afford to be less concerned with its rural community, which is now much smaller and can rely more on capital and

knowledge-intensive technologies than on subsidized ordinary inputs for production. Nevertheless, the support given to the agricultural sector and the rural community during the 1970s was an important pillar of the overall agricultural and rural development strategy. The Saemaul Undong was a remarkable Korean experience. While many features of the Saemaul Undong are specific to 1970s Korea and are not mentioned here, some universal lessons may be learned from it. The main lesson is that although it is possible to significantly improve the livelihood of the rural population, it cannot be done without government intervention. The government's role as catalyst and coordinator and its commitment in designing and initiating rural advancement programs are essential.

The effectiveness of state intervention requires the rural population to accept that the state promotes development and its agents are a source of potential assistance rather than feared exploiters. The Korean government in the 1970s was able to mobilize the population by changing their attitude toward the government. That confirms that the political commitment of the government was a key factor in the success of its development program, but its commitment would have been meaningless and the program would have failed regardless if the government's policies were not credible or if they were not compatible with the peasants' interests.

Indeed, one of the main objectives of the government's development policies was to raise the level of rural well-being. The government gradually provided all peasants in all villages with better housing, subsidized agricultural inputs, paved roads, clean water, electricity, extension services, and high-yield seeds and ensured high output prices for their products. The green revolution in grain production was an important component of the government program, and the peasants adhered to it because it was profitable for them to do so. During the 1970s, price support for farmers, especially for grain production, was maintained along with subsidized food prices for urban consumers as long as the fiscal cost was acceptable and did not contradict other major international interests of the country.

Effective local organization and institutions also are critical to the success of rural development programs. Three levels of administration were created in Korea. At the lowest level, an elected committee in each village, headed by an appointed leader, played an important role but under strong supervision of parastatal organizations. The national level was administered by the Ministry of Home Affairs, which had the power to deal with all other relevant ministries, thereby avoiding dependence on a large number of separate agencies and ministries.

Taiwan's development experience paid even more attention to this key institutional component.

In both Korea and Taiwan, parastatal organizations were part of the system and were in charge of various missions (collecting and purchasing rice, selling inputs to farmers, and providing extension services and credits to farmers). Radical land reform also was a basic factor in rural development in both countries. That does not mean that radical reform is a universally necessary condition. It is true that the relatively egalitarian land ownership structure was for a certain period a favorable factor, but what is more essential is to secure legal entitlement to assets, especially land and water, and access to markets, an idea that the International Fund for Agricultural Development supports (IFAD 2001).

In Korea the Saemaul Undong experience confirmed the benefit of a holistic approach integrating training, institution building, capital accumulation, pricing and marketing policies, and villagers' needs and challenges. It also dealt comprehensively with nonagricultural employment. Japan's and Taiwan's agricultural policies showed the importance of extension services and were based more on market incentives than direct government intervention. The Taiwanese experience also differed from the Korean because Taiwan had higher food production potential, enough to meet its domestic demand for food and to contribute to exports and generate capital and labor for industrialization.

Nevertheless, in spite of the rapid rural development and improvement in the livelihood of the rural population, Saemaul Undong was ended at the close of the 1970s. The Korean government stopped insisting on the use of high-yield rice varieties and ended the price support policy because it had become too costly and too difficult to manage. By then, Korea's policies and priorities also had changed and became more market oriented. In both Korea and Taiwan, the rapid and highly inclusive rural development process was not enough to stop the rural exodus to the cities. More than half of the rural Korean population (7.7 million of 14.4 million people) had migrated to urban areas by 1980, and the process has continued. As of 2010 Korea's rural population had been reduced to less than 7 percent, and mechanization became critical for the survival of family farming. Massive migration to urban areas also happened in Taiwan, but it was slower there because Taiwan could provide off-farm employment for rural people. As in all parts of the world, the trend is toward a much smaller rural population.

Alternative Policies and Recommendations

Tunisia has adopted many features of the rural development policies of Korea and Taiwan, including price subsidies and support, and has provided infrastructure and training, though less systematically. What it has not achieved is a comprehensive, inclusive, and consistent strategy. Significant efforts and programs were devoted to certain components of rural development while other components were either neglected or were not effectively managed. For instance, public water facilities were provided in many places but not the right price incentive for water use and access to markets. Appropriate land distribution and land property laws often were missing or poorly enforced in Tunisia.

Le Kef, Sidi Bouzid, and other regions can achieve ambitious rural development targets and very significantly improve the situation of their rural populations if more coherent strategies and holistic approaches are adopted and implemented that take into account in a realistic manner all the major obstacles and key development factors involved: natural resources, human resources, population issues, land ownership and distribution, financial needs, and incentive-compatible and efficient institutions.

In addition, other countries' experiences show that agricultural development programs and other development programs should not be designed separately. In general, a strategy based on micro-farming alone is not sustainable, at least not over the long term. Small and micro projects are beneficial in combating poverty and reducing unemployment, but they are not enough to reduce regional disparities and ensure sustainable growth based on inclusive institutions. There is a need for well-coordinated comprehensive programs combining public and private interventions and integrating public infrastructure, training and capacity development, marketing, financial resources, and institutional reforms. Coordination of all these dimensions is primarily the responsibility of government, and government intervention is indispensable.

Finally, exodus to urban areas is inevitable—even when and where rapid rural development is possible. There is no reason why this exodus should be stopped or constrained within the same region, and there is no logic for ensuring that all regions are equally urbanized and industrialized. Inevitably, in a natural process, growth will be faster in some regions and the population will move to the faster-growing regions.

References

Boughzala, Mongi. 2010. "Dynamique de l'emploi dans les gouvernorats de Gafsa et du Kef : identification des opportunités et des obstacles relatifs à la création d'emplois [Employment dynamics in the governorates of Gafsa and Kef: Identifying barriers and opportunities]." With the participation of Salah Ahmed and Mohamed Elloumi, UNDP, MDG Achievement Fund, April.

Centre National d'Etudes Agricoles (CNEA). 2008. "Etude stratégique sur le développement durable et agriculture dans les gouvernorats de Gabes, Sidi Bouzid, Nabeul, le Kef, et Bizerte, gouvernorat du Kef [Strategic study on sustainable agricultural development in the governorates of Gabes, Sidi Bouzid, Nabeul, Le Kef and Bizerte]." December. CNEA, Ministry of Agriculture.

Commissariat Régional de Développement Agricole (CRDA). 2007. "Stratégie régionale de développement du secteur agricole dans le gouvernorat du Kef [Agricultural development Regional Strategy for the Kef governorate]." October.

————. 2008a. "Projet de développement agricole intégré de la zone frontalière du gouvernorat du Kef : Phase 1 : Diagnostic de la situation actuelle et axes de développement [Integrated agricultural development project for the Kef border region; phase 1: Diagnosis and main issues]." Conseil Ingénierie et Développement, October.

————. 2008b. "Rapport annuel des activités du Commissariat Régional au Développement Agricole [Annual report of the Kef CRDA]."

Henia, Abdelhamid. 2014. "The Tunisian Midwest in the 18th and 19th Century" (in Arabic). Paper presented at a seminar organized by the University of Tunis, Faculty of Social Sciences, in collaboration with UGTT, January 10, 2014, Tunis.

International Food and Agriculture Development (IFAD). 2001. *Rural Poverty Report* 2001.

Institut National de la Statistique de Tunisie (INS, Tunisian National Statistics Institute). 2005. "Enquête nationale sur le budget, la consommation, et le niveau de vie des ménages [Household budget and consumption survey 2005]."

————. 2011. "Enquête nationale population-emploi [Labor survey], 2005, 2007, 2008, 2010, 2011."

Lipset, S. 1959. "Some Political Pre-Requisites of Democracy: Economic Development and Political Legitimacy," *American Political Science Review* 53.

Looney, K. Elizabeth. 2012. "The Rural Developmental State: Modernization Campaigns and Peasant Politics in China, Taiwan and South Korea." PhD dissertation, Harvard University, Graduate School of Arts and Science, August.

Ministère du Développement Régional et de Planification (Ministry of Regional Development and Planning). 2012. "Indicateurs de Développement Régional [Regional development indicators]." November.

Ministère de l'Environnement et du Développement Durable and G.I.Z. 2008.

Ministère de l'Equipement, de l'Habitat et de l'Aménagement du Territoire, Direction Générale de l'aménagement du territoire. 2008. "Schéma directeur d'aménagement de la région économique du nord ouest, Partie 1 Scenarii d'aménagement et de développement de la region [Master territorial plan of the northwest economic region, Part 1]." September.

Ministère de l'Agriculture. 2006. "Enquête sur les structures des exploitations agricoles [Structure of agricultural holdings survey]." 2004–05.

————. 1996. "Enquête sur les structures des exploitations agricoles [Structure of agricultural holdings survey]." Undertaken in 1994–95.

Norel, P. H. 2005. "Le développement économique est-il né en Asie? [Was economic development born in Asia?]." Centre de Recherche sur l'Intégration Economique et Financière, Université de Poitiers.

Office de Développement du Centre Ouest. 2011. "Gouvernorat de Sidi Bouzid en chiffres [Sidi Bouzid in numbers]."

Organisation des Nations Unies pour l'Alimentation et l'Agriculture [United Nations Food and Agriculture Organization (FAO)]. 2006. 28th Regional FAO Conference for Asia and the Pacific, Jakarta, Indonesia (Adjustment and restructuring of the main Asian economies and their impacts on food security and poverty in the rest of the region). May 15–19.

Park, Sooyoung. 2009. "Analysis of Saemaul Undong: A Korean Rural Development Programme in the 1970s." *Asia-Pacific Development Journal* 16, no. 2.

Peemans J-P. 2011. "Les discours sur le développement rural face aux réalités du monde et de l'Asie du Sud–Est (1945–2010) [The discourse on rural development and the reality in South East Asia]." Groupe de Recherches Asie de l'Est et du Sud Est, working paper no. 1.

Ravallion, Martin, and Dominique van de Walle. 2008. "Land and Poverty in Reforming East Asia." *Finances and Development* 45, no. 3. International Monetary Fund.

12

Agriculture and Rural Development for Inclusive Growth and Food Security in Morocco

HAFEZ GHANEM

The agriculture sector is crucial to achieving Morocco's objective of inclusive growth and poverty reduction. The government of Morocco is aware of that and has adopted an ambitious program (Plan Maroc Vert, or PMV) that aims to increase agricultural production and reduce rural poverty and rural-urban inequality. PMV is built on two pillars: the first aims to develop modern, high-productivity agriculture through large projects based on public-private partnerships; the second aims to develop family farming through projects that are mainly government financed. This chapter stresses the importance of the second pillar and argues that it needs to be complemented by the introduction of new social safety net programs based on cash transfers and by new, inclusive economic institutions that represent small farmers and ensure that they have a voice in the policymaking process.

The Arab revolutions that started in late 2010 in Tunisia and then in Egypt, Yemen, Jordan, and Morocco called for economic inclusiveness and greater social justice. Achieving these objectives requires paying particular attention to poorer and less developed regions that directly or indirectly depend mainly on agriculture for their livelihood. This is

I would like to thank Perrihan El-Rifai, Uri Dadush, Mongi Boughzala, Homi Kharas, Hideki Matsunaga, and others for comments on an earlier draft. I also benefited from discussions with Yuko Morikawa and other colleagues at the JICA office in Rabat. Moreover, the research on Morocco benefited from a research project on "agricultural production, food security, and higher value in North Africa" in which I participated thanks to support from the African Development Bank (AfDB).

especially relevant for Morocco. Rural poverty in Morocco is about three times higher than urban poverty, and the majority of the rural poor make their living directly or indirectly from agriculture.

The policies and programs recommended here to develop agriculture should be viewed as one component of a broader strategy to achieve inclusive growth. The proportion of Moroccans working in agriculture—about 40 percent—is very high relative to that in countries at a similar level of development; for example, it is about 15 percent in Tunisia, 20 percent in Algeria, and 30 percent in Egypt. The experiences of other countries indicate that the proportion will fall as rural dwellers (particularly youth) migrate to urban centers. Unless appropriate policies and programs are put in place, rapid rural-urban migration could lead to increasing urban unemployment and social discontent as new migrants join the large number of urban poor living in overcrowded slum areas with little access to basic physical and social infrastructure. Therefore, inclusive growth policies for Morocco need to include agriculture and rural development to slow migration out of rural areas as well as investments in other sectors of the economy and in urban centers to facilitate the inevitable economic and social transformation toward a more urbanized society.

The remainder of this chapter is divided into four sections. The first reviews political economy developments in Morocco and how the country was impacted by the Arab Spring. The second describes the key challenges to agriculture and rural development in Morocco. The third section discusses possible strategies to deal with those challenges, and the fourth presents the conclusion.

Political Economy Background: Why Are Agriculture and Rural Development Important?

Morocco is one of the countries affected by the Arab Spring. The country was growing at an average rate of about 5 percent a year for the ten years before 2011, which led to a decline in poverty from around 15 percent of the population to 6 percent. Yet Moroccans (especially youth) felt that the fruits of that growth were not equitably shared. They demanded more freedom, social justice, and an end to corruption. In this regard, Morocco is very similar to other Arab Spring countries (for example, Tunisia and Egypt) where youth remained discontented in spite of fairly robust economic growth and improvements in social indicators.

But Morocco is different from other Arab Spring countries, with the exception of Jordan, because it is a monarchy and the king, Mohammed VI, enjoys widespread acceptance and legitimacy as the head of state and the country's spiritual guide (Commander of the Faithful). That allowed Morocco to avoid the revolutionary chaos, civil strife, and institutional meltdown observed in other Arab Spring countries. The king held the country together. Thus, from the early days of the Arab Spring, Morocco picked a path different from that of other countries. Moroccans appeared to have decided on a gradual transition toward a more open and democratic system. They did not demand a change of regime; what they wanted was reform. In other words, it is possible to argue that Morocco chose evolution rather than revolution.

Mohammed VI led the reform process, and a new constitution was adopted by referendum in July 2011. The constitution strengthened the powers of the prime minister and of the Parliament as well as the independence of the judiciary. It enshrined more political and social rights and called for a more open and decentralized governance system, laying the groundwork for more inclusive economic growth. As prescribed by the new constitution, the king appointed as prime minister the leader of the party that had won the most seats in Parliament, in this case Abdelilah Benkiraine, leader of the moderately Islamist PJD (Justice and Development Party).

The new constitution did not significantly reduce the powers of the king, who continues to be the dominant political figure in Morocco. Mohammed VI is considered to be widely popular, and he is clearly leading the transition. Evolutionary change carries the risk of a slowdown—or even a halt—in the reform process if powerful interest groups feel threatened and attempt to block the transition. That in turn could lead to disappointment and frustration among the population, especially the youth, and hence to political unrest. Leaders of this type of change therefore need to implement reforms at a pace that is fast enough to maintain public support for the evolutionary process while avoiding abrupt changes that could result in disruption and instability.

Economic reforms that help achieve rapid and inclusive growth are important for the success of political transformation. According to the

World Bank, economic inequality is a key challenge.[1] Morocco's Gini coefficient (0.41) is high compared with that of other emerging economies. This indicates that inequality is a serious problem and it is compounded by huge disparities across regions. For example, the poverty rate in the region of Gharb-Charda-Beni Hssen is 72 percent higher than the national average. Reducing inequality and regional disparities would help increase support for the political process.

Poverty is especially high in rural areas where most people depend directly or indirectly on agriculture for their livelihood. About 10 percent of rural dwellers live below the poverty line, and they represent two-thirds of all the poor people in Morocco. They tend to live in regions with difficult geographic conditions (for example, mountains), and they lack access to basic physical infrastructure to connect them to markets as well as the social infrastructure (for example, schools, universities, and hospitals) necessary for human development.

The issue of food security and food prices also is important for Morocco. In fact, some observers argue that food price increases were among the factors that caused the revolutions in Egypt, Morocco, and Tunisia.[2] Moroccan households, on average, spend around 40 percent of their income on food. That figure is much higher for poorer households, which may spend as much as 75 percent of their income on food. A simple calculation would show that if, on average, food accounts for about 40 percent of a household's consumption basket a doubling of food prices like that which occurred in 2007–08 would lead to an almost 30 percent decline in real income. Such a sharp reduction in real income could be destabilizing, especially if it disproportionately affects the poor and vulnerable.

This discussion indicates that agricultural development is an important political priority in Morocco for two reasons. First, agriculture (and related services and processing activities) is important for increasing rural standards of living; therefore, it is an essential component of any inclusive growth strategy that aims to reduce inequality and regional disparities. Second, growth in agricultural productivity and output is a necessary component of a food security strategy. It helps to reduce import dependence and increases the country's ability to deal with large swings in international food prices and their impact on the poor and vulnerable.

---

1. World Bank (2014).
2. See, for example, AfDB (2012).

Challenges for Moroccan Agriculture and Food Security: What Needs to Change?

The agriculture sector in Morocco is called on to ensure food security for a growing population while generating incomes and jobs for rural dwellers and helping to reduce rural poverty—objectives that will have to be achieved under difficult circumstances. Since 2007, world food prices have been high and volatile, and medium-term projections by the Organization for Economic Cooperation and Development (OECD) and the Food and Agriculture Organization (FAO) indicate that volatility is likely to continue.[3] Moreover, climate change—including increasing temperatures and less precipitation—risks making agriculture yields even lower and more unstable.

High and Volatile World Food Prices

Figure 12-1 shows that after a long period of low and relatively stable food prices, things began to change at the beginning of the twenty-first century as global prices rose and became more volatile, reflecting a shift in market fundamentals. World food markets became tighter because the rate of increase in agricultural yields slowed as a result of lower investment. The annual rate of growth of global capital stock in primary agriculture fell from 1.1 percent in the period 1975–90 to 0.5 percent during 1991–2007. As a result, productivity growth declined. For example, the rate of growth in cereal yields dropped from 3.2 percent a year in the 1960s and 1970s to 1.5 percent in 2000. At the same time, the demand for food rose due to the increases in population and incomes, which led to a shift toward consuming more meat and therefore to an increase in the demand for animal feed and the derived demand for cereals.[4] The low level of food stocks around the world also contributed to higher price volatility, with many public as well as private market participants reducing the size of their inventories in order to lower costs. That meant that nearly all of the adjustment to production shocks had to be made through cuts in consumption, through higher prices, rather than through reductions in stocks, as was often the case in the past.

3. See OECD and FAO (2010).
4. See FAO (2012).

FIGURE 12-1. FAO Food Price Index, 2001–15

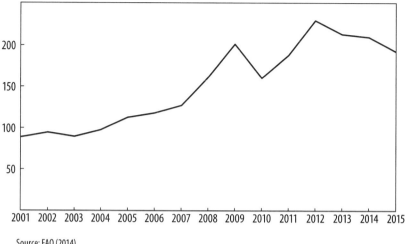

2002–04 = 100

Source: FAO (2014).

Food prices appeared to have stabilized in 2013 and 2014 and even began falling as oil prices dropped. Nevertheless, many observers and international organizations still expect food prices to remain high and volatile over the medium term, for three main reasons.[5] First, the link between the food and fuel markets is getting stronger as a result of the development of biofuels. Since world fuel prices tend to be more volatile, food prices also will be more volatile. Second, climate change and the greater frequency of extreme weather events could lead to more supply shocks and therefore to higher price volatility. Third, production is moving toward potentially more fragile regions, such as the Black Sea area, and world markets are becoming increasingly dependent on supplies from such regions. Because yields in those regions are less stable, there is more world price volatility.

Many observers also argue that increased "financialization" of commodity markets and the rise in speculation have contributed to higher food price volatility.[6] The returns on commodity futures seem to be negatively correlated to the returns on stocks and bonds. Therefore they are an attractive vehicle for portfolio diversification. Between 2006 and 2011,

5. For example, see OECD and FAO (2010).
6. For example, see Prakash (2011).

noncommercial actors (those who are not involved with the physical product) doubled their share of open positions in wheat, corn, and soybean futures. The tendency of those investors to behave as a "herd," buying or selling large quantities at the same time, has been blamed for magnifying changes in food prices and thus contributing to greater volatility. Moreover, policy measures taken by a number of governments in times of crisis (such as export restrictions or hoarding) increase international price volatility. For example, according to an analysis carried out by the FAO, the sharp increase in rice prices in 2008 can be attributed mainly to government policies.[7] Changes in market fundamentals cannot explain why rice prices doubled in 2008, and, given that there are virtually no forward markets for rice, speculators cannot be blamed for the increase.

High Dependence on Food Imports

High and volatile world prices pose a special challenge to Morocco because of its high dependence on imported food. Morocco consumes more imported than domestically produced cereal, for a cereal dependency ratio of 54 percent, more than three times the world average of 16 percent.[8] In normal times, high dependence on imported food is not necessarily a problem if the country has sufficient export revenues to cover its food import bill. Morocco spends about 20 percent of its export revenues on food imports, which is about four times higher than the world average.

High import dependence poses particular challenges in periods of high volatility in world markets. Importing countries face two types of risk: the risk of price hikes and the risk of a disruption in physical supply. Morocco's demand for food imports (particularly cereals) is highly inelastic, which means that it is unable to reduce imports in response to a price increase; therefore, it has to bear the full impact of high prices. Moreover, in times of shortages, countries sometimes impose export bans, and food supplies are susceptible to disruption by war, civil strife, and natural disasters. Thus, Morocco could face a situation in which it cannot import food at any price.

Does this mean that Morocco is food insecure? The answer is no. Food security does not require food self-sufficiency, and Morocco is

---

7. See Dawe (2010).

8. The cereal dependency ratio is defined as the ratio of imported cereal to total cereal consumption.

able to ensure its food needs through a combination of domestic production and imports. However, it is important for Morocco to continue reviewing its agriculture policies as well as its import and emergency food reserve strategies to ensure that food security for its growing population is maintained over the medium and long term.

Morocco's Twin Problems: Child Malnutrition and Obesity

Although vulnerable to changes in world markets, Morocco cannot be considered a food insecure country. Undernourishment, defined as inadequate caloric consumption, is not a major problem in Morocco. About 5 percent of Morocco's population is undernourished, which is disturbing, but is much lower than the average for developing countries. In fact, obesity appears to be a bigger problem than undernourishment. More than 17 percent of Moroccans are considered obese, which is significantly higher than the world average of 11.7 percent.

While a large segment of the population is obese, another group—mainly children under five years of age—is not receiving the nutrients necessary to grow and develop into healthy and productive adults. About 15 percent of Moroccan children under the age of five are stunted (their growth is below average for their age because of nutrient deficiency) and 2.3 percent are wasted (nutrient deficiency is causing a deterioration in their bodily functions). Child malnutrition is often caused by a mother's lack of knowledge about healthy feeding rather than lack of access to food. It is important to point out here that Morocco has made good progress over the last decade in reducing child stunting from about 23 to 15 percent. However, it is clear that 15 percent is still too high and that this effort needs to continue.

The Importance of Small Family Farmers

Improving nutrition and reducing dependence on imports can be partly achieved by developing domestic agriculture. The vast majority of agricultural production in Morocco comes from family farming, which is defined as a type of agricultural production system that is managed by one or more members of a family and that relies primarily on non-wage family labor.[9] Family farming includes agricultural, forestry, fishery, pastoral, and aquaculture activities. It often

---

9. See Abaab and others (2000).

TABLE 12-1. Share of Holdings of Less than Five Hectares

Percent

Country	Share of total holdings	Share of land area
Algeria	55.4	11.3
Egypt	98.2	70.7
Jordan	78.9	23.8
Lebanon	96.7	60.1
Morocco	69.8	23.9
Qatar	73.3	3.4
Tunisia	53.5	10.9
Yemen	93.0	43.9
Average	84.2	25.3

Source: FAO agriculture census data provided to author.

is characterized by multiple activities as the family tries to increase its income and diversify its products to protect itself from exogenous shocks. Family farmers are often, but not always, smallholders; however, nearly all smallholders tend to be family farmers. That is why most empirical work on the subject has used the size of a land holding as a proxy measure for family farming. Nearly 70 percent of all holdings in Morocco are less than five hectares and are family farms; in fact, the average size of a family farm is only about two hectares. This underlines the importance of smallholders and family farming for agricultural development and inclusive growth in Morocco. Table 12-1 and figure 12-2 indicate that Morocco's situation is similar to that of other Arab countries.

While the majority of holdings are family farms, family farms control only a small proportion of total agricultural land. About 75 percent of agricultural land in Morocco is held by relatively large, corporate-type agricultural concerns. That reflects the dualistic nature of Moroccan agriculture, in which large numbers of family farms operate alongside big, more modern entities. While family farmers tend to produce for their own consumption (subsistence farming) and to sell to local markets, the large modern farms produce for national and international markets. They tend to have higher productivity and to be more profitable than small family farms. In Morocco, the average large modern farm earns about nine times more than the average family farm.

FIGURE 12-2. Average Size of Family Farms

Hectares

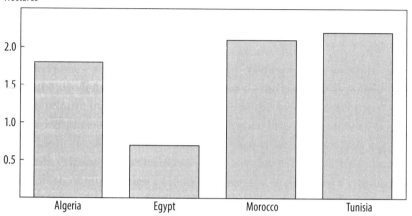

Source: FAO agriculture census data provided to author.

A 2007 study by the program RuralStruc divided Moroccan farms into three groups. The first group, productive farms, controls about 22 percent of Moroccan farmland. It consists mainly of large farms and a very few small and medium farms that operate in niche areas. The second group consists of structurally noncompetitive farms, which are basically subsistence farms and micro farms. This group comprises about 600,000 units, or 41 percent of all farms in the country, but it controls only 8.5 percent of all farmland. The remaining medium and small farms could become competitive because they have access to good land, sufficient water, and modern equipment. However, they face a host of problems that limit their ability to be profitable and to expand, including ambiguous land titles, poor transport and communication infrastructure, and lack of access to credit and to technical and marketing information.

Family farming is a major source of household employment and income in Morocco, where about 10 percent of the population is engaged in family farming. That explains the importance attached to family farming in the PMV, which tries to balance the desire to develop modern agriculture (the first pillar of the PMV) with the need to support family farmers (the second pillar). The second pillar consists of 545 projects costing about 20 billion dirhams ($2.5 billion) over a ten-year period (2008–20) that target about 950,000 farmers operating in remote and difficult areas. The projects are divided into three types: those that replace existing crops and products with new ones that provide higher value added to the farmers; those that enhance the productivity of existing products; and those that introduce new activities to increase family income and diversify its sources. The projects are designed jointly with the professional associations representing the beneficiaries, who are expected to participate in the project costs (about 30 percent) to ensure ownership and sustainability.

The PMV aims to increase the agricultural sector's competitiveness by shifting production to higher-value-added fruits and vegetables and by capitalizing on Morocco's geographic position and its proximity to European markets. It also aims to enhance crop intensification and raise yields through increased mechanization and the use of certified seeds. There has been a focus on developing and expanding high-value agrifood chains such as those for olives, citrus, and milk and dairy products.

Agriculture, Rural Development, and Economic Inclusion

Agriculture's role in Morocco's economy and society is much more important than is revealed by simply looking at its share of GDP, which is 15 percent. About 40 percent of Morocco's labor force is employed in agriculture. In addition, about 43 percent of Morocco's population lives in rural areas; residents' livelihoods are therefore either directly or indirectly affected by agriculture. Agriculture is especially important because it provides a livelihood for the majority of the poor. Poverty in Morocco is largely a rural phenomenon. Opportunities for rural youth outside of agriculture are limited. Agro-industry—such as the production of olive oil and canned juices and vegetables—remains relatively underdeveloped and contributes only 5 percent of GDP. Most services are concentrated in urban centers.

Inclusive growth that improves living standards across the different regions of the country requires investment in physical infrastructure as well as in education to create greater opportunities, especially for youth. Access to physical infrastructure has been improving. About 98 percent of rural households are connected to electricity, and 93 percent have access to clean drinking water. However, according to the World Bank, ensuring the reliability and maintenance of those services continues to be a challenge.[10]

10. World Bank (2014).

Similarly, Morocco has expanded access to education, but the quality of education remains unsatisfactory. Net school enrollment has increased; it currently is close to 100 percent. But while a larger proportion of Moroccan children are going to school than ever before, they are not learning. According to international test results, about 75 percent of primary school students fail basic tests of mathematics. Unsurprisingly, children in remote rural areas tend to be less well served by the educational system than their urban peers. Hence, they have a harder time competing in the labor market.

The Role of Women in Moroccan Agriculture

Between 23 to 35 percent of the labor on family farms is provided by women. Moreover, the role of women in family farming is increasing because more and more male family members are migrating to oil rich countries and to cities in order to earn a better living and send remittances to their families at home. Women are left to look after the family farm. As a result, family farming in Morocco is undergoing a process of feminization.

A division of labor between men and women on the family farm is commonly observed. While men will traditionally raise crops only for selling, women tend to be responsible for production of food within the household and for animal husbandry. They plant food crops, and they look after small and large ruminants and specialize in the production of eggs and milk and other dairy products. They also participate with all family members in harvesting activities. They are usually helped by their children, who take small ruminants to water and pasture and work alongside their parents at harvest time.

Women suffer more than men from lack of access to land, credit, and technology. Women landholders generally represent less than 5 percent of all landholders in Morocco. Moreover, land fragmentation poses a special problem for women, who are hampered by social norms from moving among plots that may be far from one another. Women also have even greater difficulties than men in obtaining rural credit. Often, a woman's husband must first approve the request, and his approval may not always be forthcoming. Those who sign legally binding documents must also be literate. The older women who participate most in commercial activities and could benefit readily from microcredit are the least likely to be literate. Women often have to form associations to obtain microcredit. The organizational participation requirements for obtaining microfinance can be time consuming and often require the presence of an agent in the community to act as a go-between with the banks.

Rural women have little access to extension services. Most extension programs lack qualified personnel and have limited capacity to mainstream women in policies, programs, and implementation strategies. The design of many extension programs has not taken women's cultural and time constraints into account. Consequently, the opportunities for women to express their needs and have them met are more limited than those of men. Finally, research and extension work tend to focus on cash crops rather than the subsistence food crops that women grow and own. Although women play a preponderant role in all forms of animal husbandry, including raising small ruminants, caring for cows, and preparation of all milk products, extension services for women rarely focus on those activities.

A Strategy for Food and Nutrition Security and Rural Development

Morocco can improve food and nutrition security and at the same time reduce rural poverty and make growth more inclusive by

—increasing food reserves and using financial markets to reduce commodity price risks,

—increasing support to smallholders and family farmers to link them to markets and thus increase domestic food production while raising their incomes,

—supporting the development of independent producer organizations that give smallholders a voice and also help them gain better access to input and output markets, and

—introducing social protection systems that target the rural poor through conditional or unconditional cash transfers.

Increasing Food Reserves and Using Financial Markets to Reduce Risks

Morocco will continue to be highly dependent on food imports for the foreseeable future. That should not be a problem as long as the country continues to generate sufficient export revenues to cover its import bills. In fact, it often makes more sense for a country to export high-value agricultural products and use part of the export proceeds to import lower-value food commodities.

However, Morocco still needs to develop import strategies to protect its food security in a world of high and volatile prices. Holding larger physical food reserves is one possible option. Countries need to maintain food security emergency reserves to assist the most vulnerable without disrupting normal private sector market development, which is needed for long-term food security. The size of the emergency reserves needed depends on a country's specific circumstances. Holding food stocks can be expensive. FAO and the World Bank estimate that storage of 1 metric ton of wheat costs $2.15 a month. Therefore, the costs and benefits of holding larger emergency reserves must be weighed.

Another area that deserves special attention is the use of financial markets to reduce risks. Countries around the world are increasingly using financial risk hedging instruments to ensure against volatility— Mexico, for example, has used such instruments to fix the price of its corn imports in order to avoid another "tortilla crisis." Futures contracts, which require the buyer to purchase a fixed quantity at a fixed price at a predetermined future date, are one way of managing commodity price risk. Buyers need to obtain credit or guarantees to cover the value of this contract.

Another alternative is to use options contracts. These contracts give the buyer the right—but do not impose the obligation—to purchase a fixed quantity of a commodity at a fixed price at some future date. They act like insurance against high prices: if prices fall, the buyer can decide not to use the option and thus lose only the premium, which is paid up front in cash. A famous example of the use of options comes from Malawi, which bought options to purchase maize in 2005. The price of maize increased, and Malawi exercised the option, saving about $5 million.

Increasing Domestic Production

Vulnerability to international market volatility could also be lowered by reducing dependence on those markets through higher domestic production. Since most food in Morocco is produced by smallholders and family farmers, increasing food production would imply helping those small producers increase their productivity. They are especially in need of help because yields on small farms often are lower than those on large modern farms. By supporting small family farmers, governments

TABLE 12-2. Yields of Major Crops

Hectograms per hectare

Area	Cereals	Oil crops	Vegetables	Fruits
Morocco	16.1	3.6	292	99.5
World	36.6	6.4	192	112.6

Source: FAOSTAT website.

would be fighting rural poverty and making economic growth more inclusive while reducing import dependence and enhancing food security. Increasing support to small family farmers does not mean ignoring large modern farms. Both are important for growth and food security. But because smallholders tend to face greater challenges than large farms, they may require greater support from the government in order to level the playing field.

Table 12-2 compares yields per hectare for major groups of food products in Morocco with the world average. It indicates that with the exception of vegetable production, yields in Morocco are lower than the world average. For example, cereal yields in Morocco are around 16 hectograms per hectare while the world average is about 36 hectograms per hectare. This yield gap could be considered good news in that it means that there is room for higher production. On the other hand, the low yields also reflect water scarcity and difficult climatic conditions that may be hard to resolve. In addition to enhancing food security, raising the productivity of smallholders (and hence their income) will help reduce rural poverty and make economic growth more inclusive and equitable. There are six ways in which the government could intervene to support small family farmers and help increase their yields:

—Link small farmers to domestic and international markets and help increase their share in value-added products

—Adapt financial and investment services to the needs of small family farmers

—Secure land titles

—Increase investment in research and extension services and adapt them to the needs of smallholders

—Help farmers adapt to climate change

—Launch special programs for women farmers and youth.

These are detailed below.

Link small farmers to domestic and international markets

Linking farmers to markets is essential to raising their productivity and standard of living. Raising their share in value added is an important way to improve the income of family farmers, who tend to retain a very small share of value added from their products. In addition, new marketing techniques need to be introduced to reduce the role of intermediaries in the marketing process through better organization of family farmers. For example, the government can help promote the products of family farms through special labels and information campaigns about the benefits of consuming local products. Moreover, family farmers' incomes can be raised by establishing links between family farmers and small and medium enterprises that can process the farmers' products or between farmers and traders in order to link farmers with national and international markets. Such links could be established through arrangements in which a buyer or an agro-processor ensures smallholders' access to technology and necessary inputs and also facilitates marketing of the final product. Those arrangements could take the form of contract farming or outgrower schemes. Experience indicates that in order to fully benefit from links to markets, smallholders need to become more competitive, which in turn requires better access to financing, to land, and to technology. It also requires special measures to adapt to climate change and to support youth and women farmers.

Adapt financial and investment services to the needs of small family farmers

Access to financing and investment resources is perhaps the most important constraint facing family farmers. While credit to agriculture in Morocco is about 7.4 percent of agricultural GDP, overall credit to the economy is 65 percent of total GDP, showing that agriculture's share of financing is extremely low compared with agriculture's contribution to the economy. Agriculture's share of credit (adjusted for its contribution to GDP) is nearly nine times less than the average for the whole economy.

This analysis probably underestimates the magnitude of the problem facing family farmers because a large proportion of agricultural credit goes to big modern farms. Nevertheless, the data confirm that access to financing is a major constraint facing family farmers. Even if one assumed that all the credit to agriculture is going to family farmers, one would still conclude that compared with other sectors of the economy, they are grossly underserved by the financial system. Existing financial institutions, credit instruments, and bank procedures are ill adapted to the needs of family farmers. Because many family farmers do not have notarized land titles, they are not able to provide the kind of guarantees that banks require to approve a loan. The amount of credit required by individual family farmers is usually small and therefore not of interest to banks. Moreover, many banks consider agriculture to be too risky and prefer not to lend to farmers.

To deal with similar situations, other countries have created new institutions or reinforced existing ones by adopting simplified lending procedures that take into account the realities of family farmers; put in place government lines of credit to encourage banks to lend to family farmers; developed insurance and guarantee facilities to reduce the risk in lending to agriculture; and encouraged the development and expansion of rural microcredit facilities as well as farmer-centered financial institutions in which farmers have a stake. There is also a need to increase public investment in agriculture and in rural areas to build the social and physical infrastructure necessary for the development of family farming.

There are several examples from Arab countries of initiatives to enhance financing for smallholders and family farmers. Sudan created the Micro Finance Development Facility, which is owned by the Central Bank and the Ministry of Finance and is funded mainly by donor organizations. It has supported the creation of sixteen new microfinance institutions and has reached nearly half a million beneficiaries. About 80 percent of funding under this program goes to agriculture-related activities. It funds small investments by family farmers and gives special preference to women and young graduates from agriculture and veterinary colleges. Lebanon's Disaster Fund for Agriculture is an example of an initiative that provides guarantees and reduces the riskiness of family farming. Half of the resources for this fund are provided by the government and the other half by the farmers themselves. The idea is to provide financial compensation to farms suffering from bad weather conditions or other types of natural disasters. By reducing farmers' risks, the fund also helps them obtain credit.

Secure land titles

Access to land is another important issue for small family farmers. As stated earlier, the average size of a family farm in Morocco is only about two hectares; moreover, the average size is steadily decreasing as a result of population increase. Inheritance laws that divide land among surviving children and the absence of a well-functioning land market that allows consolidation compound the problem. The small size of family farms complicates their access to technology, inputs, and markets.

Many family farmers in Morocco do not have a title to their very small holdings. In addition to making it difficult for family farmers to obtain credit, uncertainty about their ownership of land discourages them from investing. Therefore, governments could help boost investment in agriculture by facilitating land titling for farmers and in some cases distributing public and collective land to small family farmers. It is also recommended that laws and regulations be amended to protect the rights of small tenants.

Increase investment in research and extension services and adapt them to the needs of smallholders

Research and extension services should adapt to the needs of family farmers. The productivity of Moroccan family farmers is lagging in part because of lack of access to appropriate modern technologies. National institutions need to carry out their own agricultural research in order to adapt existing knowledge and techniques to local ecological, social, and economic realities. Many studies show that the return on investment in agricultural research is typically very high, an estimated 36 percent for Arab countries. However, as is shown in figure 12-3, at 0.9 percent of agricultural GDP, Morocco's investment in research, while higher than that in other North African countries, is far below the rate of about 2.4 percent observed in OECD countries and the 1.5 percent observed in successful Latin American countries.

Perhaps more important, extension services in Morocco are poorly funded and therefore ineffective. Moreover, extension workers often are not trained to communicate with family farmers and end up delivering information in a manner that is not convincing or helpful to the farmers. This appears to be a problem across the Arab world. For

FIGURE 12-3. Investment in Agricultural Research as a Percent of Agricultural GDP

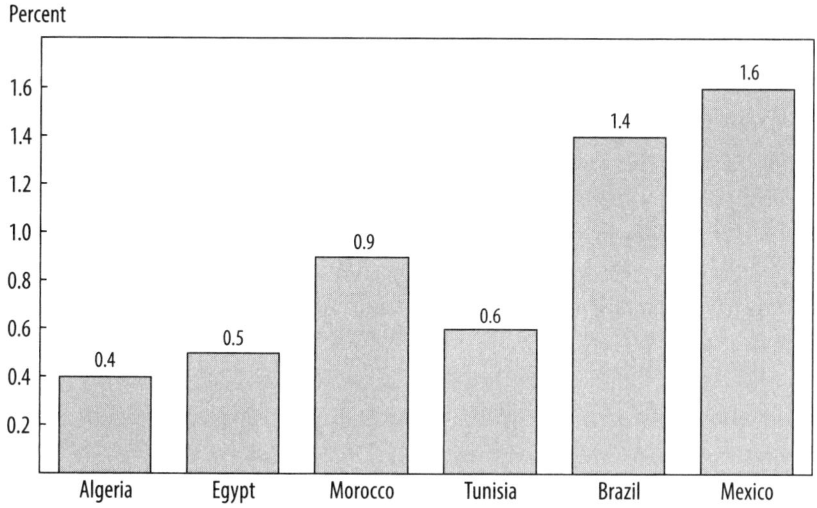

Percent

Source: World Bank, FAO, and International Fund for Agricultural Development (2009).

example, a recent study in Jordan compared the productivity of olive farmers who received support from extension services with those who received no support.[11] It concluded that receiving support from extension services had no impact on productivity, implying that even when research is successful, its results are not adequately transmitted to small family farmers.

It appears that there is a need to consider innovative types of research and extension institutions as well as new instruments for delivering information to family farmers. Innovative extension systems put family farmers at the center and do not consider them as mere end receivers. New institutions could be based on government partnerships with the private sector, family farmer–producer organizations, and civil society. Many civil society organizations have earned the trust of family farmers because they have deep knowledge of the sector and long experience working with family farmers. They increasingly use modern technologies and information and communication technologies such as mobile phones and the Internet to deliver information to family farmers.

11. See Al-Sharafat, Altarawaneh, and Altahat (2012).

Help farmers adapt to climate change

Better research and extension services are especially needed to help family farmers adapt to the impact of climate change. North Africa is considered a climate change hotspot. According to the most recent research, temperatures in the region could rise on average by 3 degrees Celsius by 2050, with rain water declining by about 10 percent and demand for water rising by 60 percent during the same period. Moreover, the rise in seawater levels would have strong effects on low-lying areas, increasing land salinity and contaminating underground water resources.

The prospect of higher temperatures, less rainfall, and increased land salinity in a country that is already suffering from insufficient water resources does not augur well for the future of agriculture. Urgent action must be taken now, and family farmers should be at the center of efforts to adapt to climate change. They are the largest food producers and creators of rural employment, and their small size and lack of investment resources make them especially vulnerable to climate change impacts and other types of shocks.

Some farmers already are adapting to higher temperatures by adjusting crop planting schedules. Research and extension can be helpful here by introducing new varieties that are more heat resistant and by informing farmers about new cropping patterns to reflect changes in climatic conditions. Morocco's biggest challenge will continue to be dealing with water shortages. Here, again, research and extension can play an important role by introducing more drought-resistant varieties of crops. These new varieties need to be accompanied by new investments in better irrigation systems to avoid water wastage and to ensure the most efficient use of limited water resources.

Launch special programs for women farmers and youth

Given their important role in agriculture and food and nutrition security, particular attention needs to be paid to the needs of women farmers.[12] The government could consider a three-pronged approach to support women farmers. First, existing laws on access to land and to credit need to be reviewed and wherever appropriate revised to remove

---

12. See FAO (2011).

biases against women farmers. Moreover, many existing procedures, particularly those for obtaining land titles and microfinance, need to be revised and simplified to reflect the realities of rural women. Second, the government could put in place special programs to provide financial services for rural women, such as an "agricultural women's bank" that would specialize in working with women farmers and catering to their banking needs. Third, extension services and programs need to be revised to better reflect the increased feminization of family farming. For example, Sudan has developed Women Farmer Schools, a program catering to the needs of rural women that includes sharing information on health and nutrition issues as well as on agricultural production and animal husbandry.

Youth unemployment, with rates of around 25 percent, is a major challenge facing all North African countries. Youth are increasingly losing interest in agriculture and are looking for jobs in urban areas. This shift is putting pressure on urban infrastructure and depriving rural areas and family farms of young people, who are important labor resources and are generally more educated and dynamic than their parents. The availability of adequate goods and services and job opportunities would convince more youth to stay closer to the family farm.

Two types of action can be pursued to encourage youth to remain in rural areas and in agriculture. First, the government needs to invest more in rural infrastructure to attract new businesses and create more opportunities for off-farm employment. Youth would benefit from the opportunity of an off-farm job that pays them a wage and also permits them to continue supporting the family farm. Second, there is a need to develop programs and projects that target young farmers specifically and provide them with privileged access to land, credit, and technical knowledge.

Supporting Inclusive Producer Organizations

Producer organizations and cooperatives can play an important role in strengthening the governance system of the agriculture sector, particularly by developing and supporting family farmers and thereby increasing the productivity of the sector. Problems caused by the large number of very small dispersed family farms in Morocco can be tackled through the development of strong producer organizations that bring farmers together to ensure that their voices are heard in policy discussions and also help to enhance their access to technology, input and output markets, information, communications, and natural resources. Compared with producer organizations and other civil society organizations that operate in rural areas in regions with similar per capita incomes (for example, Latin America and East Asia), those in Morocco are still quite weak and do not yet play their full role in supporting family farming.

Producer organizations and cooperatives should also play an important economic role, bringing family farmers together to enhance their access to technology and inputs, improve market access, and help them retain a larger share of value added. Producer organizations could encourage farmers to share their experience and know-how with each other. They could also propose and encourage programs for applied agricultural research that support family farmers, and they could help improve extension services and adapt them to the needs of family farmers. In fact, civil society organizations, including producer organizations and cooperatives, are often much better placed than government agencies to deliver extension and technical support to family farmers.

The government needs to support producer organizations, cooperatives, and other civil society organizations working with family farmers and to ensure their political and financial independence. That may require creating an enabling environment, which entails making legal and policy changes that provide more financial and operational autonomy to civil society organizations and moves them out of government control. It will also require a change in the current bureaucratic and political culture, away from centralized control and toward a much more decentralized and participatory system of governance. The government should regularly invite producer organizations and cooperative representatives to participate as equal partners in the formulation and implementation of policies and development programs.

Morocco can learn from Latin America's experience in this area. Brazil provides an example of a public–civil society partnership for food security.[13] When Luis Ignacio Lula da Silva was elected president of Brazil, fighting hunger was one of his top priorities for achieving social justice. Therefore, he created the National Food and Nutritional Security Council (Consea), which is a good example of an inclusive eco-

13. See Da Silva, Del Grossi, and De Franca (2011).

nomic institution. It had fifty-nine members—seventeen government representatives and forty-two members from civil society representing small farmers as well as poor and food insecure people—and it was chaired by a civil society representative. The council met at the president's office and made its recommendations directly to President Lula. Because the problem of hunger is intersectoral in nature, the council had a broad membership representing all sectors of the economy. Consea was also conceived as a tool to give voice to those suffering from hunger and to improve cooperation between government and civil society. Under Consea and President Lula, Brazil was extremely successful in eliminating hunger.

Conclusion

Morocco, which has maintained stable economic growth while gradually implementing democratic reforms, is considered a success story in the Arab world. Greater inclusiveness, so that all Moroccans share in the benefits of economic growth, would help ensure its continued success and economic and social stability. This chapter argues that inclusive growth is linked to food and nutrition security. Ensuring economic inclusion and poverty reduction requires providing support to the smallholder and family farmers who represent most of the poor in Morocco. At the same time, supporting those farmers and enhancing their productivity and their links to markets can lead to increased food production and improved food and nutrition security. The government of Morocco is aware of the importance of smallholder farming, and the second pillar of its Plan Maroc Vert focuses on their needs. The analysis in this chapter supports emphasizing the PMV's second pillar, arguing that the twin objectives of inclusive growth and food and nutrition security could be achieved by adopting an approach that includes

—increasing food reserves and using financial markets to reduce risks

—improving the links between markets and smallholders and family farmers and helping farmers increase domestic food production while raising their incomes, and

—supporting the development of independent producer organizations that give a voice to smallholders and also help them gain better access to input and output markets.

References

Abaab, A., and others. 2000. *Agricultures Familiales et Développement Rural en Méditerranée*. Paris: Editions Karthala.

AfDB (African Development Bank). 2012. *The Political Economy of Food Security in North Africa*. Tunis.

Al-Sharafat, A., M. Altarawaneh, and E. Altahat. 2012. "Effectiveness of Agricultural Extension Activities." *American Journal of Agricultural and Biological Sciences* 7, no. 2: 194–200.

Da Silva, J. G., M. Del Grossi, and C. De Franca. 2011. "The Fome Zero (Zero Hunger) Program: The Brazilian Experience." Brasilia: Ministry of Agrarian Development.

Dawe, D. 2010. *The Rice Crisis: Markets, Policies, and Food Security*. Rome: FAO.

FAO (Food and Agriculture Organization). 2011. *The State of Food and Agriculture: Women in Agriculture, Closing the Gender Gap*. Rome.

———. 2012. *Price Volatility from a Global Perspective*. Technical background document for the high-level event "Food Price Volatility and the Role of Speculation." Rome.

———. 2014. *State of Food and Agriculture in the Near East and North Africa Region*. Rome.

FAOSTAT (Food and Agriculture Organization of the United Nations Statistics Division) Website.

Organization for Economic Cooperation and Development (OECD) and FAO. 2010. *OECD-FAO Agricultural Output 2010–2019*. Paris and Rome.

Prakash, A., ed. 2011. *Safeguarding Food Security in Volatile Global Markets*. Rome: FAO.

Programme RuralStruc. 2007. *Dimensions Structurelles de la Liberalisation pour l'Agriculture*. Rabat.

World Bank. 2014. *Country Partnership Strategy for the Kingdom of Morocco for the Period FY2014–17*. Washington.

World Bank, FAO, and International Fund for Agricultural Development. 2009. *Improving Food Security in Arab Countries*. Washington: World Bank.

13

Improving the Quality of Basic Education in Yemen for Youth in the Future

TAKAKO YUKI and YURIKO KAMEYAMA

Regime change is what the people of the Middle East and North Africa wanted and achieved after massive demonstrations began in Tunisia in December 2010 and spread across the region during the period known as the Arab Spring. That energy now needs to be transformed into substantive action to ensure that the new governments that took power formulate and implement policies that can resolve issues and get the better results that their people want. To inform dialogue between the government of Yemen and its development partners, this chapter analyzes the issues pertaining to the quality of basic education, the foundation on which job opportunities are based and on which people develop the knowledge and skills that they need to take advantage of those opportunities. Jobs are among the top priorities for Arab youth. The unemployment rate in the Middle East and North Africa (MENA) region is among the highest in the world, especially among youth, and the duration of unemployment is worrisome.[1] The number of jobs is not growing and the majority of private sector jobs are still in the informal sector,

We received valuable comments from Hafez Ghanem, Rebecca Winthrop, Raj M. Desai, Hamoud Al-Seyani, Regina Bendokat, and others. Md. Shamsuzzoha provided research assistance in data management. We are very grateful for the valuable advice and data received from the Ministry of Education in the Republic of Yemen and its development partners, such as the World Bank and GTZ.

1. For TIMSS mathematics assessments in 1995, 2003, and 2007, see Masood Ahmed, "Youth Unemployment in the MENA Region: Determinants and Challenges," International Monetary Fund, June 2012 (www.imf.org/external/np/vc/2012/061312.htm).

especially in Yemen (Angel-Urdinola and Tanabe 2012). As the youth population of Yemen grows, competition for public sector jobs will increase, making such jobs difficult to obtain (Assaad and others 2009).

Human resources—along with other factors such as the business regulatory environment and (micro) finances—are an important factor in fostering private sector businesses. What are the key issues in human resource development in the MENA region? The first issue is the relevance of education and skills to the labor market. Overall, Arab countries have succeeded in increasing the supply of their educated labor force through expansion of education services. During the last decade (1999–2010), the MENA region (at all income levels) increased, on average, the gross enrollment ratio from 97 percent to 104 percent in primary education, from 68 percent to 77 percent in secondary education, and from 22 percent to 31 percent in tertiary education.[2] However, a good share of firms in the region still report skill shortages as a major constraint in doing business.[3] These shortages call for continuing the commitment to expanding education services while increasing attention to the relevance of the education offered. The education sector needs to produce workers with the types and levels of competencies and skills that are demanded by the labor market. Policies should address training that will help adolescents meet the challenges of the twenty-first century and provide mechanisms to improve the transition from the education system to the labor market.[4] Yemen, which has not yet caught up with other MENA countries in the development of either education services or private firms, also needs to prepare for the future demand for skills.

The second issue in the region is the quality of basic education, which affects the future trainability of youth and thus the relevance of education. Growing evidence on learning achievement confirms the existence of quality issues within the education sector. For example, not only Yemen but all of the thirteen Arab countries that participated

2. Education Statistics (http://data.worldbank.org/data-catalog/ed-stats).
3. Enterprise Surveys (www.enterprisesurveys.org/).
4. For Yemen, a case study of students at the third level of the secondary education system indicates that the majority of those who participated in the knowledge and skills measurement examination did not have the skills needed for the twenty-first century, including skills in problem solving, written communications, technology use, and searching for information (Republic of Yemen 2012a; Mohammed bin Rashid Al Maktoum Foundation and UNDP 2012).

in Trends in International Mathematics and Science Studies (TIMSS) testing scored significantly lower than the TIMSS average of 500 in 2007, in grade 4 or grade 8 (or both) (Mullis, Martin, and Foy 2008).[5] The 2011 TIMSS results indicate more or less the same results (Mullis and others 2012). All of the nine Arab countries that participated in the 2011 grade 4 assessment ranked among the bottom ten countries on the country-average math scale. The Arab region's common concern with student learning is underscored by the Doha Declaration on Quality of Education in the Arab World in 2010.[6] Insufficient mastery of basic reading and numeracy can have negative effects on skills learning in technical and vocational education and training (King 2011).

Furthermore, inequity in access remains a potential obstacle to improving the quality of learning for those already enrolled unless the amount and/or efficiency of the public budget is increased. The situation is challenging for Yemen in particular. While the country increased the net enrollment rate (NER) in primary education from 57 percent in 1999 to 78 percent in 2010,[7] much effort is required to achieve the international target of 100 percent net enrollment and compliance with the national compulsory basic education policy, particularly for girls and rural children.[8] Yemen's female enrollment rate is below that of many other low-income countries. The primary school net attendance rate for girls was estimated to be 53 percent in rural and 80 percent in urban areas in 2008 (Ministry of Health and Population and UNICEF 2008, p. 100), and the primary education completion rate for boys and girls was 42 percent in rural areas in 2006.[9] The availability and quality of learning resources tend to be lower in rural schools. Given the

5. Some countries participated only in grade 8, some only in grade 4, and some in both grades.

6. The declaration emphasizes different issues: actual teaching and learning factors, student learning assessments, reliable monitoring and evaluation methods, accountability in the sector, and collaboration with stakeholders (http://go.worldbank.org/GI7C2VQXY0).

7. Millennium Development Goals Indicators, UNDP (http://mdgs.un.org/unsd/mdg/Data.aspx).

8. Compulsory education is defined as eight to nine years of education in most Arab countries, including Yemen. For Yemen, after basic school, the system separates students into secondary school and post-basic vocational training centers. Then the system tracks students into universities (degree or diploma courses), community colleges (two years), or postsecondary vocational training centers.

9. Education Statistics (http://data.worldbank.org/data-catalog/ed-stats).

TABLE 13-1. Public Education Expenditure and Primary Enrollment Rate, Selected Countries, circa 2010[a]

Indicators	Yemen	Senegal	Ghana	Vietnam	Lao
Public expenditure on education as % of GDP	5.2[b]	5.6	5.5	5.3[b]	3.3
Public recurrent spending on total education as % of total public recurrent spending	16.0[b]	45.8[c]	n.a.	n.a.	11.4[c]
Public expenditure per pupil as a % of GDP per capita, primary	18.2[c]	16.4	11.4	19.4[b]	n.a.
Total net enrollment rate, primary	77.6	75.5	84.0[c]	98.0	96.8
Total net enrollment rate, primary, female	70.0	77.7	84.4	n.a.	95.4
Gender parity index for net enrollment rate, primary	0.83	1.06	1.01	n.a.	0.97
GDP per capita (current US$)	1,291	1,034	1,319	1,224	1,158

Sources: World Bank online data; UNESCO Institute for Statistics online data, accessed December 2012; Global Partnership for Education, 2012, pp. 283, 310; and Education for All Fast Track Initiative, 2010, p. 87.
a. Most data are for 2010; exceptions are noted below.
b. Data are for 2008.
c. Data are for 2011.

government's tuition-free policy and the low share of private primary schools,[10] effective public finance management is the key to improving quality, access, and achievement for all and to ensuring the trainability of all youth in the future. In fact, as table 13-1 shows, the amount that Yemen spends on education is comparable with the amount spent by other countries in terms of total education expenditure (5 percent of GDP in 2010) and expenditure per pupil in primary education (18 percent of GDP per capita in 2011); there has, however, been a decline in the total education expenditure since the early 2000s (9 percent of GDP). Overall public sector governance was considered weak for Yemen as well as other MENA countries (World Bank 2003, 2009).

This chapter focuses on the challenges to improving the quality of education in Yemen, which at the same time needs to rapidly increase access to education for underserved children. The next section analyzes learning outcomes and factors correlated with those outcomes. The third section analyzes the quality of Yemen's basic education policies and governance to identify the issues and reforms needed to achieve better education results. The last section presents policy implications.

---

10. The private share is a little higher at the tertiary level (20.1 percent), while it was only 4 percent at the primary level in 2010 (World Bank, Education Statistics, http://data.worldbank.org/data-catalog/ed-stats).

FIGURE 13-1. Mathematics Achievement in Middle- and High-Income Countries, 2011[a]

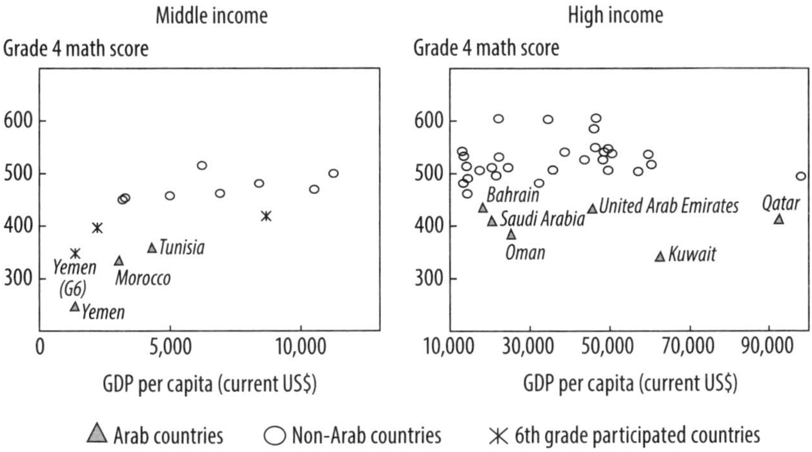

Source: TIMMS 2011; GDP per capita (current US$) from World Bank online database.
a. Three countries participated at the grade 6 level: Botswana, Honduras, and Yemen. Countries are classified based on GDP per capita (current US$) for 2011. For Bahrain, the data are for 2010.

Quality of Learning Outcomes in Yemen and Other Countries

Growing evidence indicates that Yemen as well as the other Arab countries needs to improve the quality of education outcomes. The Trends in International Mathematics and Science Study indicates a relatively low level of student achievement in the region. As figure 13-1 shows, all nine participating Arab countries, both low- and high-middle-income countries, performed far below the international TIMSS average of 500 on the grade 4 mathematics exam in 2011. Yemeni achievement was marked the lowest among participating countries while the country's economic level also was marked the lowest. Yemen also assessed its grade 6 students on the grade 4 exam in 2011, and while the achievement for the grade 6 students was still low, it was above the average for the grade 4 students (Mullis and others 2012). Cross-country comparisons show that the Yemeni score is not high even compared with that of other low- and lower-middle-income countries, although there are only small differences (see figure 13-2). However, such results should be used cautiously because of their methodological limitations (Altinok 2010).

With respect to gender differences in performance, grade 4 girls outperformed boys on the TIMSS mathematics assessments in 1995, 2003,

FIGURE 13-2. Primary Education Scores and GDP per Capita in Low- and Middle-Income
Countries

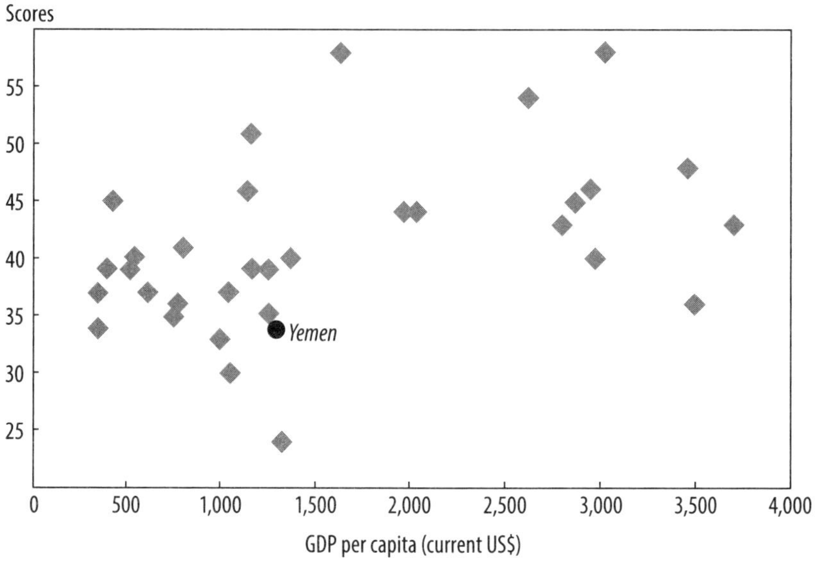

Source: Global Partnership for Education, 2012; original from Altinok (2010); World Bank online database.

and 2007 in all but one of the participating Middle Eastern countries
(Ezzine, Thacker, and Chamlou 2011), yet girls' performance was still
low (and remains the same in the 2011 TIMSS assessment). The TIMSS
also highlights the quality issues not only in math and science but also
in reading. For Yemen, while about 40 percent of the 2007 test items
were covered by the curriculum, less than half of the responses were
correct due to the literacy problem (Al-Mekhlafy 2009, p. 85). The
literacy problem also appears to be an issue for the other Arab countries. In her analyses of the fifteen MENA countries that participated
in the TIMSS 2003 or 2007 grade 8 test, Bouhlila (2011) emphasizes
language ability as the most serious issue.

New information on understanding the status of language acquisition is becoming available globally through the Early Grade Reading
Assessment (EGRA), a set of oral assessments implemented in many
developing countries (Gove and Cvelich 2011). In Yemen, the EGRA
assessed students in forty schools in three governorates and found that
the proportion of students who were not able to read a single word
(that is, those scoring zero in oral reading fluency) was 42 percent for

FIGURE 13-3. Mathematics Scores, Grade 4, Yemen

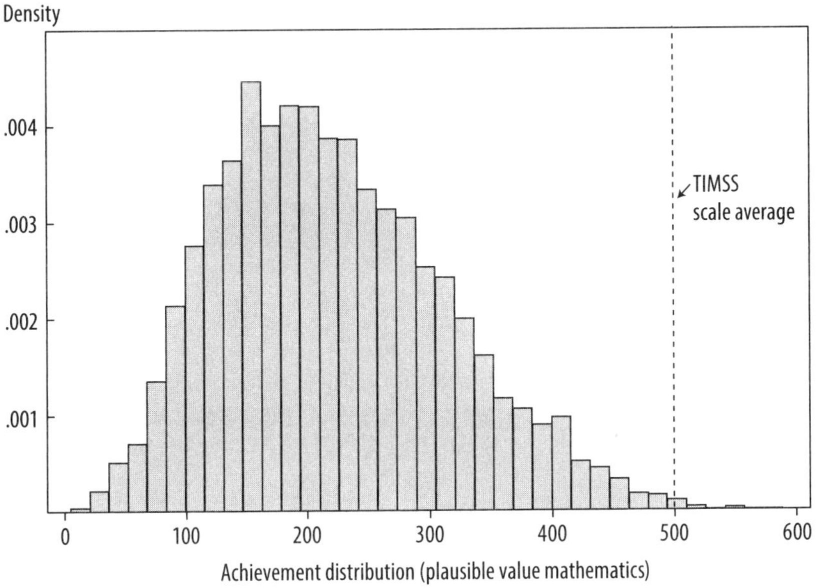

Source: TIMMS 2007.

grade 2 and 27 percent for grade 3 (Collins and Messaoud-Galusi, 2012, p. 2). Among students who could read at least one word, the rate of words of text read per minute was less than one-quarter of the recommended rate for adequate comprehension, and the students accurately read only approximately half of the words that they attempted. In Morocco, with a similar method, 34 percent of grade 2 students and 17 percent of grade 3 students were unable to read any words in a narrative text of fifty-eight words (Messaoud-Galusi and others 2012, p. 36). To improve reading instruction in early grades in Yemen, there is a need to improve the provision of reading materials, parental involvement in schooling, and pre- and in-service teacher training on the basic components of reading that should begin in grade 1.

As shown in figure 13-3, while the majority of grade 4 students are below the TIMSS international scale of 500, there is still variation among students. Al-Mekhlafy (2009) compares the average scores between students grouped by various pupil-related teaching and school-related variables to find possible determinants of student scores. He finds that the gender of students and class size were significantly

TABLE 13-2. Student-to-Teacher Ratio and Population Density, Selected Countries

	Primary education, student-to-teacher ratio		Population density (per km²)
	2000 or circa	2010 or circa	2010 or circa
Yemen	22	31	46
Egypt	23	26	81
Jordan	20	...	68
Morocco	29	26	72
Tunisia	23	17	68
Ghana	34	31	107
Lao PDR	30	29	27
Senegal	51	34	65
Vietnam	30	20	280

Source: World Bank online data, accessed December 2012.

related to performance, while qualification and experience of teachers had mixed implications, partly because many younger (and thus less experienced) teachers tend to have higher education.

Class size—or the student-to-teacher ratio (STR)—is internationally recognized as an important factor affecting the quality of education, and therefore it is important to see how it has evolved in Yemen. Empirical results on the effectiveness of smaller class sizes or STRs are mixed, depending on the country context (for example, developing or developed country), the student's grade, and teacher quality. Some studies point out that students' achievement in developing countries may have been lowered by the steep increase in access to basic education (UNESCO 2011; Hungi and others 2010) and by a high ratio of students to less qualified teachers. In fact, the Yemeni data indicate a notable increase in STR in primary education over the last decade, from 22:1 in 2000 to 31:1 in 2010, which is higher than in many countries in the region (table 13-2). This increase is good news for the efficiency of public resources as it is nearing the target of 35:1 set in the early 2000s for the year 2015 by the Fast Track Initiative plan for universal primary education (Government of Yemen and World Bank 2004).[11] However, the increase in the average STR can result in a decrease in the quality

11. This is a multidonor initiative, to which the government of Japan also contributes. It is now called the Global Partnership for Education (GPE).

FIGURE 13-4. Distribution of Class Size, Grade 4, Yemen

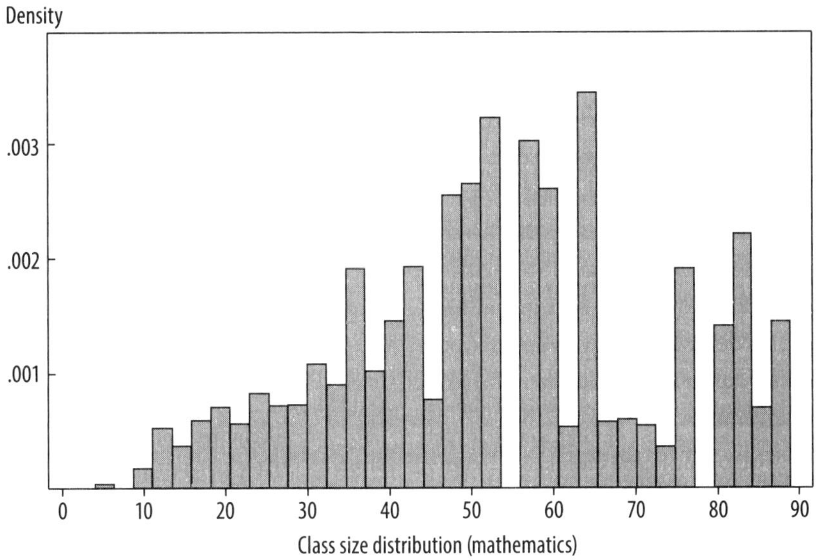

Density

Class size distribution (mathematics)

Source: TIMMS 2007.

of teaching, especially if teachers who are less qualified have to teach a larger number of students whose learning readiness also varies more because of the increased access of disadvantaged children.

One should also note that the actual class size can be higher than the STR: the average is not a maximum number. The TIMSS 2007 shows that Yemen's average class size for grade 4 mathematics was forty-six students, almost double the international average of twenty-six students (Mullis, Martin, and Foy 2008, pp. 268–69). Class size varies greatly among the sample schools of Yemen (figure 13-4), and the standard error is large relative to that for the other countries.

We prepared a statistical estimation model based on the descriptive analyses of Al-Mekhlafy (2009) to further assess the factors correlated to student achievement in Yemen. We adopted the production function approach (for example, Hanushek 1995; Fuller and Clarke 1994). As table 13-3 shows, the ordinary least squares (OLS) estimation results for the 2007 TIMSS Yemeni scores[12] indicate that class

12. The TIMSS sample schools are randomly selected according to an international sampling guideline, which sets a minimum class size in order to be selected

TABLE 13-3. OLS Estimation of Mathematics Examination Scores, Grade 4, Yemen

Specification	1	2
Student's gender (1: female, 0: male)	16.556***	16.734***
Household goods[a]	5.642***	6.021***
Building shortage is a lot (1: yes, 0: otherwise)	−16.158***	−17.544***
Ask parents to raise funds (1: yes, 0: otherwise)	10.487***	10.219***
Enrichment math (1: yes, 0: otherwise)	29.618***	29.930***
Less qualified teacher[b]	5.708	5.963
Class size (math)	−0.544***	−0.511***
Class size × (less qualified teacher)	−0.366***	−0.375***
Rural (1: rural, 0: urban)	...	4.713
Observations	4,601	4,601
Adjusted R^2	0.0777	0.0778

Source: TIMSS 2007 for Yemen.
a. Availability of four goods in student's home (presence of calculator, computer, study desk, dictionary).
b. 1 is equal to or less than teacher institute's diploma, 0 is equal to or higher than university diploma.
$+p < 0.10, *p < 0.05, **p < 0.01, ***p < 0.001$

size is significantly and negatively associated with student achievement, even after we controlled for urban-rural differences. The negative effect of a larger class size also tends to increase when associated with lower educational qualifications of mathematics teachers.[13] Yet lower teacher qualification alone is not significantly associated with student achievement. Our estimate indicates a significantly negative association between student performance and the school director's perception of the shortage of school buildings. Parental involvement, measured as whether a school asks parents to raise funds for the school, has a significant and positive association. Although basic education is tuition free, given the shortages of school amenities funded by the government,

---

and thus excludes many of the small rural schools in Yemen. For this study, the Ministry of Education (MOE) provided the information on TIMSS sample schools and the research team merged them with the Annual Education Survey (AES) data of 2004–05, 2007–08, and 2009–10 for basic indicators (for example, number of students and teachers). The merged total number of schools is 141.

13. To directly tackle poor results, a pilot program called the General Education Improvement Program Yemen (GEIP 2012), assisted by the GTZ, supports training for teachers in pilot schools in order to improve student achievement. Their students appear to have performed better in the TIMSS 2011 grade 4 mathematics test.

TABLE 13-4. OLS Estimation of Mathematics Examination Scores, Grades 5 and 6, Dhamar Governorate, Yemen

Specification	1	2	3
GPI change in enrollment, 2004–07, (1: high, 0: other)	−4.030***	−4.030***	−3.762***
GPI change in enrollment, 2007–10	−3.820*	−5.494**	
Enrollment growth rate from 2007–10 (grades 1–6)			−4.183**
Student's gender dummy (1: female, 0: male)	1.605**	1.183	1.680**
(Female) × (GPI change)		3.807	
Student's grade (1: grade 6, 0: grade 5)	1.529**	1.560**	1.545**
Variable group concerning the student's home environment[a]			
Student's arithmetic homework dummy (1: every day, 0: other)	0.607	0.596	0.602
Frequency of supervisor's visit	2.124***	2.132***	2.070***
Other characteristics of school			
Presence/absence of a workshop on the quality of education attended by parents	2.590***	2.573***	2.385***
Time of establishing fathers' council (1: 5 or more years ago, 0: otherwise)	7.492***	7.510***	7.243***
Education fees paid by parents (grade 6 students)	3.294***	3.294***	3.336***
Number of students per teacher	−0.119***	−0.120***	−0.093***
Characteristics of arithmetic teacher			
Number of years in teaching	0.459***	0.456***	0.478***
Training experience (1: yes, 0: no)	1.136	1.181	1.171
Teaching method: frequency of teaching equations for word problems	1.324***	1.314***	1.652***
Observations	1,159	1,159	1,159
Adjusted R^2	0.2324	0.2325	0.233

Source: 2011 JICA/ERDC survey in Yemen.

a. It controls the variable group, including the housing environment (for example, presence or absence of electricity and desks, parents' education and vocation).

+$p < 0.10$, *$p < 0.05$, **$p < 0.01$, ***$p < 0.001$

parental contributions could have made a practical difference among schools. Great attention needs to be paid to the relatively poor communities where such contributions are less feasible.

More recent data on rural schools also indicate the association of various supply-side factors and parental involvement to student achievement. Table 13-4 shows the OLS estimate of mathematics scores with data collected in 2011 from schools in underserved areas of Dhamar governorate, where the Gender Parity Index (GPI) sharply increased

FIGURE 13-5. Female-to-Male Student Ratio, Grades 1–6, Yemen

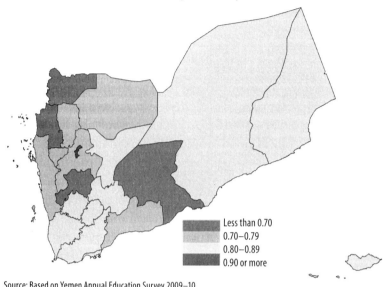

Less than 0.70
0.70–0.79
0.80–0.89
0.90 or more

Source: Based on Yemen Annual Education Survey 2009–10.

from less than 0.6 in 2004 to nearly 0.8 in 2009 (see figure 13-5) but the net enrollment ratio was still as low as 55 percent for girls (Republic of Yemen 2012b, p. 55).[14] The results indicate that higher enrollment and a better GPI are negatively associated with student achievement. (Statistical appendix tables appear at the end of this chapter.) That seems to imply that a high-achieving school with respect to educational access might be less able to ensure the quality of learning resources per student and learning achievement for either girls or boys. A higher student-to-teacher ratio is also negatively associated with student achievement. Yet some related measures mitigate these negative associations. For example, having supervisors visiting schools and holding workshops on school improvement with communities has a positive association with

14. The 2011 survey was conducted by JICA and the Education Research and Development Center (ERDC) under the MOE and merged with the AES data. All sampled rural schools were randomly selected to represent schools in underserved districts with a low base in terms of GPI in 2004–05. They were then split into two groups according to their medium-term improvement in GPI between 2004–05 and 2007–08. Group 1 represents the high-achieving group and Group 2 the low-achieving group. Students (grades 5 and 6) were tested on mathematics using the 2007 TIMSS questions.

student learning. The roles of parents, communities, and local administrations in enhancing school improvements are already important factors for improving gender parity in access (for example, JICA 2010), and they could also be vital for improving student learning.

Quality of Systems and Policies

To address the various issues in improving the quality of learning, what policy reforms need to be considered further? This section examines the quality of Yemeni policies in comparison with global empirical evidence and best practices, mainly using the conceptual framework, diagnostic tools, and policy database developed by the World Bank and its partners under the program System Approach for Better Education Results (SABER).[15]

Assessment Systems

Many countries provide either an examination or a standardized assessment during the so-called primary cycle, but that is not the case with the current assessment system in Yemen (see table 13-5).[16] At the final year of basic education (grade 9), Yemen has a regional examination to qualify for a graduation certificate.[17] The graduates who pass the grade 9 exams have the right to enroll in public secondary schools (from grade 10 on), and they are to be accepted by public schools on a first-come, first-served basis (in practice, better-scoring students go on to secondary education, while the others may go into vocational training, the

15. The SABER is an initiative that helps countries systematically examine and strengthen the performance of their education systems to achieve learning for all. The SABER works on about fifteen policy domains (education issues or subsectors) to design key policy indicators based on existing empirical evidence of good practices and diagnostic tools that enable data collection, scoring, and assessment. The results are often summarized as a country or regional report. For details, see http://go.worldbank.org/NK2EK7MKV0.

16. The categories of assessment are according to the SABER framework (Clarke, Liberman, and Ramirez 2012).

17. The certificates for grades 1 to 8 of basic education and grades 10 to 11 of secondary education are issued by the schools; only certificates for grades 9 and 12 are issued by the MOE. If students want to move from one school to another within the same district, they need to get the approval of the District Education Office; if students want to move to another school in another district but within the same governorate, they need to get the approval of the Governorate Education Office.

TABLE 13-5. National Examination and Assessment System, Yemen and Selected Countries, 2010–11

	Arab countries				Asian countries	
Education characteristic	Yemen	Jordan	Tunisia	Egypt	Japan	Indonesia
Years of education						
Primary or basic	9[a]	10[a]	6	6	6	6
Secondary (lower + upper)	3	2	3 + 4	3 + 3	3 + 3	3 + 3
Years of compulsory education	9	10	11	9	9	9
Standardized assessments of student learning						
Primary cycle or up to grade 6	n.a	Assess (grade 5)	Assess (grade 4)	Assess (grade 4) Exam (grade 6)	Assess (grade 6)	Exam (grade 6)
Lower secondary	Exam (grade 9)	Assess (grade 8) Exam (grade 10)	Exam (grade 9)	Assess (grade 8) Exam (grade 9)	Assess (grade 9) Exam (grade 9)	Exam (grade 9)
Upper secondary	Exam (grade 12)	Exam (grade 12)	Exam (after grade 12)	Assess (grade 10) Exam (grade 11/12)	Exam (grade 12)	Exam (grade 12)

Sources: SABER—teacher online database (accessed June 2012); UNESCO, 2011; World Bank, 1999. For Japan, information on the National Assessment of Academic Ability is available at www.nier.go.jp.

a. The duration of lower secondary is considered as grades 7–9 for Yemen and grades 7–10 for Jordan in this table for comparison. Exam: Either national or regional examination that decides for completion or entry into the next level of the specific level of education. Assess: Nationwide all or representative sample learning assessment (which does not decide pass or fail at grade or specific level of education).

labor market, and so forth).[18] This system is quite different from that in some East Asian countries, such as Japan and Indonesia, which have competitive selection systems for admission to public senior secondary schools. At the end of (upper) secondary education, Yemeni students need to pass a national examination to receive a graduation certificate in either an art or a science field. The scores are used as selection criteria to enter public and private universities. New graduates need to wait for one year before being enrolled. Competitive departments, such

18. Although in practice lower-scoring students go to vocational training, they have to go through a selection process. This selection process is not due to vocational education being selective but due to the limited number of vocational institutes, which are concentrated in urban areas (Al-Seyani 2012).

as medicine and engineering, often require students to take additional entrance examinations. There are always possibilities for students who passed their graduation examinations to enter universities, provided that they do not have a strong preference for which department they study in or object to paying additional fees for evening shifts at public or private universities.

To fill the information gap on learning achievement at the primary level, Yemen is considering introducing a national assessment at the lower grades of basic education in its Updated Sector Plan 2013–2015 (Republic of Yemen 2012a), although it is not yet sure where it is to be implemented. In terms of international large-scale assessments, the government participated in three rounds of TIMSS and plans to use TIMSS as a monitoring tool to raise student achievement in light of international standards (Republic of Yemen 2012a). However, questions are raised by development partners on the necessity of having Yemen join the next round of TIMSS given the lack of relevance of its curriculum to TIMSS and its low performance (Al-Seyani 2012). While this may be a good opportunity to consider the relevance of TIMSS for Yemen, there is a risk of dropping it without having any alternative assessment opportunity.

Classroom assessments could provide swift feedback for improving teaching and learning activities (Clarke, Liberman, and Ramirez 2012). In Yemen at the basic education level, the results of two classroom examinations are used as a pass-fail test for promotion to the next grade (Al-Seyani 2012). The exceptions are for grades 1 to 3, from which students can move to the next grade regardless of scores, but this policy is now being reconsidered for possible revision.

Teachers

The SABER program on teacher policies classifies and analyzes education systems around the world according to eight core teacher policy goals that all education systems should aim to achieve. These goals were selected because

—they are related to either student performance or teacher performance through theory or evidence

—they are priorities for resource allocation

—they are actionable (that is, governments can have a direct influence on them through policy reform).

TABLE 13-6. Status of Teacher Policies, Yemen and Selected Countries

Policy goal	Yemen	Egypt	Jordan	Tunisia
1 Setting clear expectations for teachers	◉◉◉○	◉◉◉○	◉◉◉○	◉◉◉○
2 Attracting the best into teaching	◉○○○	◉◉◉○	◉◉◉○	◉◉◉○
3 Preparing teachers with useful training and experience	◉◉◉○	◉◉◉◉	◉◉◉○	◉◉◉◉
4 Matching teachers' skills with students' needs	◉○○○	◉◉◉◉	◉◉◉◉	◉◉◉○
5 Leading teachers with strong principals	◉○○○	◉◉◉○	◉○○○	◉◉◉○
6 Monitoring teaching and learning	◉◉◉○	◉◉◉◉	◉◉◉○	◉◉○○
7 Supporting teachers to improve instruction	◉○○○	◉◉◉○	◉◉◉○	◉◉◉◉
8 Motivating teachers to perform	◉○○○	◉◉◉○	◉◉○○	◉◉◉○

Source: World Bank SABER online database, 2010–11.
Note: ◉○○○ latent; ◉◉○○ emerging; ◉◉◉○ established; ◉◉◉◉ advanced.

Education systems are classified according to their level of achievement of each of these goals. The four levels of classification are "latent," "emerging," "established," and "advanced."

According to the SABER teacher database,[19] Yemeni teacher policies are assessed as "established" on the three policy goals but "latent" on the others (table 13-6). Benchmarking with global good practices suggests that it is important for Yemen to improve the quality of teacher policies and their implementation so that teachers are assigned to even hard-to-staff schools, are motivated to attend and perform at school, and are supported to improve instruction through better training.

For the goal of "matching teachers' skills with students' needs," Yemeni policies are classified as "latent." Yemen faces difficulties in recruiting teachers with the needed skills (World Bank 2011a). Finding teachers who are willing to work in rural areas is hard. No regulation mandates that public school teachers work in hard-to-staff schools at some point in their career, and incentives for teachers to work at hard-to-staff schools are also assessed as latent. According to the 1999 law for teachers working in rural areas, only monetary bonuses or allowances are to be provided, depending on an area's remoteness. It is difficult to fire teachers who reject rural assignments. As a short-term

19. Data as of August 2012 are available for fifty countries on the website, SABER: System Approach for Better Education Results (http://saber.worldbank.org/index.cfm?indx=8&tb=1).

measure, the government or schools hire teachers who may not have the required qualifications, especially if they are female and/or if they are in the same rural area as the schools needing teachers. However, this approach also makes equality a quality issue to be tackled as soon as possible.

Policies with the goal of "supporting teachers to improve instruction" also are latent for Yemen. Yemen does not require professional development training although the government has conducted a series of refresher courses or has upgraded in-service training (World Bank 2007). Yemen is also latent for one sub-indicator regarding the extent to which entry-level teachers are required to be familiar with classroom practices. There also are plans for training a certain number of teachers with an emphasis on classroom performance (Republic of Yemen 2012a). The Ministry of Education management information system would be designed to include data on teacher training experiences so that it could be used for personnel management (Al-Seyani 2012). It is crucial to use such information for ensuring the quality standards for teachers among schools.

Among policies with the goal of "motivating teachers to perform," a basic but important challenge is teacher absenteeism. Although Yemeni policies, as in the other Arab countries, mandate penalties for teacher absenteeism, there are many issues regarding the practical mechanisms implementing these policies (World Bank 2011a). A survey found that the absenteeism rate, defined as the percentage of teachers who are absent on the day of a survey visit without prior approval of leave, was 14 percent on average among teachers in basic education schools (World Bank 2006). The absence rate defined as the percentage of teachers who are absent on the day of a visit with an official or unofficial excuse was 19 percent on average. This teacher absence rate is fairly significant compared with that in several other countries with similar social and economic indicators. Smaller schools tend to have greater teacher absenteeism than larger schools because on average, a teacher in a small school teaches more subjects than a teacher in a larger school: 4.2 and 1.7 subjects, respectively. Teacher absenteeism can also have a more severe effect on students in rural areas than in urban areas because rural schools have fewer registered teachers and it is difficult to find substitute teachers for the teachers who are absent. Above all, the number of teachers on a payroll was much larger than the number of teachers in the annual education survey (198,671 versus 171,101), implying a serious issue with ghost teachers (nearly 30,000 salaried persons who are not recognized by any school director at all) (World Bank 2006). Recently governorates started salary reductions to punish teachers for absenteeism and the use of the remaining budget for other items in school operations (Al-Seyani 2012). To our knowledge, no information is yet available on whether that measure has reduced teacher absenteeism or removed ghost teachers from the payroll system.

Policies seeking to evaluate how well students learn are relatively well assessed, because Arab countries, including Yemen, have some student evaluations, but few policies address teacher performance in relation to the results of these evaluations, thus making feedback on teachers insufficient (World Bank 2011a). Teacher evaluations are to be conducted by subnational and local authorities every year; however, these evaluations are not required for all teachers nor do they take into account progress in student learning (World Bank 2011b). As in the other Arab countries, Yemen does not have a policy for feedback from parents (World Bank 2011a). The mechanism of parental feedback to teacher performance is not clearly defined in the Updated Sector Plan 2013–2015 (Republic of Yemen 2012a), although the involvement of parents and communities in school is emphasized. The role of school committees, including fathers' and mothers' councils, is to include monitoring teacher absences but not teaching performance (Al-Seyani 2012). In fact, one survey notes that schools with fathers' and mothers' councils suffer 5 percent less teacher absenteeism on average than schools without them (World Bank 2006, p. 34), underscoring the importance of parental and community involvement.

Curriculum and Textbooks

The official total of instruction hours per academic year is short in Yemen, as in some other Arab countries (World Bank 2011a; World Bank 2011b), but actual teaching time is known to be even shorter. Yemen has 729.6 hours of teaching per year in primary and 864 hours in secondary schools, which is only 70 percent of the time of "high-performing systems" at the secondary education level. Moreover, the time to deliver the curriculum is often constrained due to high levels of teacher absenteeism and limited hours of operations of schools, particularly in rural areas (World Bank and the Republic of Yemen 2010).[20] Although short instructional time has an effect on students' learning skills and knowledge, instructional time itself does not seem to be a topic of reform in the Updated Sector Plan 2013–2015 (Republic of Yemen 2012a), which is based on the Basic Education Development Strategy (BEDS 2003–2015). Instead, the policy focuses on measures to increase the actual instructional time to meet the official requirement of good quality (180 to 190 days), for example, by training and supervising teachers (Al-Seyani 2012).

The difference between policy intent and implementation also appears to be a matter of concern for curriculum content. For example, the TIMSS 2007 shows that the "intended curriculum" of Yemen covers the TIMSS mathematics items at more or less the same level as the international average—the same level, for example, as Japan (Mullis, Martin, and Foy 2008). However, "taught" mathematics topics cover only 46 percent of all items, the smallest percentage among the participant countries. It generally seems that high-scoring countries such as Singapore have a high percentage of "taught" items (Mullis, Martin, and Foy 2008). The contents of classroom activities are an issue if the country wants to make the education system perform in line with international standards.[21]

Actual teaching practice may not catch up with a reformed curriculum in Yemen. Although the policy intends to provide one set of textbooks per student in basic education, the 2011 JICA-ERDC survey shows that in the surveyed rural schools, only 67 percent of students in grades 5 and 6 and 71 percent of those in grades 8 and 9 have all the

20. Research on actual student learning days vis-à-vis official instructional days indicates that actual learning days are only 77.9 percent of official days in Tunisia and 71.1 percent in Morocco due to school closures, teacher absences, teacher available days, classroom task days, and student absences (Abadzi 2007, p. 22). In the case of Morocco, there are positive correlations between rural schools and school closures, inert instructional time, and time for classroom management. The results suggest that schools in rural and poor environments have fewer learning days than schools in urban and more advantaged communities (Abadzi 2007).

21. The issue is not only about subject coverage but also test method. Most of Yemeni grade 4 students are not familiar with the type of questions and implementation method used in TIMSS (that is, most students have not taken any test prepared by external agencies or test that includes items that are not specifically taught in class (Al-Seyani 2012).

textbooks that they are supposed to have. Similarly, despite the existence of a teacher's guide with instructions for teaching a competence-based curriculum, the guidebooks are delivered at the end of the academic year. Furthermore, the guidebooks are difficult to comprehend due to a number of errors and mistakes in their content. The contents of materials for teaching and learning, references, and books in the libraries are inconsistent (quoted in World Bank and Republic of Yemen 2010).

School Autonomy, Community Participation, and Accountability

The SABER program on school autonomy and accountability classifies and benchmarks school-based management policies with the goal of promoting better conditions for learning and thereby improving student performance. As pointed out by Bruns, Filmer, and Patrinos (2011), if school autonomy and accountability are deepened, schools can redefine their incentive structure to create better conditions for learning and teaching. In the process, parents become clients of the education system and partners in the management of education at the school level. There are five main indicators of policy goals for better school autonomy and accountability, and each of them has a set of sub-indicators, all of which are assessed and scored (see table 13-7).

According to SABER's school autonomy and accountability scale, Yemeni policies overall are low on school autonomy and accountability (table 13-7). The Yemeni government has a policy of decentralizing public primary education expenditure management to the governorate level but not to the school level. In practice, the key responsibilities for both personnel and operational budgets remain at the central level, as discussed below. Still, local authorities, schools, and communities share responsibilities, and they all play an important part in helping children learn. In terms of personnel matters, public school regular teachers are hired by regional governments (governorates) according to the number of new hires approved by the central government in Yemen. As discussed above regarding teacher policies, teacher evaluations also are conducted by subnational and local authorities although communities and parents contribute to monitoring teacher absenteeism.

While contract teachers normally follow the same rules as regular teachers, there are some exceptions: schools or school management councils may contract with teachers using funds provided by communities

TABLE 13-7. School Autonomy and Accountability, Yemen and Selected Countries

	Autonomy in budget	Autonomy in personnel management	Role of school council on school governance	School and student assessment	Accountability
Yemen[a]	◉○○○	◉◉○○	◉○○○	◉○○○	◉○○○
Senegal	◉○○○	◉○○○	◉○○○	◉◉◉○	◉○○○
Lao PDR	◉◉○○	◉○○○	◉◉○○	◉◉○○	◉○○○
Vietnam	◉◉○○	◉○○○	◉○○○	◉◉○○	◉◉○○
Mexico	◉◉○○	◉○○○	◉○○○	◉◉○○	◉◉○○
Indonesia	◉◉○○	◉○○○	◉◉◉○	◉◉◉○	◉◉◉○
Malaysia	◉◉○○	◉○○○	◉◉◉○	◉◉◉○	◉◉◉○
Thailand	◉◉○○	◉○○○	◉◉◉○	◉◉◉○	◉◉◉○

Source: Prepared by author, using data from the World Bank SABER website, Patrinos, Shibuya, and Arcia (2012) for Senegal, and Al-Seyani (2012) for Yemen.
a. Yemen data were collected only for this paper, not validated by the World Bank SABER team.
Note: ◉○○○ latent; ◉◉○○ emerging; ◉◉◉○ established; ◉◉◉◉ advanced.

or external donors. This method of contracting teachers has been used especially in remote areas, where regular teachers are reluctant to go and where schools prefer to have local teachers. One of the typical issues is the difficulty of changing the status of contract teachers to regular teachers due to the presence of many decisionmakers, fiscal constraints, and low qualifications of school- or community-contracted teachers. Unlike in some other countries—for example, Kenya (Duflo, Dupas, and Kremer 2011)—no evidence is so far available on whether contract teachers perform better or worse than regular teachers in Yemen.

The nonsalary operational budget is also mostly managed by central or regional governments in Yemen. The Ministry of Education (MOE) prints new textbooks and distributes them to district education offices so that each student receives a set of textbooks each semester. School directors are supposed to pick them up and distribute them to students; some school managers use school fees to rent trucks to deliver textbooks (World Bank 2006; World Bank and Republic of Yemen 2010). However, due to delays in printing and lack of a distribution budget, the full packages of textbooks often do not reach the students on time; other teaching materials, such as chalk and flipcharts, rarely reach basic schools. Budgets do not allocate funds for utilities such as water tanks. Shortages of operational funds often are filled by so-called community participation fees, which are collected by schools. However, these fees have been eliminated for all students in grades 1 to 3 as well as for girls in grades 4 to 6 (Republic of Yemen 2012a). The fee waivers often have been associated with school grant schemes in African countries, such as Kenya and Uganda (Fredriksen 2007).[22] Yemen also approved a Cabinet decree on school operation budgets (school grants) in 2008, although it has not yet been enacted or actually budgeted by the Ministry of Finance.

For school grants, the MOE has experimented with participatory school-based management programs with development partners, namely UNICEF for Child Friendly Schools (since 2008), World Bank and its co-financers for a whole school development program (since 2009), and JICA for a project, Broadening Regional Initiative for Developing Girls' Education (BRIDGE) (since 2005).[23] The three programs have been piloted in different areas under different guidelines. Yet all share similar features to facilitate school councils, including having representatives of fathers, mothers, and communities prepare and implement school improvement plans with grants and voluntary contributions (summarized in table 13-8). Fathers' and mothers' councils are parts of the school committees that manage the school grants, and thus parents have the right to review the financial report. The results are promising, although challenges remain. For example, BRIDGE worked to improve gender parity rapidly, but to maintain progress, it appeared that local administrations would need to continue monitoring and facilitating schools and communities for gender parity (Yuki and others 2012). The government of Yemen now has plans for

22. Teacher salaries account for the majority of public education budgets while communities contribute to nontuition costs such as examination and certification fees. The amount is not large but it is known to be a burden, especially for poor families who have many school-age children; consequently, the government has started exempting them from community contribution fees.

23. The three programs were built on earlier efforts by the MOE for institutionalizing community and parental participation. The government started institutionalizing and developing its community participation capacity in the late 1990s. For example, with the assistance from donors such as the GTZ and the World Bank, the government established a community participation unit in the Ministry of Education and promoted mothers' and fathers' councils, whose responsibilities are to care for school facilities, monitor teachers' attendance, and assist needy children in their schools (for example, World Bank 2004; Jones 2005).

TABLE 13-8. Participatory School-Based Management Programs with School Grants, Yemen

Project or program name	BRIDGE 1[a]	Basic Education Development Project (BEDP) 1 component 3.2, Community Participation and Literacy	Child Friendly School (CFS)	Updated sector plan 2013–15 School-based development
Partner	JICA	IDA, DFID, Netherlands	UNICEF	MOE with all partners
Years and targets	2005–06 to 2008–11 59 schools in Taiz governorate	2008– (implementation started in 2009) 60 schools: 30 schools each in Hadramout and Al Mahrah governorates Plan to expand 120–150 schools	2008– 110 schools in 11 districts in 5 governorates (Hodeidah, Taiz, Ibb, AlDhale, Lahej)	2013–15 700 schools in 2012 and 2013 to cover all basic and secondary schools
Tools to directly support schools	Grant $3,000 based on school plan prepared by school committee	School grant US$1,500	US$1,000 grant per year (the year 2007)	300,000 YER (about US$1,500) per school

Source: JICA (2008, 2009); World Bank (2004); Republic of Yemen (2012a), p. 54; Republic of Yemen (2012b).
a. BRIDGE 2 (2009–) is currently suspended for security reasons. It is for Dhamar and Taiz governorates.

various measures to scale up these experiments—for example, by standardizing the manuals of similar projects, enacting a decree to provide operational budgets to schools (as school grants), facilitating the establishment of fathers' and mothers' councils, and implementing activities for raising awareness of gender equality and quality of learning activities (Republic of Yemen 2012a).

Table 13-7 indicates that school accountability (measured in terms of availability and use of education and finance information) also is low in Yemen. It is important to help schools become accountable for results in order to ensure continuous community involvement in school management and to provide schools with more resources and responsibilities. Information is available at the central government level in terms of basic data, such as the number of students by gender and facility;[24] however, there appears to be no standardized system to report such information, originally collected at the school level, back to the communities and parents. Test scores are currently communicated at the student level; there are no comparisons between schools and thus no way to judge whether schools are doing well or whether they can or should do better. There are no criteria within the MOE to assess schools. Schools do not use student assessments to make pedagogical adjustments or to change school materials. The results of national exams at grades 9 and 12 are made available to students who take the exams, but comparisons are not made among schools or over time.[25]

Comparisons among governorates, which have a certain decentralized budget authority, often are made, but the analyses rarely report changes over the years, nor are they used for improving budget allocations and implementation. For the BEDS (2003–15) and the Updated Sector Plan 2013–2015, the MOE has prepared a projection model of basic inputs for target enrollments at the national level but not for each governorate. Although there was a plan to prepare an action plan by governorate, only a few governorates that benefited from external technical assistance prepared action plans.[26]

Policy Implication for a New Education Plan

The Arab Spring brought great attention from the international community to the needs of Arab youth and thus to the need to increase the relevance of higher education and vocational training so that they can find good jobs or create their own businesses. The trainability and employability of young people can and should be ensured by a good-quality education in earlier grades. Making efforts to improve the quality of education for all girls and boys is imperative for inclusive

24. Four out of the six target indicators have data on education-related Millennium Development Goals for 2010, according to the UNDP database. According to the UNESCO statistical database (UIS), 40 percent of the 346 indicators have data for 2010. The proportion is not low compared with that of several other countries in the Arab region (see statistical appendix tables for details).

25. Students also can access the results through the Internet. The data are for individual students. Data by school are not available online (Al-Seyani 2012).

26. Hajah and Mareb governorates prepared their plans based on the Medium-Term Result Framework for the years 2011–15 with support from the GTZ. Hadramout governorate also has an annual plan (Al-Seyani 2012).

development. Greater and more urgent efforts are especially needed in Yemen because it is the poorest country in the Arab region and also is affected by political conflicts. The country's recent conflicts are reported to have negative effects on learning—for example, by displacing 64,000 children from six to fourteen years of age and by arresting 13,000 school teachers and managers (Office for the Coordination of Humanitarian Affairs 2011, p. 57). Schools also are used for shelter by displaced people or taken as bases by armed groups (UNICEF 2012).

How is the new government going to address these enormous challenges in education? The government has committed itself to developing the National Education Vision for Yemen (NEVY), which is expected to be finalized by mid-2015. This master plan would implement one overall education strategy to guide the plans of the different subsectors (including basic, secondary, and higher education and vocational training). The schedule for developing NEVY gives the government and its development partners time to formulate better policies and ensure their implementation along with citizens, who can now be involved more actively than before. To accomplish this before 2015, the Updated Sector Plan 2013–2015 was recently updated and discussed with the development partners.

As discussed earlier, the Sector Plan proposes various reforms to improve basic education quality and calls for partners' support to fill the financing gaps. The government as a whole should be strongly committed to its implementation and supported by its development partners, both financially and technically, so that the country can avoid any trade-off between expansion of access to education and improvement of the quality of education. On the basis of our analyses of student achievement and quality of policies, we want to underscore three types of actions, among many, that should be enhanced in the short run and carried out continuously to improve the quality of learning for all.

First, teacher management policies need to be strengthened and implemented by all the stakeholders, including administrations, schools, and communities, to ensure that students, even in disadvantaged areas, learn from motivated teachers who fully teach the intended curriculum, in a class of a reasonable size. Specific policy measures may include

—micro-planning of teacher needs for schools and assigning teachers to rural schools, with greater attention to current and potential variations in class size to further reach out-of-school children

—monitoring actual teacher placement and daily attendance to reduce the number of ghost teachers and absenteeism

—linking teacher placement and attendance to actual salary received and providing the needed teaching in difficult areas, in a transparent way

—improving supervision to assess and guide schools

—improving recordkeeping and information on teachers in order to give priority to teachers who need professional development and in-service training the most

—facilitating involvement of parents and communities in monitoring the attendance of school directors and teachers.

Second, nonpersonnel school resources need to be improved, especially in relatively disadvantaged areas where schools may have difficulty requesting parental or community funding and voluntary contributions. With donors' support, Yemen could scale up the existing mechanisms for school grants to reward communities and schools that aim to improve access for girls and disadvantaged students and enhance the quality of learning. Currently, only a limited number of basic schools are to receive such school grants, although according to a Cabinet decree the Sector Plan aims to cover all schools by 2015. Such resources should ideally be provided by domestic funds. However, the use of external funds can be justified to cope with the recent crisis and to better achieve the international goal of universal primary education without sacrificing the quality of learning. Providing sufficient grants for schools is key for inclusive development and economic growth. In fragile countries, school grants can be used not only as operational or recurrent budgets but also as investment budgets. Meanwhile, it is important, by comparing experiences of governorates, to refine mechanisms that would improve administrative efficiency in transferring funds to schools and targeting (for example, differentiating grant amounts by school size and community poverty level) and in monitoring and advising schools and communities on school improvement plans. Such mechanisms should also develop the institutional capacity of communities to participate in school governance and increase their access to school information and their involvement in improving student learning opportunities and outcomes.

Third, there is also a need to improve schools' transparency and accountability regarding school resources and results. In the short term, the MOE can and should promote the use of available data by schools and local administrations to self-assess their current status and over-year changes in key educational resources and outcomes and to compare them with those of other schools and localities. As a feasible starting point, the MOE can post, on its website, a list of all schools with basic indicators, such as the number of students by gender and per teacher, by using the annual education surveys (AES) conducted since 1999.[27] The MOE should also distribute the list of schools to local administrations that do not yet have online access and encourage them to discuss the information with schools. Although schools themselves must know what the issues are, less systematic information is available to indicate how each school and/or its district is doing over time and in comparison with others and to advise them on how to improve. Such information also should be made available to community-level stakeholders—such as fathers' and mothers' councils and school management committees, where such institutionalized bodies are functioning. It is also important for the central government and its development partners to efficiently allocate and possibly increase resources based on needs and progress. All stakeholders should be able to get information on progress in implementation of the teacher management policies discussed above as well as school-level management reforms. Such information would greatly help to link schools, communities, all levels of administration, and development partners in efforts to improve education in Yemen.

While the quality and timely availability of AES data are expected to improve, increasing access to and use of the available data can motivate stakeholders to accurately submit their school data in yearly data collection. The MOE and other related agencies could also advance data comparability between the AES and other databases on data related to examinations, personnel management, finance, child population, and so forth by standardizing the software used as well as the identification

---

27. The school list could and should include at least each school's name, ID number, location, the names of the directors who responded or were supposed to respond to the survey, and enrollment figures by gender and for teachers. (An example is available on the homepage of the Ministry of Education for Uganda.) Then, the MOE can gradually add lists of schools with the same ID numbers for previous years, which would enable users to know trends over time for specific schools or regions of interest.

numbers of schools and localities. This move would allow the MOE to add more key indicators to its school- and locality-level database for wider use and to increase transparency and accountability at all levels, which are necessary for inclusive development.

Development partners often support the development of project-specific monitoring databases and/or collection of baseline/endline survey data, focusing on their pilot schools and control schools. If such databases were designed in advance to make the data comparable and merged into the MOE's education management information system (EMIS) (for example, by using the same school and district IDs), it would facilitate both long-term comprehensive monitoring and short-term use of MOE data and improve data quality. This move could also help reduce the cost of monitoring for development partners because an improved EMIS could be used for project-specific performance comparison with a nontreatment group. Other than specific projects, donors also support theme-specific surveys, such as TIMSS, which could help not only education researchers but also administrators in monitoring and guiding schools and teachers if the results and instruments (for example, TIMSS math test items in Arabic) are disseminated widely. While the government is planning to introduce new national learning assessment surveys in basic education, it is important to develop such an assessment, learning from experiences with TIMSS and other relevant surveys in terms of not only survey contents but also use of the assessment results.

The Yemeni government needs to use various types of information to regularly monitor the implementation of the education strategy's key outcomes and input indicators, such as student-teacher ratios and coverage of textbooks, in order to ensure that the national average targets are being translated into practice and to help determine how action plans and budgets need to be revised to support inclusive development, paying attention to the areas in greater need. Articulating the strategy's targets, financial commitments, and progress would show the strong commitment of the central leadership to all stakeholders, including local communities, schools, and administrations—all of which have important roles in the strategy to improve the quality and equity of basic education—and thus improve its implementation.

TABLE 13A-1. OLS Estimation of GPI Changes, BRIDGE and Non-BRIDGE schools

	Coefficient	Standard error
Female-to-male student ratio (grades 1–6), 2004	−0.455	0.051***
Female share in teachers, 2004	0.498	0.241**
BRIDGE 1 pilot (1 = yes, 0 = no)	0.097	0.059*
_cons	0.130	
R-squared	0.376	
Number of observations, schools	174	

Source: AES 2004, 2007.
Note: The dependent variable is point change in the school's female-to-male student ratio (grades 1–6) from 2004 to 2007 in Maqbanah and Mahwiya districts. This estimation controls for district effects.
***$p < .01$, **$p < 0.05$, *$p < 0.1$

TABLE 13A-2. MDG Education and Gender Equality, Yemen and Selected Countries

	2.1. Net enrollment ratio in primary education		2.2. Proportion of pupils starting grade 1 who reach last grade of primary		2.3. Literacy rate of 15- to 24-year-olds, women and men	
	2000	2010	2000	2010	2000	2010
Egypt	91.8	96.3	n.a.	n.a.	n.a.	87.5
Jordan	92.2	90.7	96.5[a]	n.a.	n.a.	98.8
Morocco	71.0	94.1	73.3	90.5	n.a.	79.5
Saudi Arabia	n.a.	89.9[a]	n.a.	n.a.	95.9	97.8
Tunisia	94.9	99.4[a]	88.3	n.a.	n.a.	n.a.
Yemen	56.7[a]	78.2	68.8[a]	n.a.	n.a.	85.2

	3.1. Gender parity index in					
	Primary level enrollment		Secondary level enrollment		Tertiary level enrollment	
	2000	2010	2000	2010	2000	2010
Egypt	0.92	0.96	0.92	0.96	n.a.	0.91
Jordan	1.01	1.00	1.04	1.06	1.15	1.16
Morocco	0.84	0.94	0.79	n.a.	0.72	0.87[a]
Saudi Arabia	n.a.	0.99	n.a.	0.95	1.27	1.12
Tunisia	0.93	0.96[a]	1.03	1.06[a]	0.96[a]	1.51[a]
Yemen	0.63	0.82	0.41	0.62	0.27	n.a.

Source: UNDP MDGs on-line data, accessed August 2012.
a. 1999 or 2001 (not 2000), 2009 or 2011 (not 2010).
n.a. = Not available.

TABLE 13A-3. Number of Education Indicators Available in UNESCO Database, Yemen and Selected Countries

	All levels				Primary education			
	2000		2010		2000		2010	
Egypt[a]	214	20%	199	19%	129	37%	67	19%[a]
Jordan	395	37%	307	29%	147	42%	138	40%
Morocco	471	44%	473	44%	193	56%	168	49%
Saudi Arabia	132	12%	409	38%	10	3%	85	25%
Tunisia[b]	369	34%	36	3%[b]	172	50%	10	3%[b]
Yemen	283	26%	308	29%	125	36%	138	40%
Total indicators	1,071		1,071		346		346	

Source: UNESCO Institute for Statistics on-line data, accessed August 2012.

a. In 2009, 144 indicators for primary education were available.

b. For Tunisia, 383 indicators for all levels were available in 2008, 318 in 2009; 162 indicators for primary education were available in 2008, 132 in 2009.

References

Abadzi, Helen. 2007. "Absenteeism and Beyond: Instructional Time Loss and Consequences." Washington: World Bank.

Altinok, Nadir. 2010. "Do School Resources Increase School Quality?" Working Paper DT 2010/3. Dijon: Institute for Research in the Sociology and Economics of Education (May).

Angel-Urdinola, Diego F., and Kimie Tanabe. 2012. "Micro-Determinants of Informal Employment in the Middle East and North Africa Region." SP Discussion Paper 1201. Washington: World Bank.

Assaad, Ragui, and others. 2009. "Youth Exclusion in Yemen: Tackling the Twin Deficits of Human Development and Natural Resources." Wolfensohn Center for Development, Brookings, and Dubai School of Government.

Bouhlila, Donia S. 2011. "The Quality of Secondary Education in the Middle East and North Africa: What Can We Learn from TIMSS' Results?" *Compare* 41, no. 3: 327–52.

Bruns, Barbara, Deon Filmer, and Harry Anthony Patrinos. 2011. "Making Schools Work: New Evidence on Accountability Reforms." Washington: World Bank.

Clarke, Marguerite, Julia Liberman, and Maria-Jose Ramirez. 2012. "Student Assessment." In *Strengthening Education Quality in East Asia: SABER System Assessment and Benchmarking for Education Results*, edited by Harry A. Patrinos. Washington: World Bank.

Collins, Penelope, and Souhila Messaoud-Galusi. 2012. "EdData II: Student Performance on the Early Grade Reading Assessment (EGRA) in Yemen." Research Triangle Park, N.C.: RTI International.

Duflo, Esther, Pascaline Dupas, and Michael Kremer. 2011. "Peer Effects, Pupil-Teacher Ratio, and Teacher Incentives: Evidence from a Randomized Evaluation in Kenya." *American Economic Review* 101 (August 2011): 1739–74.

Ezzine, Mourad, Simon Thacker, and Nadereh Chamlou. 2011. "An Exception to the Gender Gap in Education: The Middle East?" MENA Knowledge and Learning Quick Notes Series 41. Washington: World Bank.

Fredriksen, Birger. 2007. "School Grants: One Efficient Instrument to Address Key Barriers to Attaining Education for All." Capacity Development Workshop, "Country Leadership and Implementation for Results in the EFA FTI Partnership," Cape Town, South Africa, July 16–19.

Fuller, Bruce, and Prema Clarke. 1994. "Raising School Effects While Ignoring Culture? Local Conditions and the Influence of Classroom Tools, Rules, and Pedagogy." *Review of Educational Research* 64, no. 1: 119–57.

General Education Improvement Program (GEIP). 2012. "Intervention: FGI Foundation Grade Initiative." Printout distributed at "Republic of Yemen: Second Basic Education Development Project: Yemen Education Mission," Amman, Jordan, July 1–10, 2012.

Gove, Amber, and Peter Cvelich. 2011. "Early Reading: Igniting Education for All: A Report by the Early Grade Learning Community of Practice," rev. ed. Research Triangle Park, N.C.: Research Triangle Institute.

Government of Yemen and World Bank. 2004. "Republic of Yemen: Education for All by 2015—Fast Track Initiative." Country Credible Plan. Sana'a, Yemen: Ministry of Education.

Hanushek, Eric A. 1995. "Interpreting Recent Research on Schooling in Developing Countries." *World Bank Research Observer.* Washington: World Bank.

Hungi, Njora, and others. 2010. "SACMEQ III Project Results: Pupil Achievement Levels in Reading and Mathematics." Working Document 1. Southern and Eastern Africa Consortium for Monitoring Educational Quality.

Japan International Cooperation Agency (JICA). 2010. "Baseline Analysis Report for the JICA Broadening Regional Initiative for Developing Girls' Education (BRIDGE) Phase II Project." Tokyo.

Jones, Adele. 2005. "Conflict Development and Community Participation in Education: Pakistan and Yemen." *International Asian Forum* 36, no. 3–4: 289–310.

King, Kenneth. 2011. "Eight Proposals for a Strengthened Focus on Technical and Vocational Education and Training (TVET) in the Education for All (EFA) Agenda." Background paper prepared for the Education for All Global Monitoring Report 2012. Paris: UNESCO.

Al-Mekhlafy, Tawfig A. 2009. "Performance of Fourth Graders of the Republic of Yemen in TIMSS 2007: A Secondary Analysis." Sana'a, Yemen.

Messaoud-Galusi, Souhila, and others. 2012. "EdData II: Student Performance in Reading and Mathematics, Pedagogic Practice, and School Management in Doukkala Abda, Morocco." Research Triangle Park, N.C.: RTI International.

Ministry of Health and Population and UNICEF. 2008. "Yemen Multiple Indicator Cluster Survey 2006: Final Report."

Mohammed bin Rashid Al Maktoum Foundation and UNDP. 2012. "Arab Knowledge Report 2010/2011: Preparing Future Generations for the Knowledge Society." United Arab Emirates.

Mullis, Ina V. S., Michael O. Martin, and Pierre Foy. 2008. "TIMSS 2007 International Mathematics Report: Finding from IEA's Trends in International Mathematics and Science Study at the Fourth and Eighth Grades." Boston: TIMSS and PIRLS International Study Center, Lynch School of Education, Boston College.

Mullis, Ina V. S., and others. 2012. "TIMSS 2011 International Results in Mathematics. TIMSS and PIRLS International Study Center, Lynch School of Education, Boston College.

Office for the Coordination of Humanitarian Affairs (OCHA). 2011. Yemen: 2011 Humanitarian Response Plan. New York. United Nations.

Patrinos, Harry A., Kazuro Shibuya, and Gustavo Arcia. 2012. *SABER School Autonomy and Accountability Senegal.* SABER Country Report 2012. Washington: World Bank.

Republic of Yemen. 2012a. Updated Sectors Plan 2013–2015: Medium-Range Results Framework." Sana'a, Yemen: Ministry of Education.

———. 2012b. "Second Medium-Term Result Framework for the Years 2011–2015." Sana'a, Yemen: Ministry of Education.

Al-Seyani, Hamoud M. 2012. "Memo to Japan International Cooperation Agency Research Institute." Sana'a, Yemen. November 9.

UNESCO (United Nations Educational, Scientific, and Cultural Organization). 2011. "EFA Global Monitoring Report 2011: The Hidden Crisis: Armed Conflict and Education." Paris.

UNICEF (United Nations Children's Fund). 2012. "UNICEF Yemen Situation Report: Reporting Period: April 2012."

World Bank. 2003. "Better Governance for Development in the Middle East and North Africa: Enhancing Inclusiveness and Accountability." Washington.

———. 2004. "Project Appraisal Document: Yemen Basic Education Development Project." Washington.

———. 2006. "Tracking Basic Education Expenditures in Yemen: Analyses of Public Resource Management and Teacher Absenteeism." Washington.

———. 2007. "Implementation Completion and Results Report: Yemen for a Basic Education Expansion Project." Washington.

———. 2009. "Middle East and North Africa Region: 2008 Economic Developments and Prospects: Regional Integration for Global Competitiveness." Washington.

———. 2011a. "MENA Regional Synthesis on the Teacher Policies Survey: Key Findings from Phase I." Washington.

———. 2011b. "SABER-Teachers: Country Report Yemen." Washington.

World Bank and Republic of Yemen. 2010. "Education Status Report: Challenges and Opportunities." Washington: World Bank.

Yuki, Takako, and others. 2011. "Promoting Gender Parity Lessons from Yemen: A JICA Technical Cooperation Project in Basic Education." Japan International Cooperation Agency Background Paper for the 2012 World Development Report on Gender Equality and Development.

Contributors

MONGI BOUGHZALA
University of Tunis El-Manar

EMMANUEL COMOLET
Agence Française de Développement

HAFEZ GHANEM
World Bank (former Brookings
    Institution)

MOHAMED TLILI HAMDI
University of Sfax (Tunisia)

YURIKO KAMEYAMA
Japan Cooperation International
    Agency Research Institute

MAYADA MAGDY RAGHEB
Japan Cooperation International
    Agency, Egypt Office

HIDEKI MATSUNAGA
Japan Cooperation International
    Agency

YUKO MORIKAWA
Japan Cooperation International
    Agency

AKIRA MURATA
Japan International Cooperation
    Agency

KEI SAKAMOTO
Japan International Cooperation
    Agency

SEIKI TANAKA
University of Amsterdam

MASANORI YOSHIKAWA
Japanese International Cooperation
    Agency

TAKAKO YUKI
Global Link Management

Index

Boxes, figures, and tables are indicated by "b," "f," and "t" following page numbers.